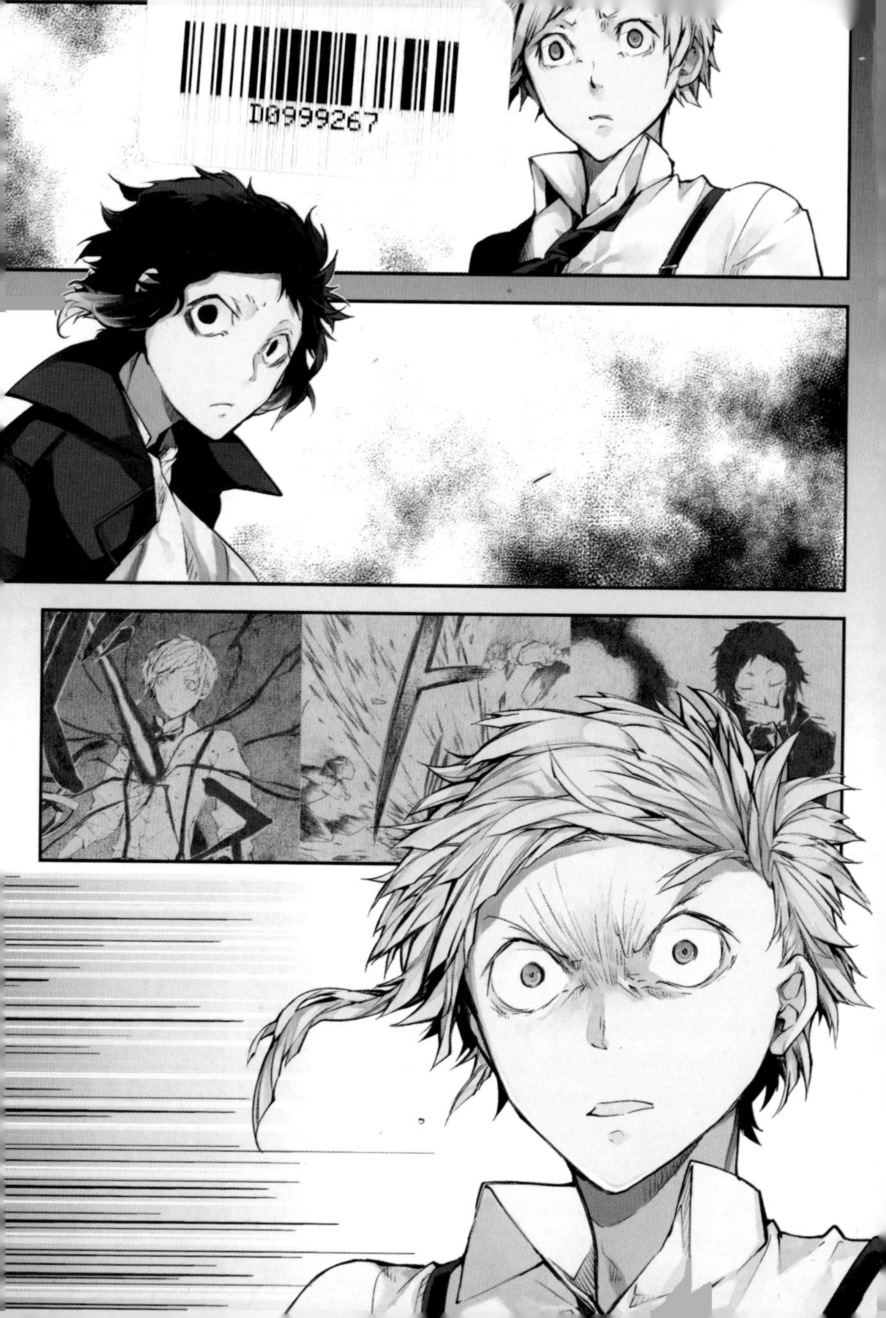

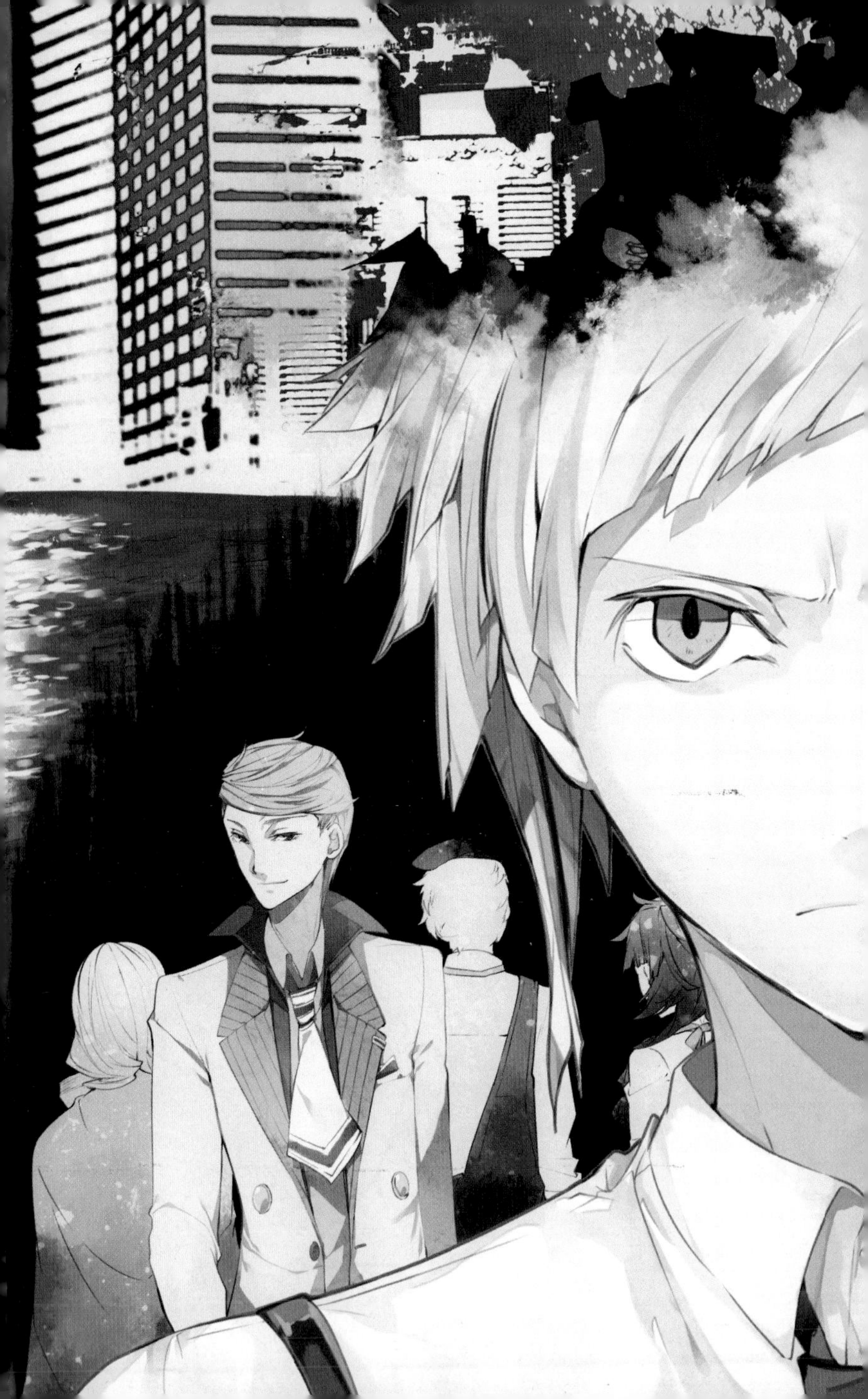

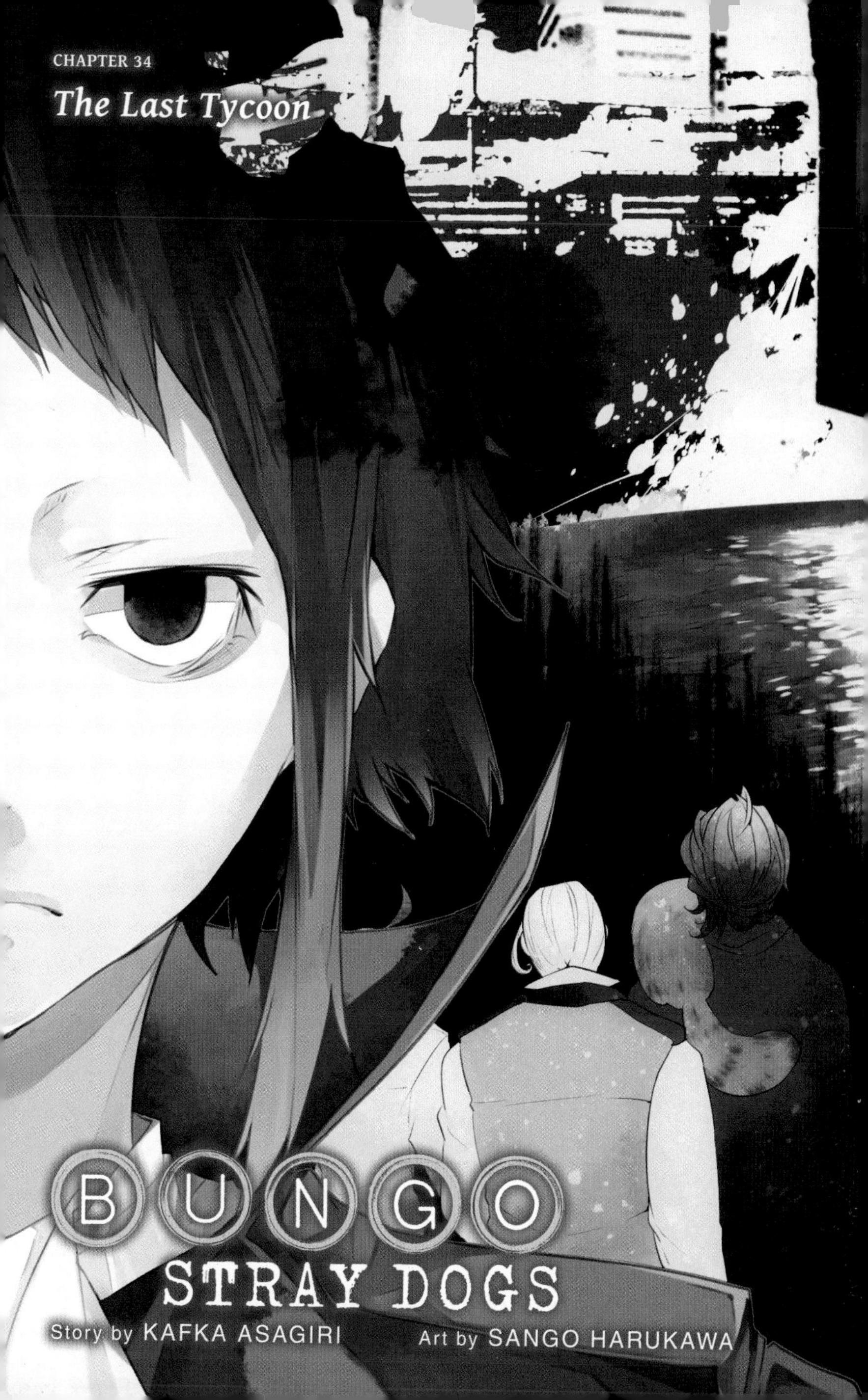
CHAPTER 34
The Last Tycoon
BUNGO
STRAY DOGS
Story by KAFKA ASAGIRI
Art by SANGO HARUKAWA

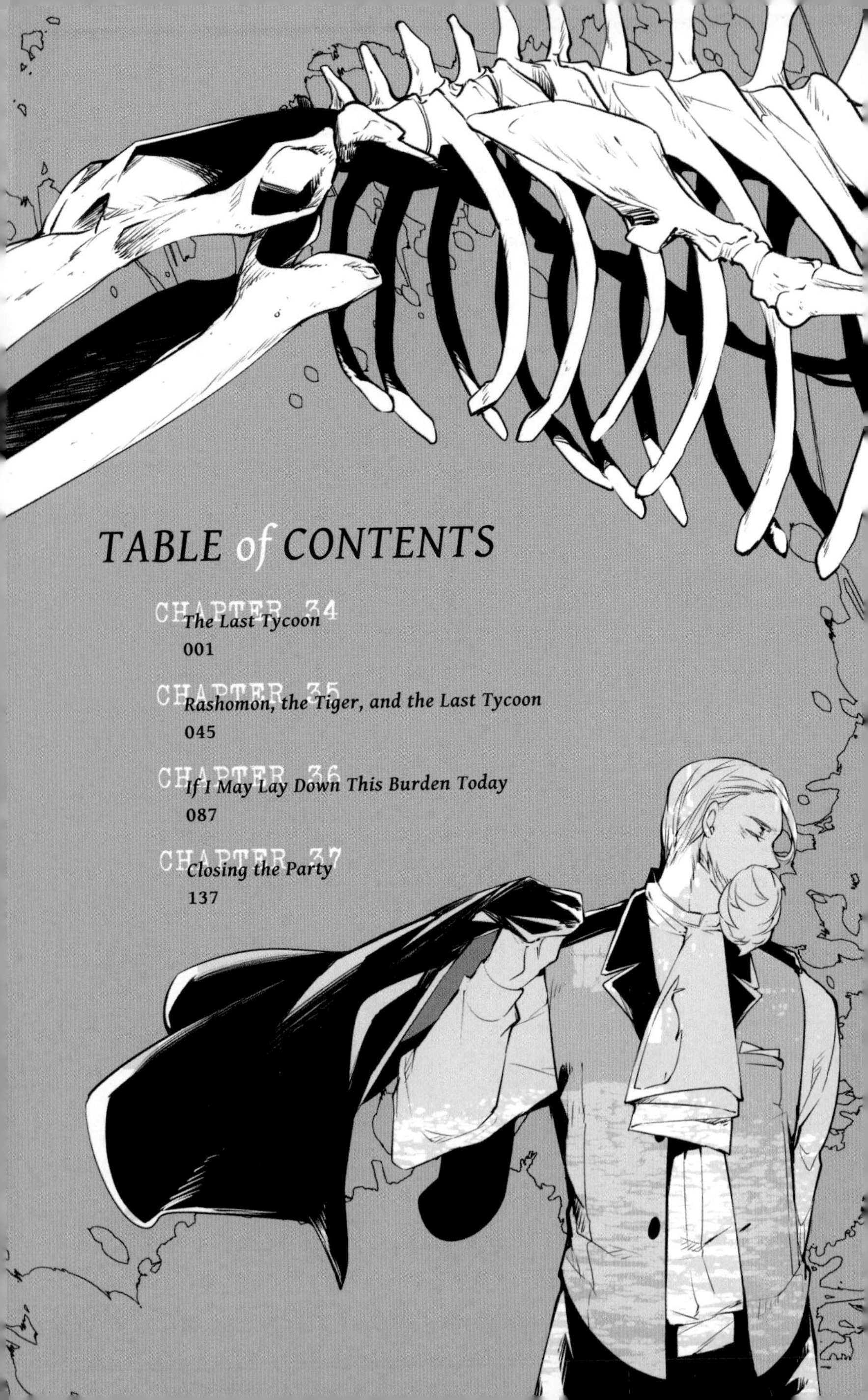

TABLE *of* CONTENTS

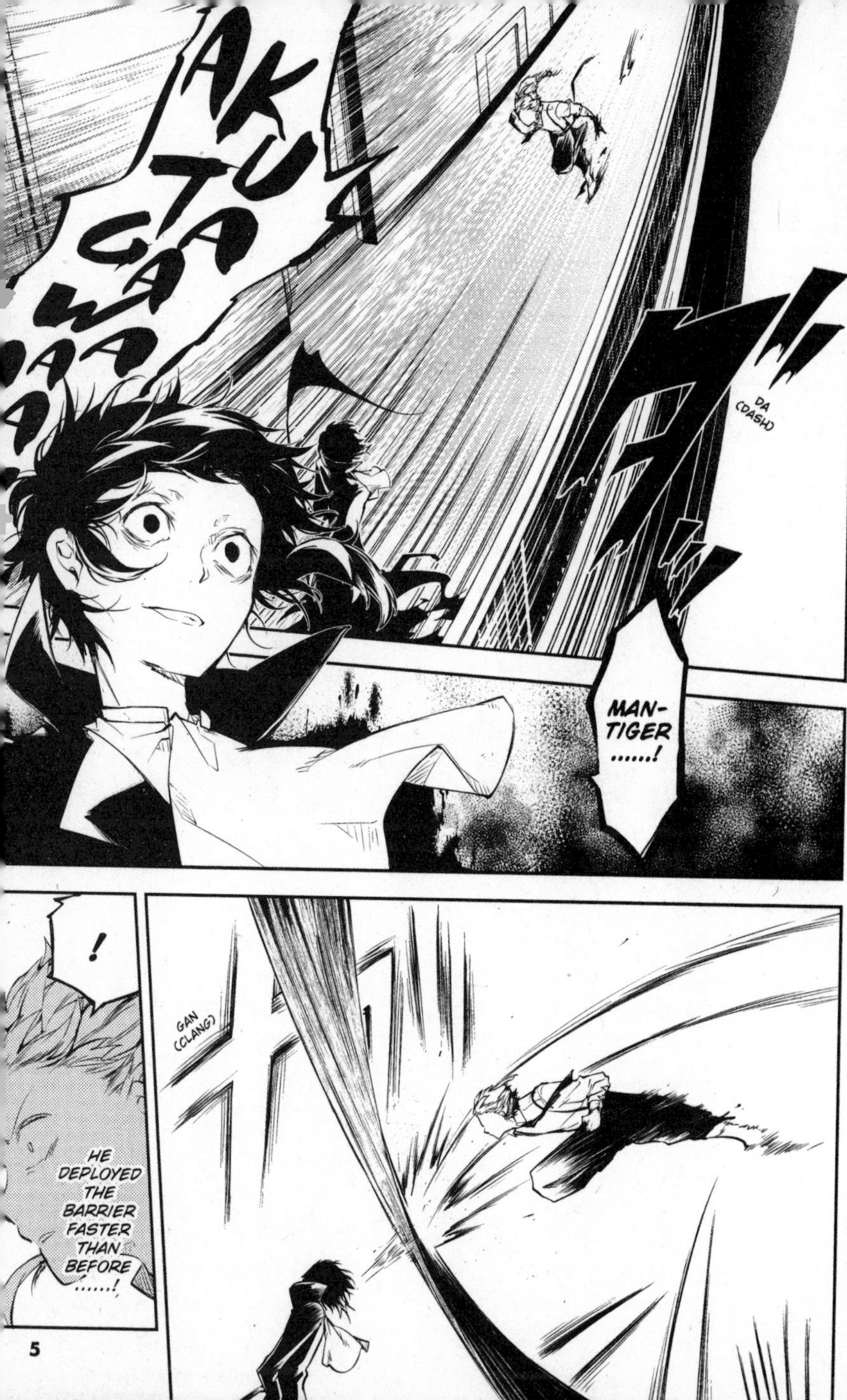

AKUTAGAWAAA...
DA (DASH)
MAN-TIGER......!
GAN (CLANG)
!
HE DEPLOYED THE BARRIER FASTER THAN BEFORE......!

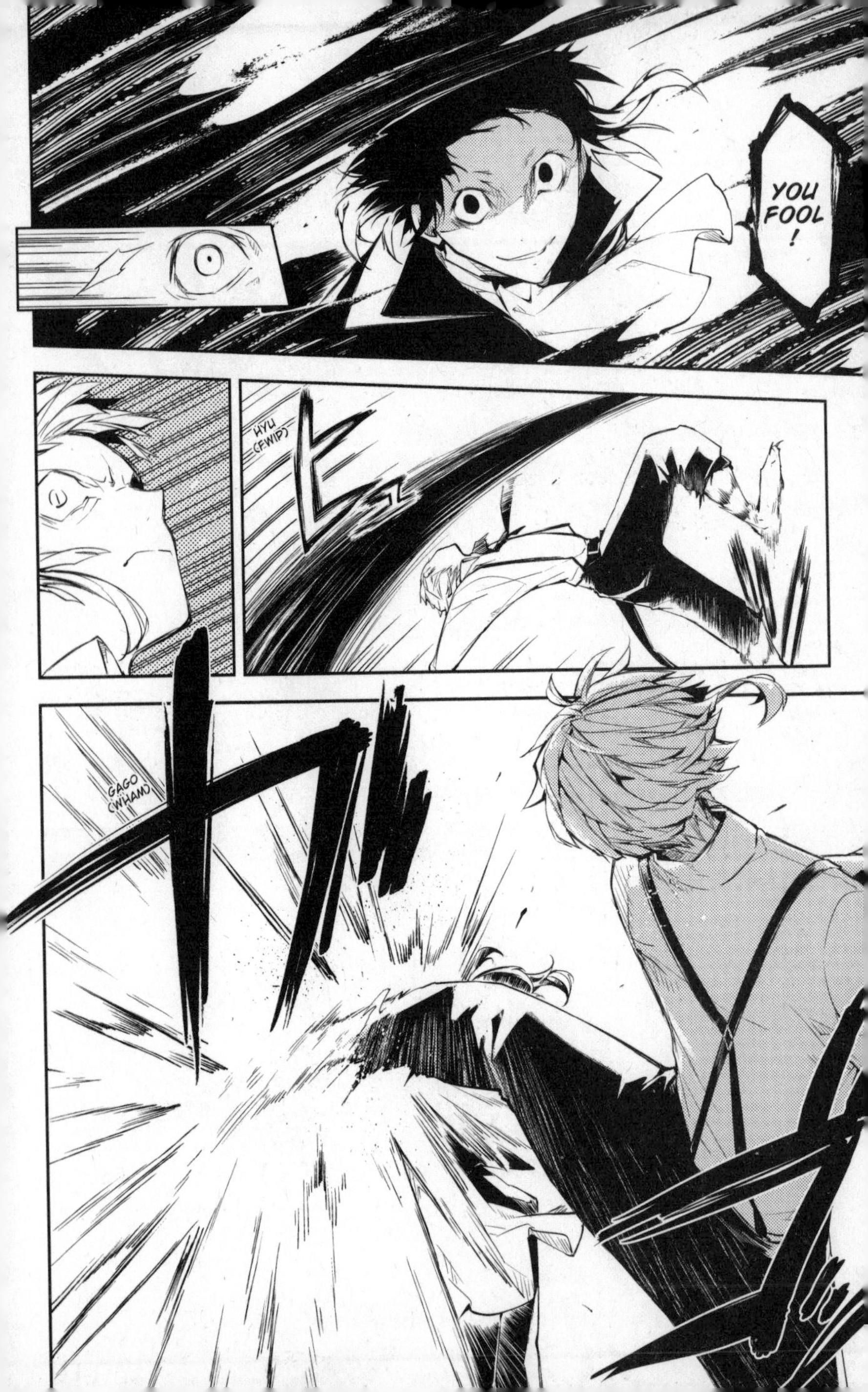
YOU FOOL!
HYU (FWIP)
GAGO (WHAM)

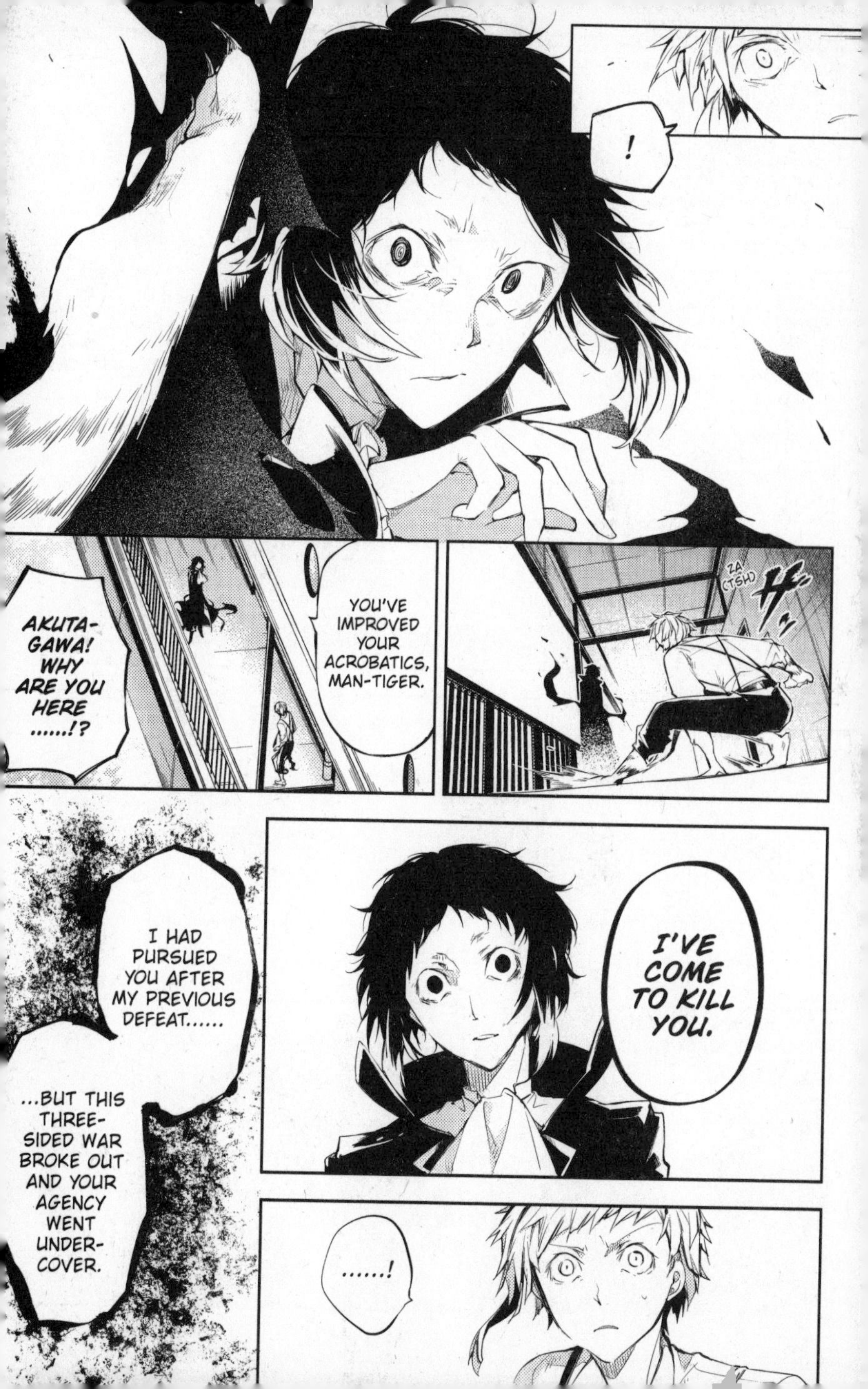
!
ZA (TSH)
YOU'VE IMPROVED YOUR ACROBATICS, MAN-TIGER.
AKUTA-GAWA! WHY ARE YOU HERE ......!?
I'VE COME TO KILL YOU.
I HAD PURSUED YOU AFTER MY PREVIOUS DEFEAT......
...BUT THIS THREE-SIDED WAR BROKE OUT AND YOUR AGENCY WENT UNDER-COVER.
......!

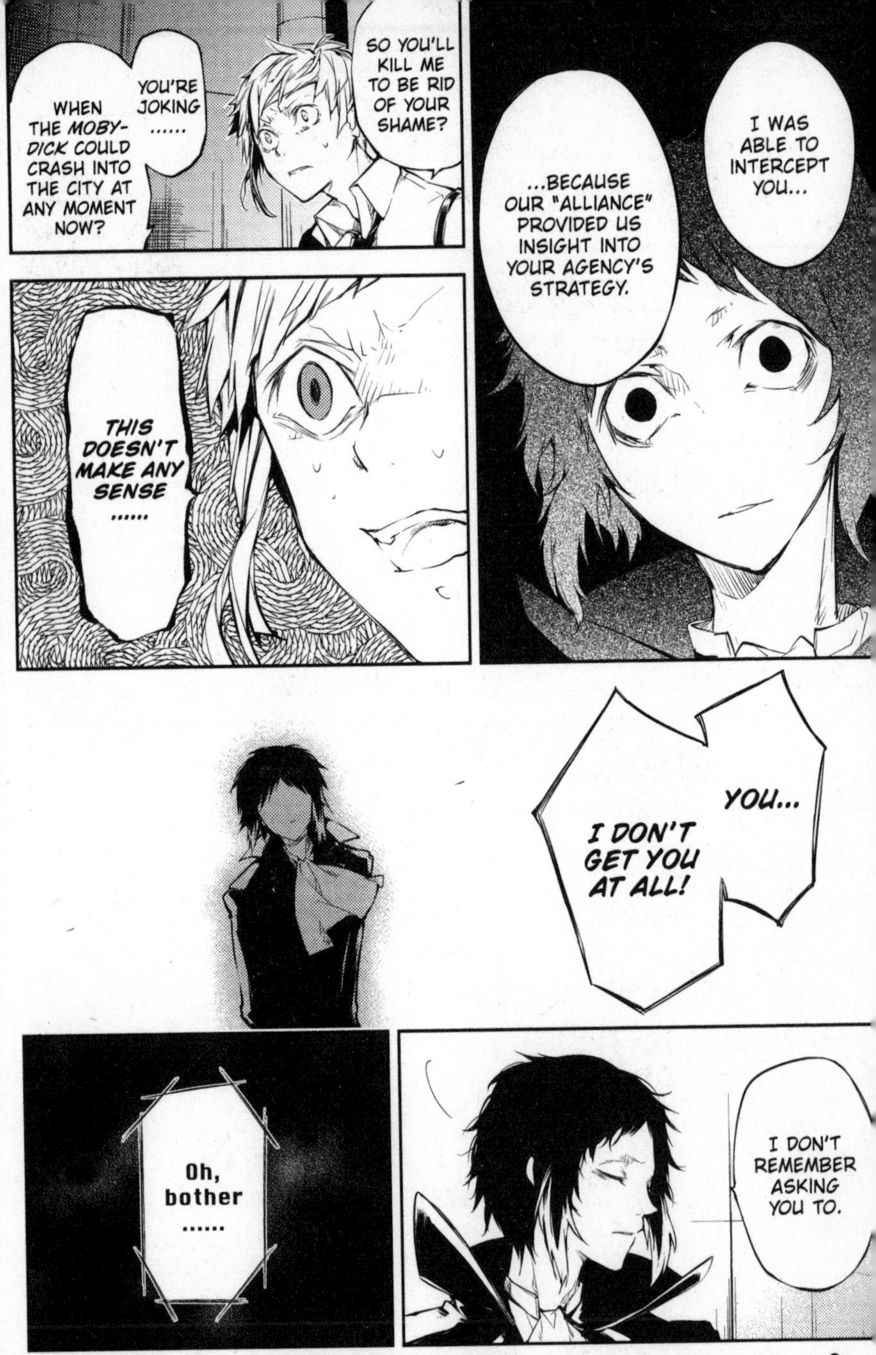
I WAS ABLE TO INTERCEPT YOU...
...BECAUSE OUR "ALLIANCE" PROVIDED US INSIGHT INTO YOUR AGENCY'S STRATEGY.
SO YOU'LL KILL ME TO BE RID OF YOUR SHAME?
YOU'RE JOKING......
WHEN THE *MOBY-DICK* COULD CRASH INTO THE CITY AT ANY MOMENT NOW?
THIS DOESN'T MAKE ANY SENSE......
YOU... I DON'T GET YOU AT ALL!
I DON'T REMEMBER ASKING YOU TO.
Oh, bother......

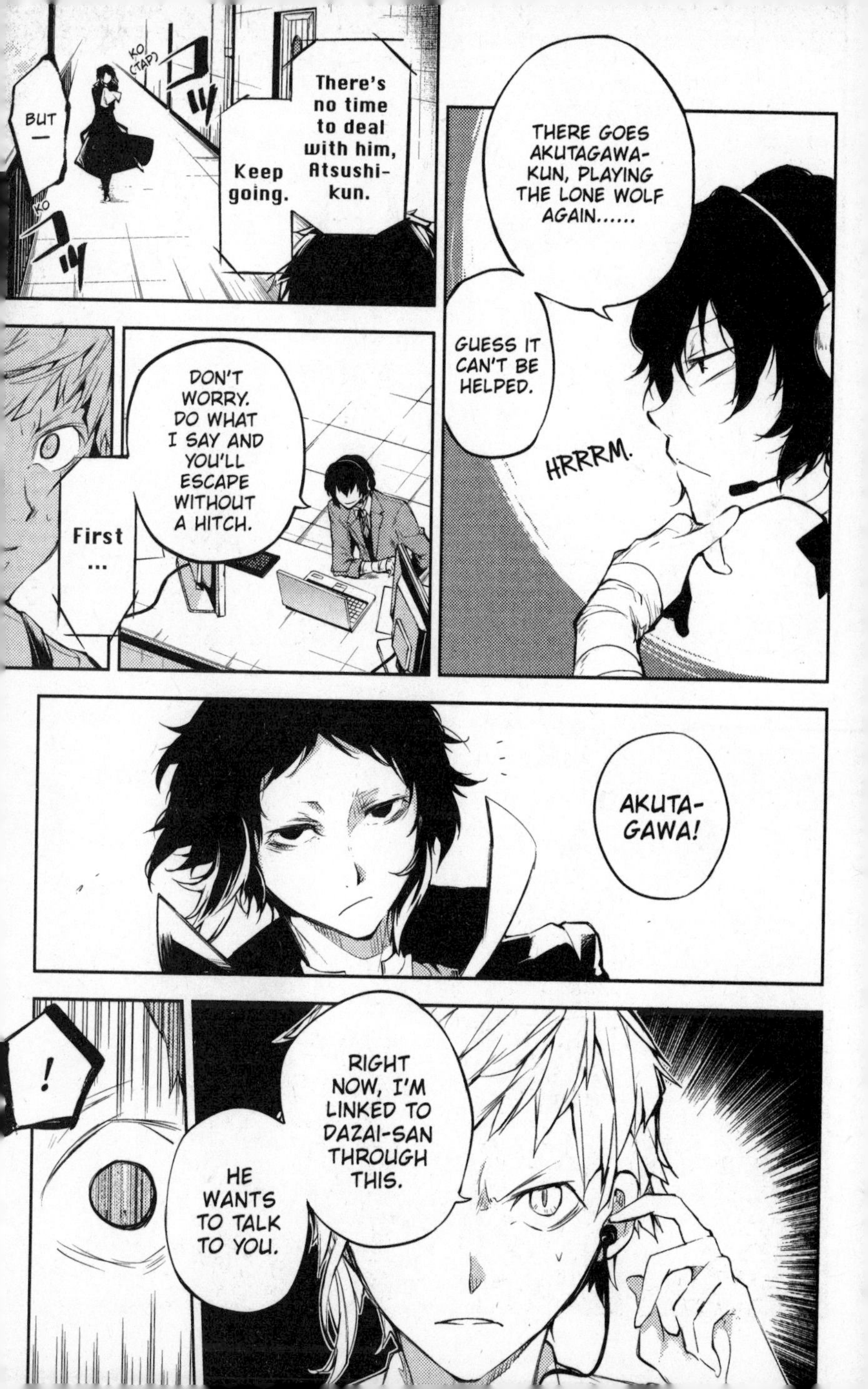
THERE GOES AKUTAGAWA-KUN, PLAYING THE LONE WOLF AGAIN......
GUESS IT CAN'T BE HELPED.
HRRRM.
There's no time to deal with him, Atsushi-kun.
Keep going.
KO (TAP)
BUT—
KO
DON'T WORRY. DO WHAT I SAY AND YOU'LL ESCAPE WITHOUT A HITCH.
First ...
AKUTA-GAWA!
RIGHT NOW, I'M LINKED TO DAZAI-SAN THROUGH THIS.
HE WANTS TO TALK TO YOU.
!

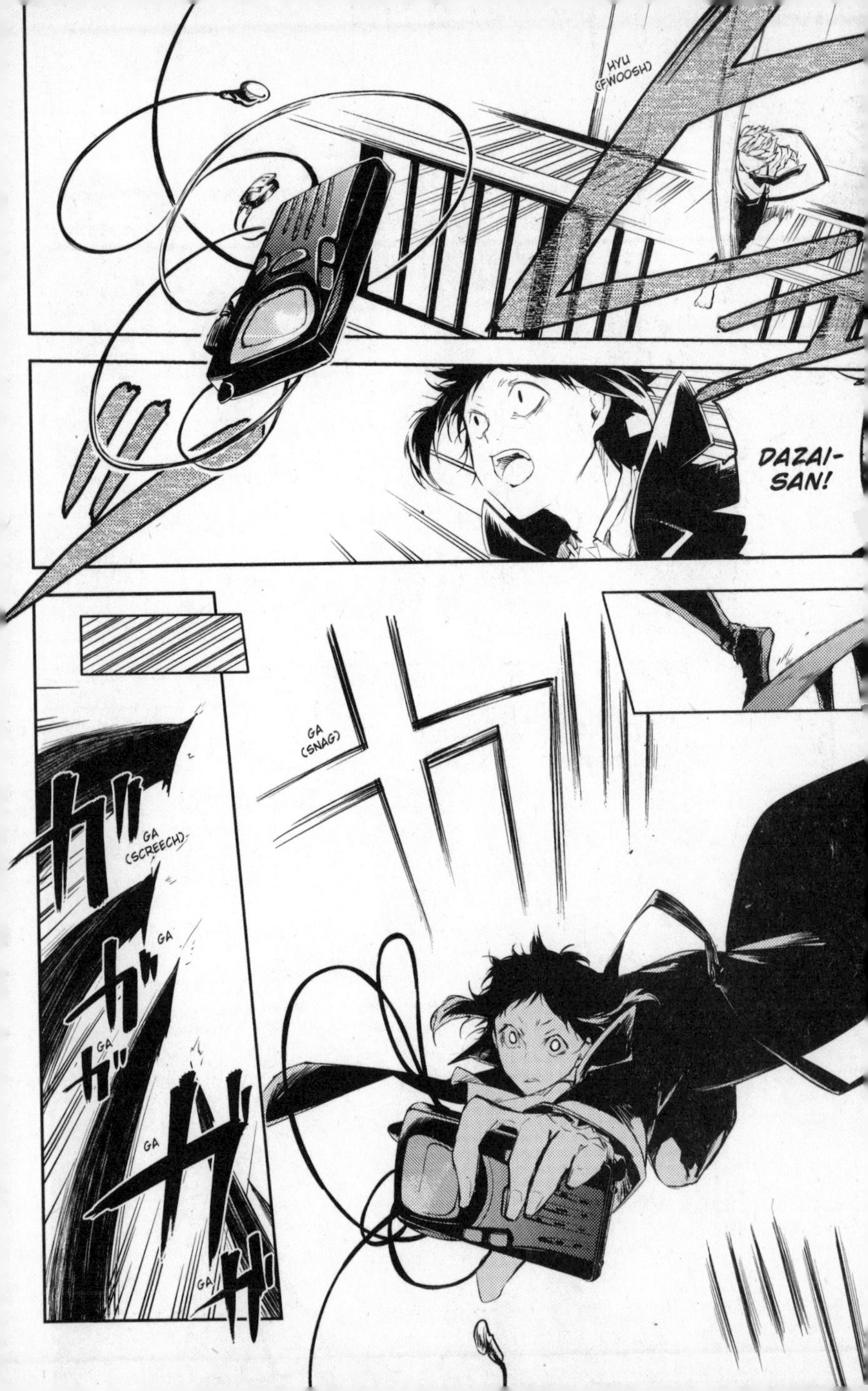
HYU (FWOOSH)
DAZAI-SAN!
GA (SNAG)
GA (SCREECH)
GA
GA
GA
GA

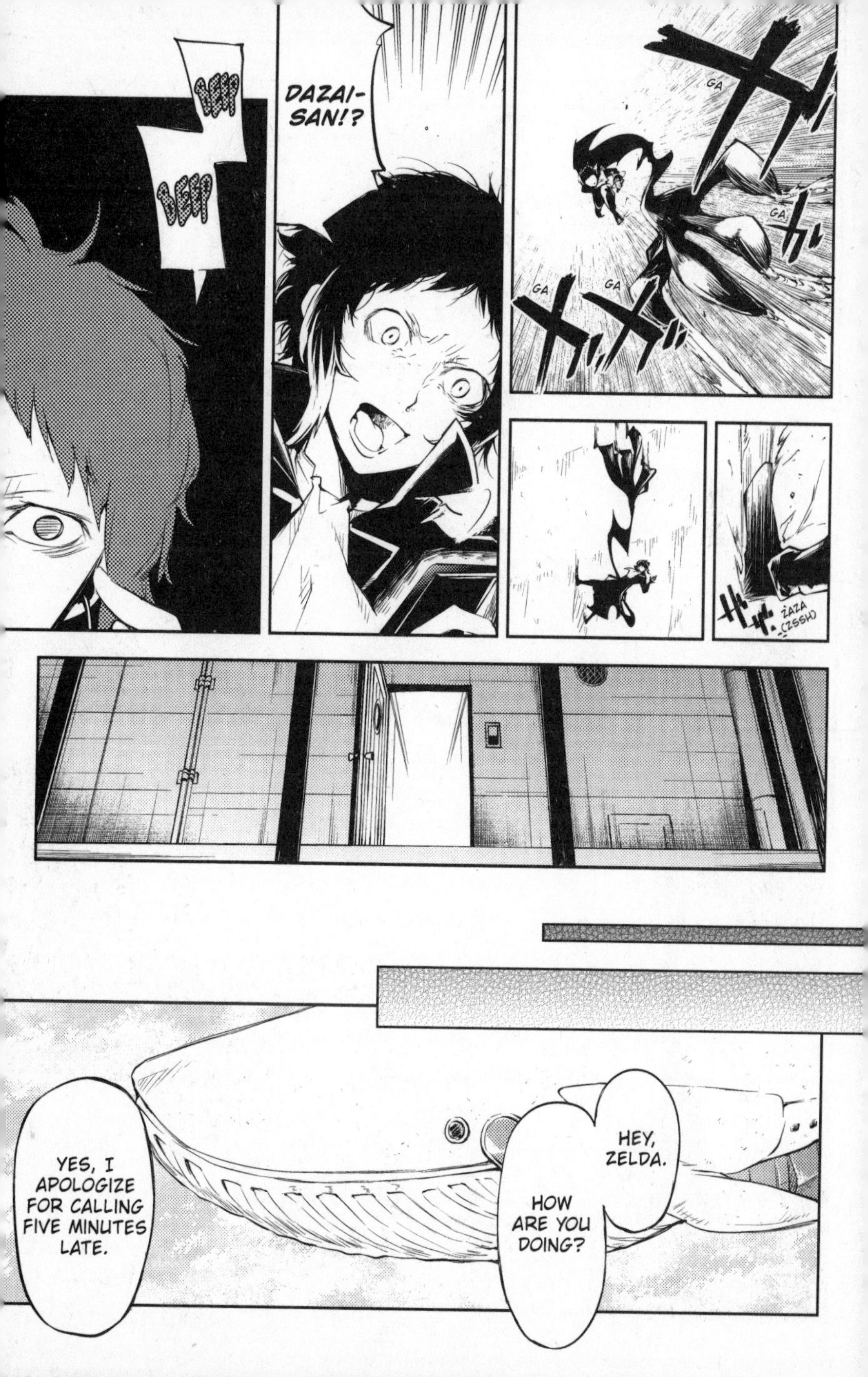
GA
GA
GA
GA
ZAZA (ZSSH)
DAZAI-SAN!?
BEEP
BEEP
HEY, ZELDA.
HOW ARE YOU DOING?
YES, I APOLOGIZE FOR CALLING FIVE MINUTES LATE.

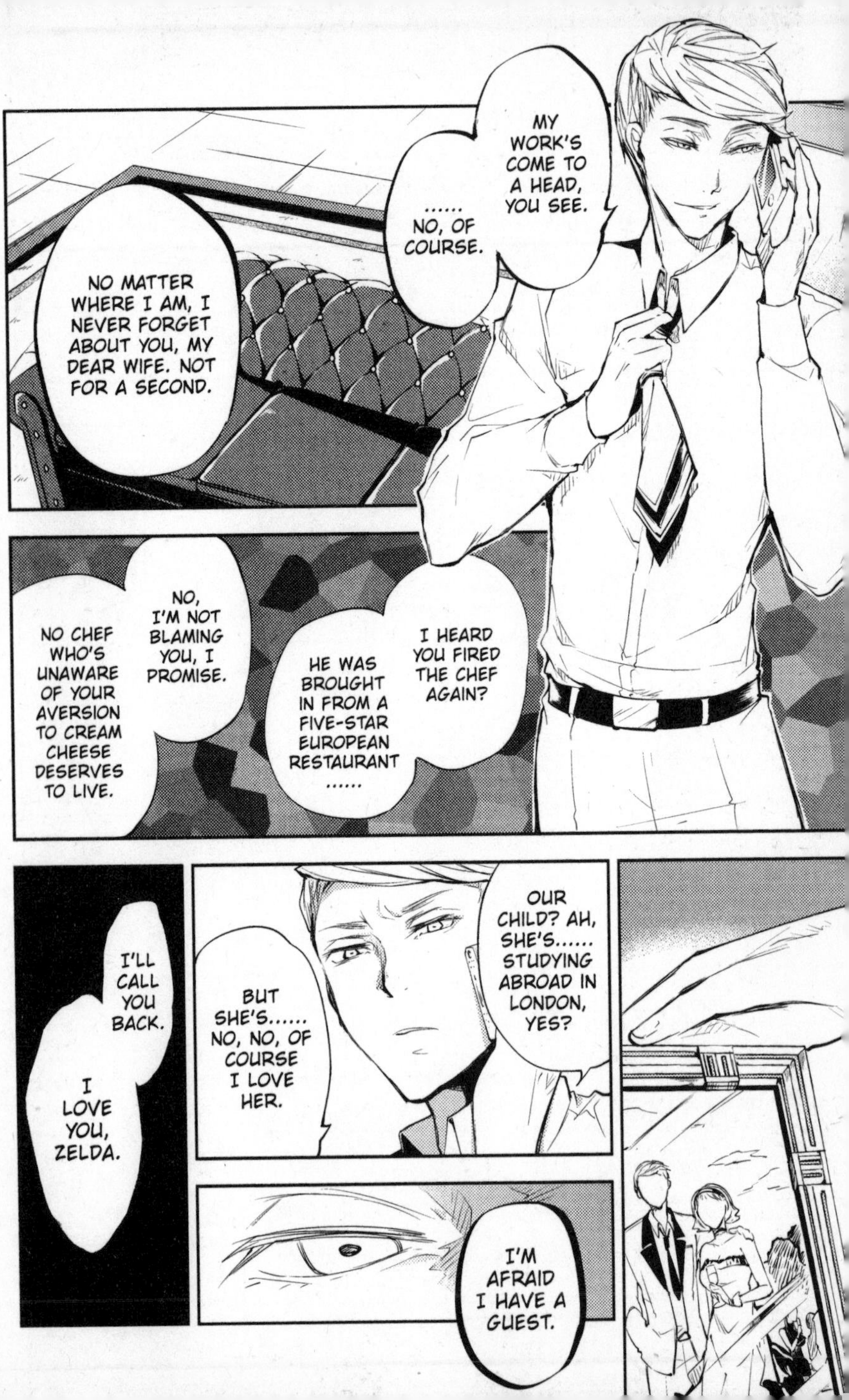
MY WORK'S COME TO A HEAD, YOU SEE.
...... NO, OF COURSE.
NO MATTER WHERE I AM, I NEVER FORGET ABOUT YOU, MY DEAR WIFE. NOT FOR A SECOND.
I HEARD YOU FIRED THE CHEF AGAIN?
HE WAS BROUGHT IN FROM A FIVE-STAR EUROPEAN RESTAURANT ......
NO, I'M NOT BLAMING YOU, I PROMISE.
NO CHEF WHO'S UNAWARE OF YOUR AVERSION TO CREAM CHEESE DESERVES TO LIVE.
OUR CHILD? AH, SHE'S...... STUDYING ABROAD IN LONDON, YES?
BUT SHE'S...... NO, NO, OF COURSE I LOVE HER.
I'M AFRAID I HAVE A GUEST.
I'LL CALL YOU BACK.
I LOVE YOU, ZELDA.

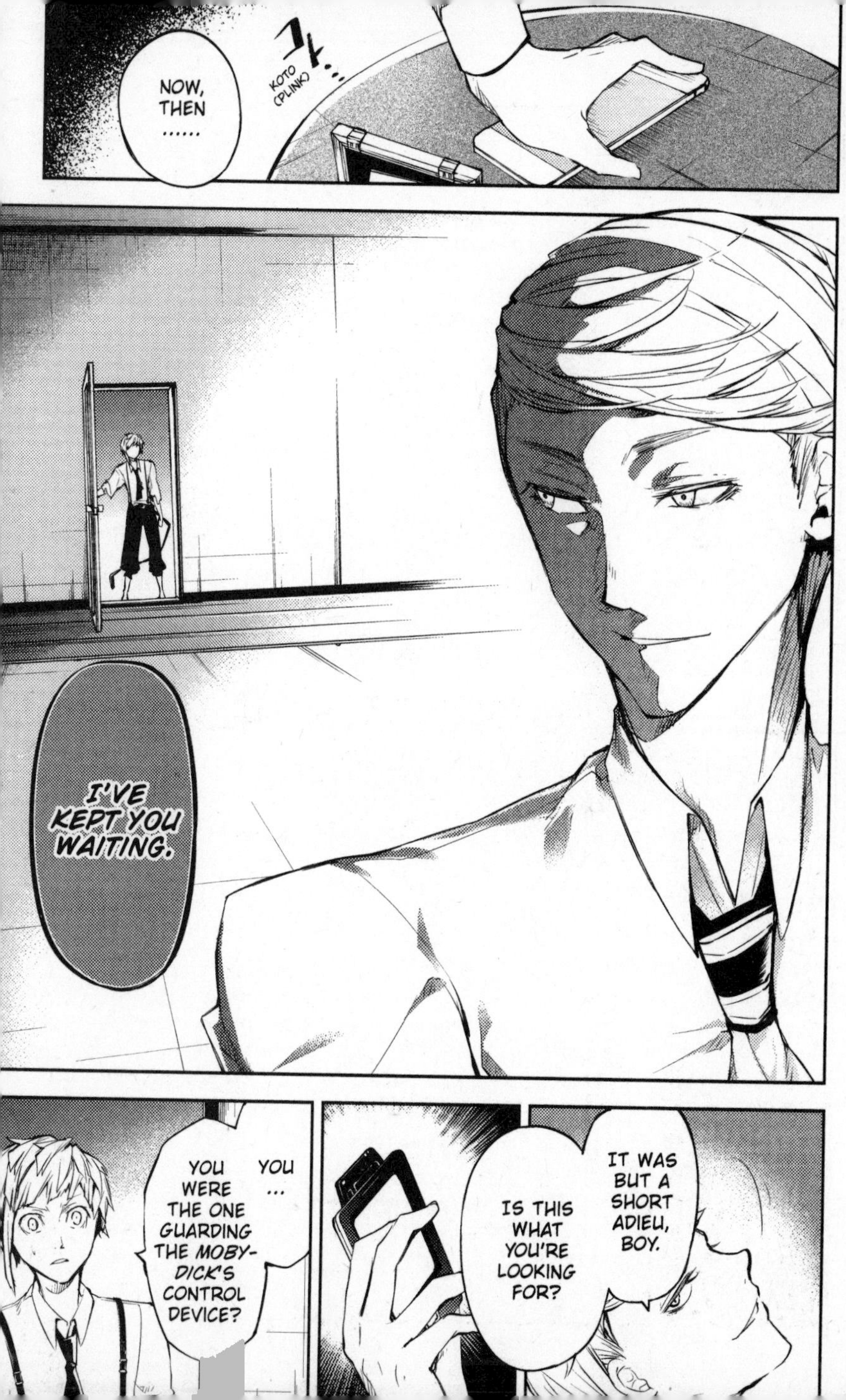
KOTO (PLINK)
NOW, THEN ......
I'VE KEPT YOU WAITING.
IT WAS BUT A SHORT ADIEU, BOY.
IS THIS WHAT YOU'RE LOOKING FOR?
YOU ...
YOU WERE THE ONE GUARDING THE MOBY-DICK'S CONTROL DEVICE?

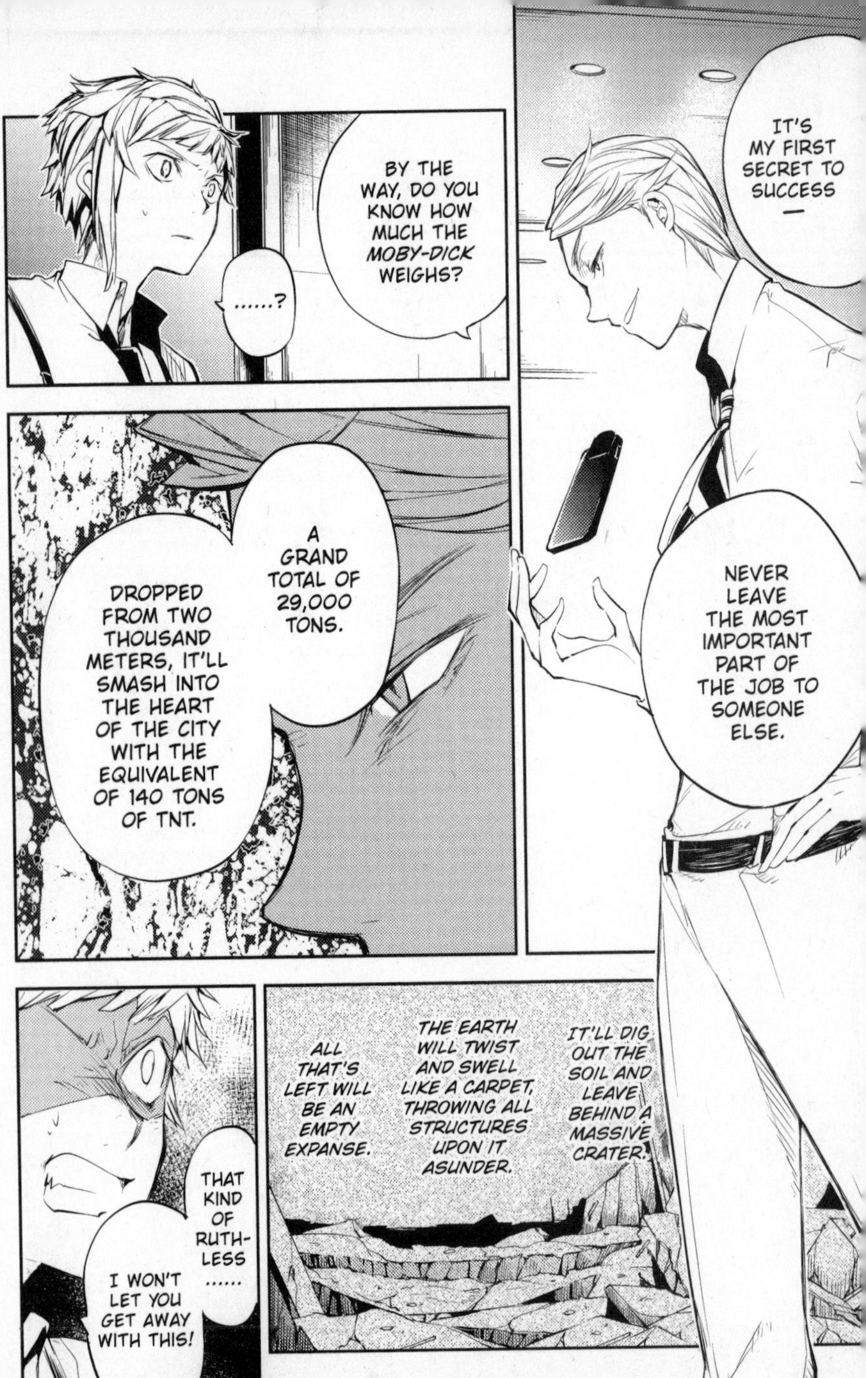
IT'S MY FIRST SECRET TO SUCCESS —
NEVER LEAVE THE MOST IMPORTANT PART OF THE JOB TO SOMEONE ELSE.
BY THE WAY, DO YOU KNOW HOW MUCH THE *MOBY-DICK* WEIGHS?
......?
A GRAND TOTAL OF 29,000 TONS.
DROPPED FROM TWO THOUSAND METERS, IT'LL SMASH INTO THE HEART OF THE CITY WITH THE EQUIVALENT OF 140 TONS OF TNT.
IT'LL DIG OUT THE SOIL AND LEAVE BEHIND A MASSIVE CRATER.
THE EARTH WILL TWIST AND SWELL LIKE A CARPET, THROWING ALL STRUCTURES UPON IT ASUNDER.
ALL THAT'S LEFT WILL BE AN EMPTY EXPANSE.
THAT KIND OF RUTH-LESS ......
I WON'T LET YOU GET AWAY WITH THIS!

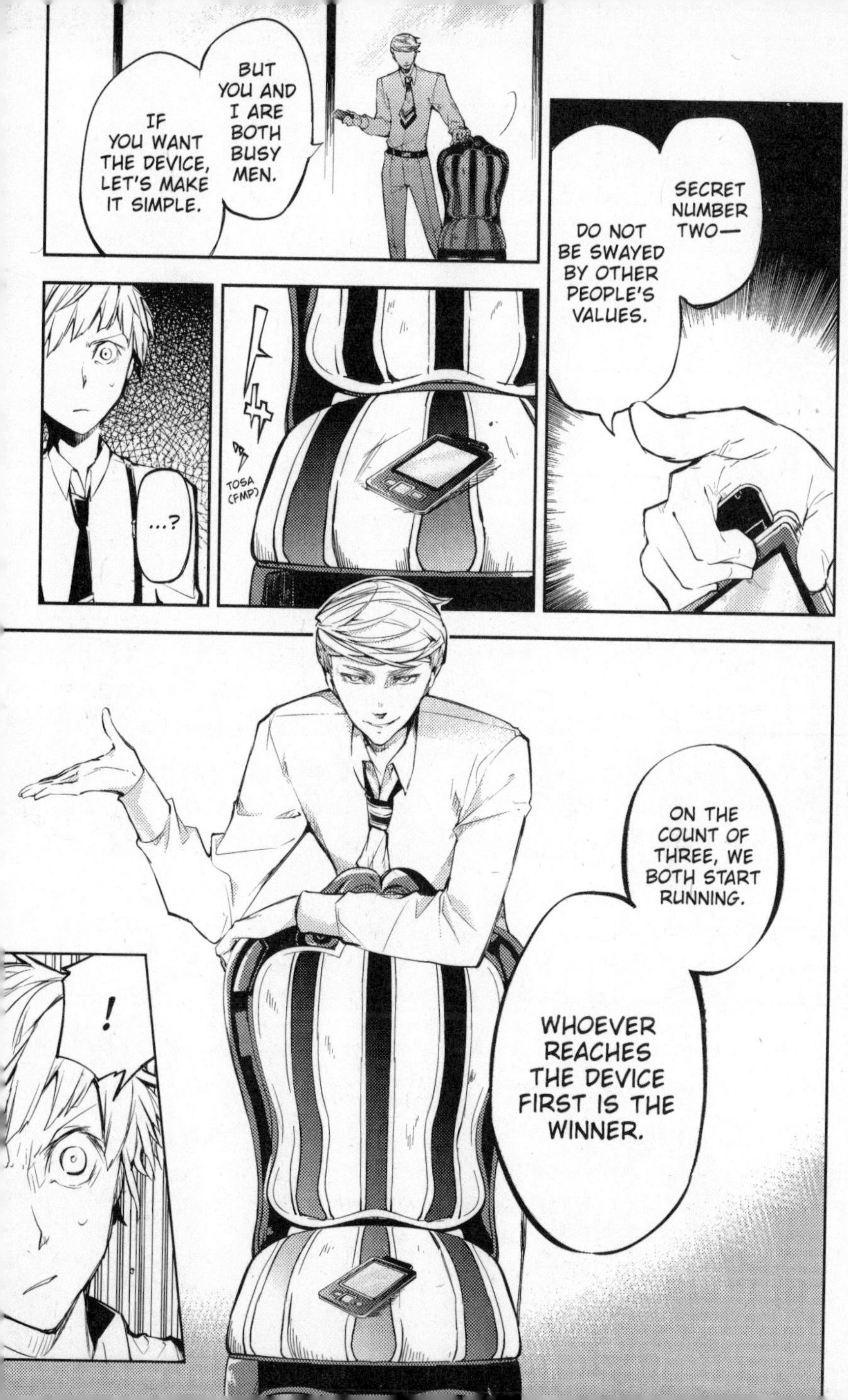
BUT YOU AND I ARE BOTH BUSY MEN.
IF YOU WANT THE DEVICE, LET'S MAKE IT SIMPLE.
SECRET NUMBER TWO—
DO NOT BE SWAYED BY OTHER PEOPLE'S VALUES.
TOSA (FMP)
...?
ON THE COUNT OF THREE, WE BOTH START RUNNING.
WHOEVER REACHES THE DEVICE FIRST IS THE WINNER.
!

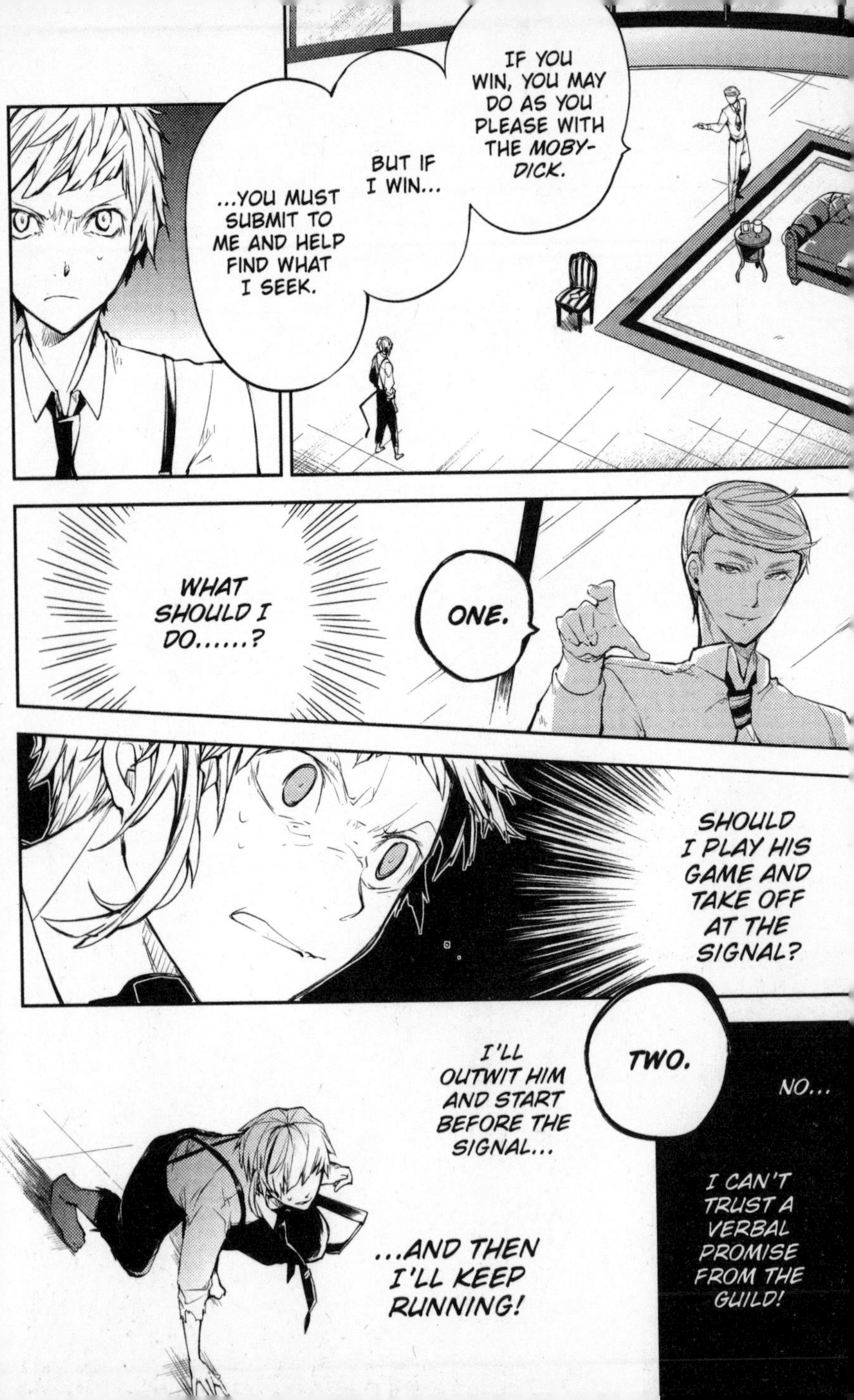
IF YOU WIN, YOU MAY DO AS YOU PLEASE WITH THE *MOBY-DICK*.
BUT IF I WIN...
...YOU MUST SUBMIT TO ME AND HELP FIND WHAT I SEEK.
ONE.
WHAT SHOULD I DO......?
SHOULD I PLAY HIS GAME AND TAKE OFF AT THE SIGNAL?
TWO.
NO...
I CAN'T TRUST A VERBAL PROMISE FROM THE GUILD!
I'LL OUTWIT HIM AND START BEFORE THE SIGNAL...
...AND THEN I'LL KEEP RUNNING!

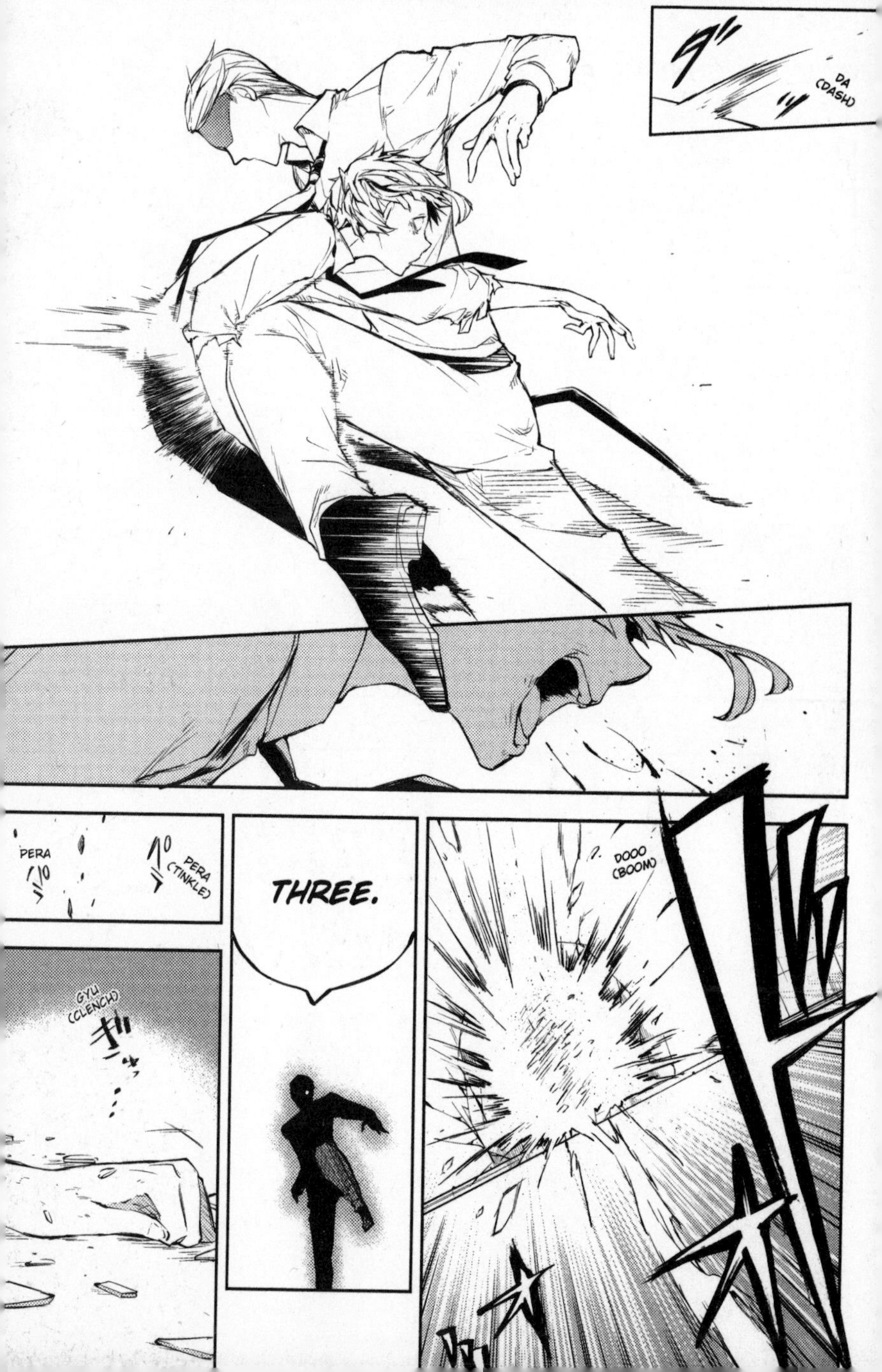
DA (DASH)
DOOO (BOOM)
THREE.
PERA
PERA (TINKLE)
GYU (CLENCH)

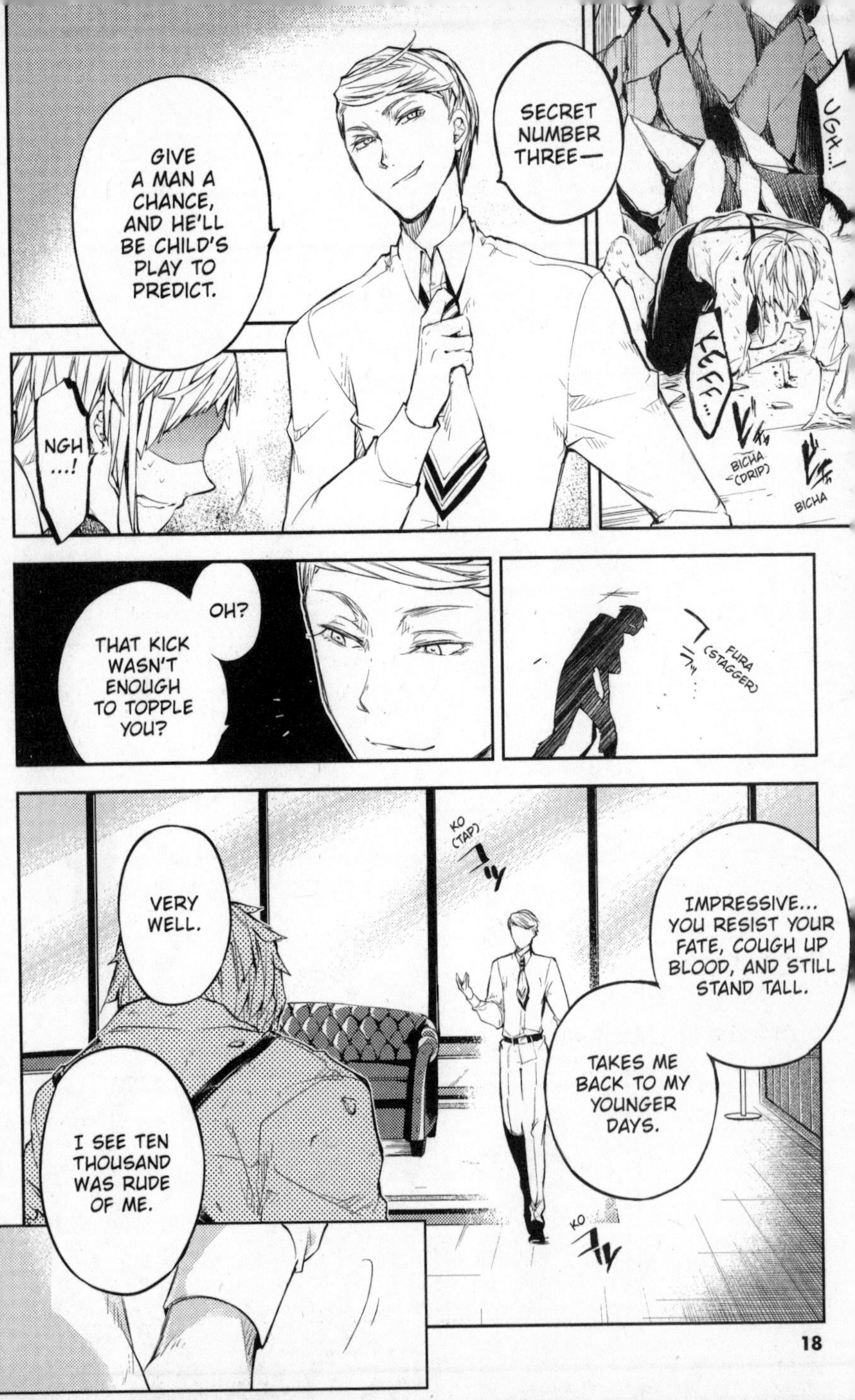
UGH...!
KEFF...
BICHA (DRIP)
BICHA
SECRET NUMBER THREE—
GIVE A MAN A CHANCE, AND HE'LL BE CHILD'S PLAY TO PREDICT.
NGH ...!
FURA (STAGGER)
OH?
THAT KICK WASN'T ENOUGH TO TOPPLE YOU?
IMPRESSIVE... YOU RESIST YOUR FATE, COUGH UP BLOOD, AND STILL STAND TALL.
TAKES ME BACK TO MY YOUNGER DAYS.
KO (TAP)
KO
VERY WELL.
I SEE TEN THOUSAND WAS RUDE OF ME.

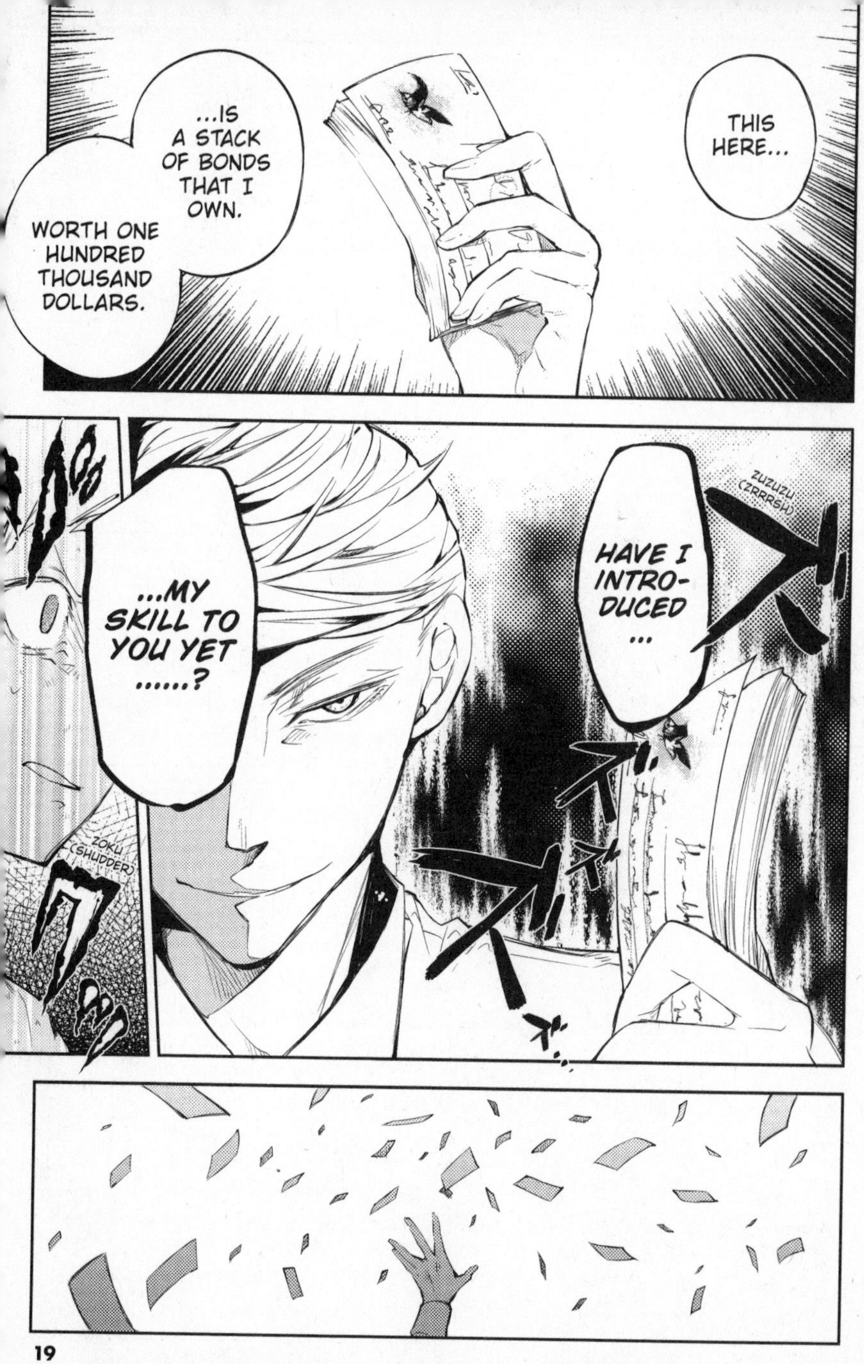
THIS HERE...
...IS A STACK OF BONDS THAT I OWN.
WORTH ONE HUNDRED THOUSAND DOLLARS.
ZUZUZU (ZRRRSH)
HAVE I INTRODUCED...
...MY SKILL TO YOU YET......?
ZOKU (SHUDDER)

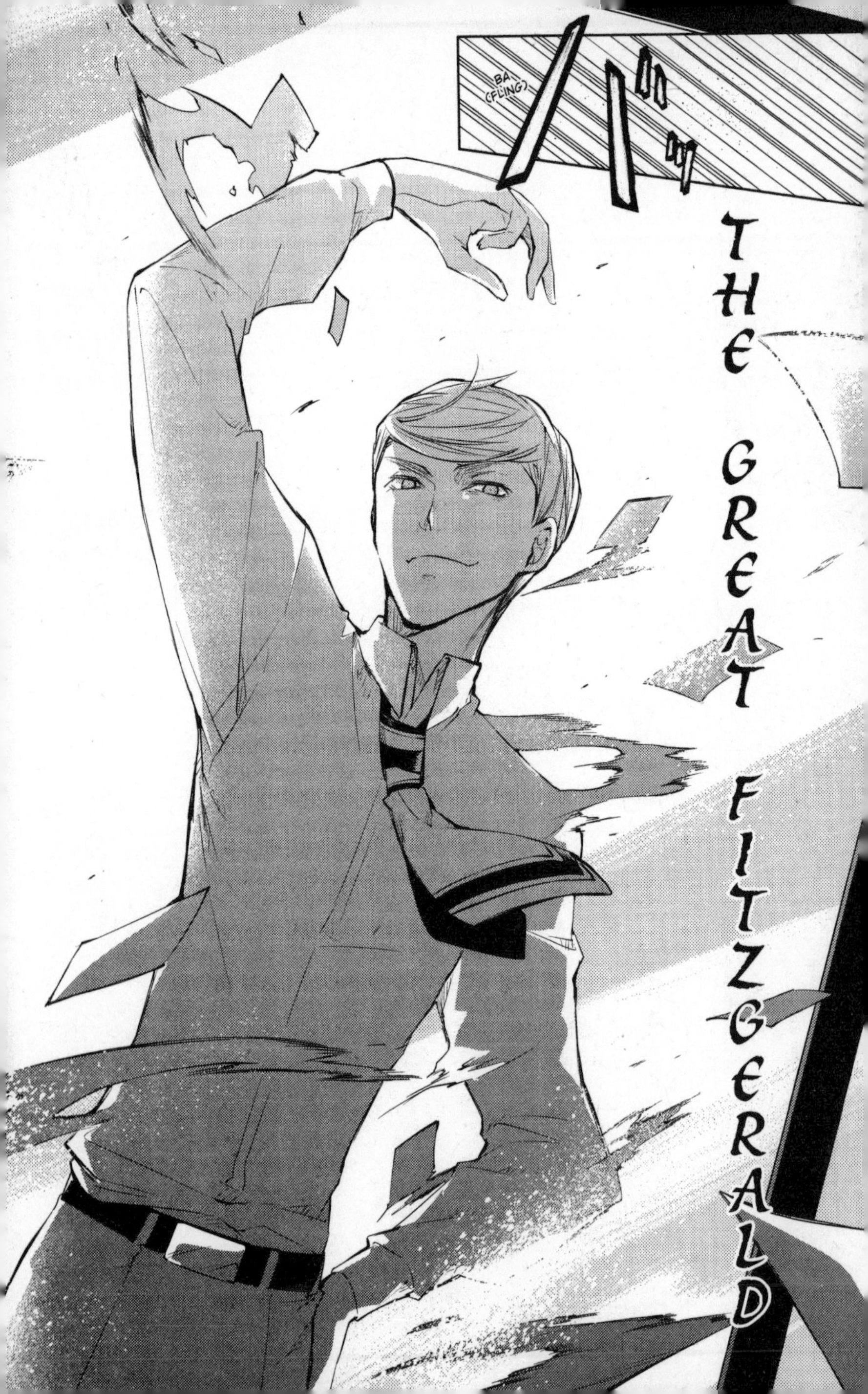
BA (FLING)
THE GREAT FITZGERALD

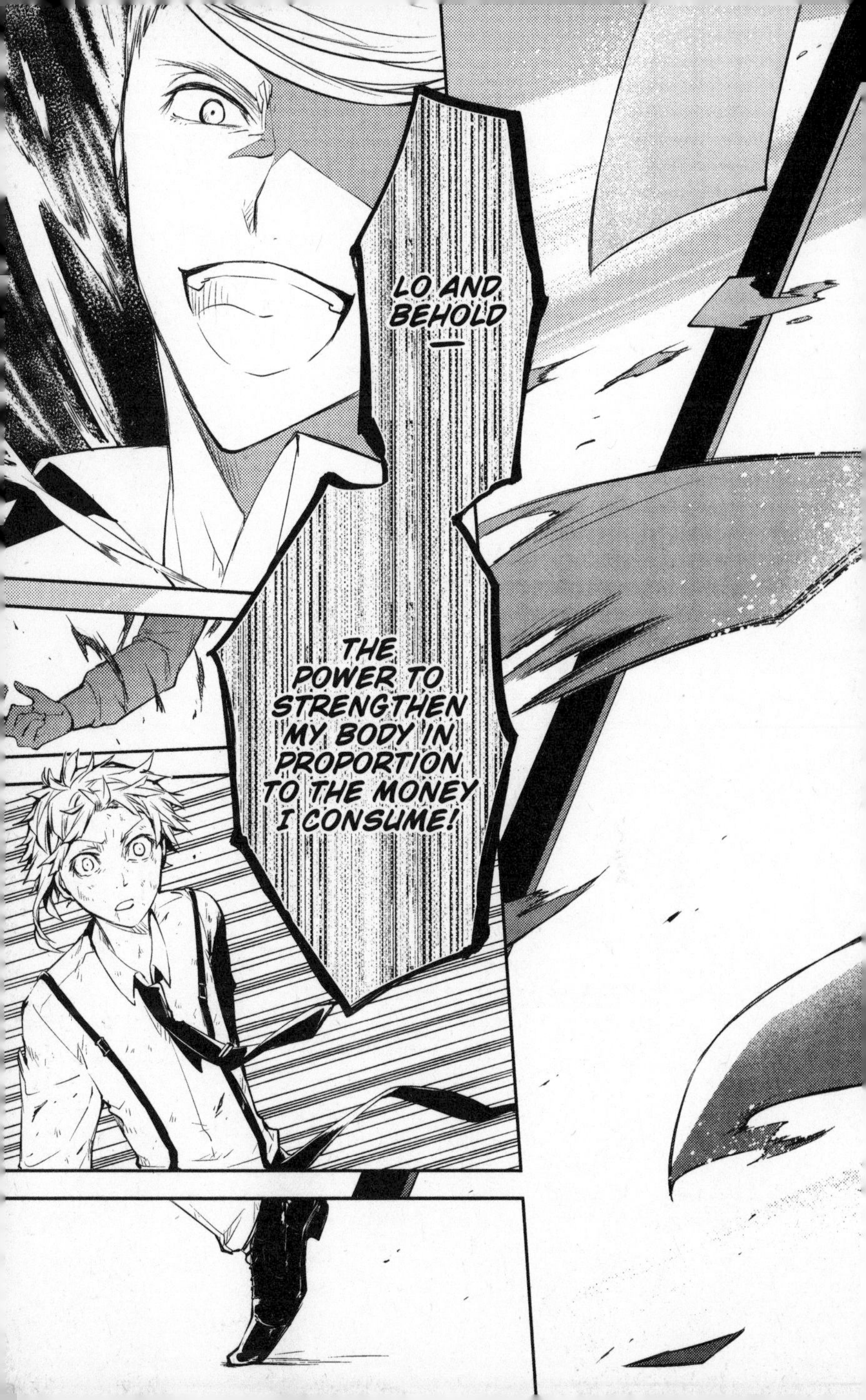
LO AND BEHOLD —
THE POWER TO STRENGTHEN MY BODY IN PROPORTION TO THE MONEY I CONSUME!

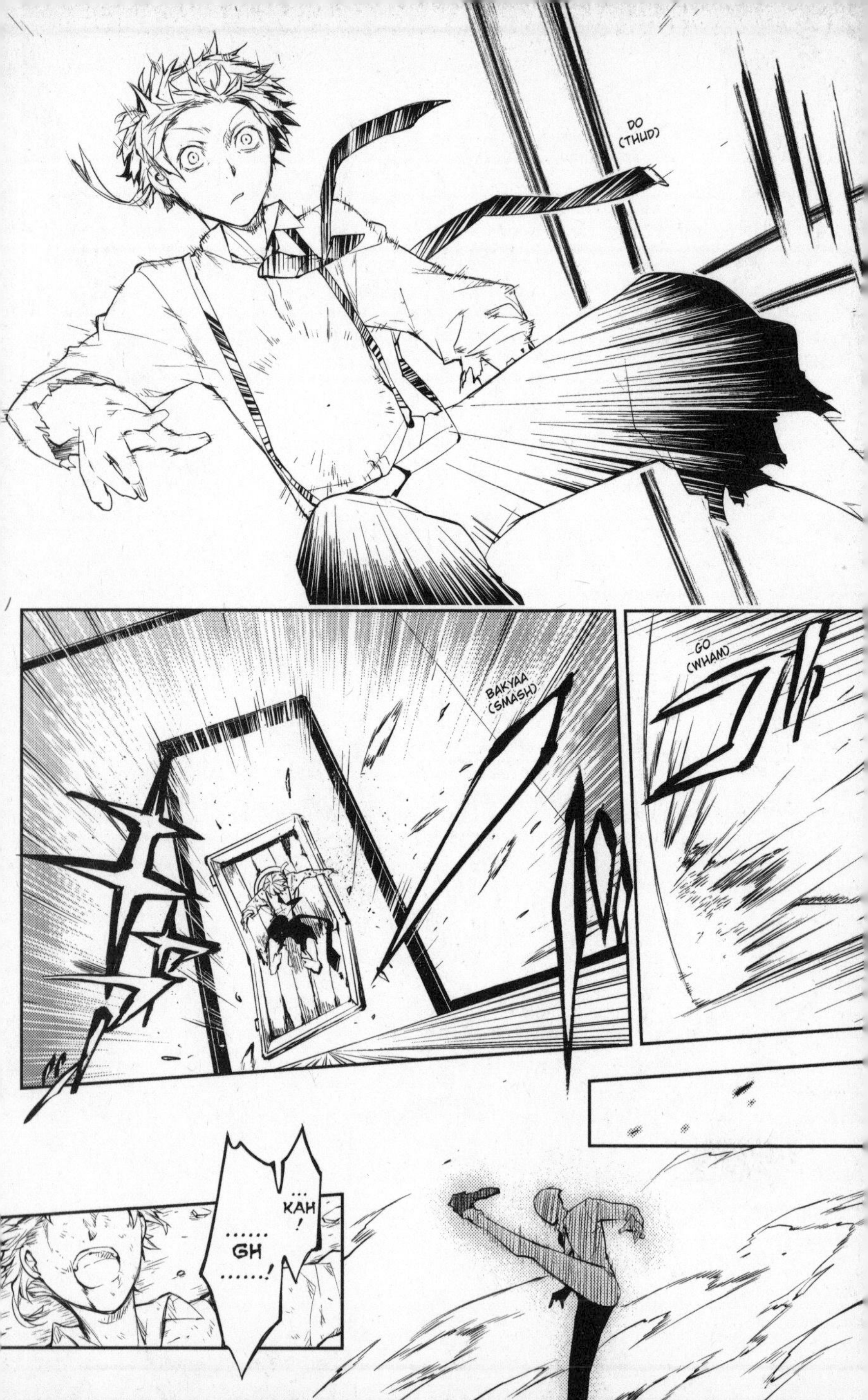
DO (THUD)
GO (WHAM)
BAKYAA (SMASH)
...KAH!
.......GH.......!

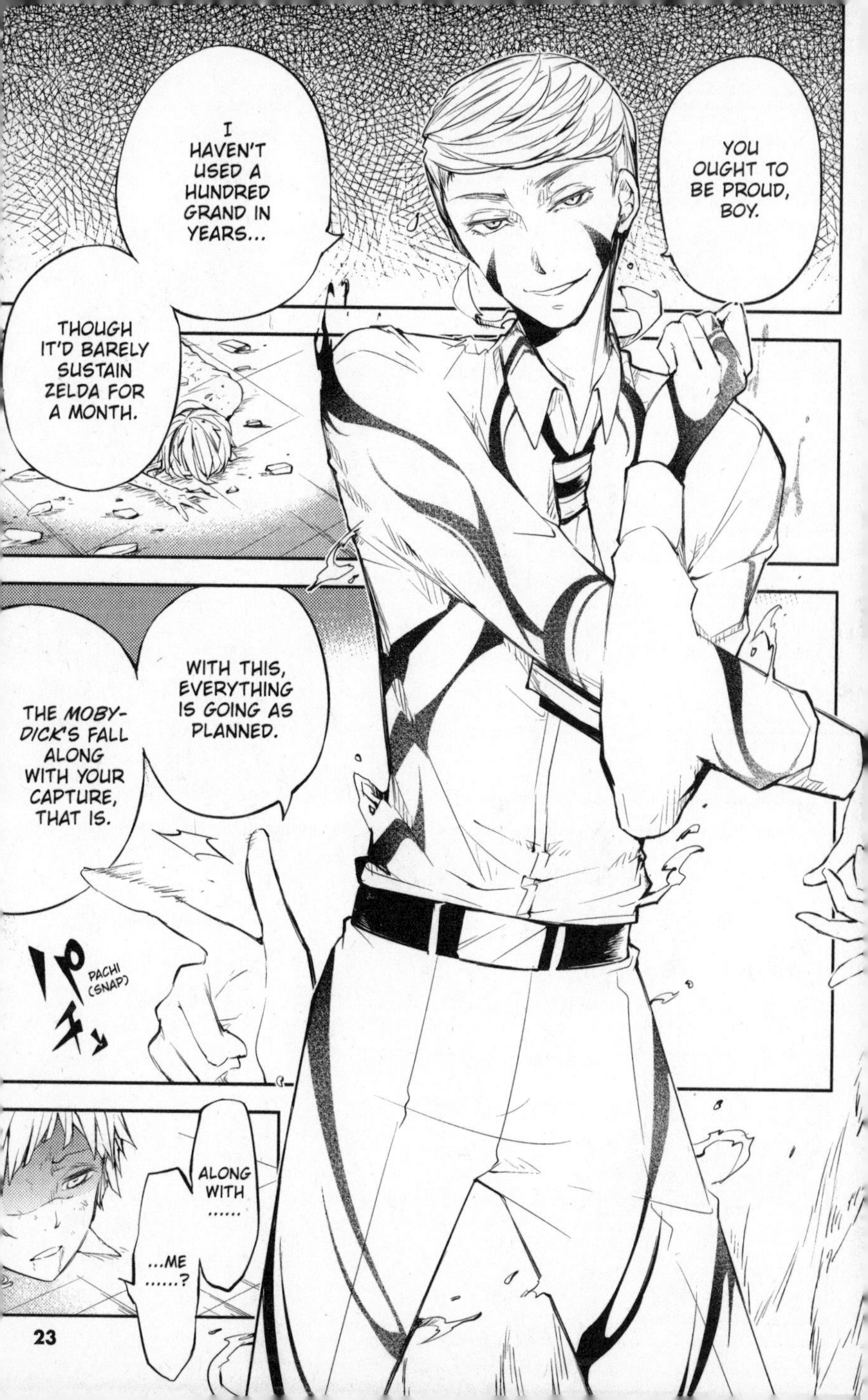
YOU OUGHT TO BE PROUD, BOY.
I HAVEN'T USED A HUNDRED GRAND IN YEARS...
THOUGH IT'D BARELY SUSTAIN ZELDA FOR A MONTH.
WITH THIS, EVERYTHING IS GOING AS PLANNED.
THE *MOBY-DICK*'S FALL ALONG WITH YOUR CAPTURE, THAT IS.
PACHI (SNAP)
ALONG WITH ......
...ME ......?

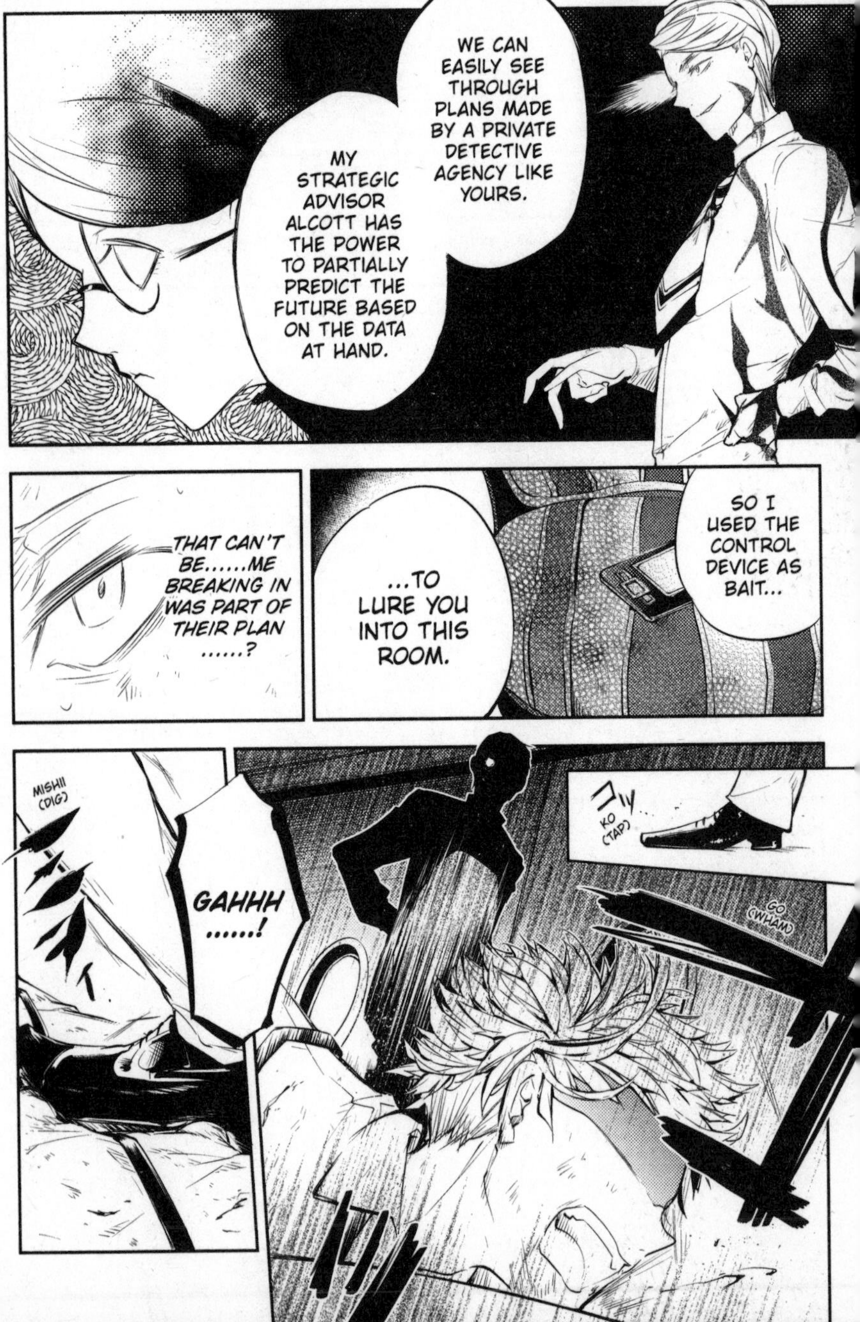

WE CAN EASILY SEE THROUGH PLANS MADE BY A PRIVATE DETECTIVE AGENCY LIKE YOURS.
MY STRATEGIC ADVISOR ALCOTT HAS THE POWER TO PARTIALLY PREDICT THE FUTURE BASED ON THE DATA AT HAND.
SO I USED THE CONTROL DEVICE AS BAIT...
...TO LURE YOU INTO THIS ROOM.
THAT CAN'T BE......ME BREAKING IN WAS PART OF THEIR PLAN......?
コッ...
KO (TAP)
GO (WHAM)
GAHHH......!
MISHII (DIG)

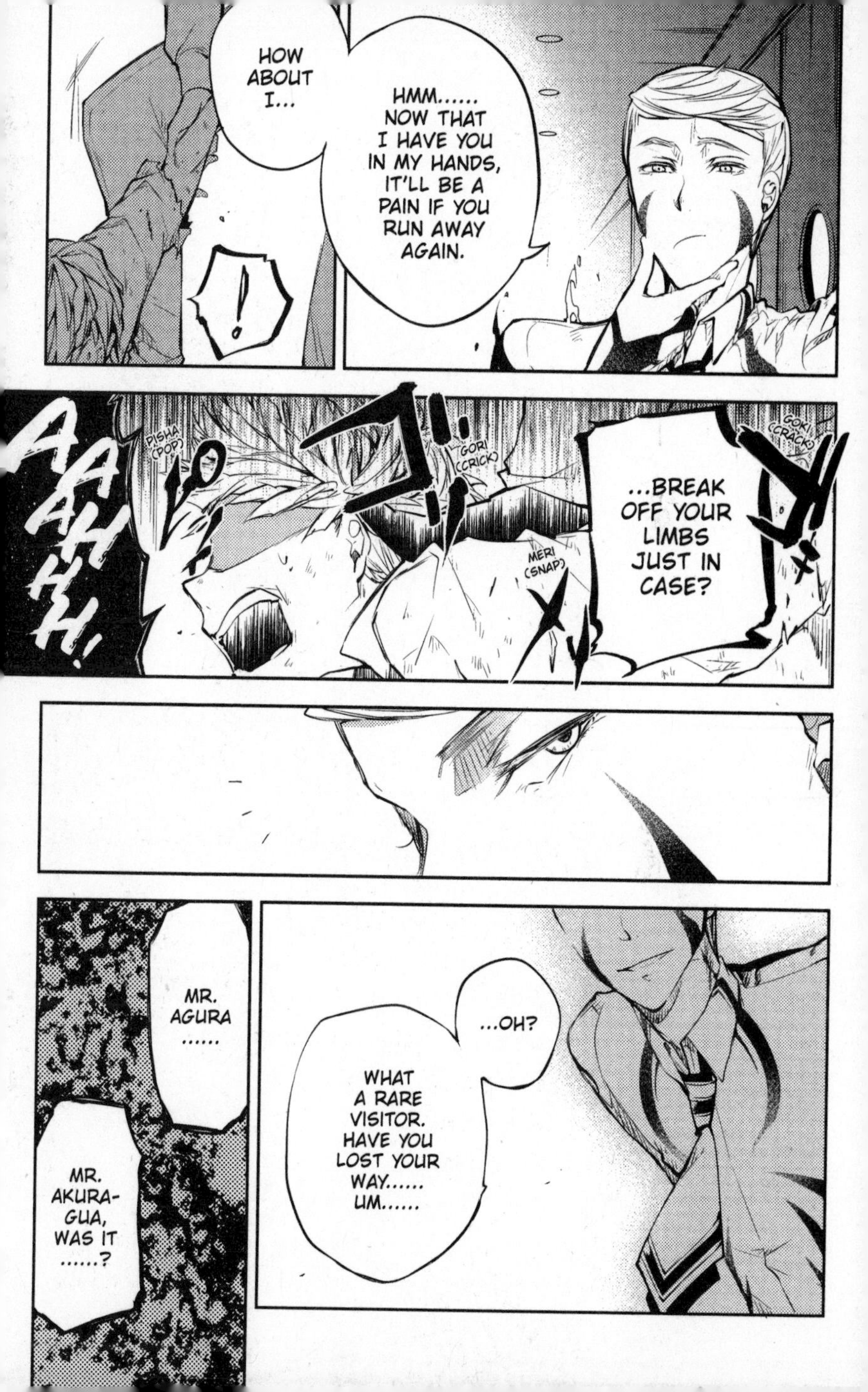
HMM...... NOW THAT I HAVE YOU IN MY HANDS, IT'LL BE A PAIN IF YOU RUN AWAY AGAIN.
HOW ABOUT I...
!
...BREAK OFF YOUR LIMBS JUST IN CASE?
GOKI (CRACK)
MERI (SNAP)
GORI (CRICK)
PISHA (POP)
AAAHHHH!
...OH?
WHAT A RARE VISITOR. HAVE YOU LOST YOUR WAY...... UM......
MR. AGURA ......
MR. AKURA-GUA, WAS IT ......?

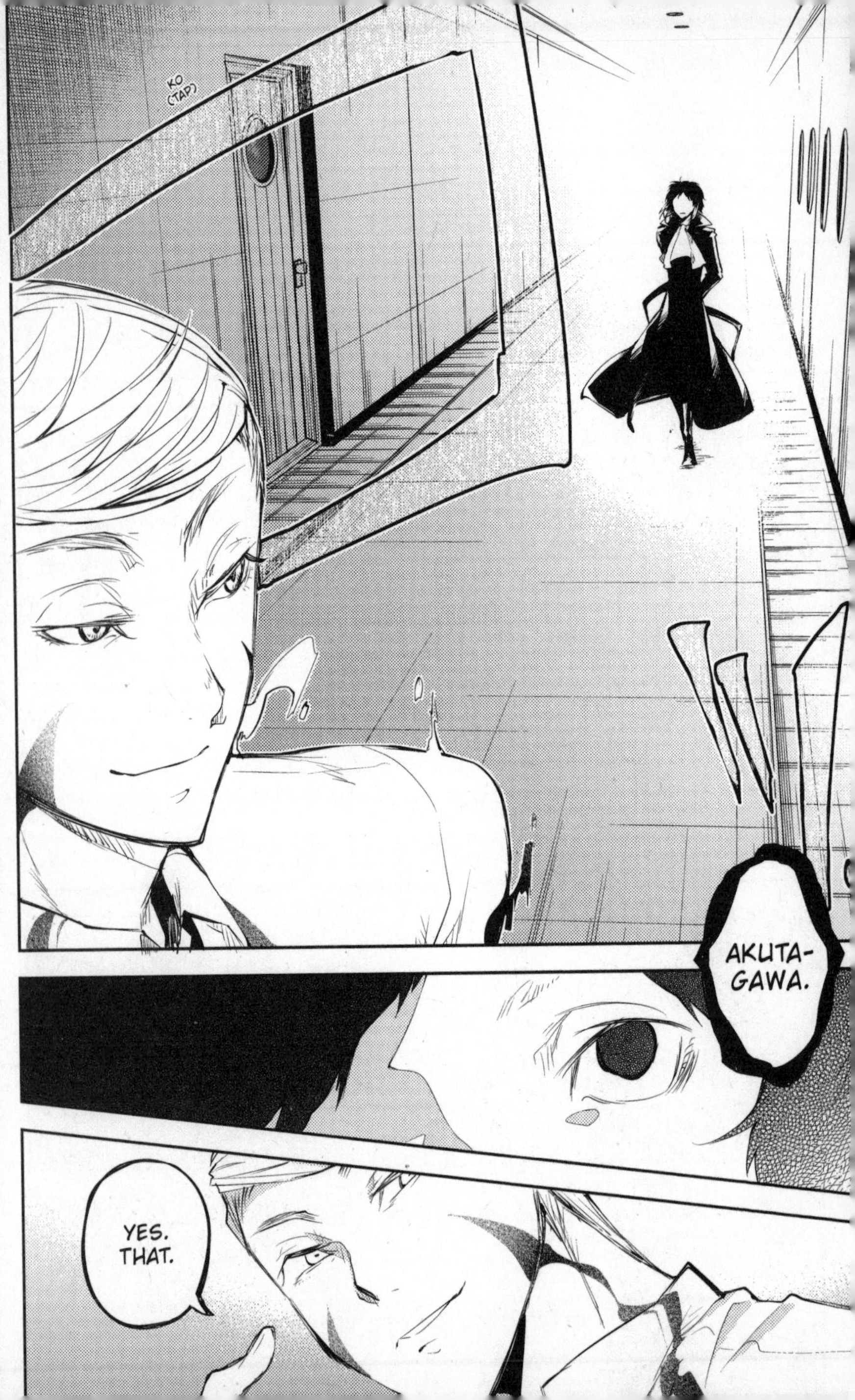
KO
(TAP)
AKUTA-
GAWA.
YES.
THAT.

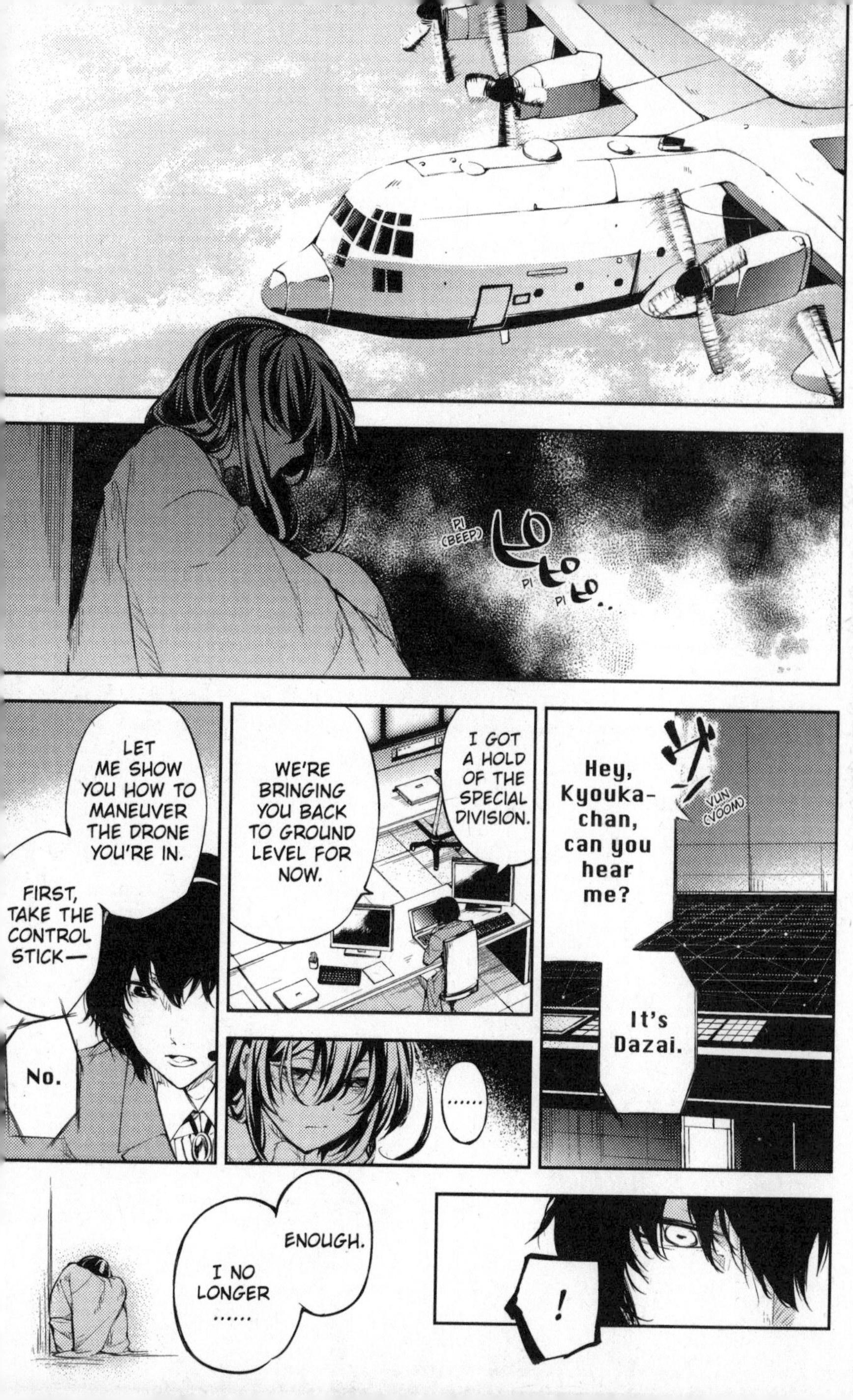
PI (BEEP)
PI
PI
VUN (VOOM)
Hey, Kyouka-chan, can you hear me?
It's Dazai.
I GOT A HOLD OF THE SPECIAL DIVISION.
WE'RE BRINGING YOU BACK TO GROUND LEVEL FOR NOW.
......
LET ME SHOW YOU HOW TO MANEUVER THE DRONE YOU'RE IN.
FIRST, TAKE THE CONTROL STICK—
No.
!
ENOUGH.
I NO LONGER ......

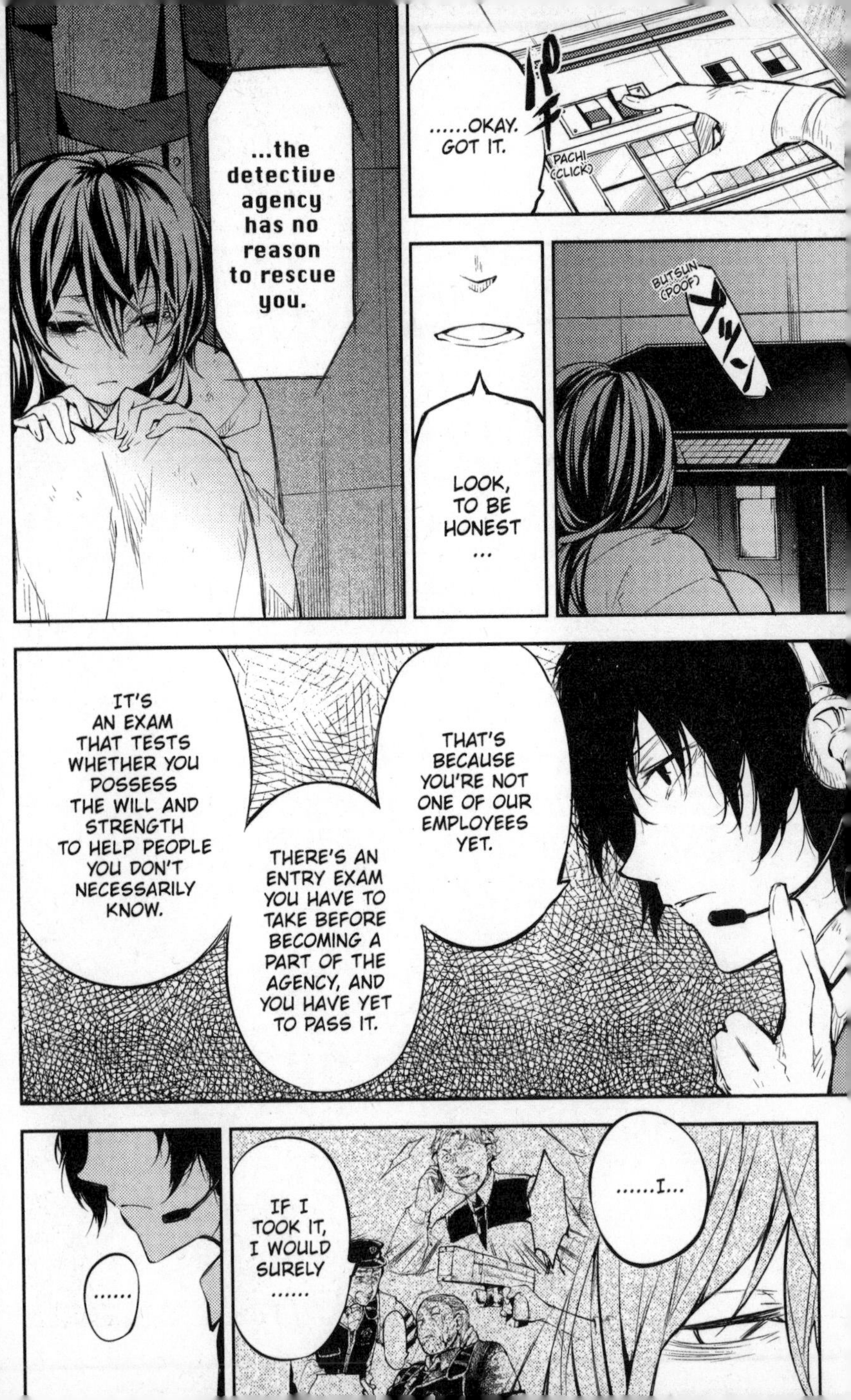
......OKAY. GOT IT.
PACHI (CLICK)
BUTSUN (POOF)
LOOK, TO BE HONEST ...
...the detective agency has no reason to rescue you.
THAT'S BECAUSE YOU'RE NOT ONE OF OUR EMPLOYEES YET.
THERE'S AN ENTRY EXAM YOU HAVE TO TAKE BEFORE BECOMING A PART OF THE AGENCY, AND YOU HAVE YET TO PASS IT.
IT'S AN EXAM THAT TESTS WHETHER YOU POSSESS THE WILL AND STRENGTH TO HELP PEOPLE YOU DON'T NECESSARILY KNOW.
......I...
IF I TOOK IT, I WOULD SURELY ......
....

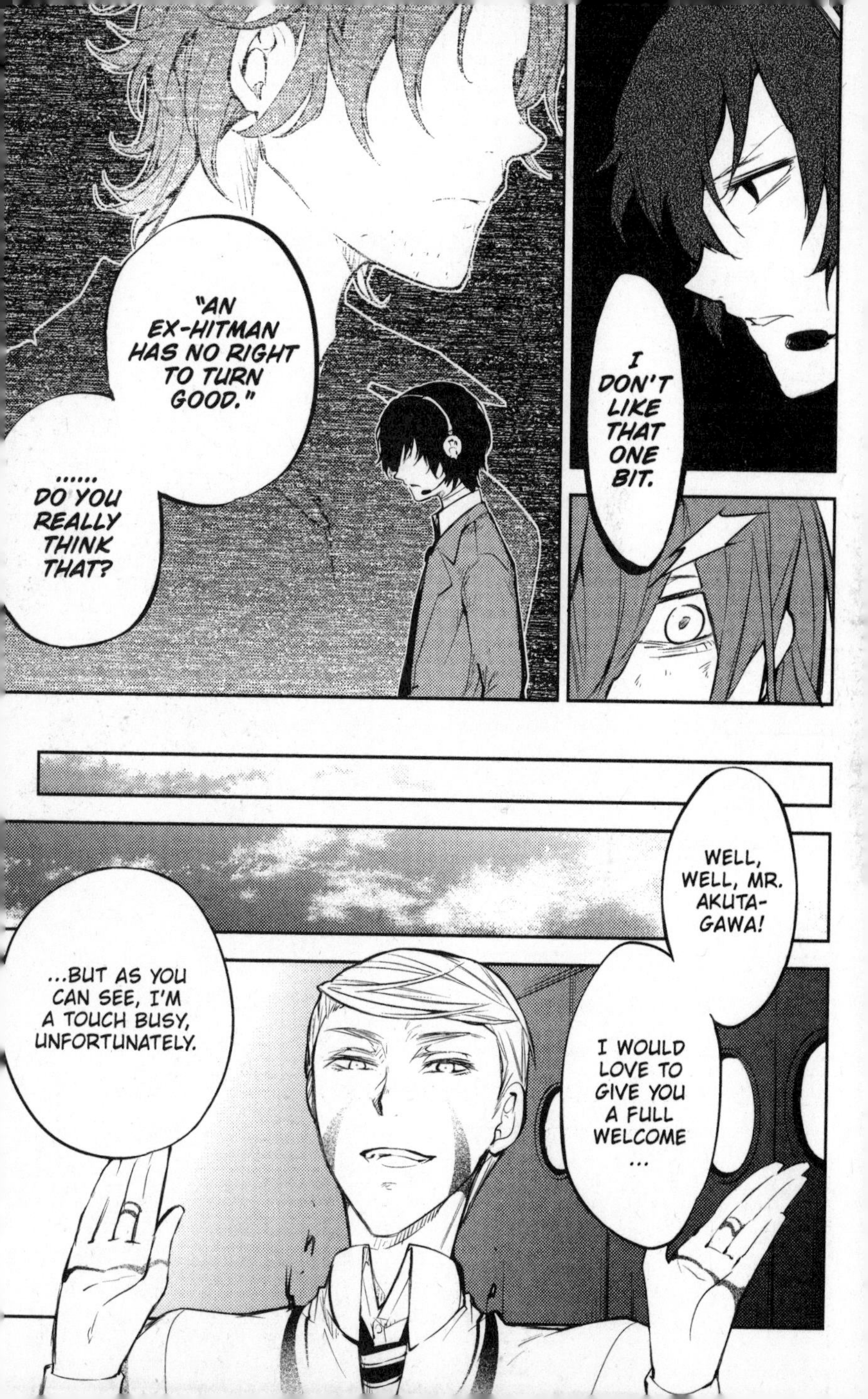
I DON'T LIKE THAT ONE BIT.
"AN EX-HITMAN HAS NO RIGHT TO TURN GOOD."
...... DO YOU REALLY THINK THAT?
WELL, WELL, MR. AKUTA-GAWA!
I WOULD LOVE TO GIVE YOU A FULL WELCOME ...
...BUT AS YOU CAN SEE, I'M A TOUCH BUSY, UNFORTUNATELY.

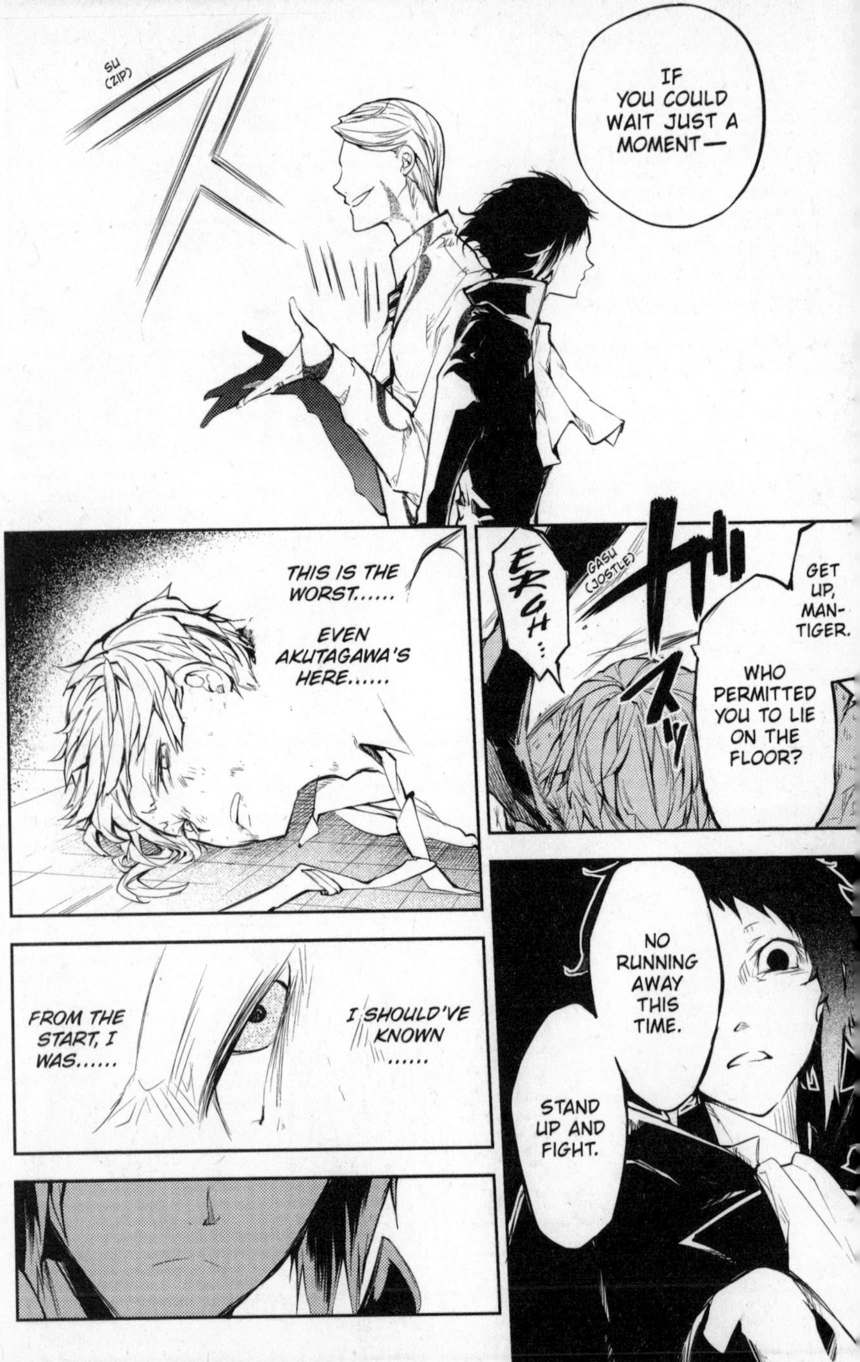
IF YOU COULD WAIT JUST A MOMENT—
SU (ZIP)
GET UP, MAN-TIGER.
WHO PERMITTED YOU TO LIE ON THE FLOOR?
GASU (JOSTLE)
ERGH...
THIS IS THE WORST......
EVEN AKUTAGAWA'S HERE......
NO RUNNING AWAY THIS TIME.
STAND UP AND FIGHT.
I SHOULD'VE KNOWN ......
FROM THE START, I WAS......

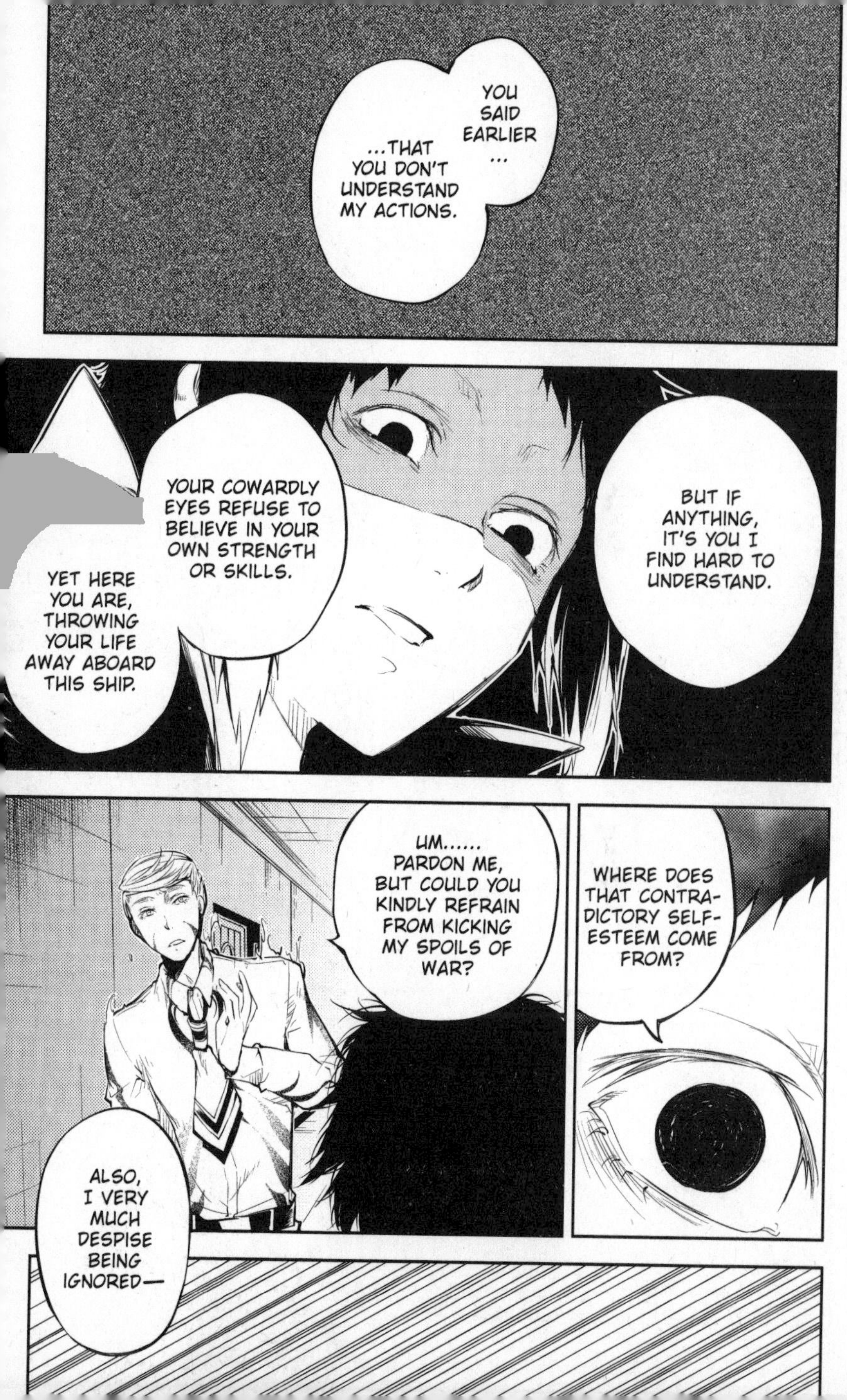
YOU SAID EARLIER...
...THAT YOU DON'T UNDERSTAND MY ACTIONS.
BUT IF ANYTHING, IT'S YOU I FIND HARD TO UNDERSTAND.
YOUR COWARDLY EYES REFUSE TO BELIEVE IN YOUR OWN STRENGTH OR SKILLS.
YET HERE YOU ARE, THROWING YOUR LIFE AWAY ABOARD THIS SHIP.
WHERE DOES THAT CONTRA-DICTORY SELF-ESTEEM COME FROM?
UM...... PARDON ME, BUT COULD YOU KINDLY REFRAIN FROM KICKING MY SPOILS OF WAR?
ALSO, I VERY MUCH DESPISE BEING IGNORED—

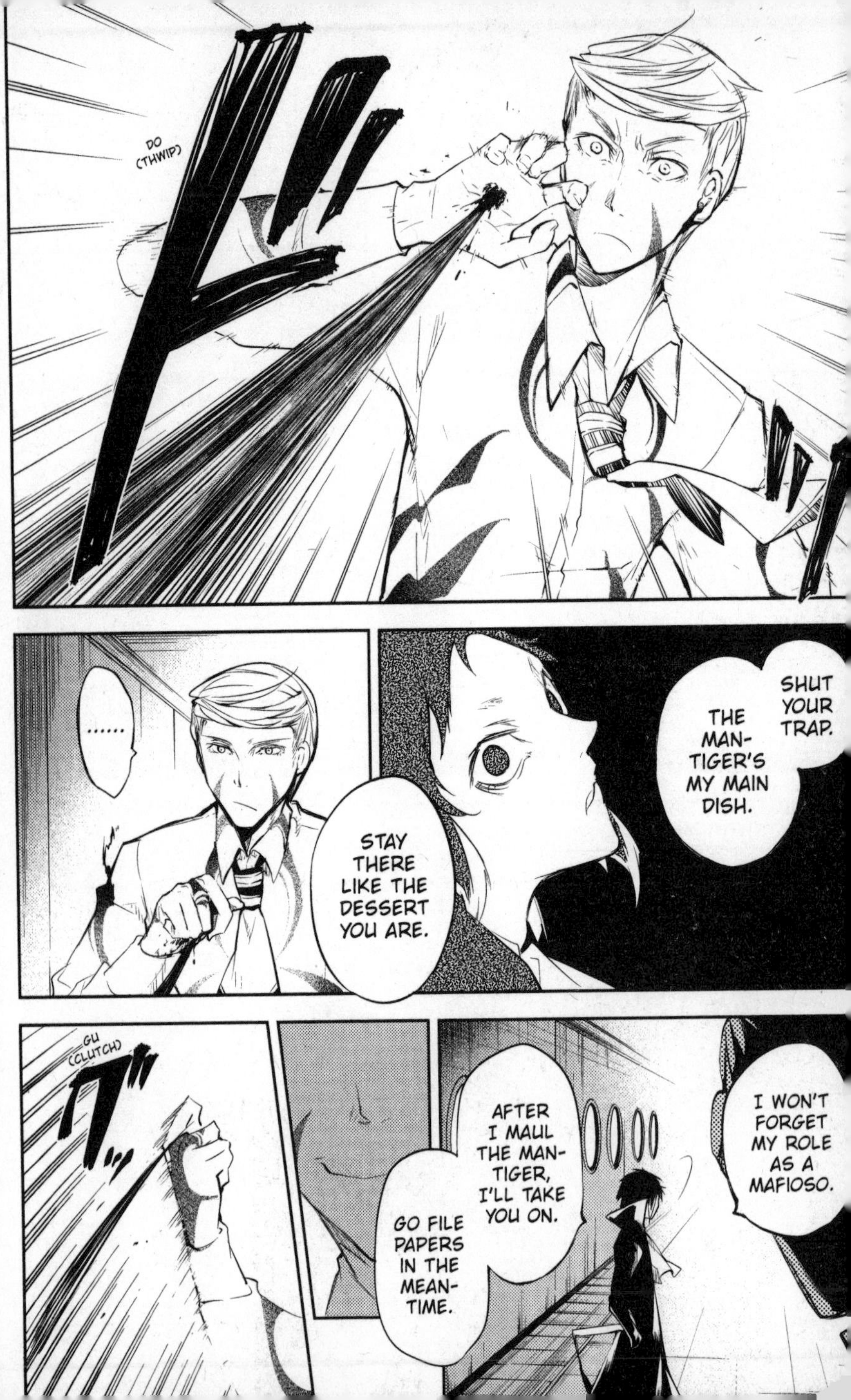
DO (THWIP)
SHUT YOUR TRAP.
THE MAN-TIGER'S MY MAIN DISH.
STAY THERE LIKE THE DESSERT YOU ARE.
......
I WON'T FORGET MY ROLE AS A MAFIOSO.
AFTER I MAUL THE MAN-TIGER, I'LL TAKE YOU ON.
GO FILE PAPERS IN THE MEAN-TIME.
GU (CLUTCH)

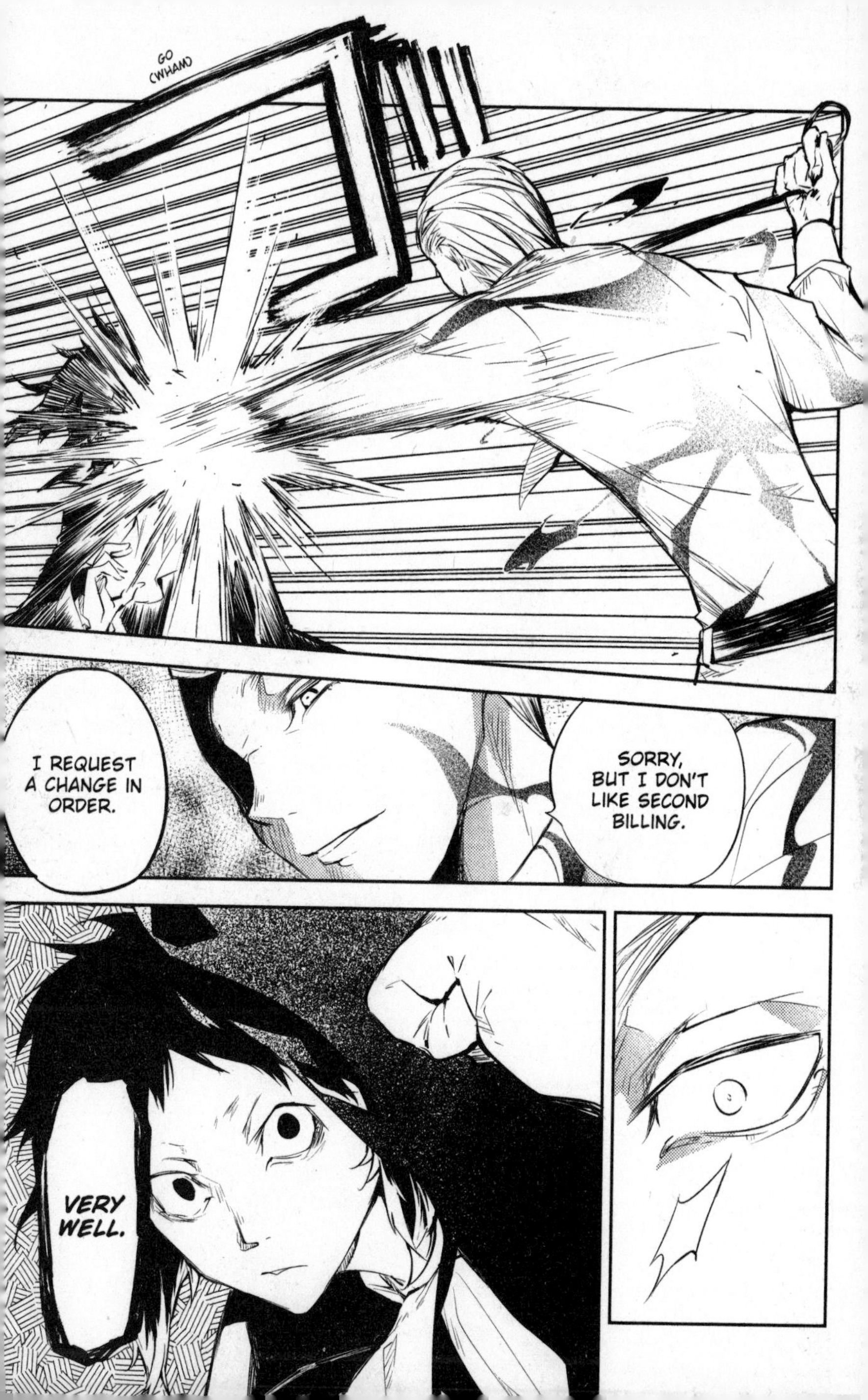
GO
(WHAM)
SORRY, BUT I DON'T LIKE SECOND BILLING.
I REQUEST A CHANGE IN ORDER.
VERY WELL.

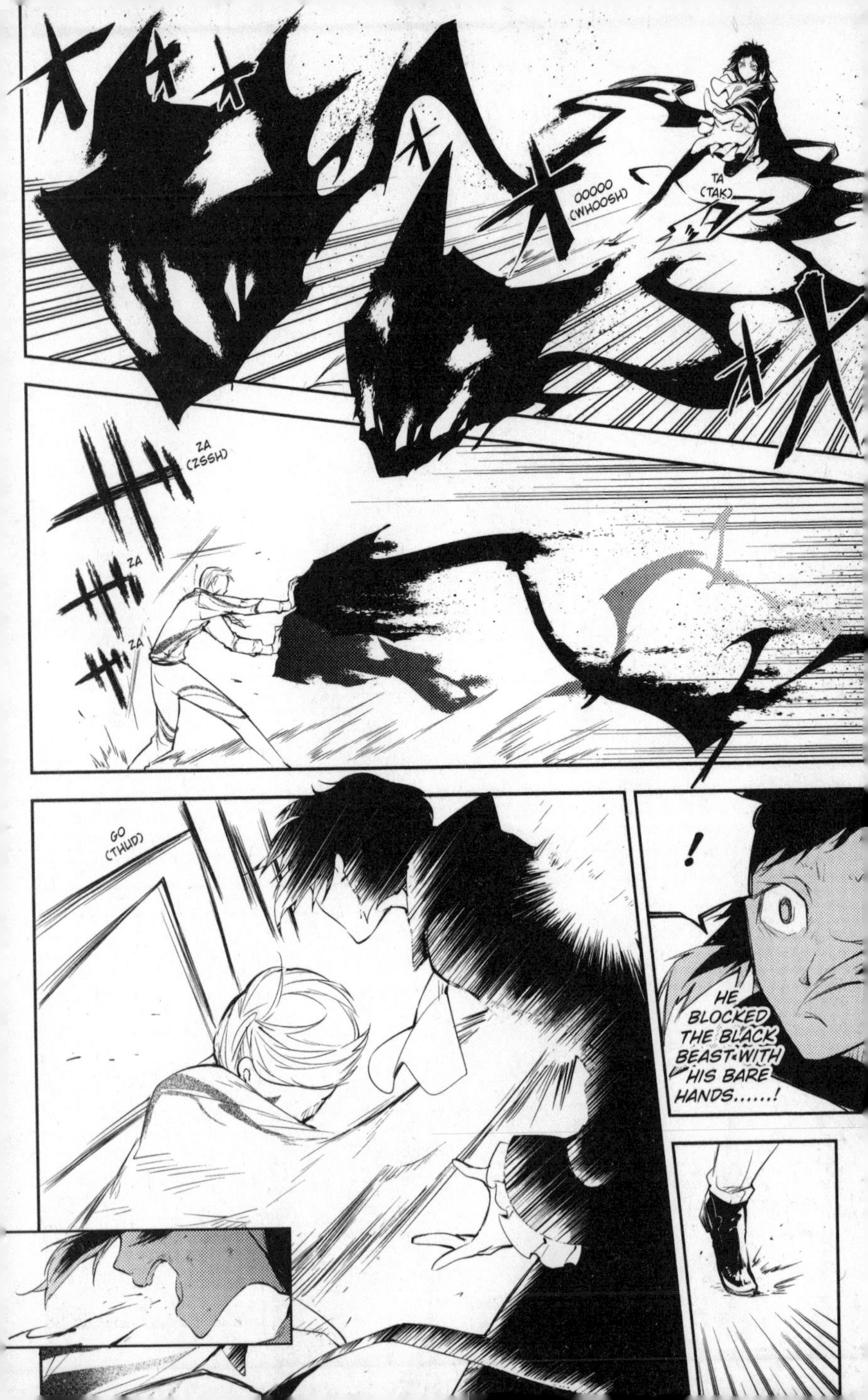
TA
(TAK)
OOOOO
(WHOOSH)
ZA
(ZSSH)
ZA
ZA
!
HE BLOCKED THE BLACK BEAST WITH HIS BARE HANDS......!
GO
(THUD)

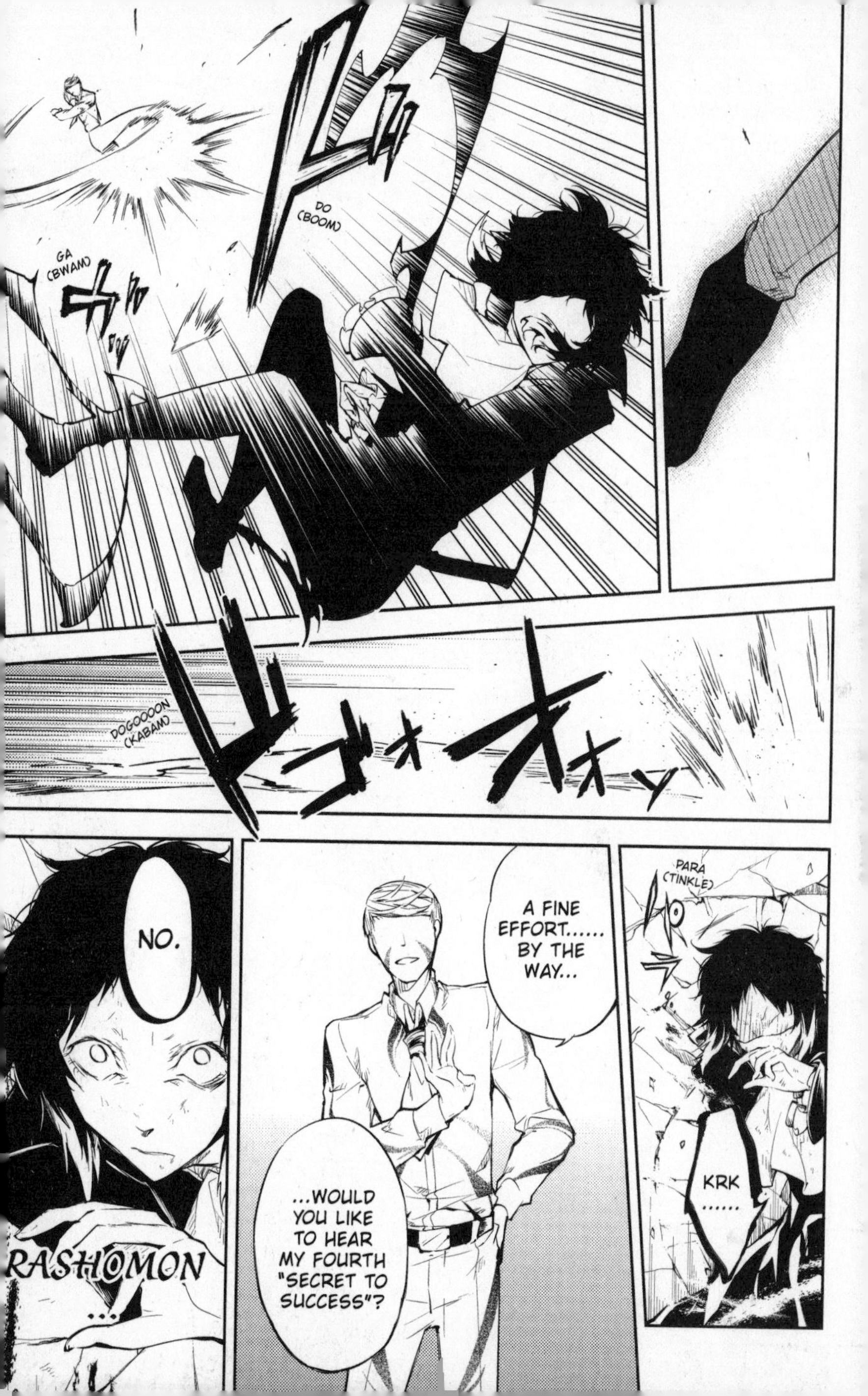
DO (BOOM)
GA (BWAM)
DOGOOOON (KABAM)
PARA (TINKLE)
KRK ......
A FINE EFFORT...... BY THE WAY...
...WOULD YOU LIKE TO HEAR MY FOURTH "SECRET TO SUCCESS"?
NO.
RASHOMON ...

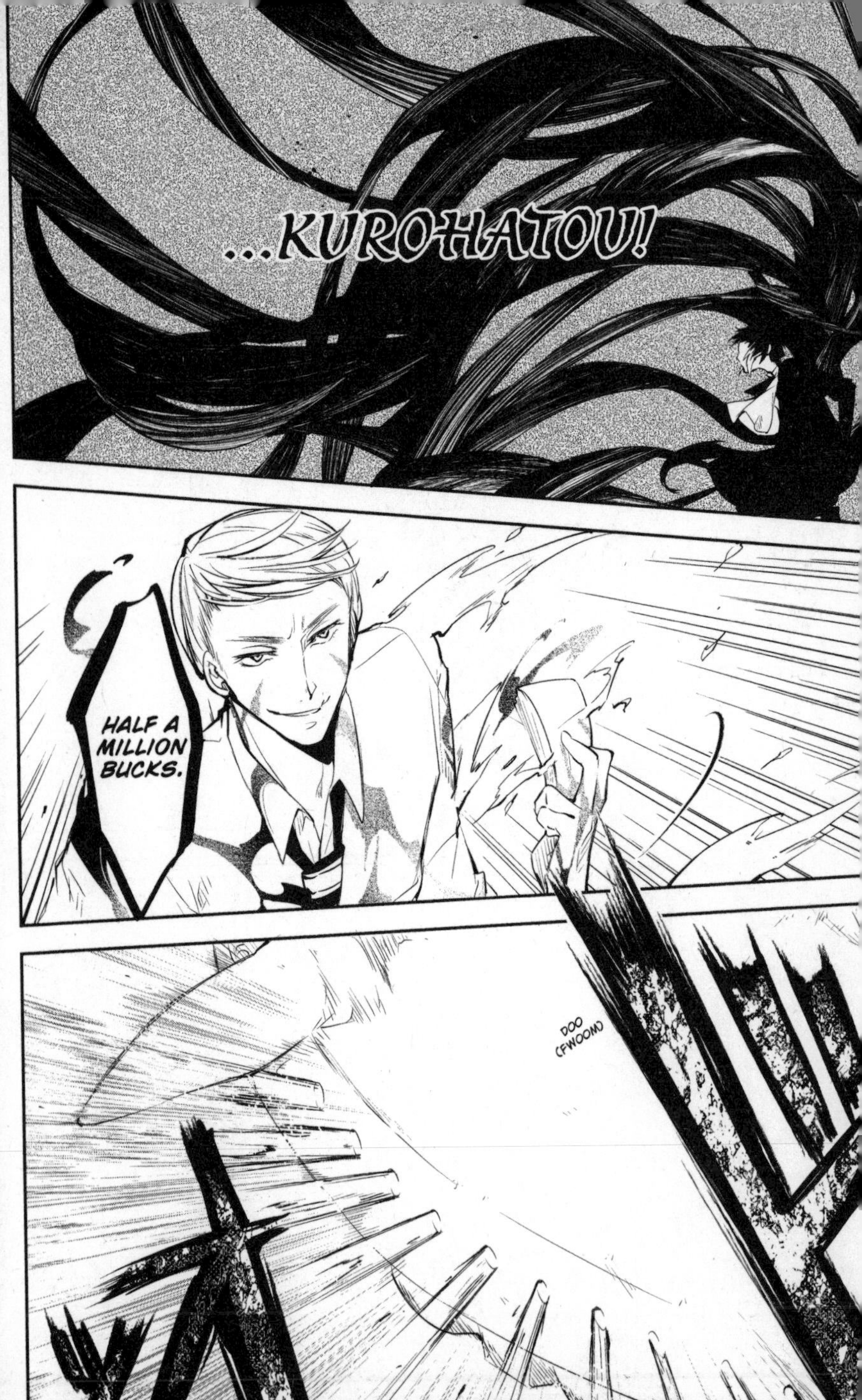
...KURO-HATOU!
HALF A MILLION BUCKS.
DOO (FWOOM)

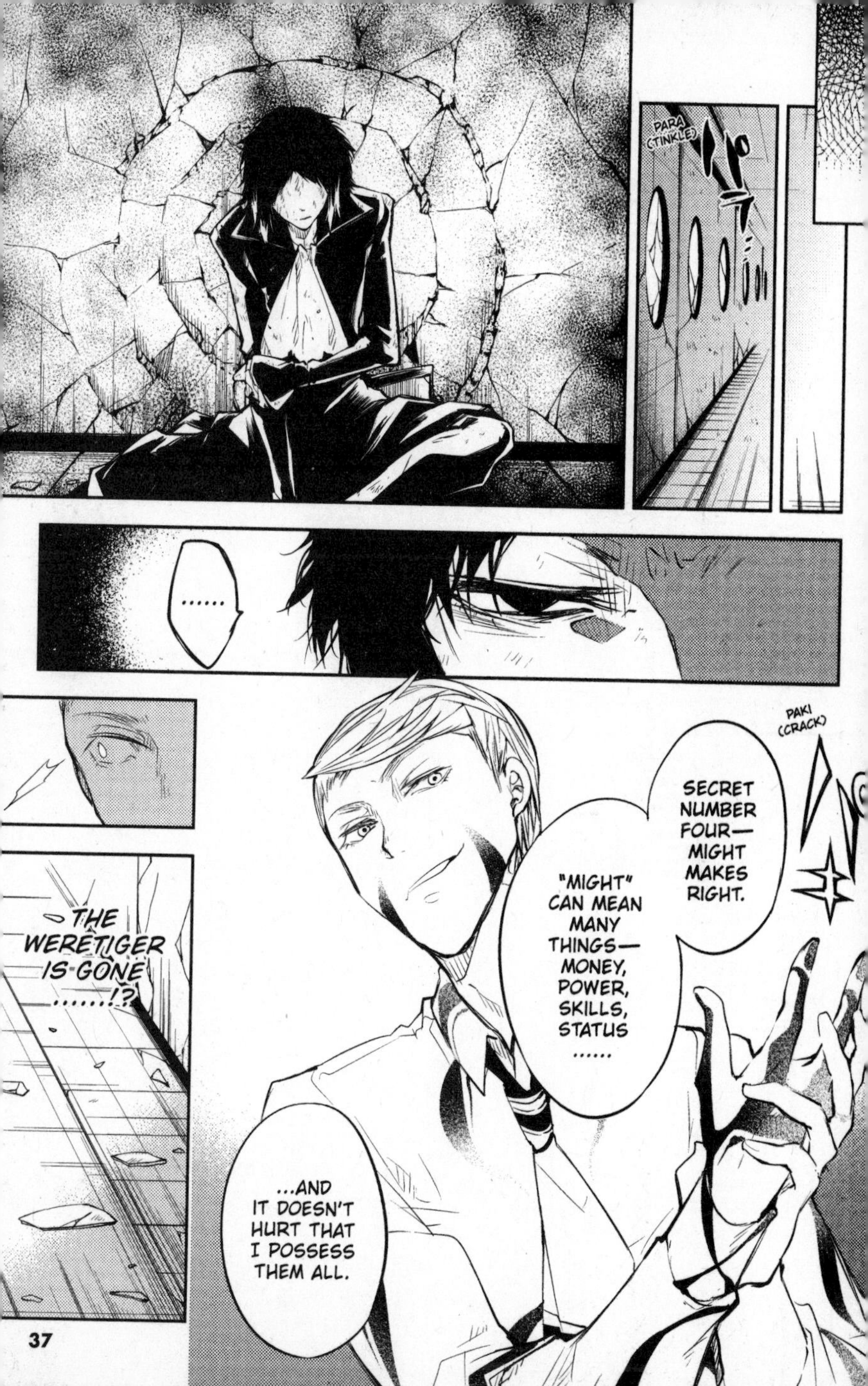
PARA (TINKLE)
......
PAKI (CRACK)
SECRET NUMBER FOUR— MIGHT MAKES RIGHT.
"MIGHT" CAN MEAN MANY THINGS— MONEY, POWER, SKILLS, STATUS ......
...AND IT DOESN'T HURT THAT I POSSESS THEM ALL.
THE WERETIGER IS GONE ......!?

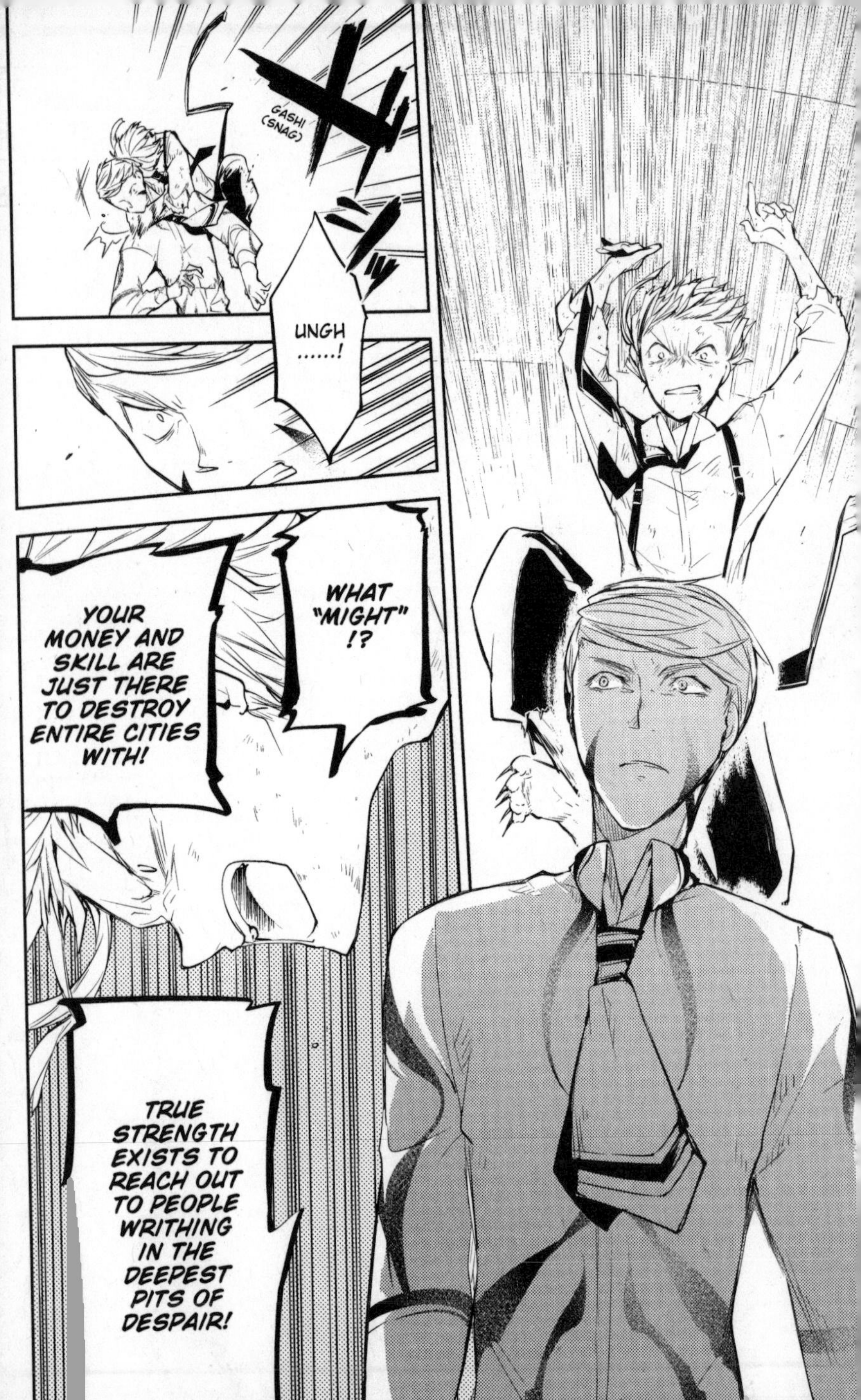
GASHI (SNAG)
UNGH ......!
WHAT "MIGHT" !?
YOUR MONEY AND SKILL ARE JUST THERE TO DESTROY ENTIRE CITIES WITH!
TRUE STRENGTH EXISTS TO REACH OUT TO PEOPLE WRITHING IN THE DEEPEST PITS OF DESPAIR!

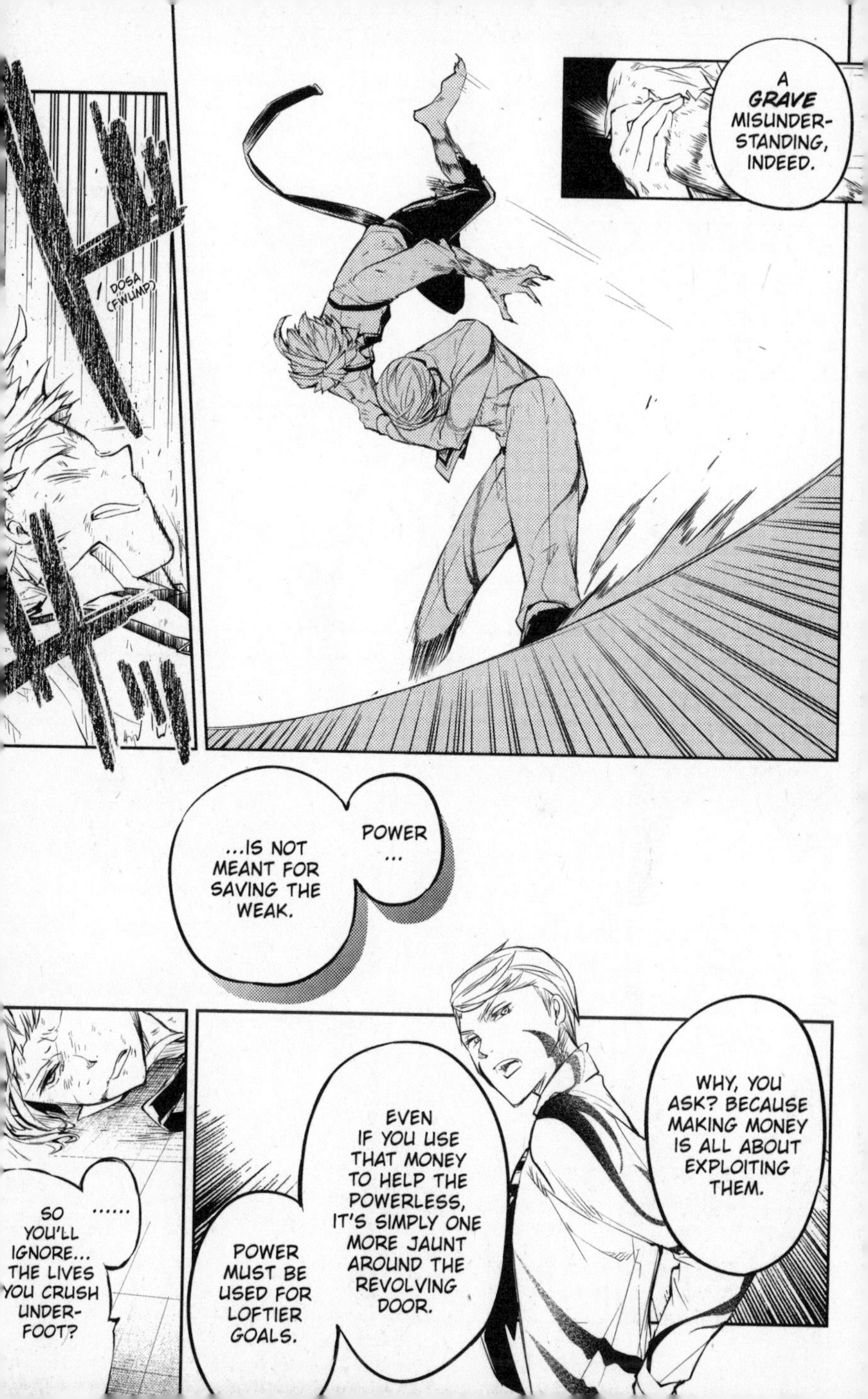
A GRAVE MISUNDERSTANDING, INDEED.
DOSA (FWUMP)
POWER...
...IS NOT MEANT FOR SAVING THE WEAK.
WHY, YOU ASK? BECAUSE MAKING MONEY IS ALL ABOUT EXPLOITING THEM.
EVEN IF YOU USE THAT MONEY TO HELP THE POWERLESS, IT'S SIMPLY ONE MORE JAUNT AROUND THE REVOLVING DOOR.
POWER MUST BE USED FOR LOFTIER GOALS.
......
SO YOU'LL IGNORE... THE LIVES YOU CRUSH UNDERFOOT?

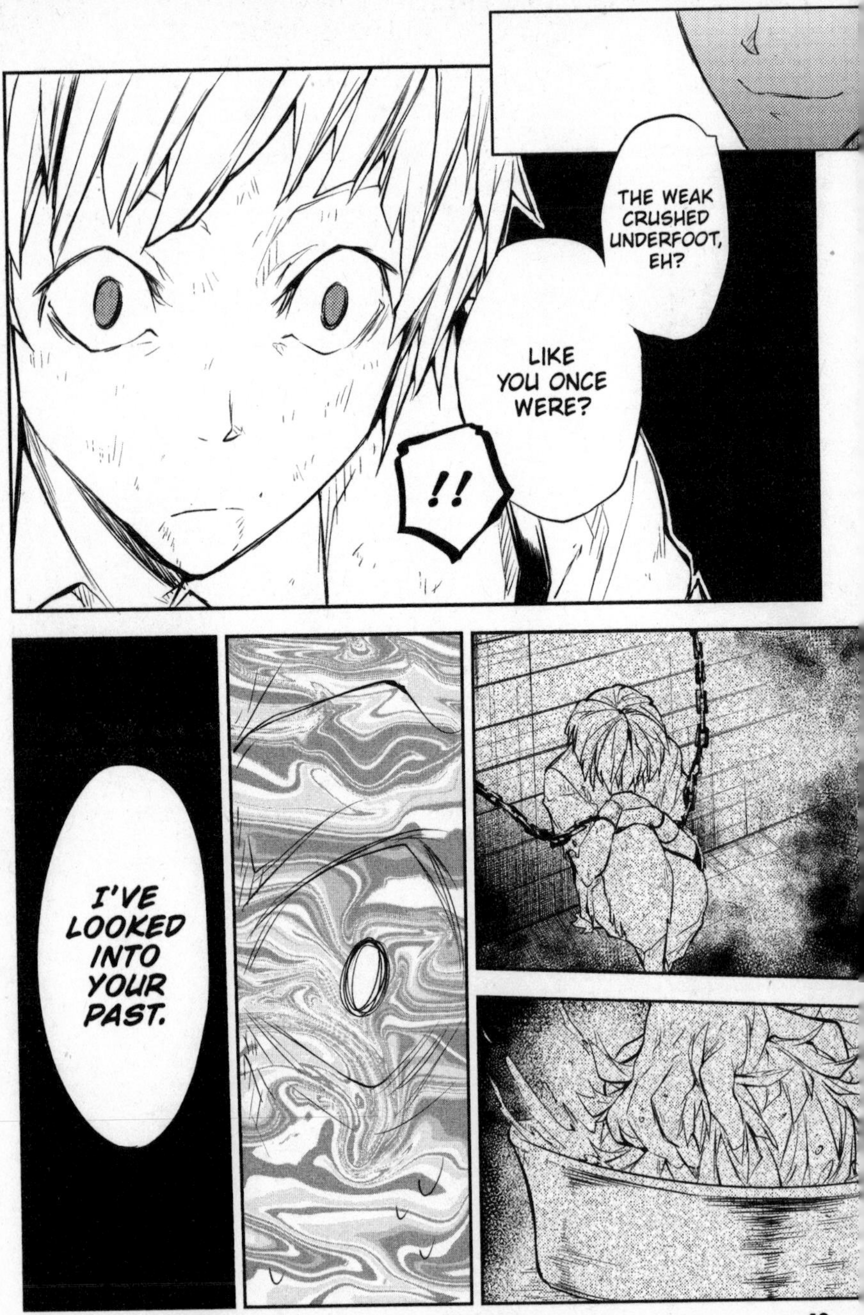
THE WEAK CRUSHED UNDERFOOT, EH?
LIKE YOU ONCE WERE?
!!
I'VE LOOKED INTO YOUR PAST.

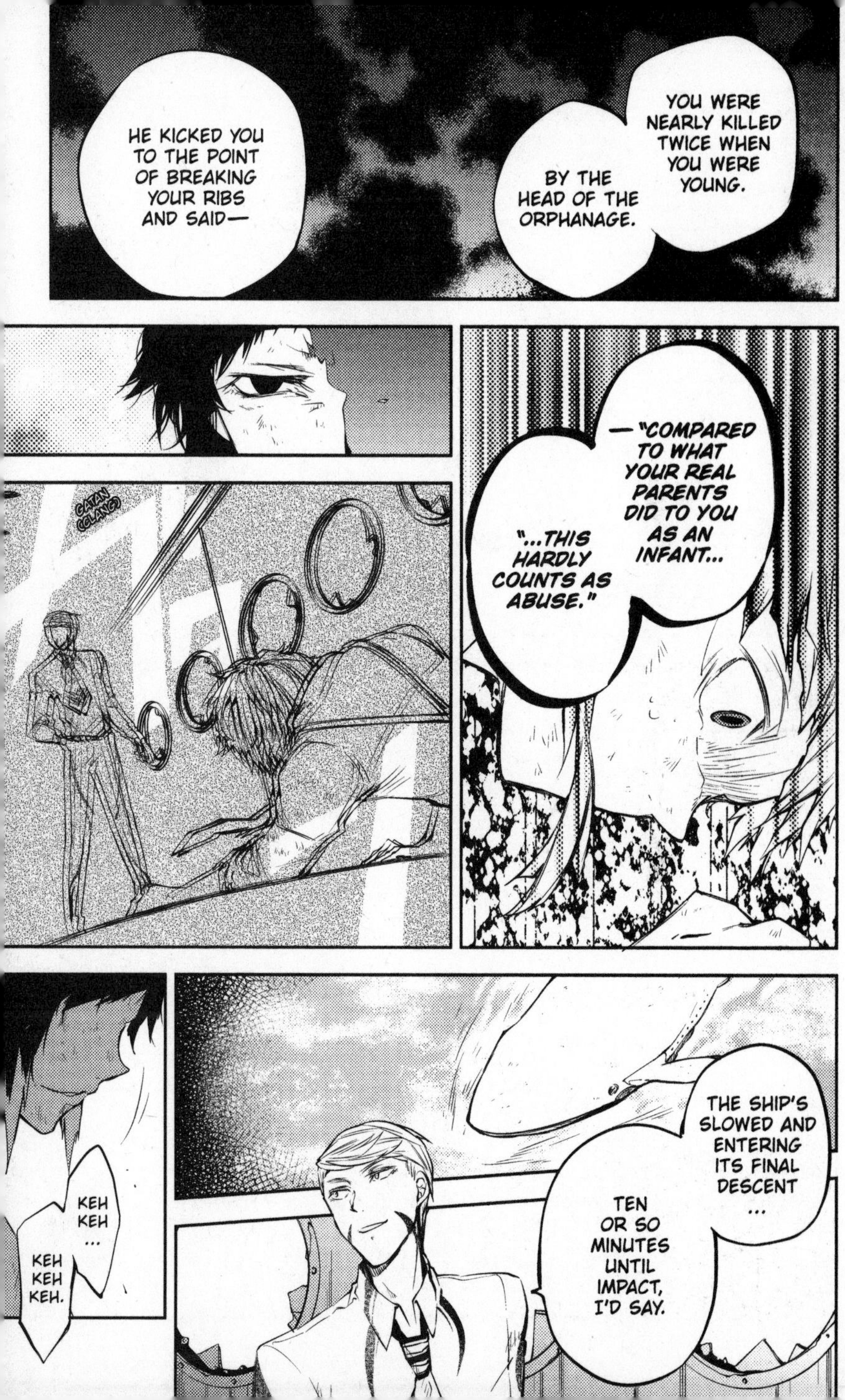
YOU WERE NEARLY KILLED TWICE WHEN YOU WERE YOUNG.
BY THE HEAD OF THE ORPHANAGE.
HE KICKED YOU TO THE POINT OF BREAKING YOUR RIBS AND SAID—
—"COMPARED TO WHAT YOUR REAL PARENTS DID TO YOU AS AN INFANT...
"...THIS HARDLY COUNTS AS ABUSE."
GATAN (CLANG)
THE SHIP'S SLOWED AND ENTERING ITS FINAL DESCENT ...
TEN OR SO MINUTES UNTIL IMPACT, I'D SAY.
KEH KEH ...
KEH KEH KEH.

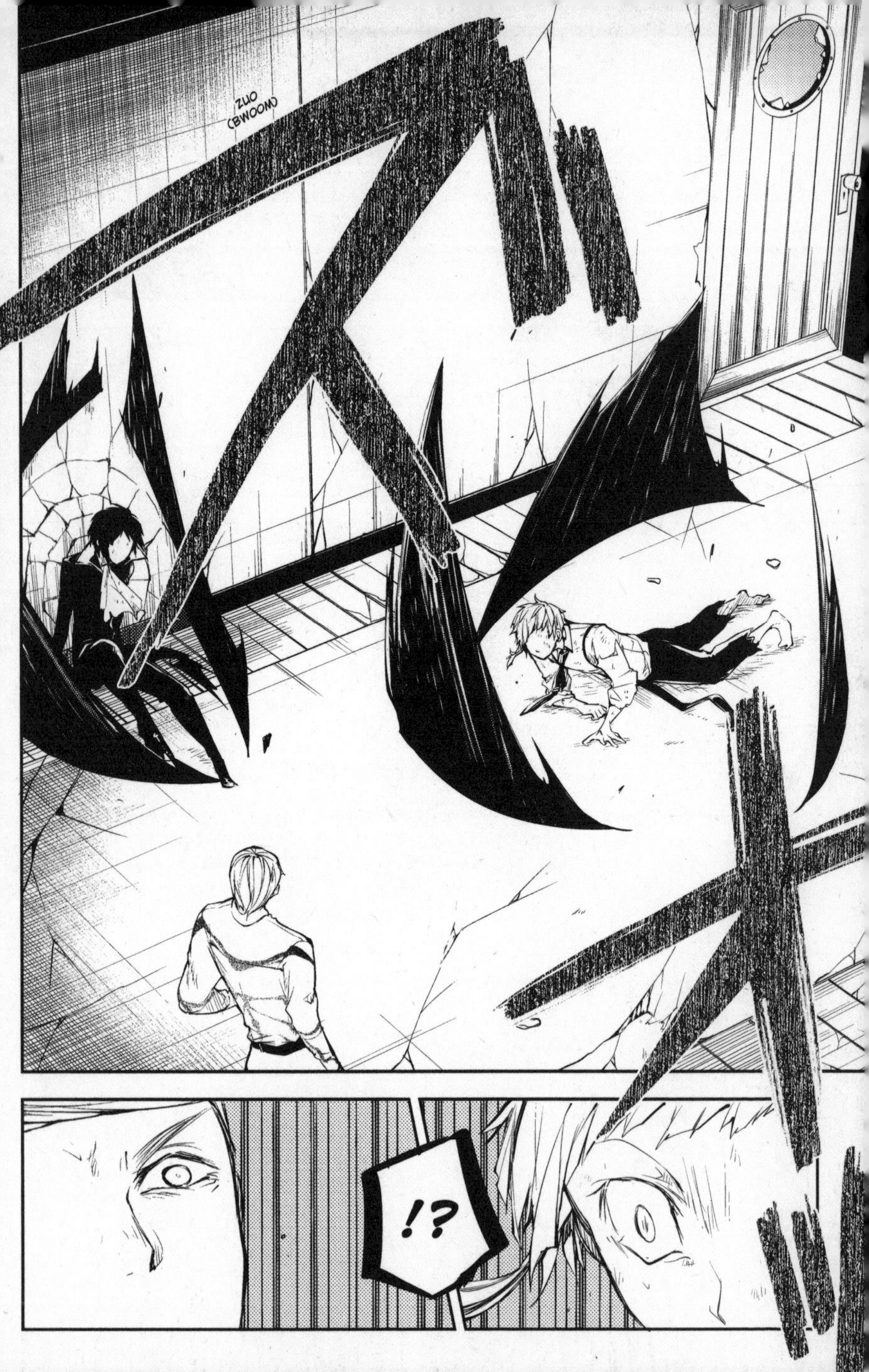
ZUO
(BWOOM)
!?

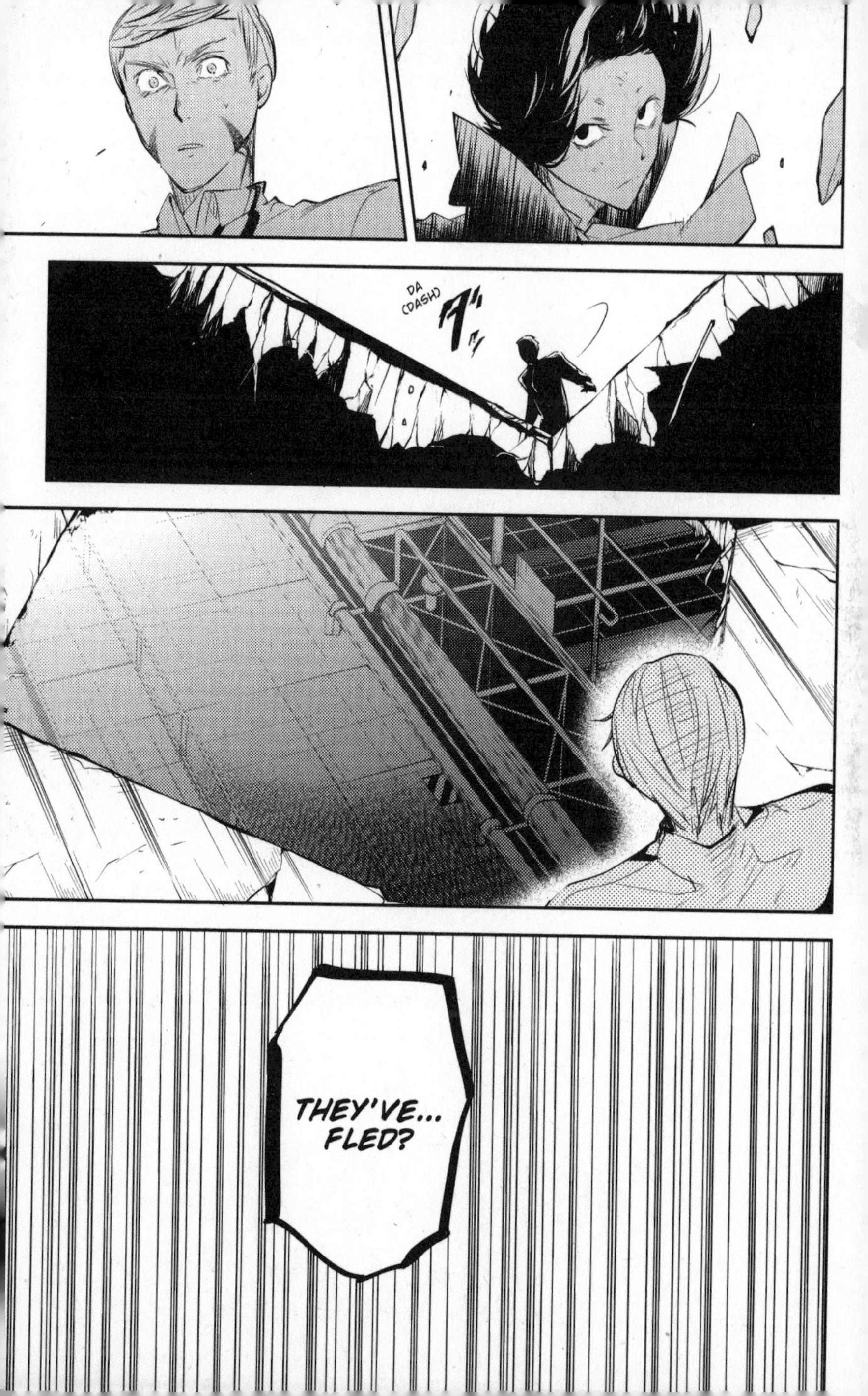
DA (DASH)
THEY'VE... FLED?

BUNGO
STRAY DOGS

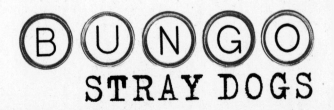

CHAPTER 35
Rashomon, the Tiger, and the Last Tycoon

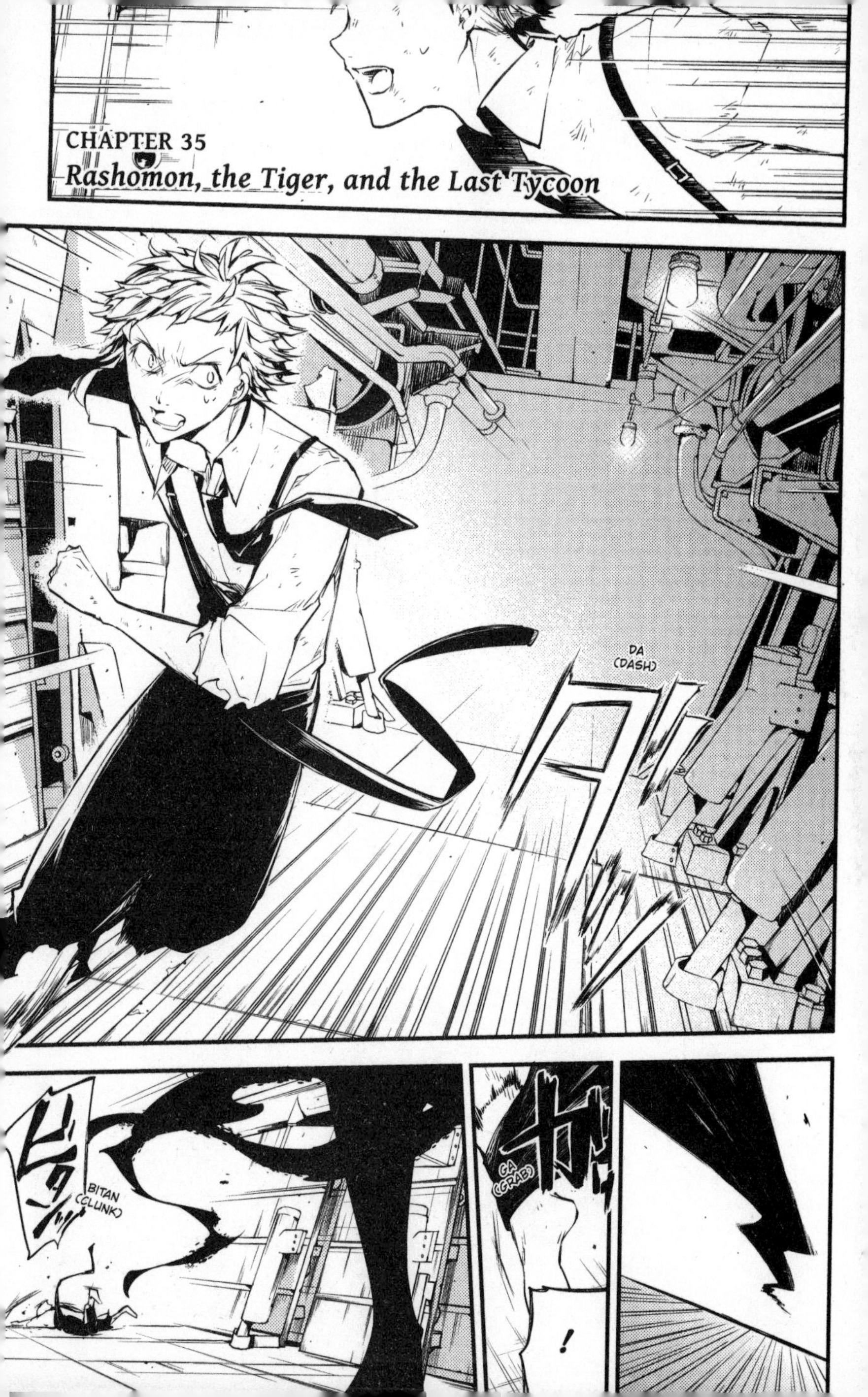
DA
(DASH)
GA
(GRAB)
!
BITAN
(CLUNK)

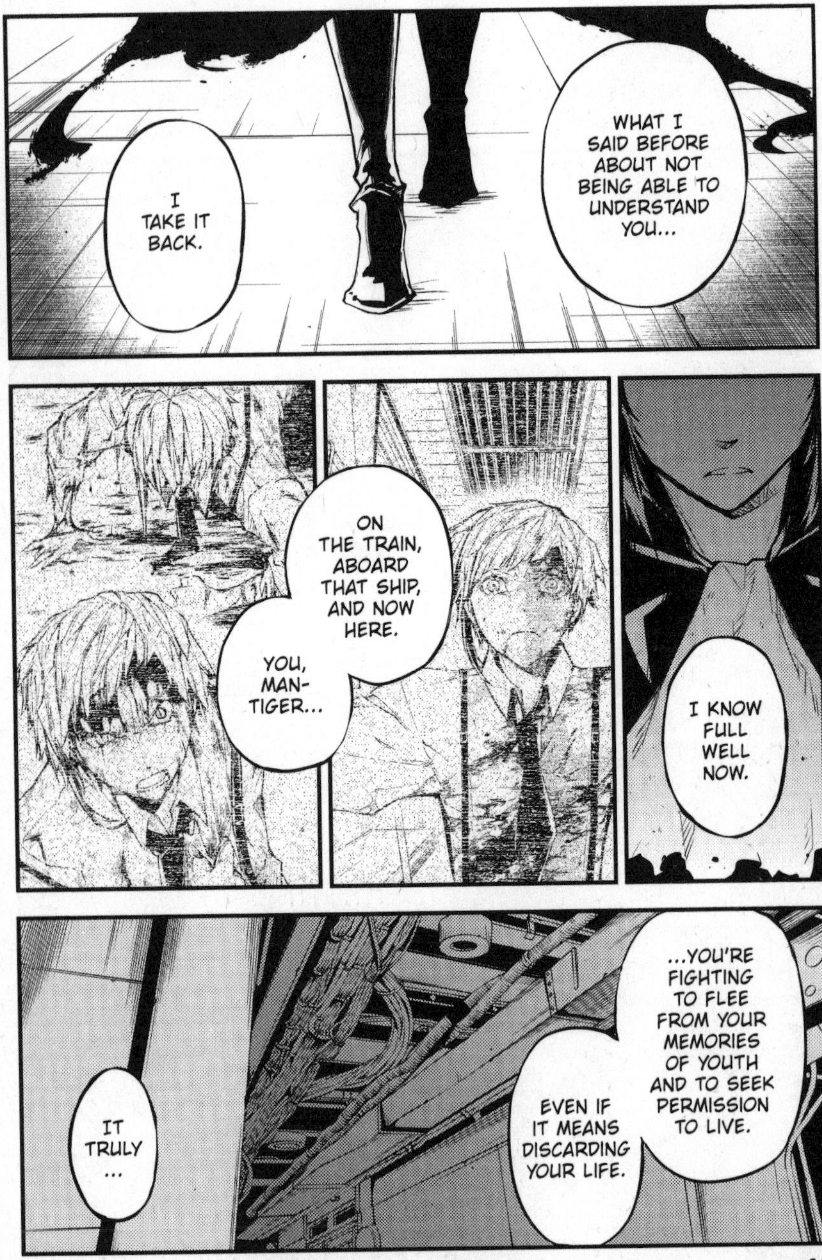
WHAT I SAID BEFORE ABOUT NOT BEING ABLE TO UNDERSTAND YOU...
I TAKE IT BACK.
I KNOW FULL WELL NOW.
ON THE TRAIN, ABOARD THAT SHIP, AND NOW HERE.
YOU, MAN-TIGER...
...YOU'RE FIGHTING TO FLEE FROM YOUR MEMORIES OF YOUTH AND TO SEEK PERMISSION TO LIVE.
EVEN IF IT MEANS DISCARDING YOUR LIFE.
IT TRULY ...

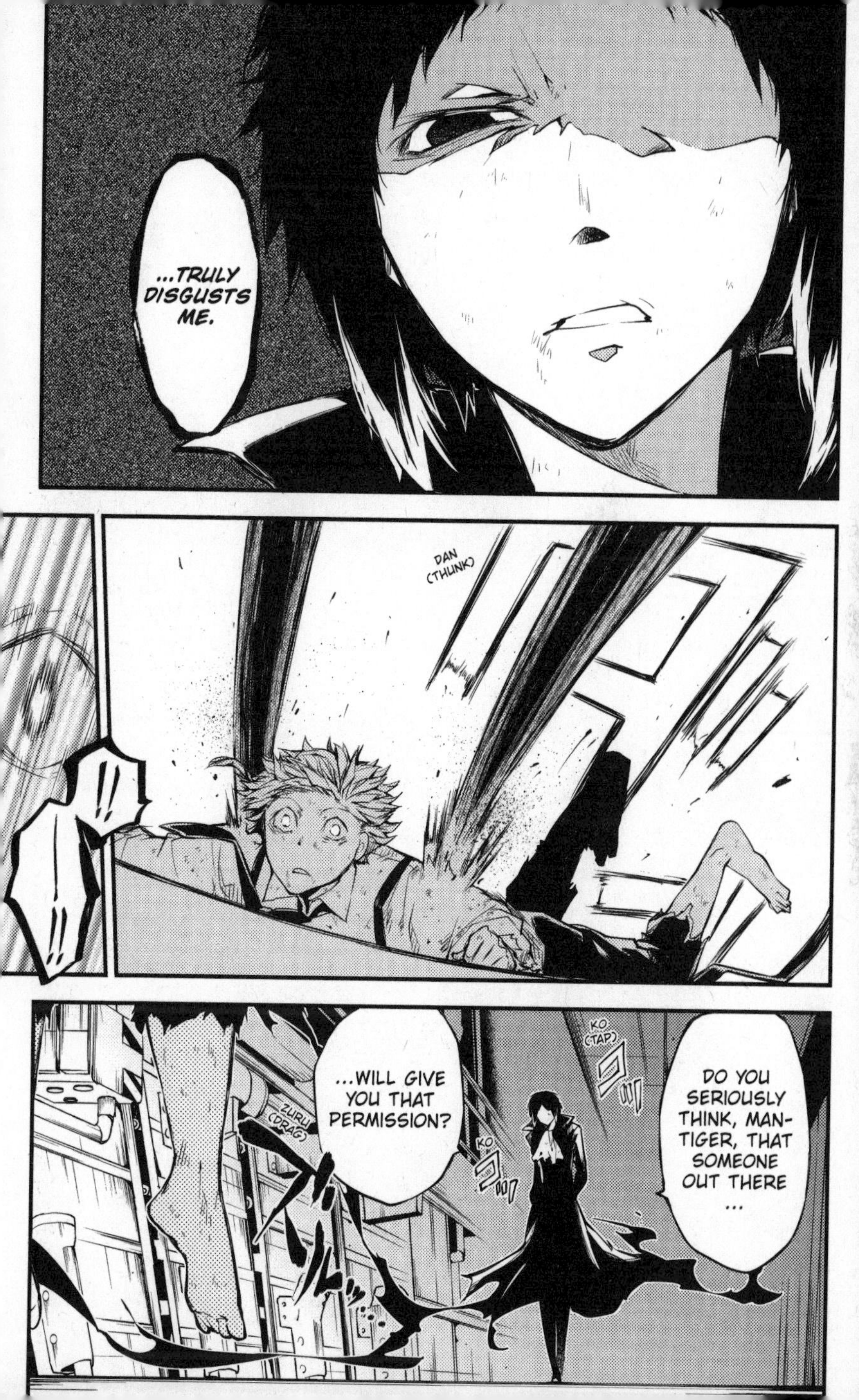
...TRULY DISGUSTS ME.
DAN (THUNK)
!!
!!
DO YOU SERIOUSLY THINK, MAN-TIGER, THAT SOMEONE OUT THERE ...
KO (TAP)
KO
...WILL GIVE YOU THAT PERMISSION?
ZURU (DRAG)

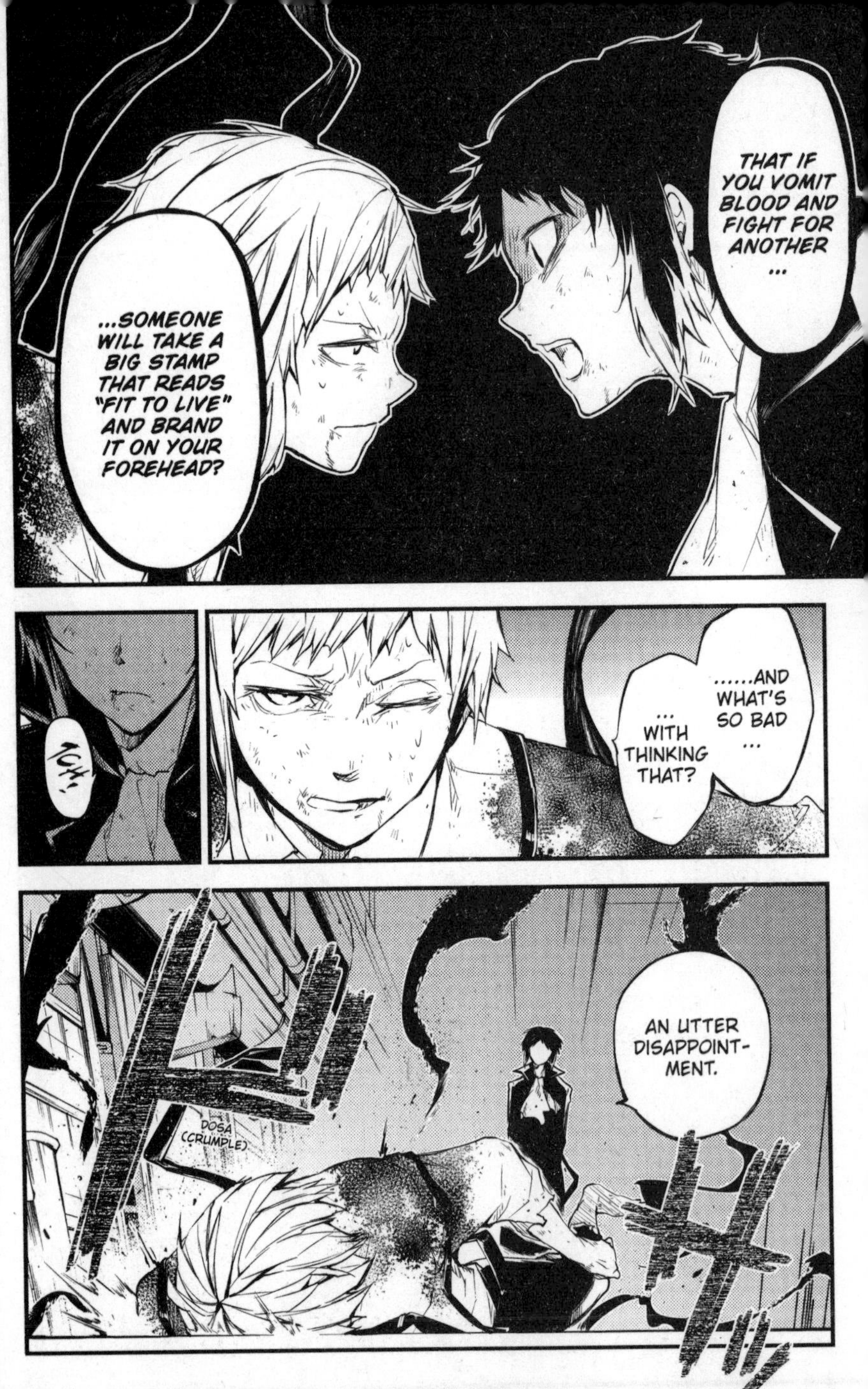
THAT IF YOU VOMIT BLOOD AND FIGHT FOR ANOTHER ...
...SOMEONE WILL TAKE A BIG STAMP THAT READS "FIT TO LIVE" AND BRAND IT ON YOUR FOREHEAD?
......AND WHAT'S SO BAD ...
... WITH THINKING THAT?
TCH!
AN UTTER DISAPPOINT-MENT.
DOSA (CRUMPLE)

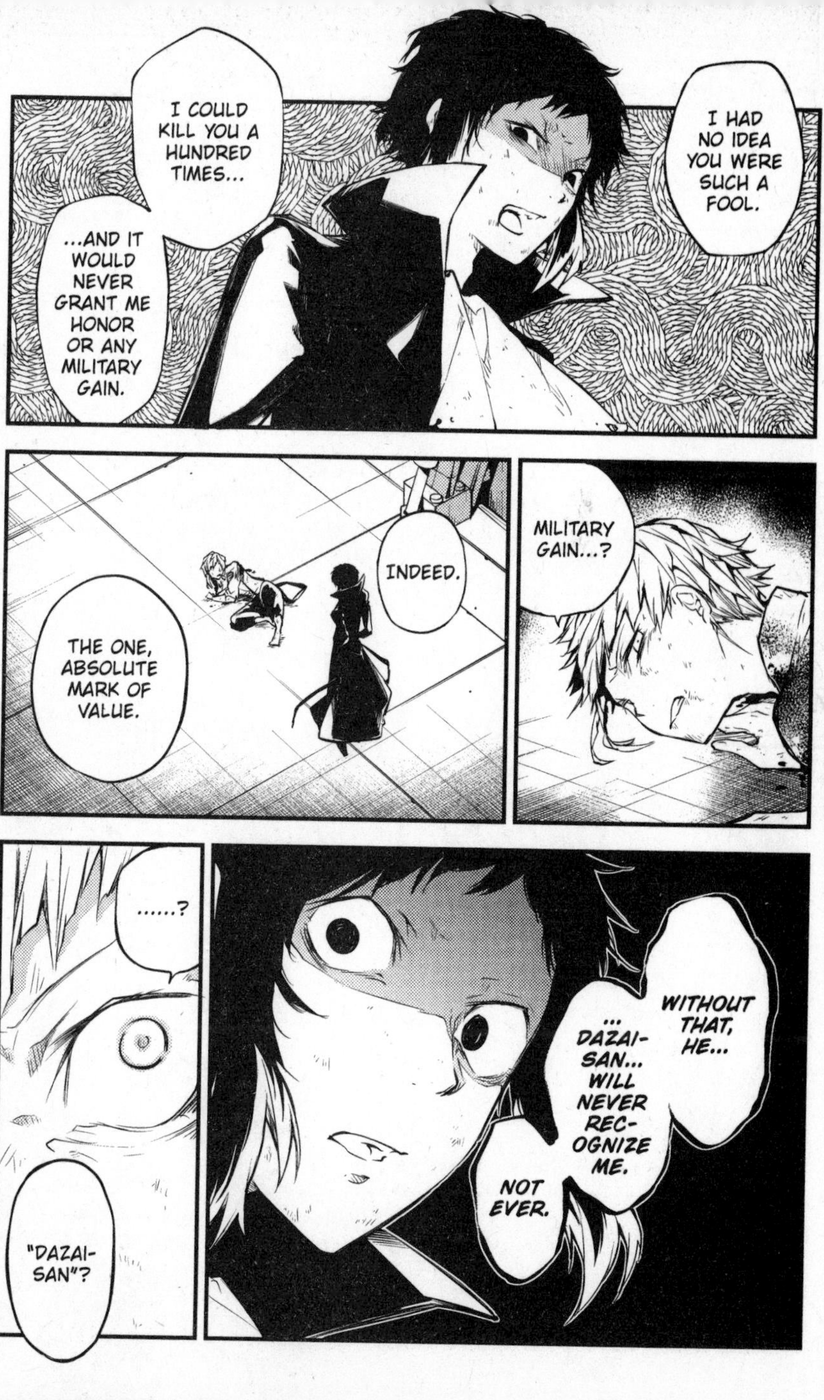
I HAD NO IDEA YOU WERE SUCH A FOOL.
I COULD KILL YOU A HUNDRED TIMES...
...AND IT WOULD NEVER GRANT ME HONOR OR ANY MILITARY GAIN.
MILITARY GAIN...?
INDEED.
THE ONE, ABSOLUTE MARK OF VALUE.
WITHOUT THAT, HE...
...DAZAI-SAN... WILL NEVER REC-OGNIZE ME.
NOT EVER.
......?
"DAZAI-SAN"?

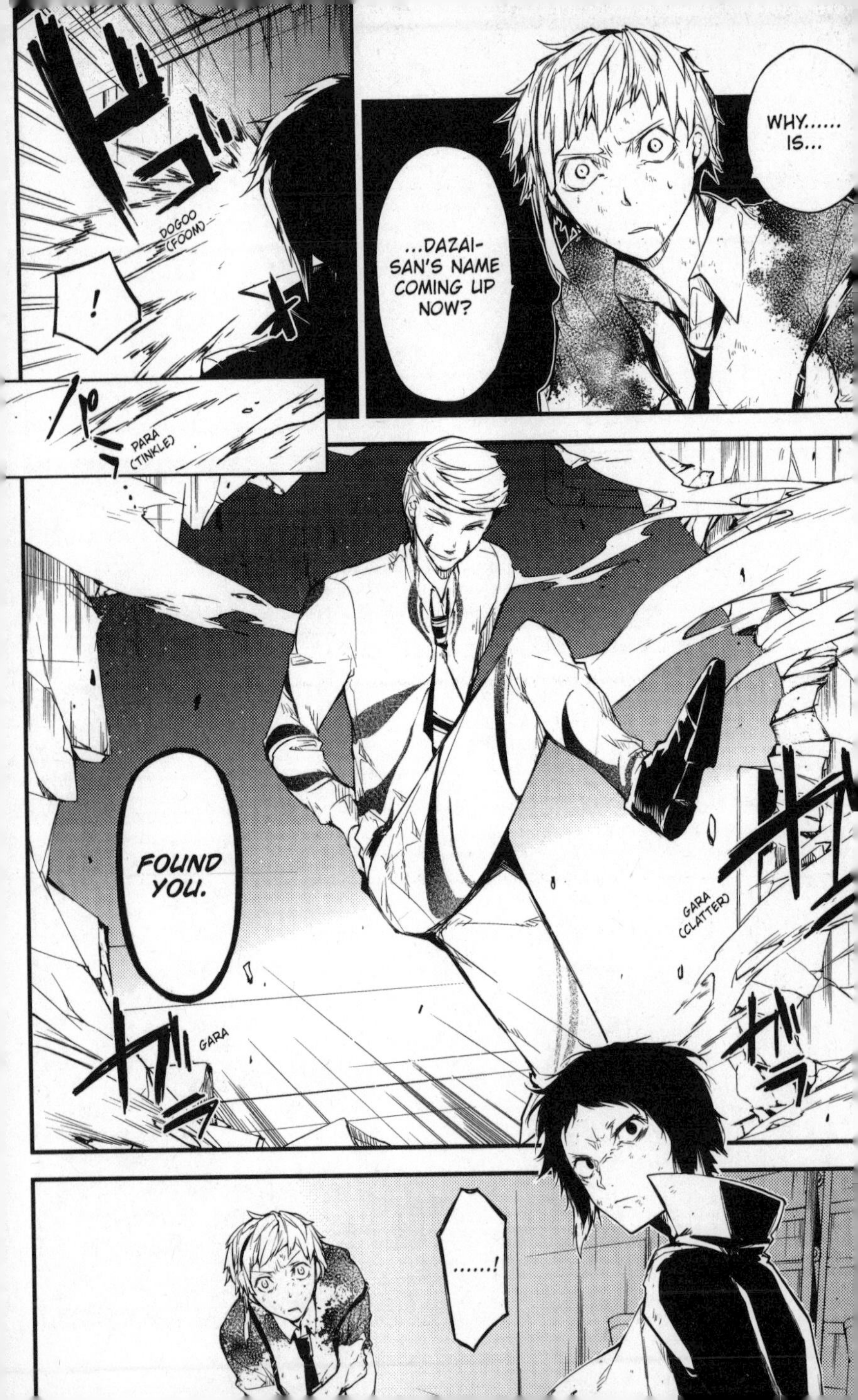
WHY...... IS...
...DAZAI-SAN'S NAME COMING UP NOW?
DOGOO (FOOM)
!
PARA (TINKLE)
FOUND YOU.
GARA (CLATTER)
GARA
......!

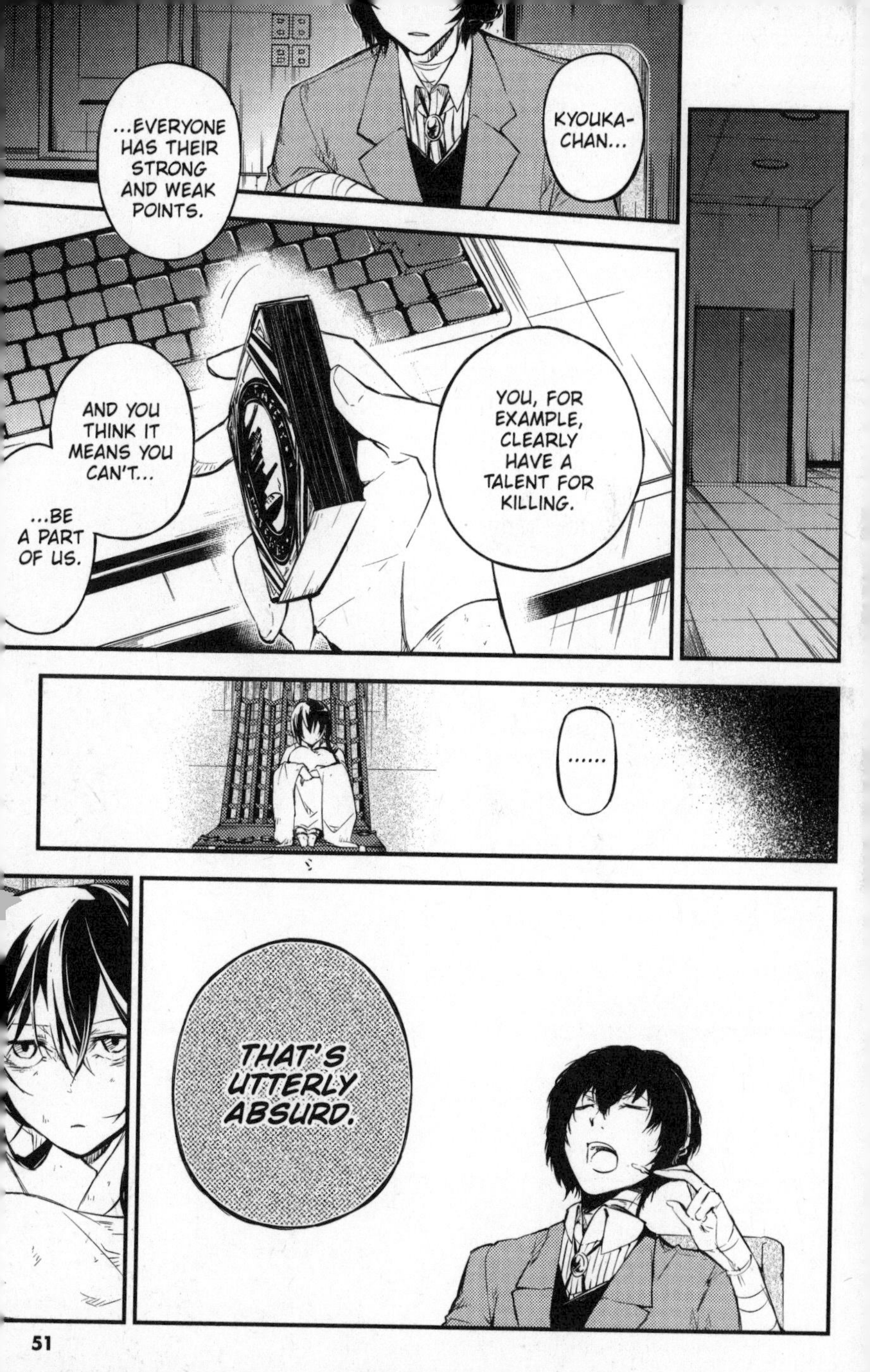
KYOUKA-CHAN...
...EVERYONE HAS THEIR STRONG AND WEAK POINTS.
YOU, FOR EXAMPLE, CLEARLY HAVE A TALENT FOR KILLING.
AND YOU THINK IT MEANS YOU CAN'T...
...BE A PART OF US.
......
THAT'S UTTERLY ABSURD.

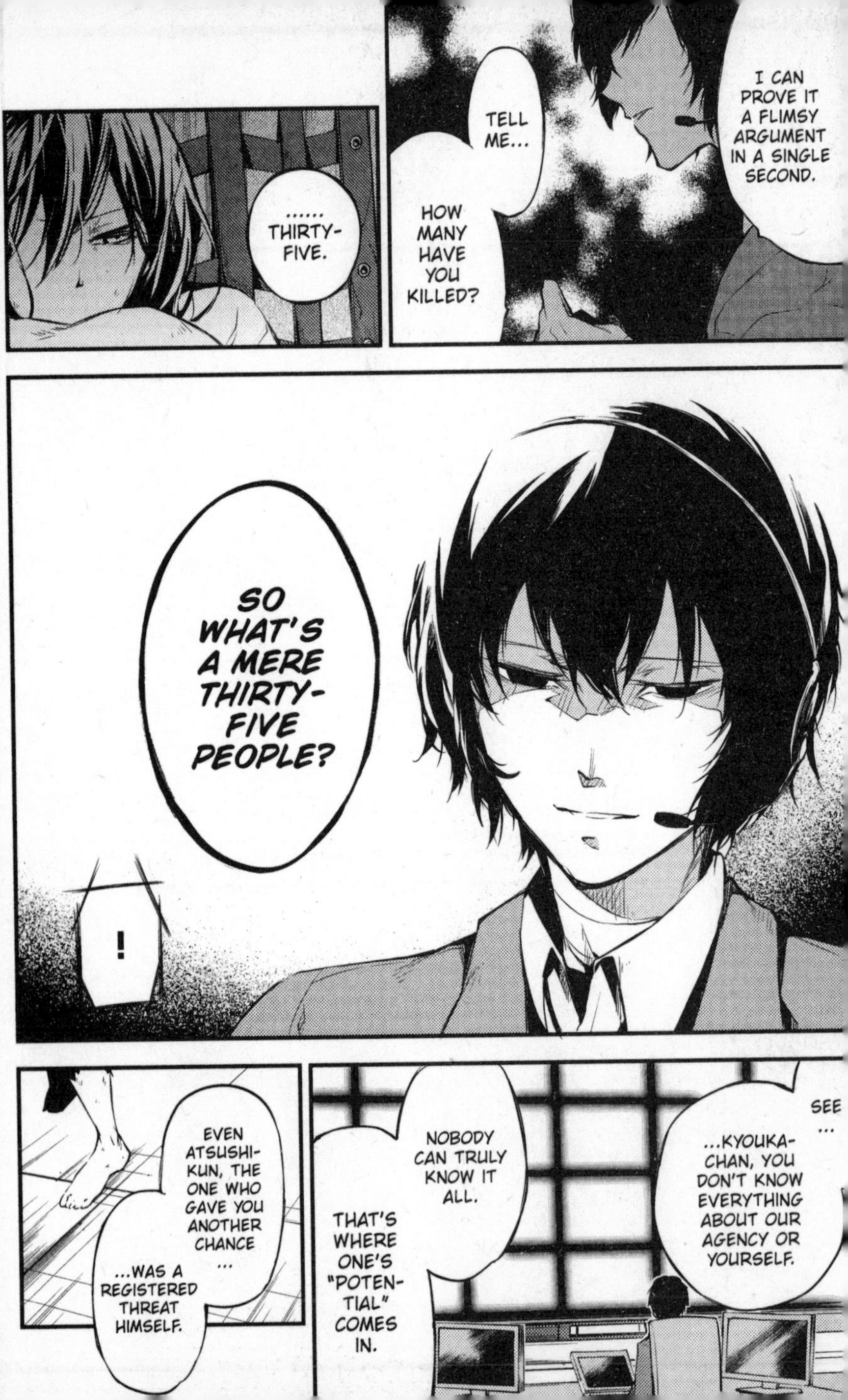
I CAN PROVE IT A FLIMSY ARGUMENT IN A SINGLE SECOND.
TELL ME...
HOW MANY HAVE YOU KILLED?
......THIRTY-FIVE.
SO WHAT'S A MERE THIRTY-FIVE PEOPLE?
!
SEE ...
...KYOUKA-CHAN, YOU DON'T KNOW EVERYTHING ABOUT OUR AGENCY OR YOURSELF.
NOBODY CAN TRULY KNOW IT ALL.
THAT'S WHERE ONE'S "POTENTIAL" COMES IN.
EVEN ATSUSHI-KUN, THE ONE WHO GAVE YOU ANOTHER CHANCE ...
...WAS A REGISTERED THREAT HIMSELF.

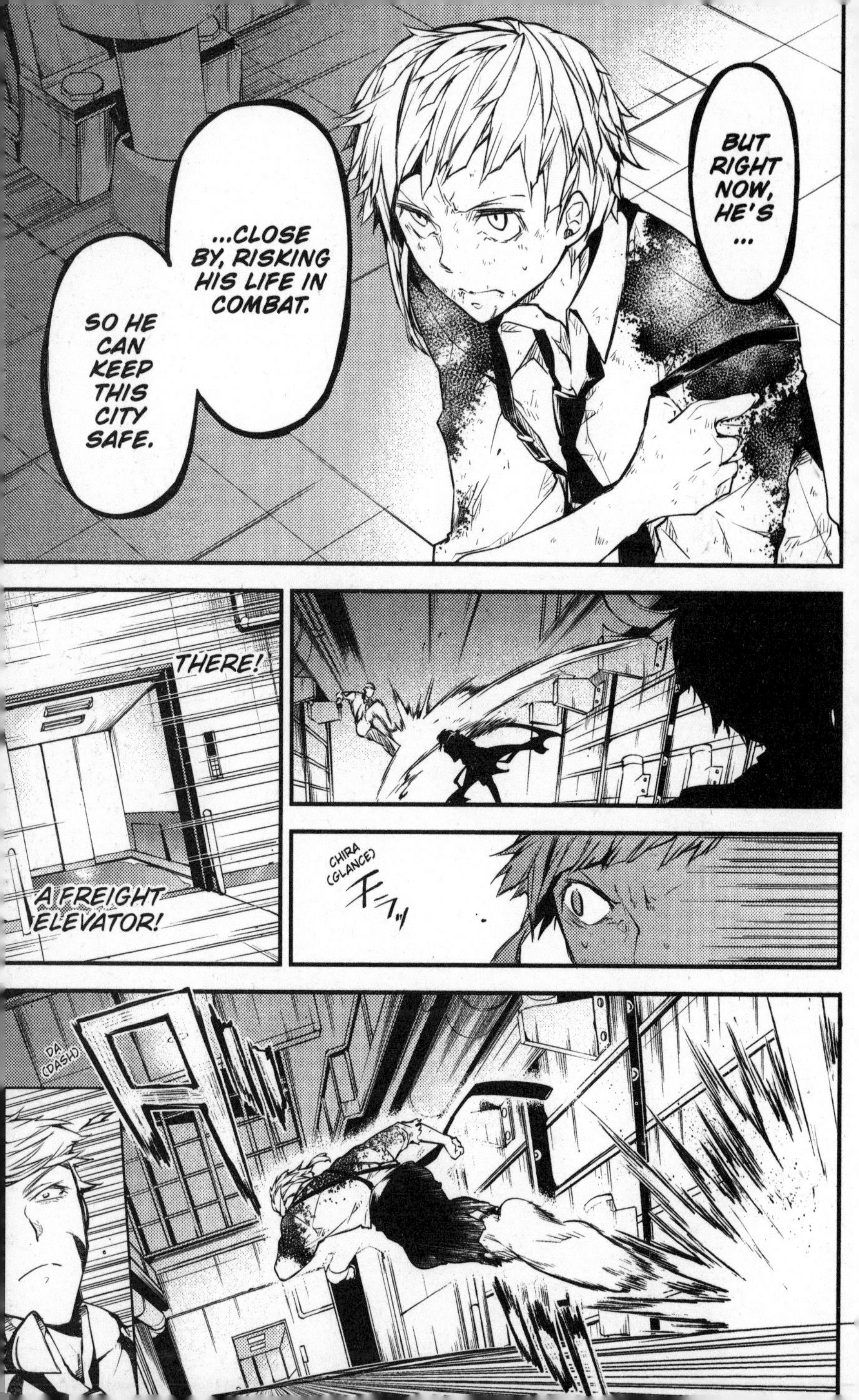
BUT RIGHT NOW, HE'S ...
...CLOSE BY, RISKING HIS LIFE IN COMBAT.
SO HE CAN KEEP THIS CITY SAFE.
CHIRA (GLANCE)
THERE!
A FREIGHT ELEVATOR!
DA (DASH)

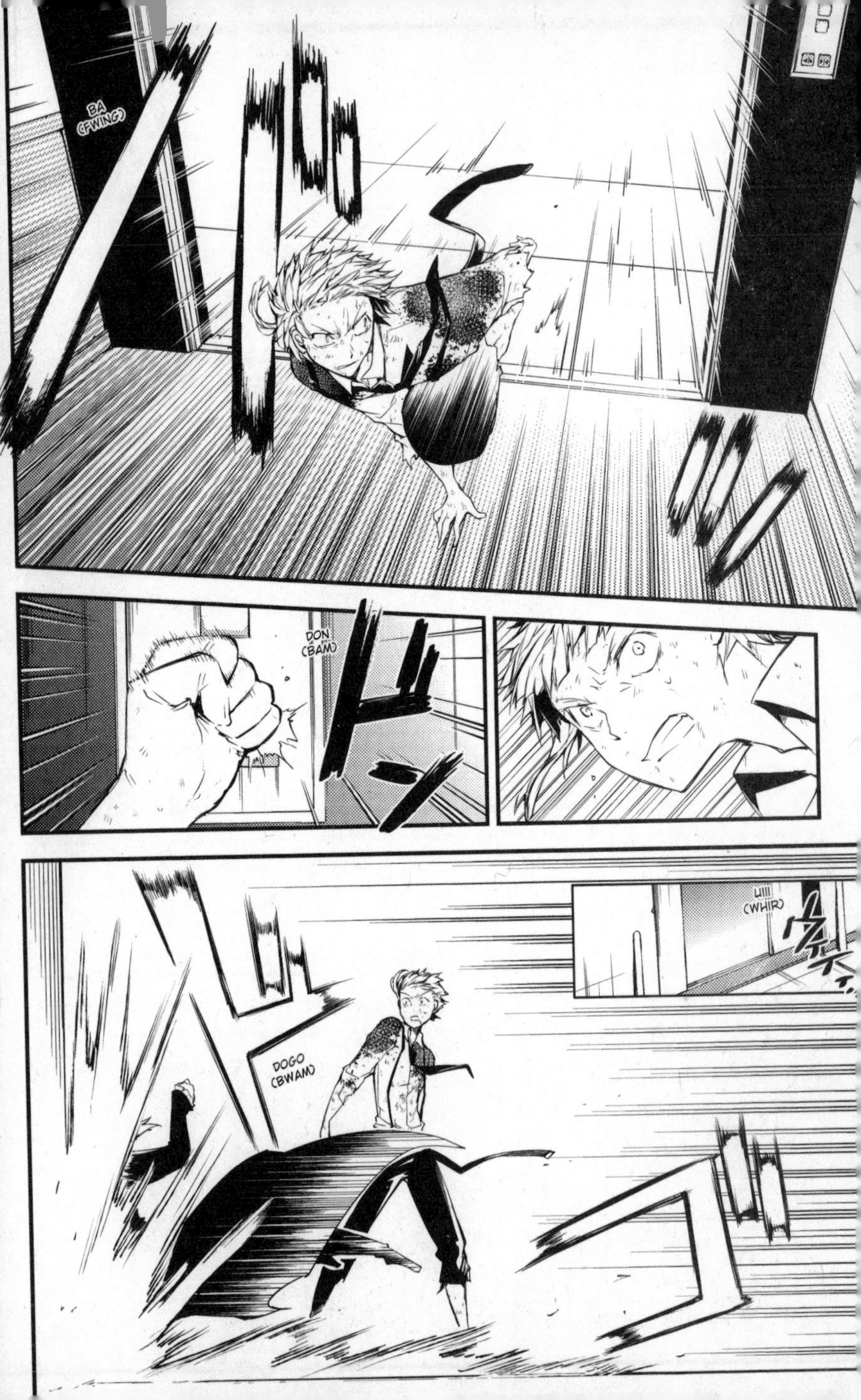
BA
(FWING)
DON
(BAM)
UIII
(WHIR)
DOGO
(BWAM)

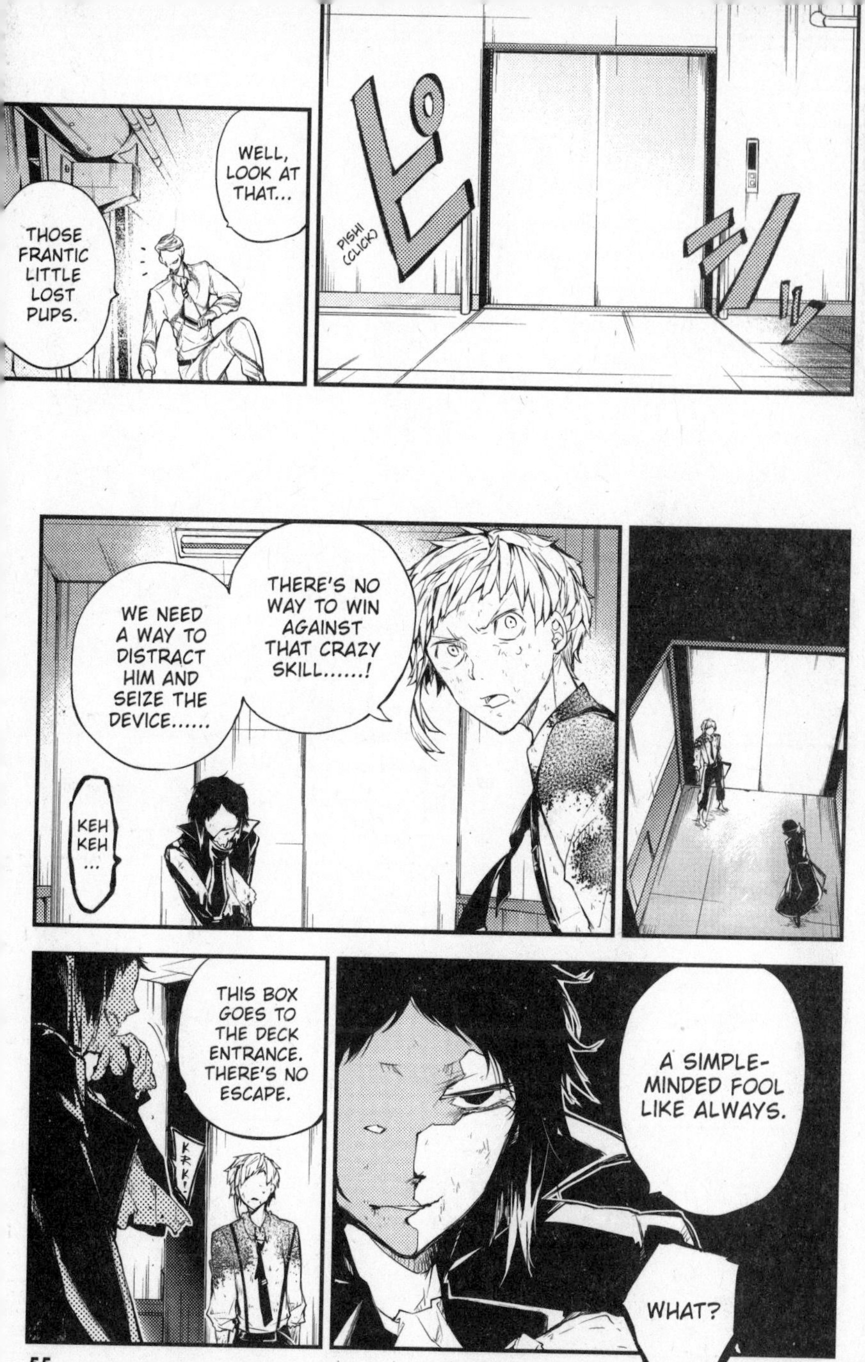
PISHI (CLICK)
WELL, LOOK AT THAT...
THOSE FRANTIC LITTLE LOST PUPS.
THERE'S NO WAY TO WIN AGAINST THAT CRAZY SKILL......!
WE NEED A WAY TO DISTRACT HIM AND SEIZE THE DEVICE......
KEH KEH ...
A SIMPLE-MINDED FOOL LIKE ALWAYS.
WHAT?
THIS BOX GOES TO THE DECK ENTRANCE. THERE'S NO ESCAPE.

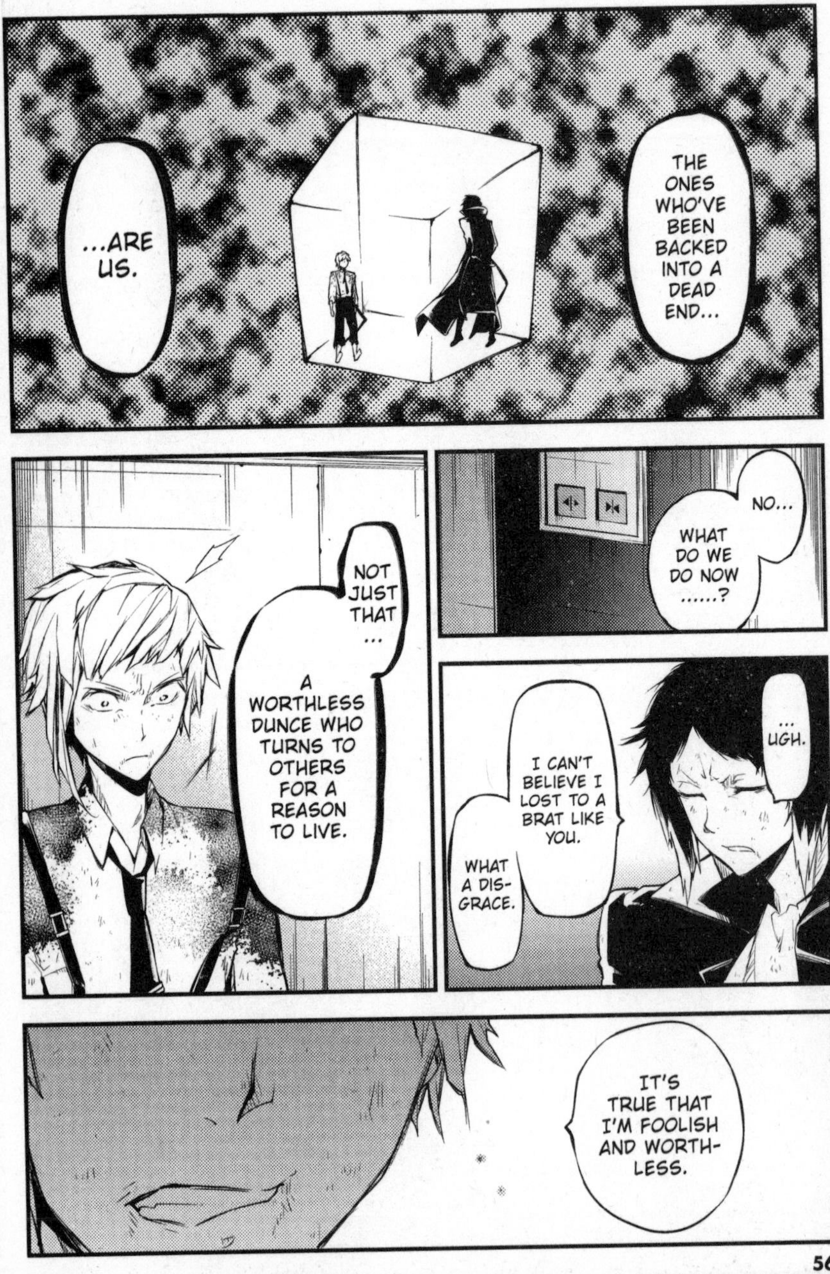
THE ONES WHO'VE BEEN BACKED INTO A DEAD END...
...ARE US.
NO...
WHAT DO WE DO NOW ......?
... UGH.
I CAN'T BELIEVE I LOST TO A BRAT LIKE YOU.
WHAT A DIS-GRACE.
NOT JUST THAT ...
A WORTHLESS DUNCE WHO TURNS TO OTHERS FOR A REASON TO LIVE.
IT'S TRUE THAT I'M FOOLISH AND WORTH-LESS.

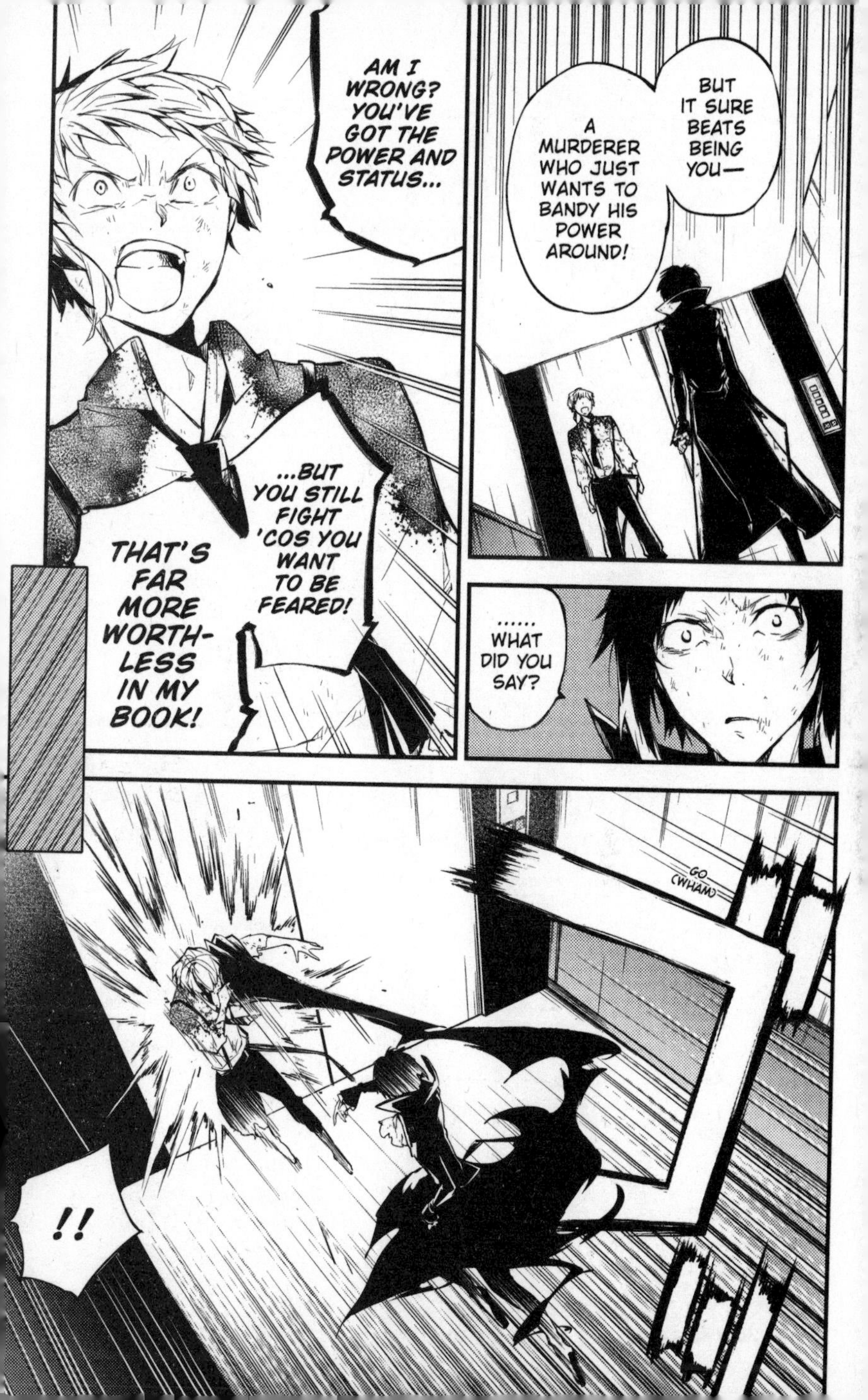
BUT IT SURE BEATS BEING YOU—
A MURDERER WHO JUST WANTS TO BANDY HIS POWER AROUND!
......WHAT DID YOU SAY?
AM I WRONG? YOU'VE GOT THE POWER AND STATUS...
...BUT YOU STILL FIGHT 'COS YOU WANT TO BE FEARED!
THAT'S FAR MORE WORTH-LESS IN MY BOOK!
GO (WHAM)
!!

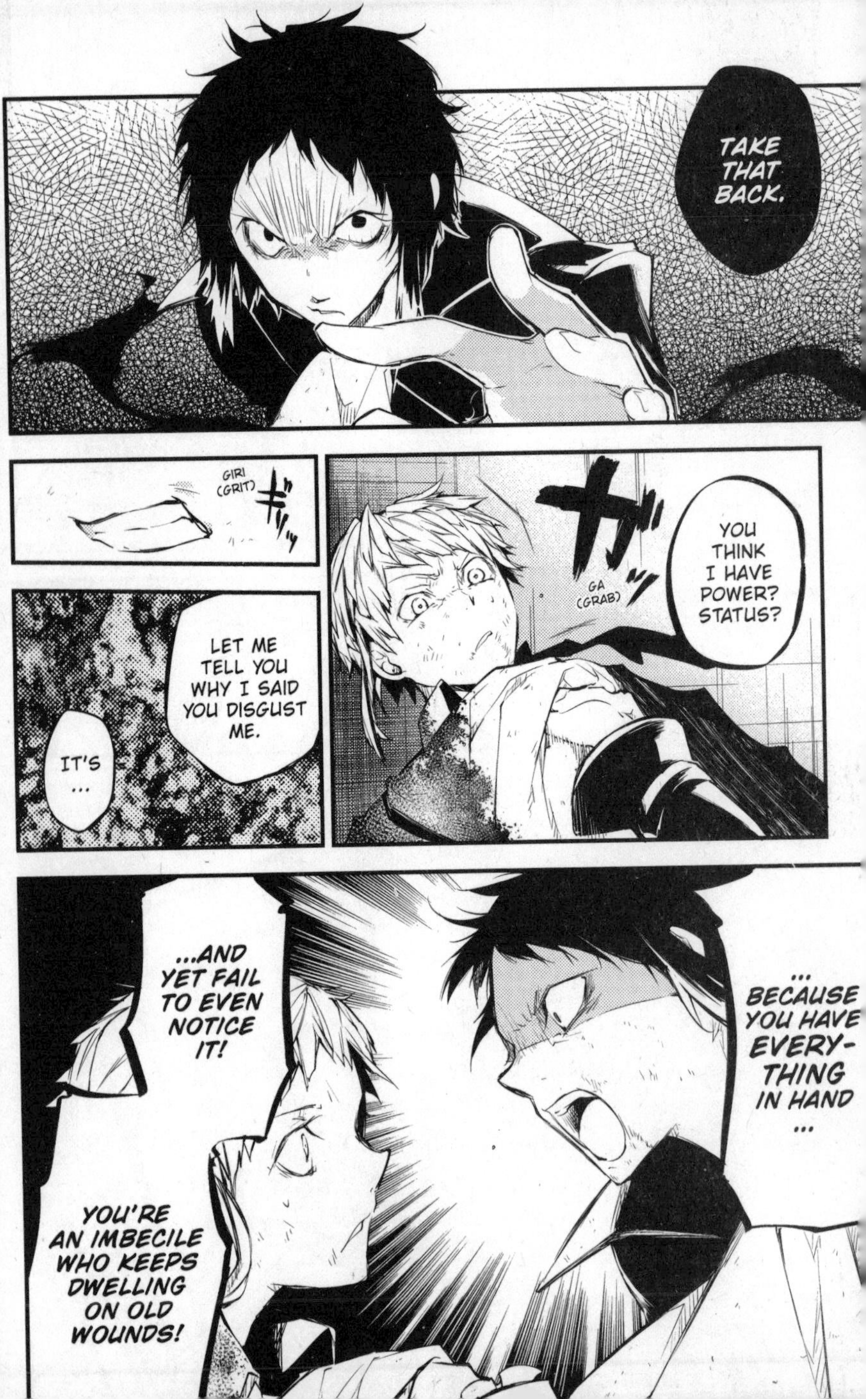
TAKE THAT BACK.
GA (GRAB)
YOU THINK I HAVE POWER? STATUS?
GIRI (GRIT)
LET ME TELL YOU WHY I SAID YOU DISGUST ME.
IT'S ...
... BECAUSE YOU HAVE EVERY-THING IN HAND ...
...AND YET FAIL TO EVEN NOTICE IT!
YOU'RE AN IMBECILE WHO KEEPS DWELLING ON OLD WOUNDS!

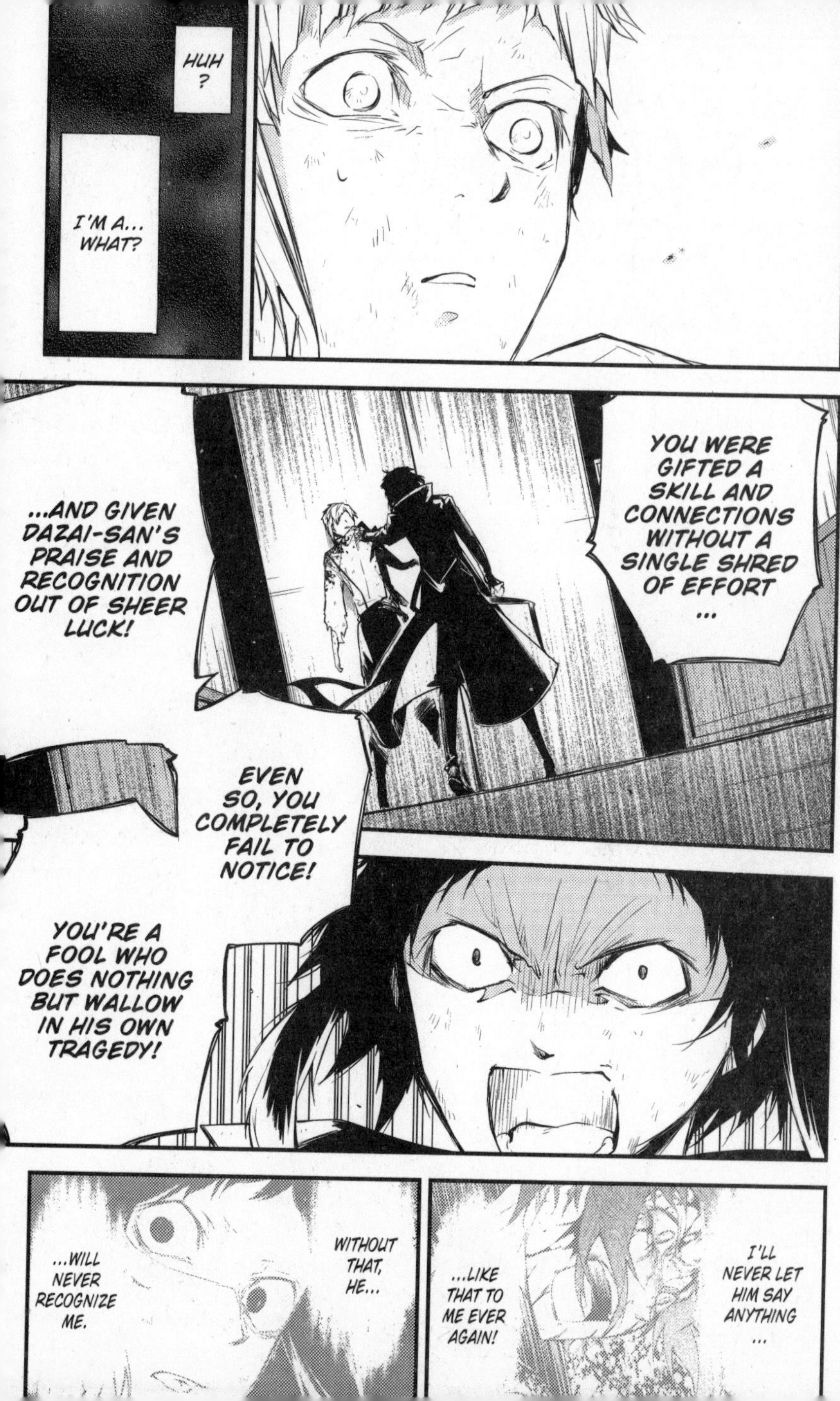
HUH ?
I'M A... WHAT?
YOU WERE GIFTED A SKILL AND CONNECTIONS WITHOUT A SINGLE SHRED OF EFFORT ...
...AND GIVEN DAZAI-SAN'S PRAISE AND RECOGNITION OUT OF SHEER LUCK!
EVEN SO, YOU COMPLETELY FAIL TO NOTICE!
YOU'RE A FOOL WHO DOES NOTHING BUT WALLOW IN HIS OWN TRAGEDY!
I'LL NEVER LET HIM SAY ANYTHING ...
...LIKE THAT TO ME EVER AGAIN!
WITHOUT THAT, HE...
...WILL NEVER RECOGNIZE ME.

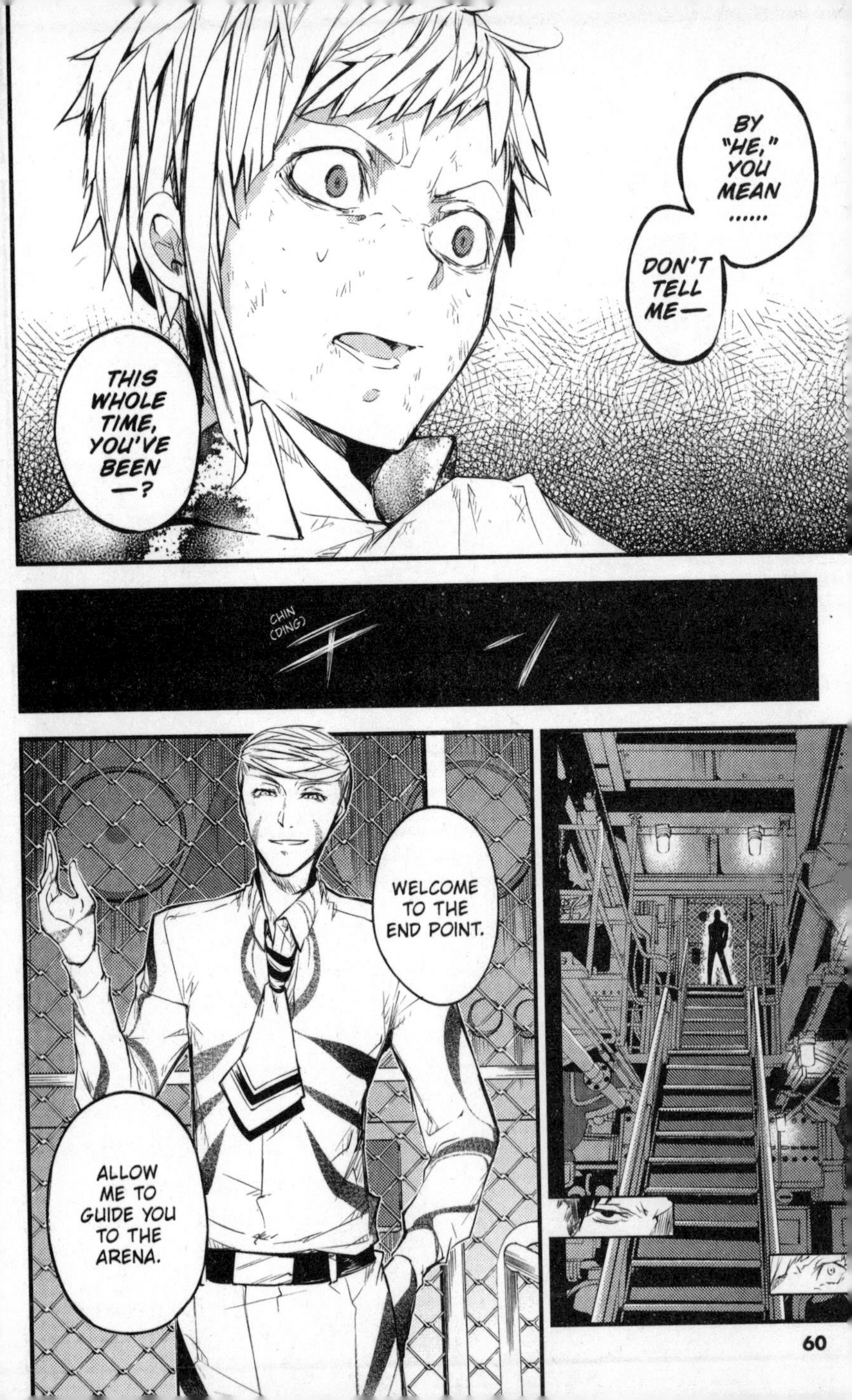
BY "HE," YOU MEAN ......
DON'T TELL ME—
THIS WHOLE TIME, YOU'VE BEEN —?
CHIN (DING)
WELCOME TO THE END POINT.
ALLOW ME TO GUIDE YOU TO THE ARENA.

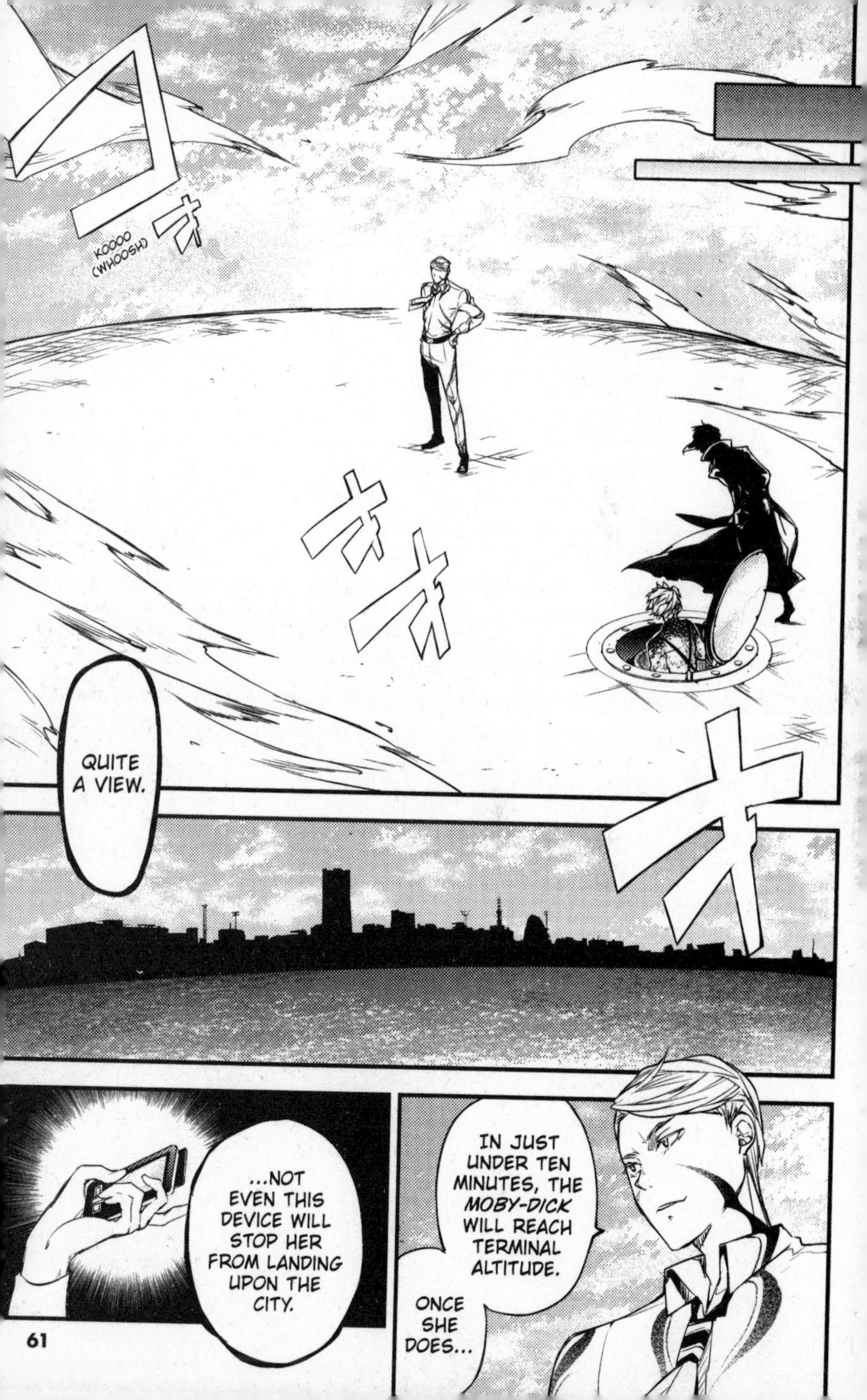
KOOOO (WHOOSH)
QUITE A VIEW.
IN JUST UNDER TEN MINUTES, THE *MOBY-DICK* WILL REACH TERMINAL ALTITUDE.
ONCE SHE DOES...
...NOT EVEN THIS DEVICE WILL STOP HER FROM LANDING UPON THE CITY.

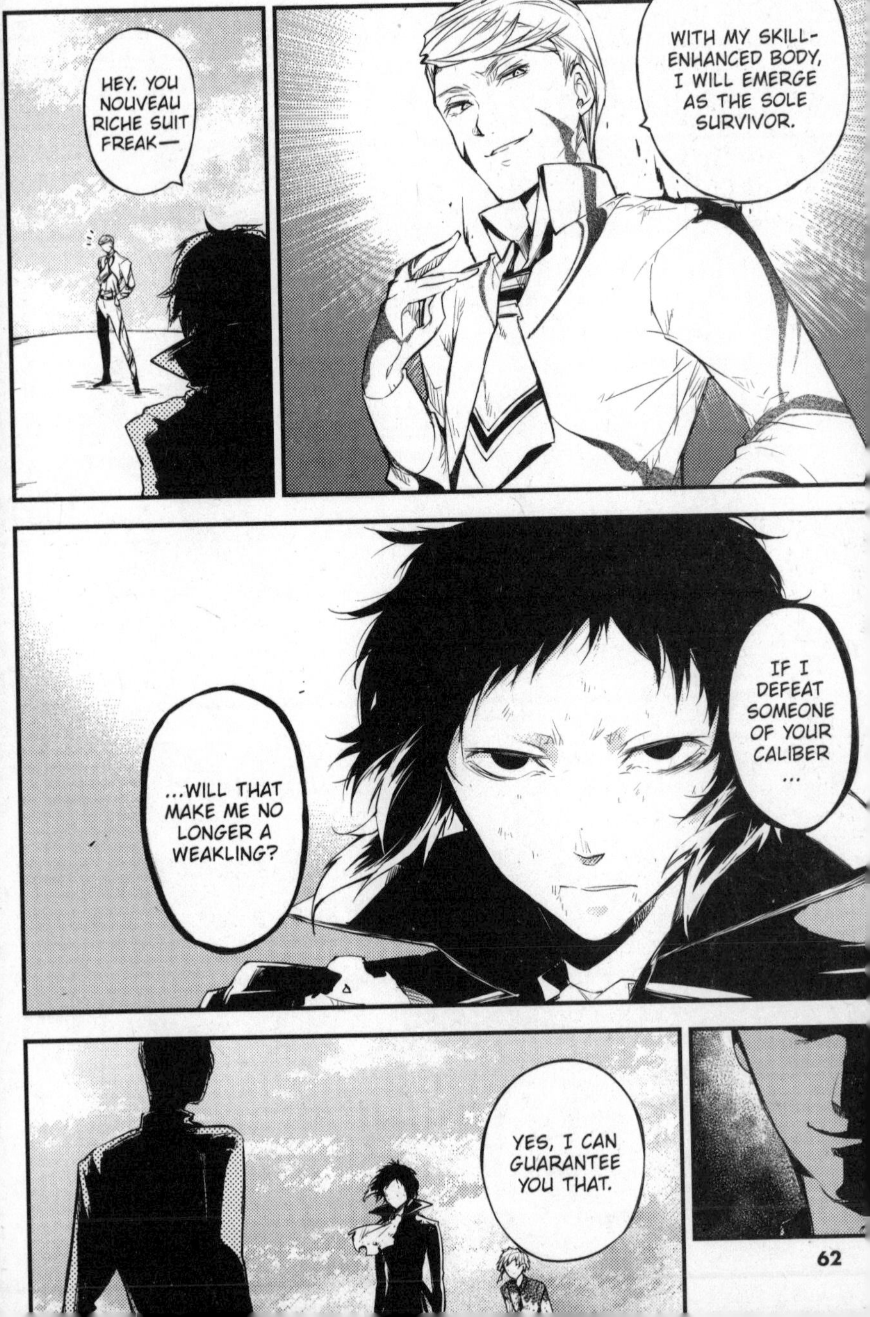
WITH MY SKILL-ENHANCED BODY, I WILL EMERGE AS THE SOLE SURVIVOR.
HEY. YOU NOUVEAU RICHE SUIT FREAK—
IF I DEFEAT SOMEONE OF YOUR CALIBER ...
...WILL THAT MAKE ME NO LONGER A WEAKLING?
YES, I CAN GUARANTEE YOU THAT.

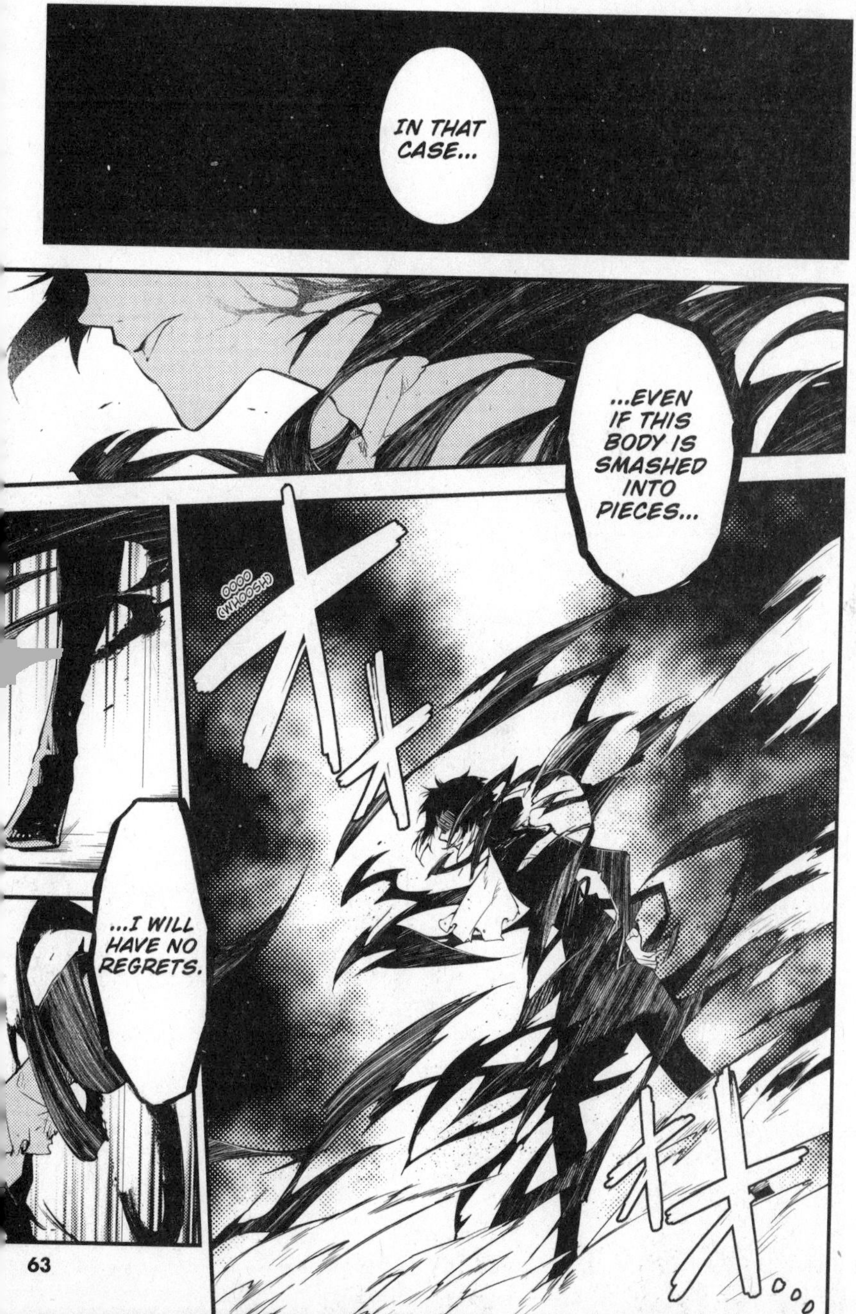
IN THAT CASE...
...EVEN IF THIS BODY IS SMASHED INTO PIECES...
(WHOOSH) OOOO
OOO
...I WILL HAVE NO REGRETS.

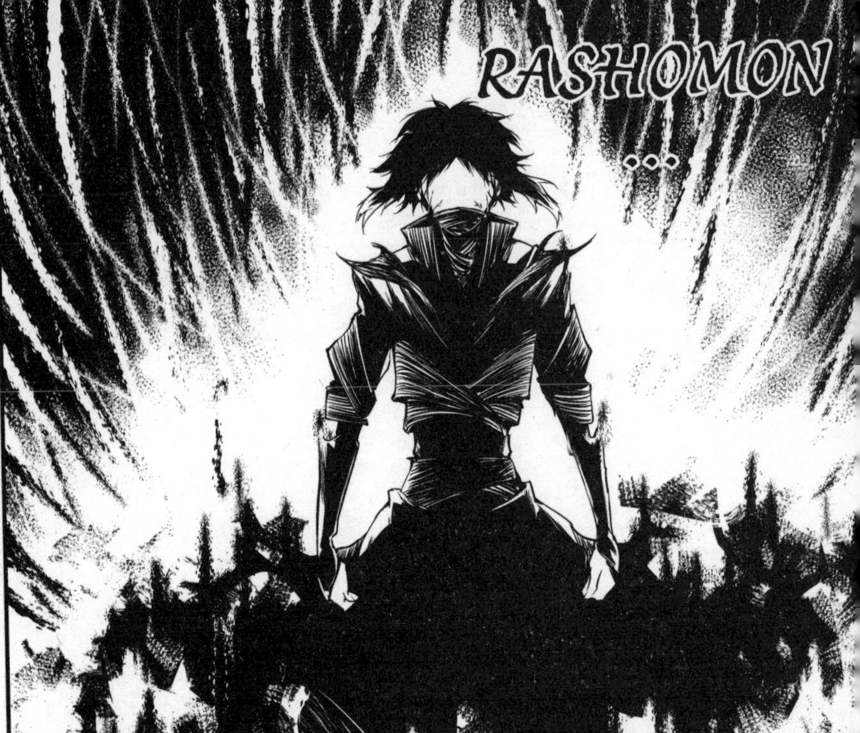
RASHOMON ...
...TENMA TENGAI!
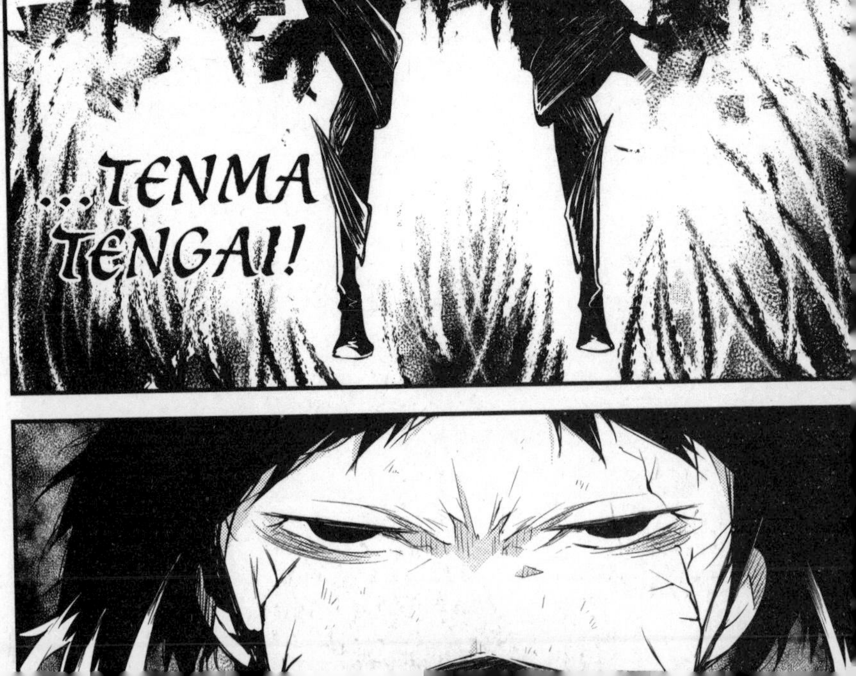

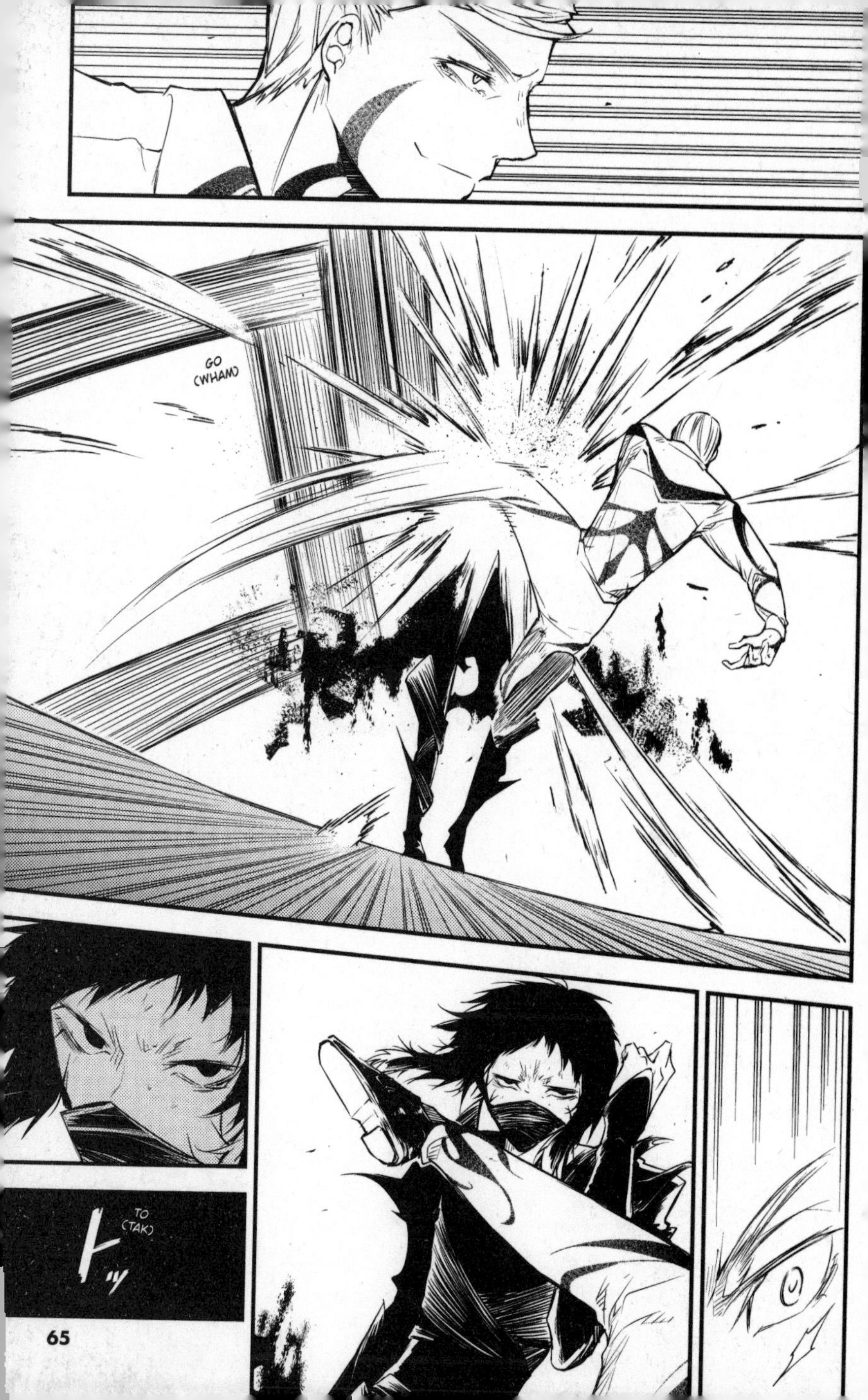
GO
(WHAM)
トッ
TO
(TAK)

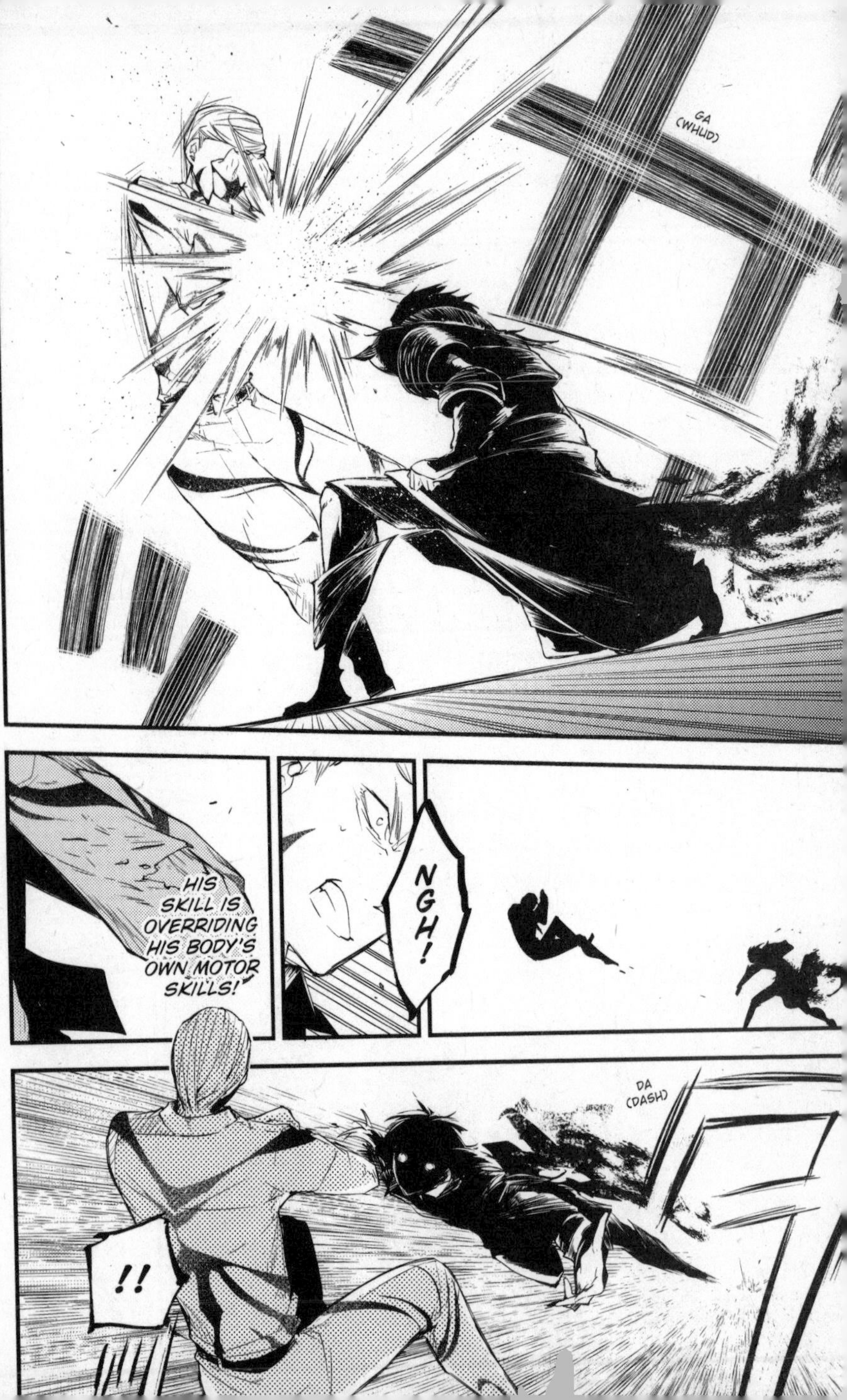
GA
(WHUD)
NGH!
HIS SKILL IS OVERRIDING HIS BODY'S OWN MOTOR SKILLS!
DA
(DASH)
!!

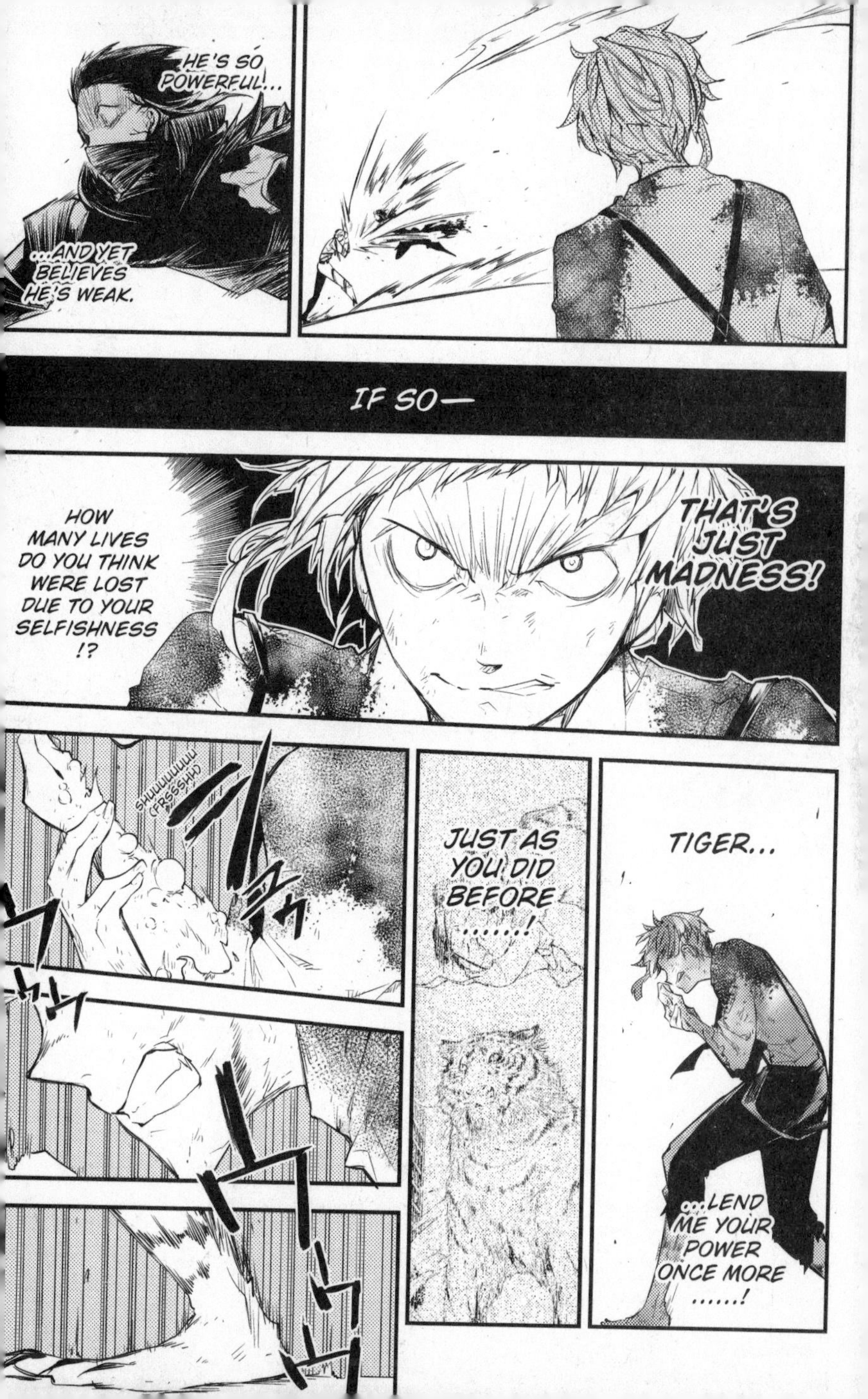
HE'S SO POWERFUL!...
...AND YET BELIEVES HE'S WEAK.
IF SO—
THAT'S JUST MADNESS!
HOW MANY LIVES DO YOU THINK WERE LOST DUE TO YOUR SELFISHNESS!?
TIGER...
...LEND ME YOUR POWER ONCE MORE ......!
JUST AS YOU DID BEFORE ......!
SHUUUUUUUU (FRSSSHH)

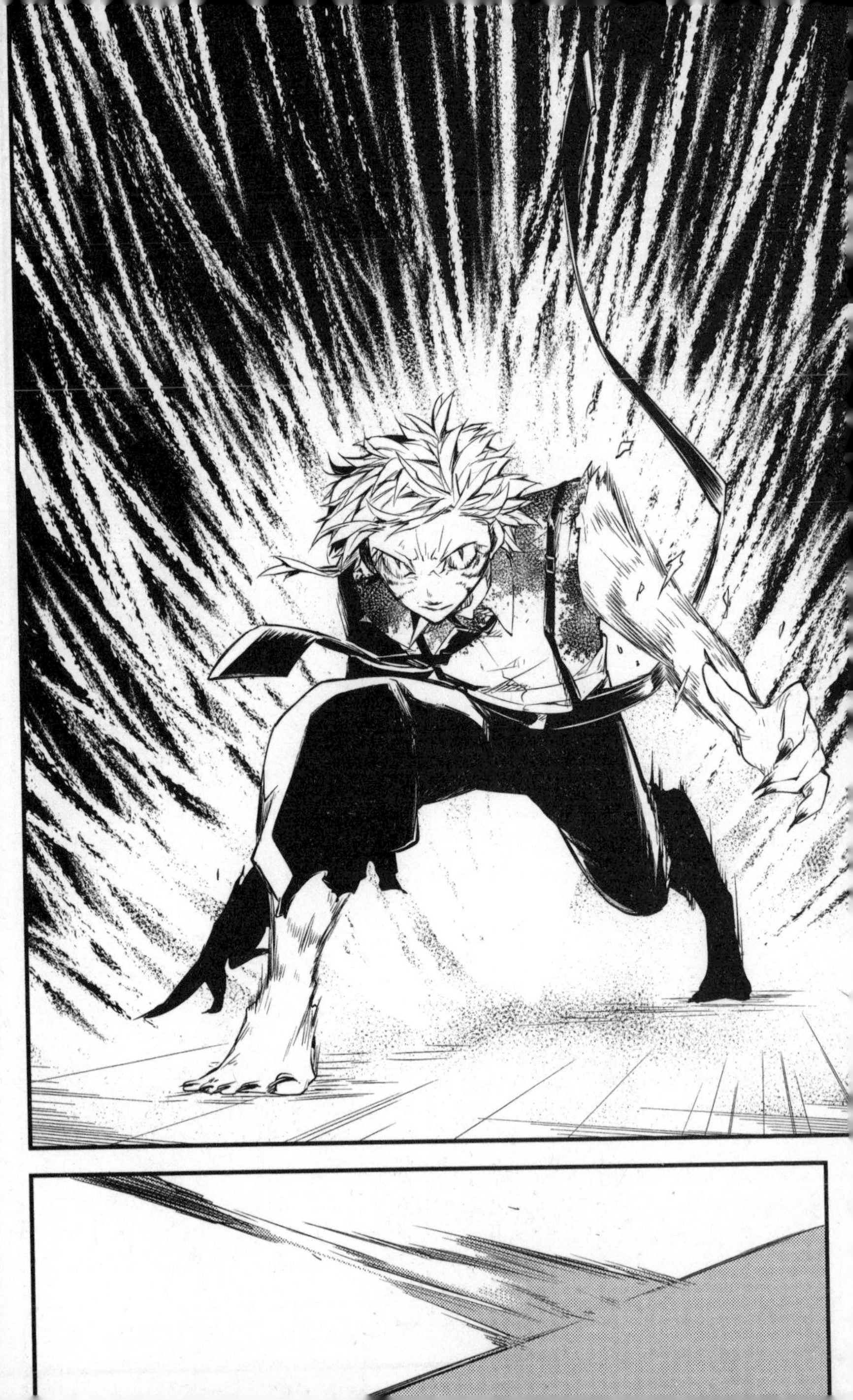

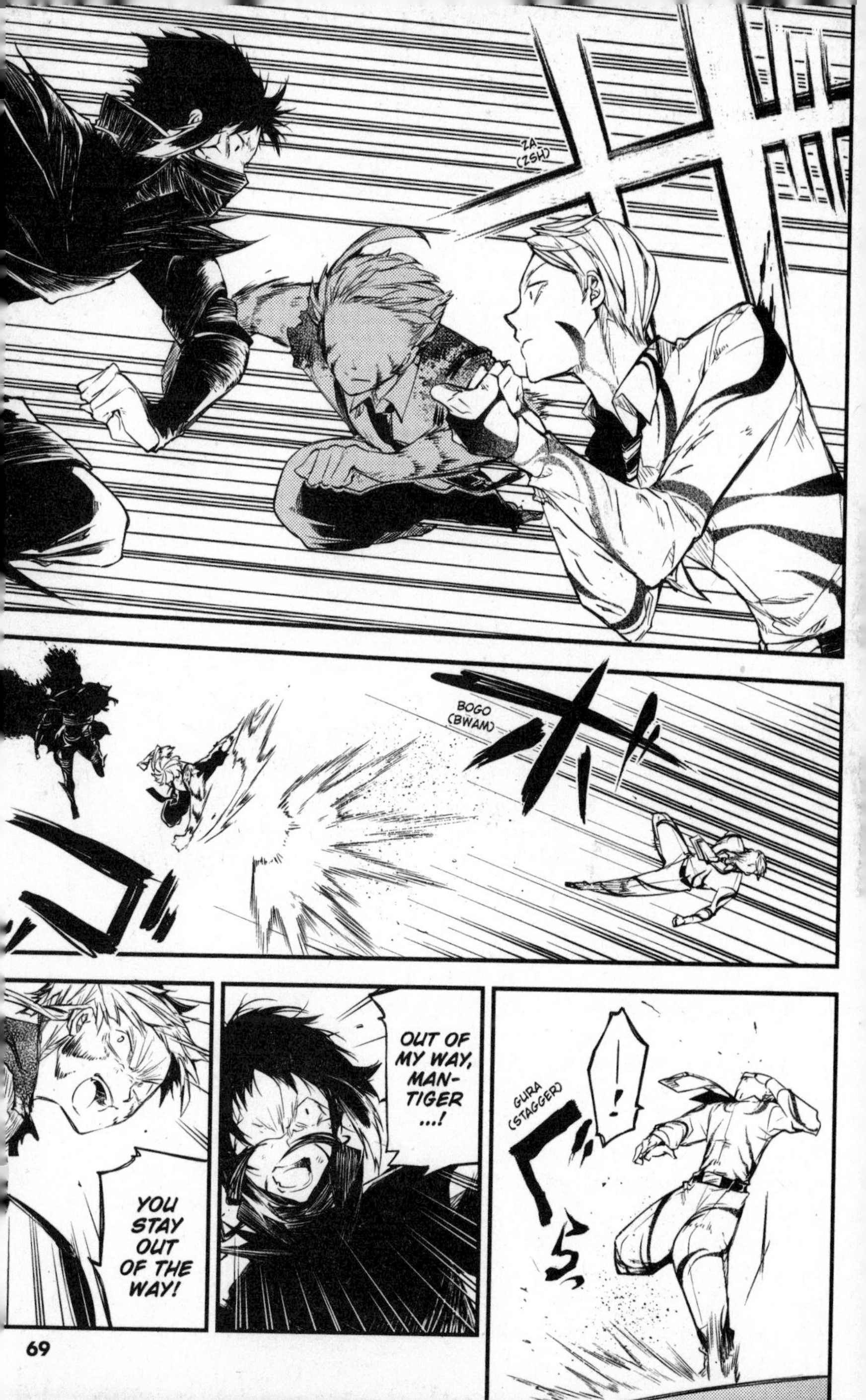
ZA (ZSH)
BOGO (BWAM)
GURA (STAGGER)
!
OUT OF MY WAY, MAN-TIGER ...!
YOU STAY OUT OF THE WAY!

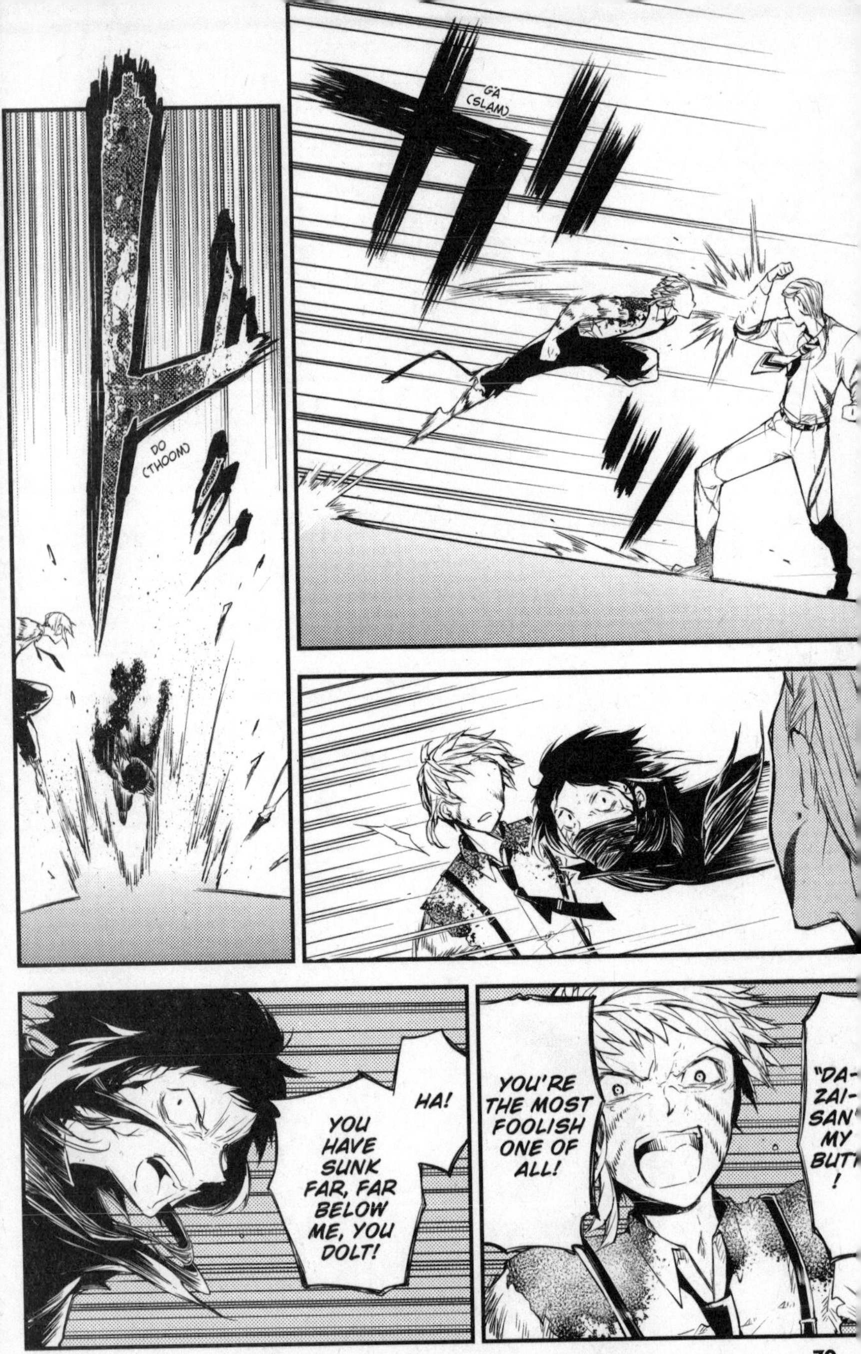
GA (SLAM)
DO (THOOM)
"DAZAI-SAN" MY BUT!
YOU'RE THE MOST FOOLISH ONE OF ALL!
HA!
YOU HAVE SUNK FAR, FAR BELOW ME, YOU DOLT!

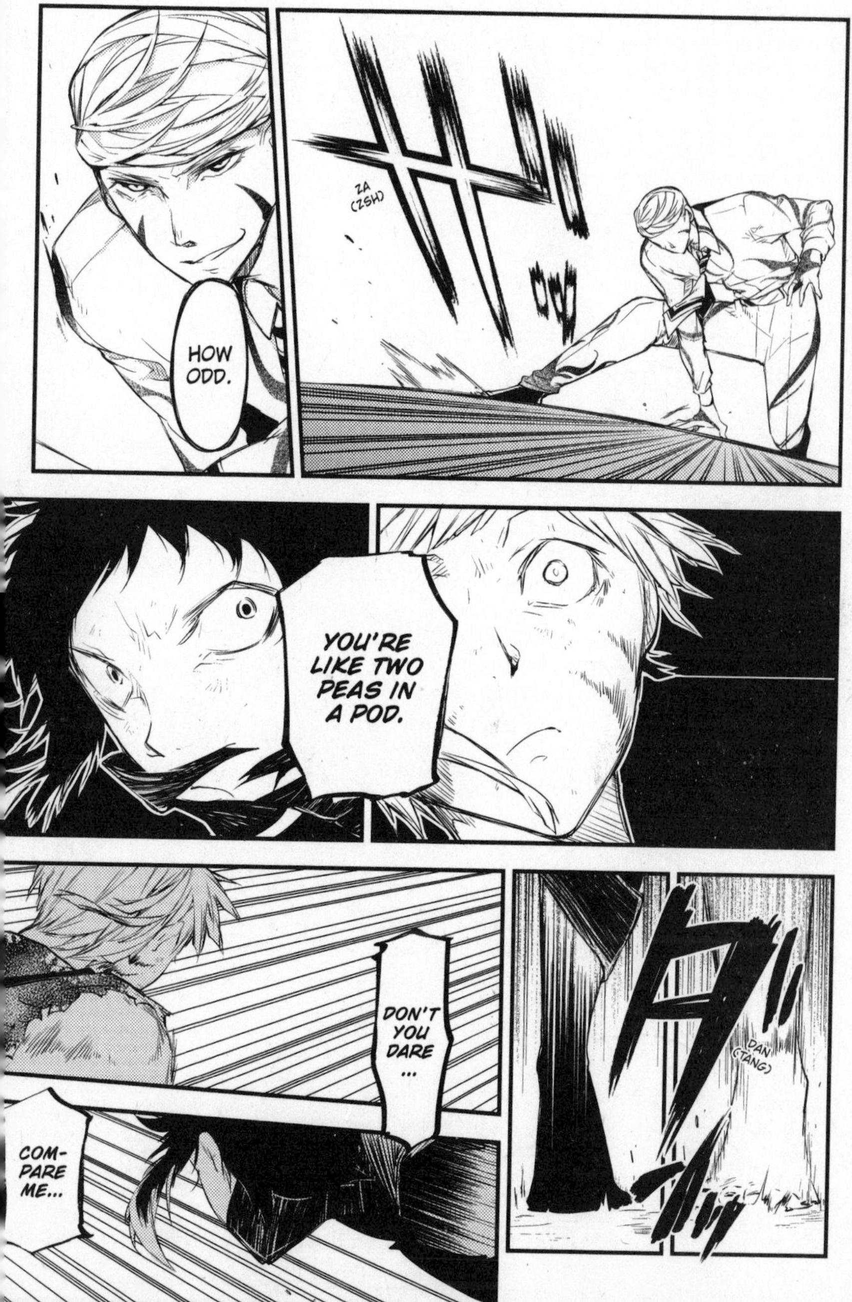
ZA
(ZSH)
HOW ODD.
YOU'RE LIKE TWO PEAS IN A POD.
DAN
(TANG)
DON'T YOU DARE...
COM-PARE ME...

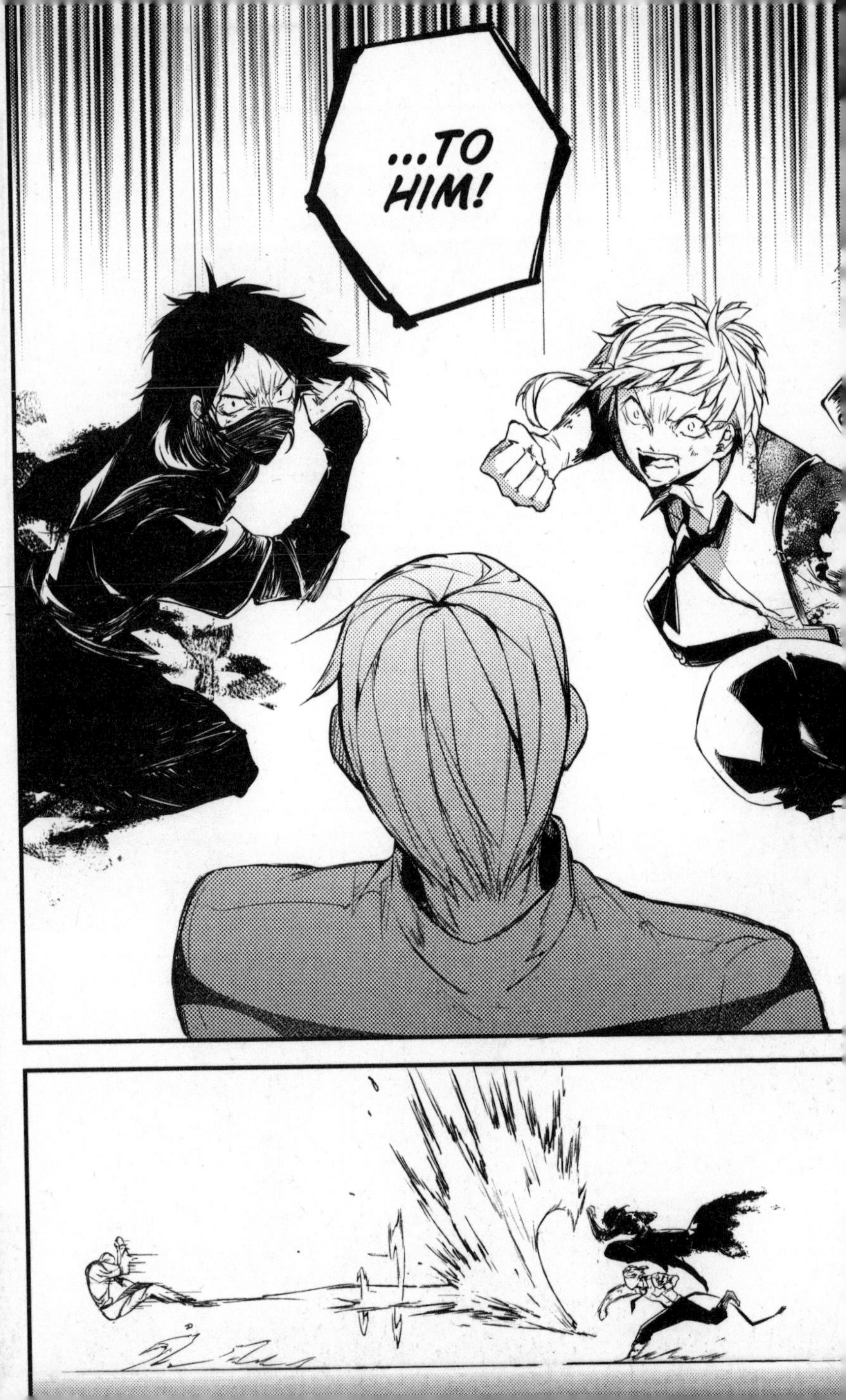
...TO HIM!

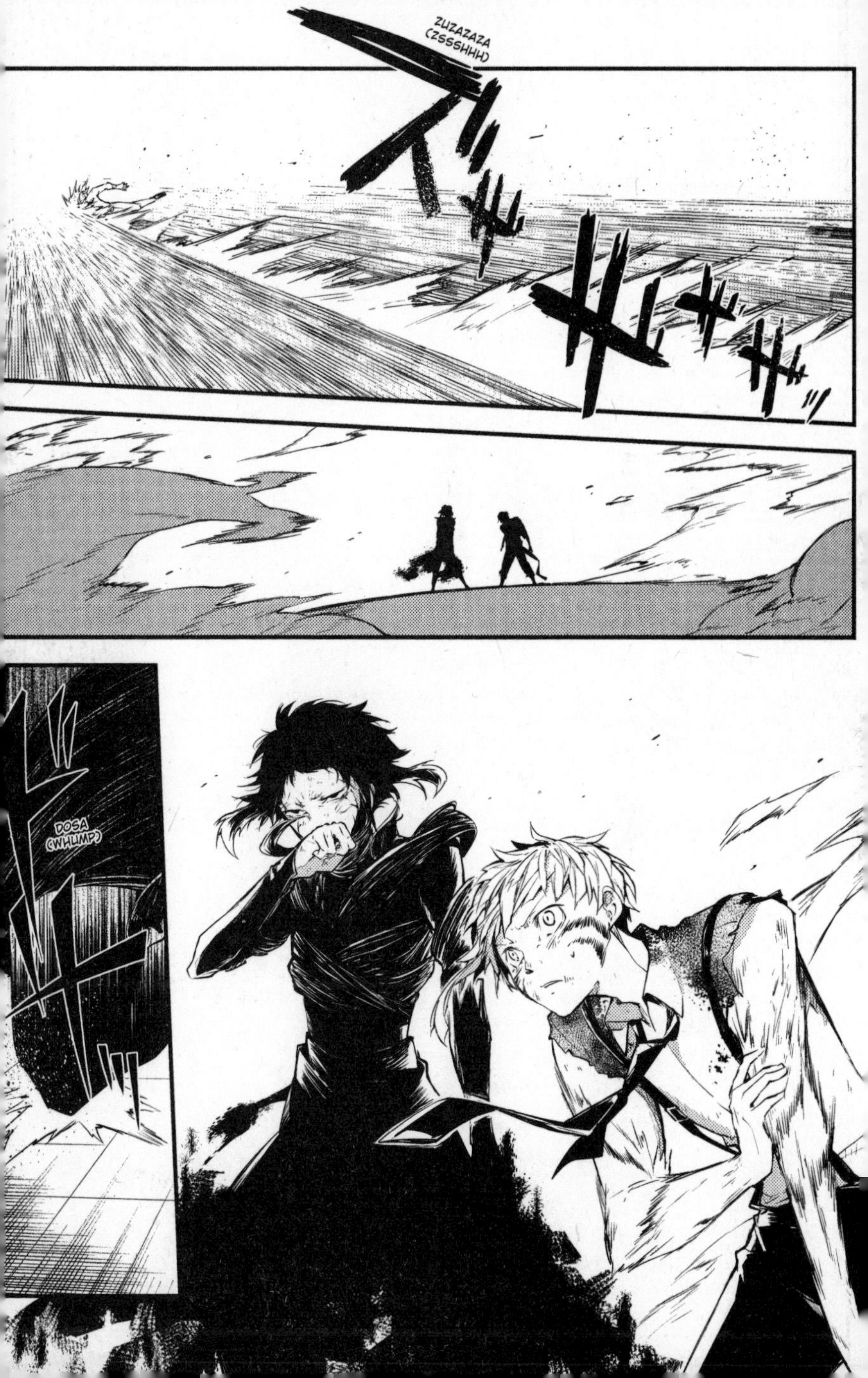
ZUZAZAZA
(ZSSSHHH)
DOSA
(WHUMP)

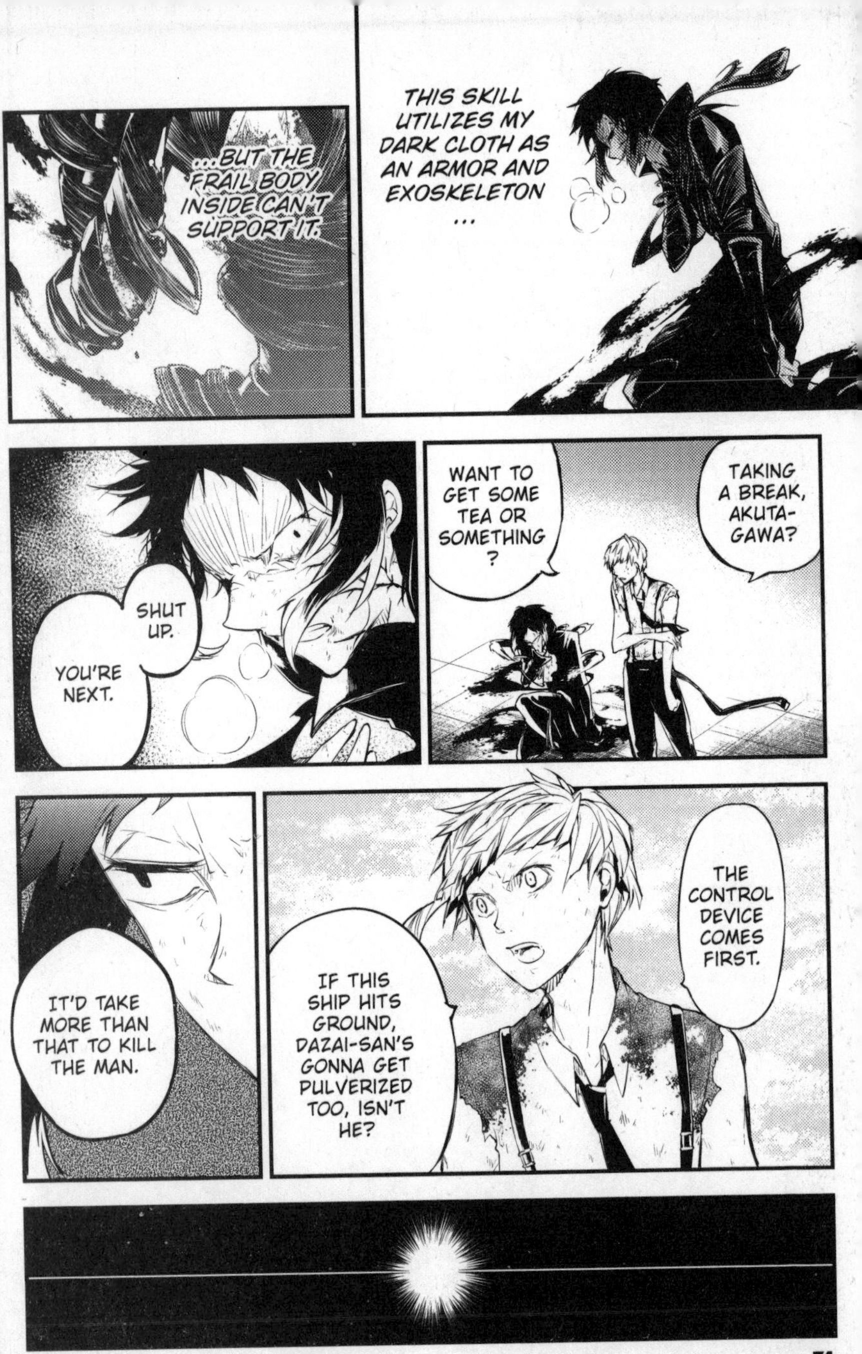
THIS SKILL UTILIZES MY DARK CLOTH AS AN ARMOR AND EXOSKELETON ...
...BUT THE FRAIL BODY INSIDE CAN'T SUPPORT IT.
TAKING A BREAK, AKUTAGAWA?
WANT TO GET SOME TEA OR SOMETHING?
SHUT UP.
YOU'RE NEXT.
THE CONTROL DEVICE COMES FIRST.
IF THIS SHIP HITS GROUND, DAZAI-SAN'S GONNA GET PULVERIZED TOO, ISN'T HE?
IT'D TAKE MORE THAN THAT TO KILL THE MAN.

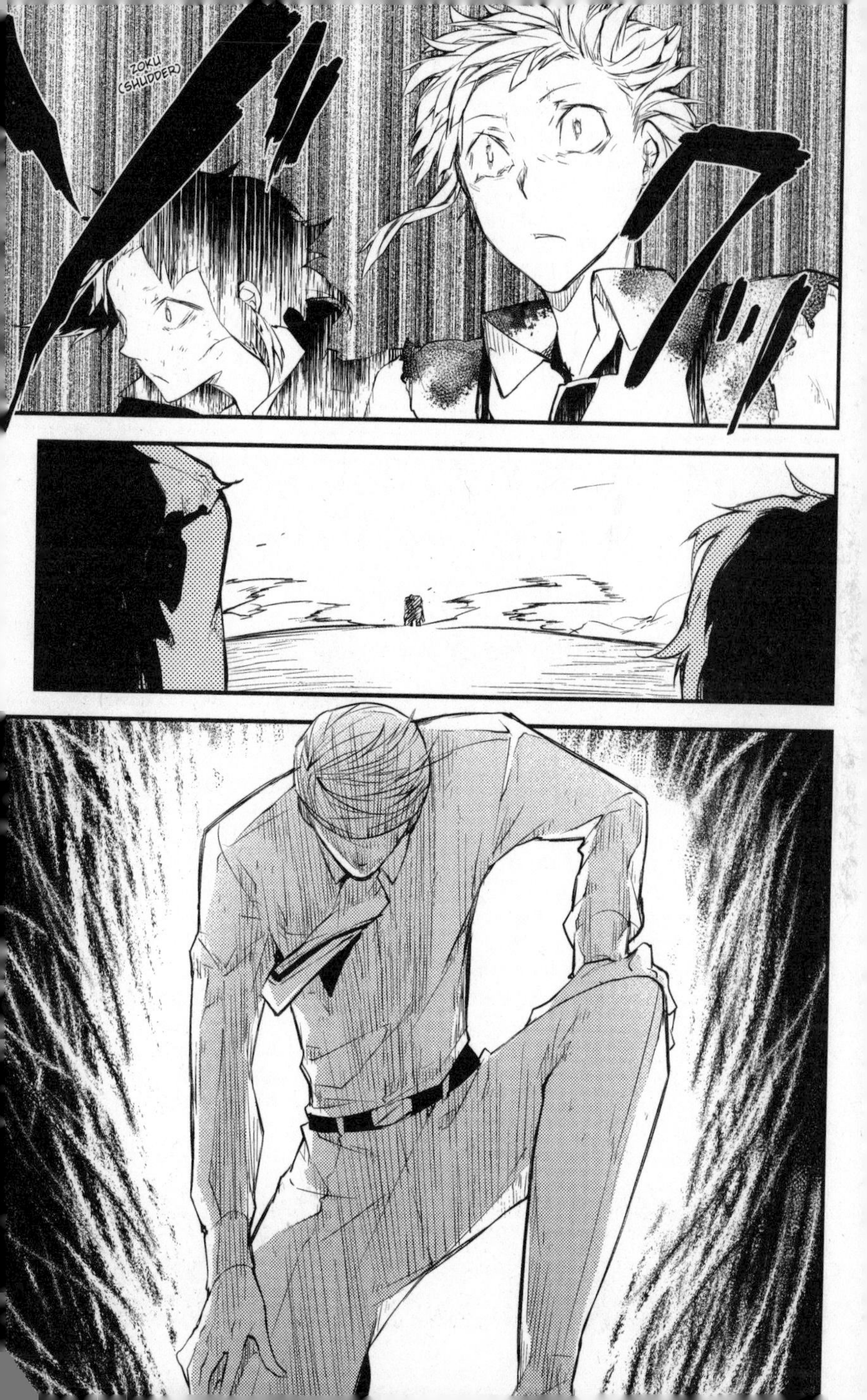
ZOKU (SHUDDER)

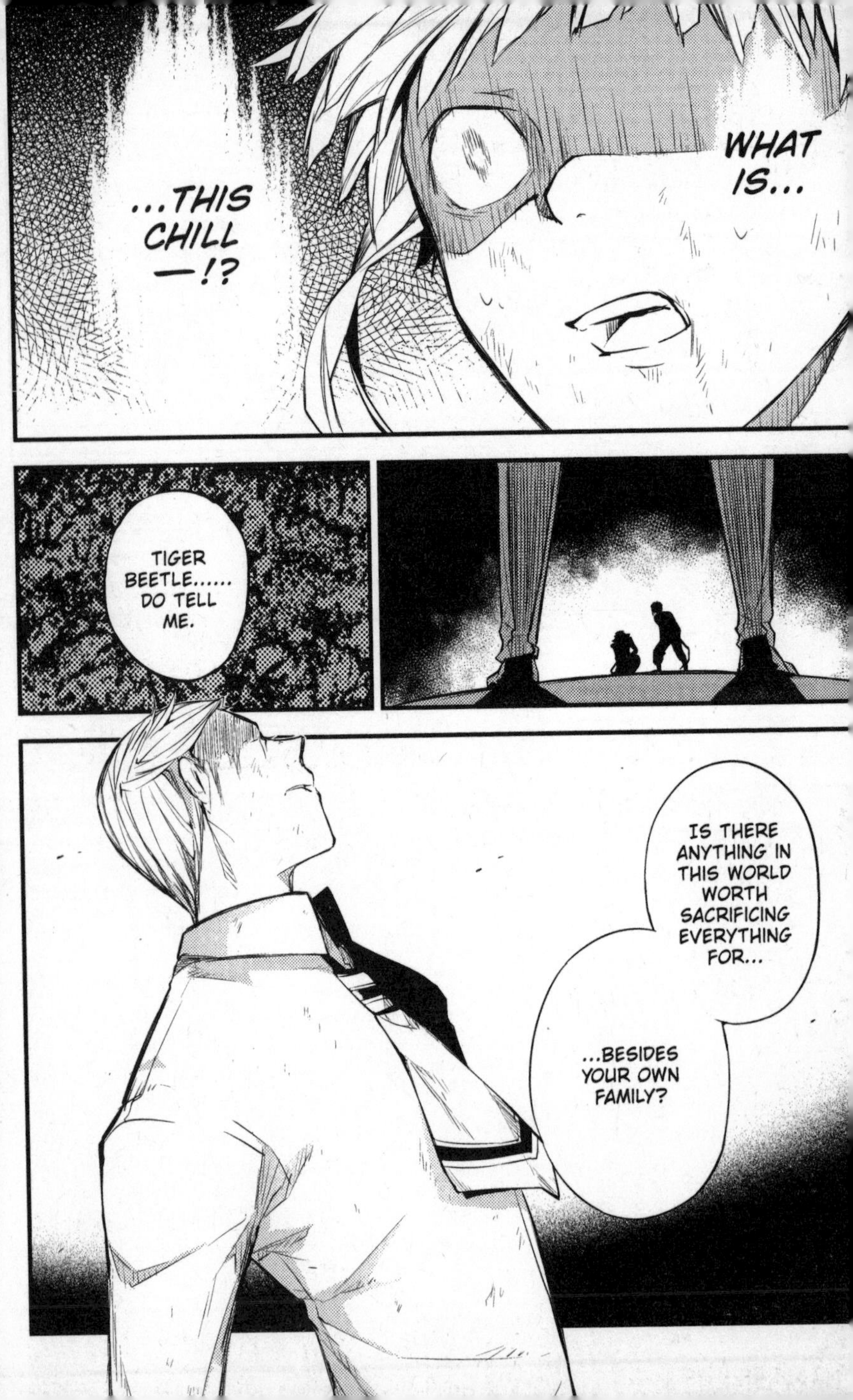
WHAT IS...
...THIS CHILL—!?
TIGER BEETLE...... DO TELL ME.
IS THERE ANYTHING IN THIS WORLD WORTH SACRIFICING EVERYTHING FOR...
...BESIDES YOUR OWN FAMILY?

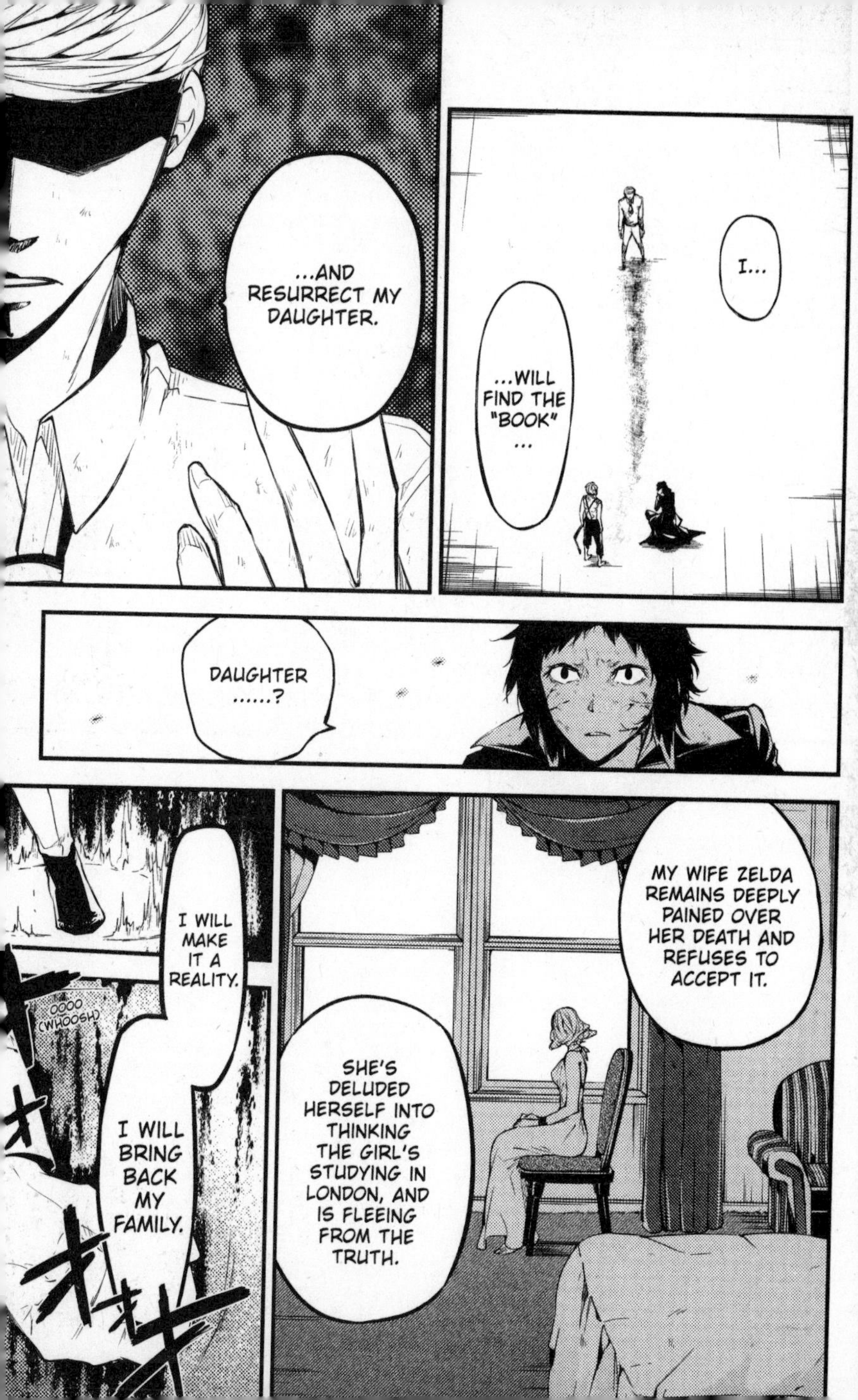
I...
...WILL FIND THE "BOOK" ...
...AND RESURRECT MY DAUGHTER.
DAUGHTER ......?
MY WIFE ZELDA REMAINS DEEPLY PAINED OVER HER DEATH AND REFUSES TO ACCEPT IT.
SHE'S DELUDED HERSELF INTO THINKING THE GIRL'S STUDYING IN LONDON, AND IS FLEEING FROM THE TRUTH.
I WILL MAKE IT A REALITY.
OOOO (WHOOSH)
I WILL BRING BACK MY FAMILY.

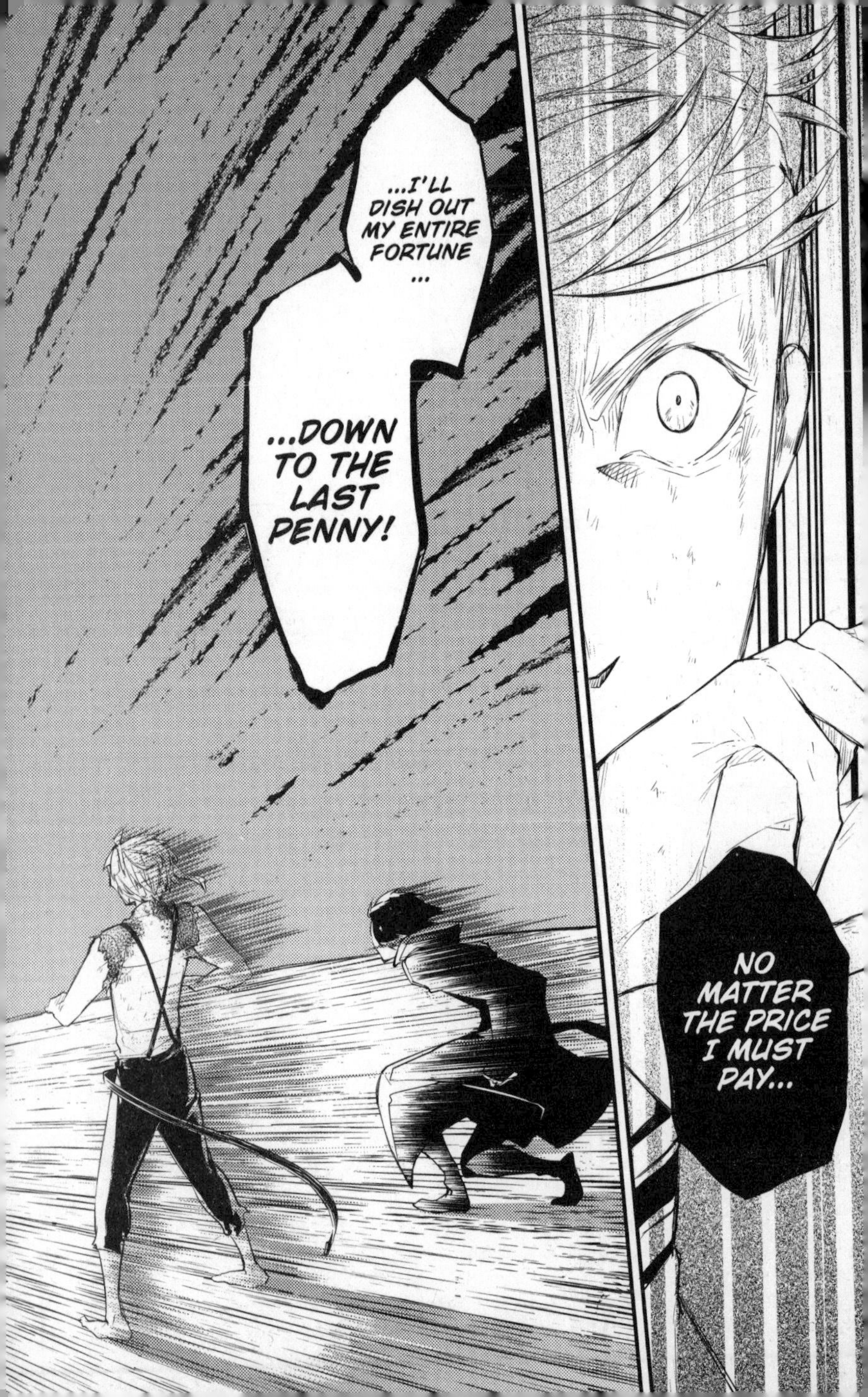
...I'LL DISH OUT MY ENTIRE FORTUNE ...
...DOWN TO THE LAST PENNY!
NO MATTER THE PRICE I MUST PAY...

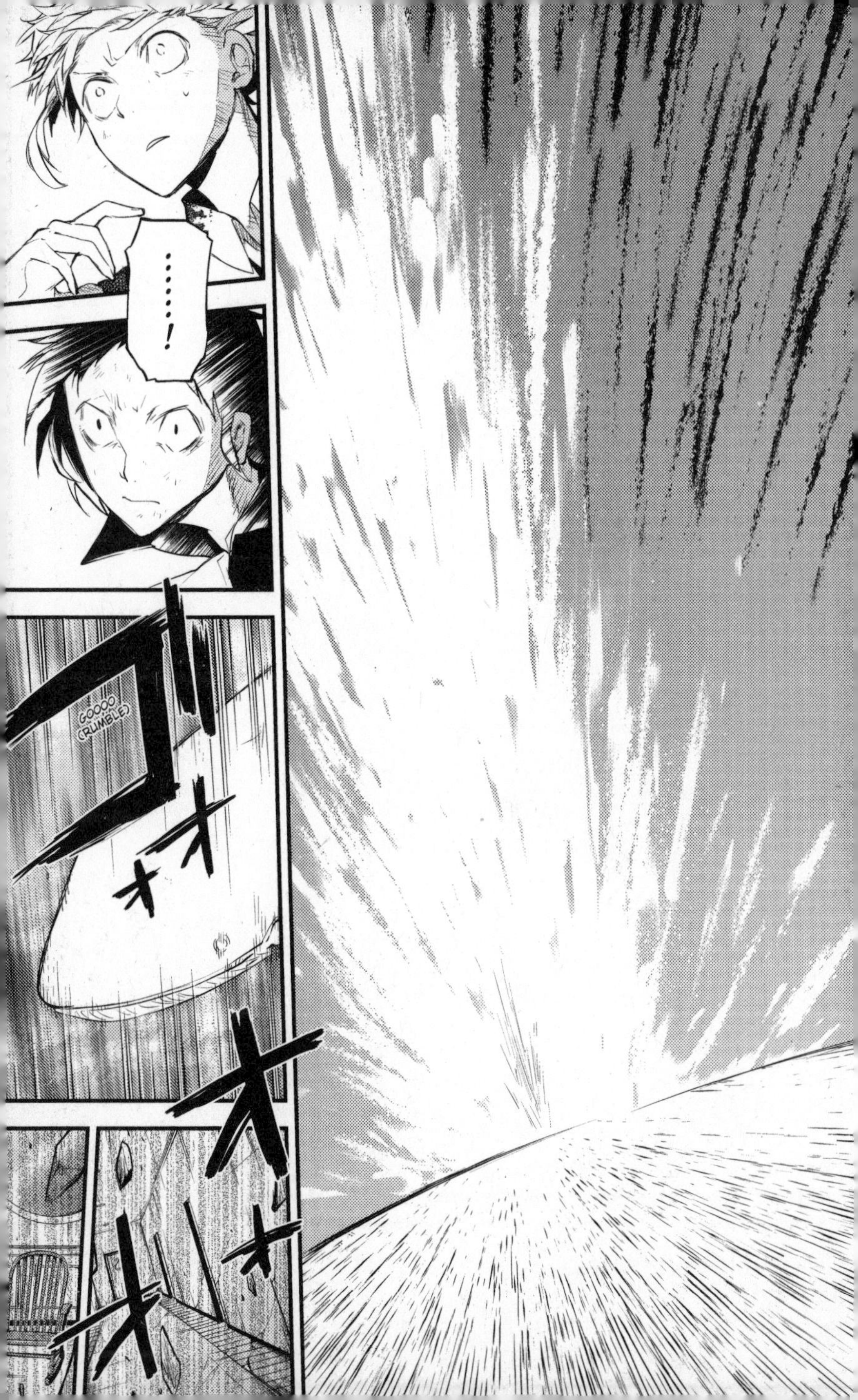
......!
GOOOO (RUMBLE)

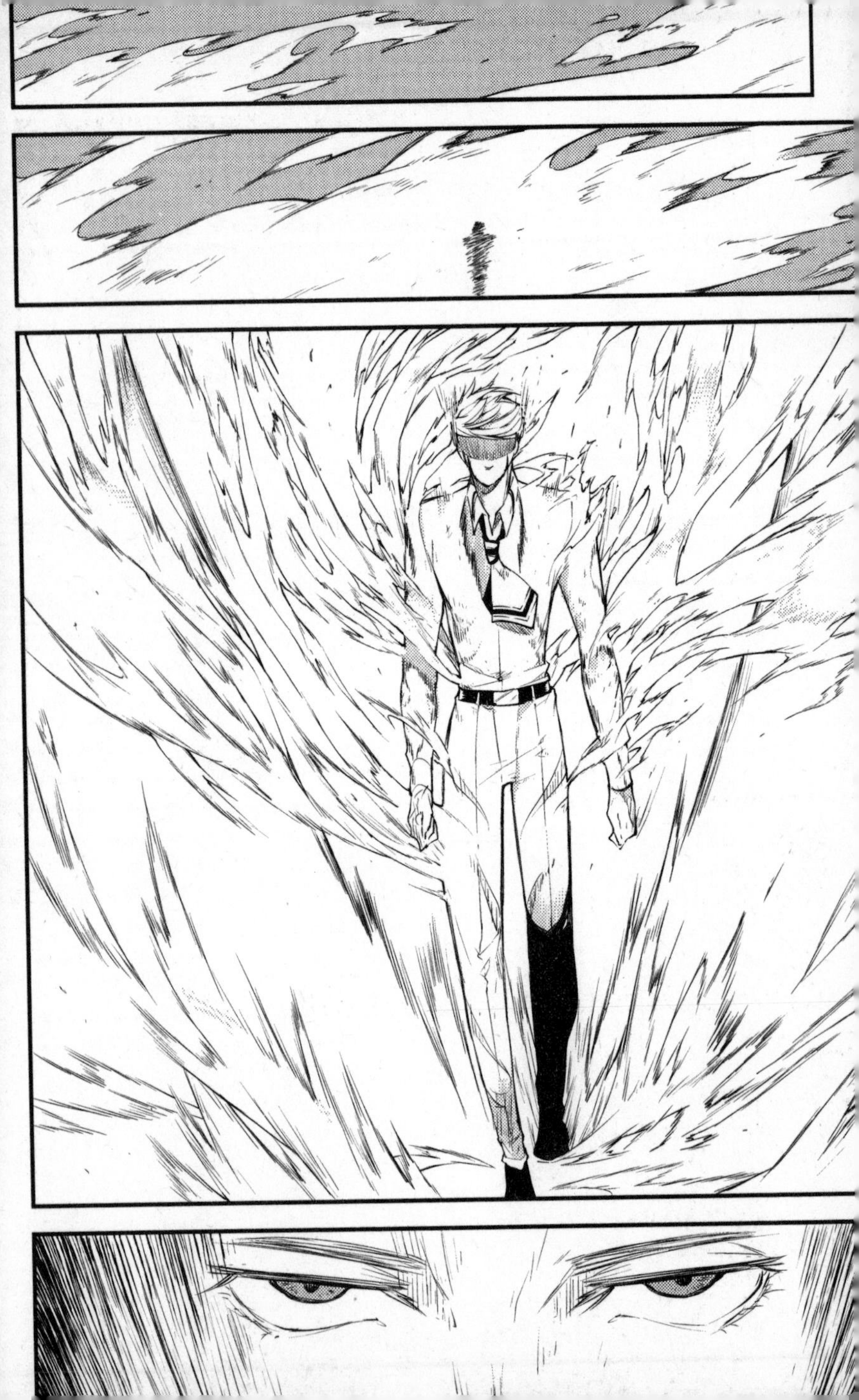

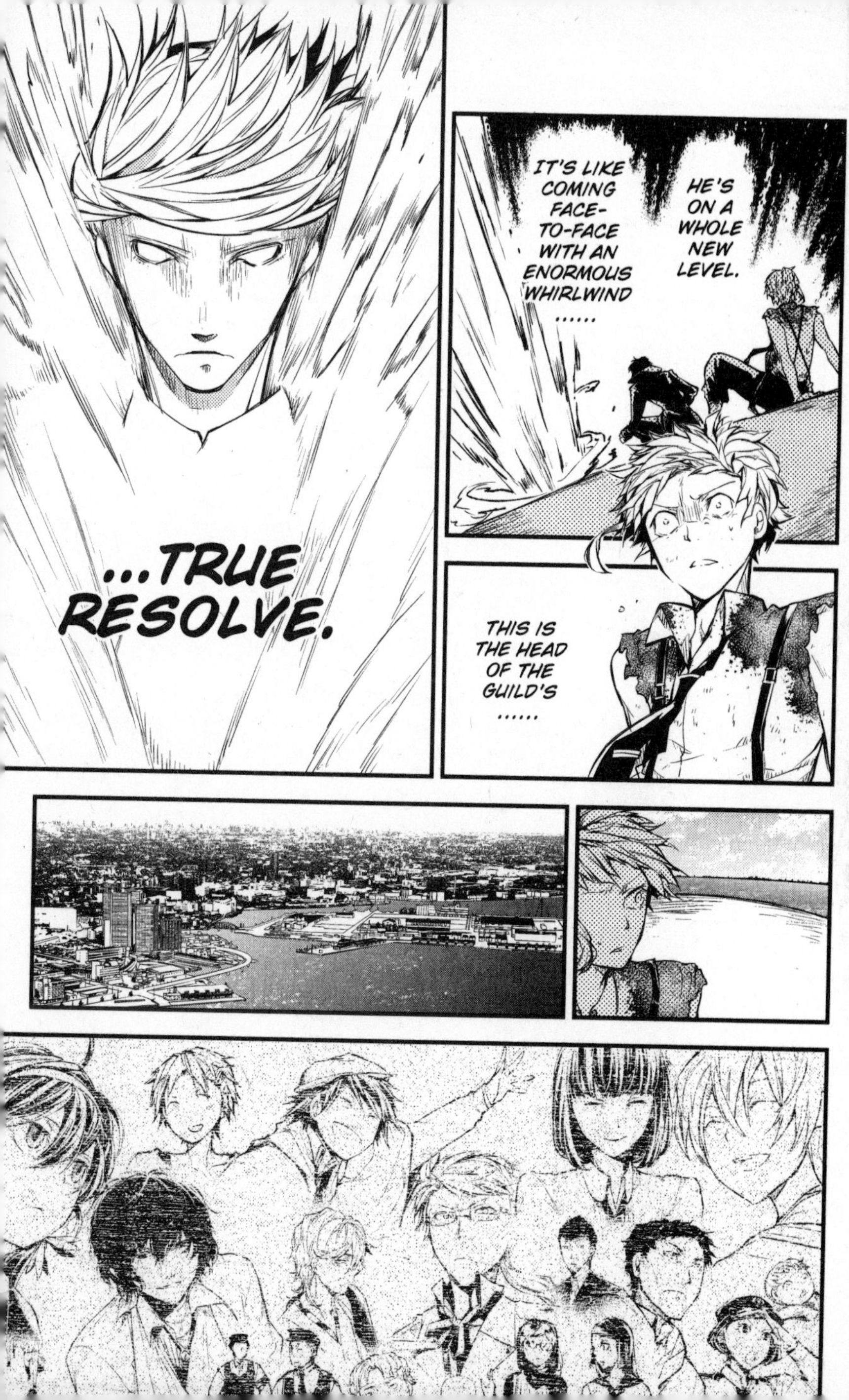
HE'S ON A WHOLE NEW LEVEL.
IT'S LIKE COMING FACE-TO-FACE WITH AN ENORMOUS WHIRLWIND......
THIS IS THE HEAD OF THE GUILD'S......
...TRUE RESOLVE.

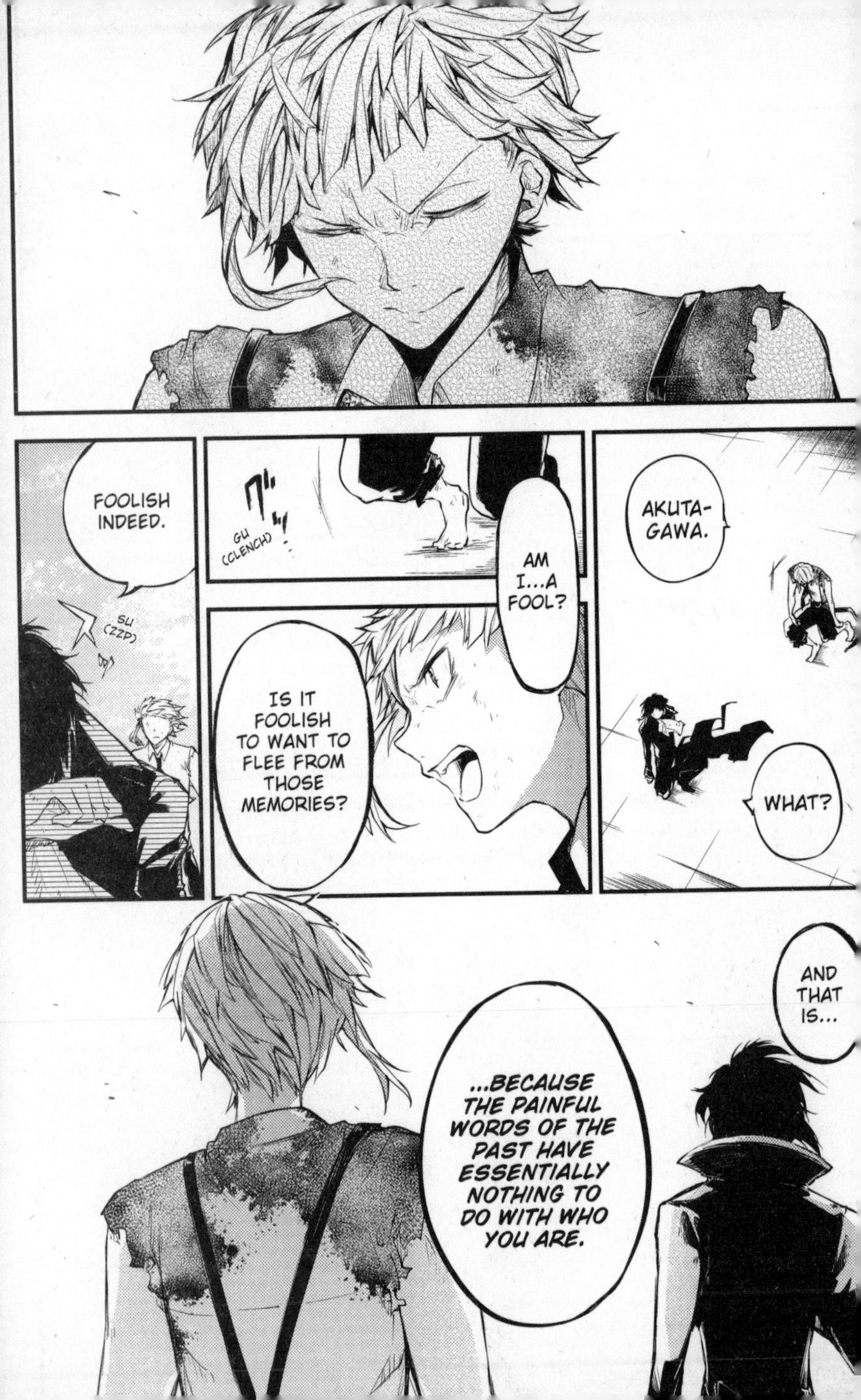
AKUTA-GAWA.
WHAT?
AM I...A FOOL?
GU (CLENCH)
IS IT FOOLISH TO WANT TO FLEE FROM THOSE MEMORIES?
FOOLISH INDEED.
SU (ZZP)
AND THAT IS...
...BECAUSE THE PAINFUL WORDS OF THE PAST HAVE ESSENTIALLY NOTHING TO DO WITH WHO YOU ARE.

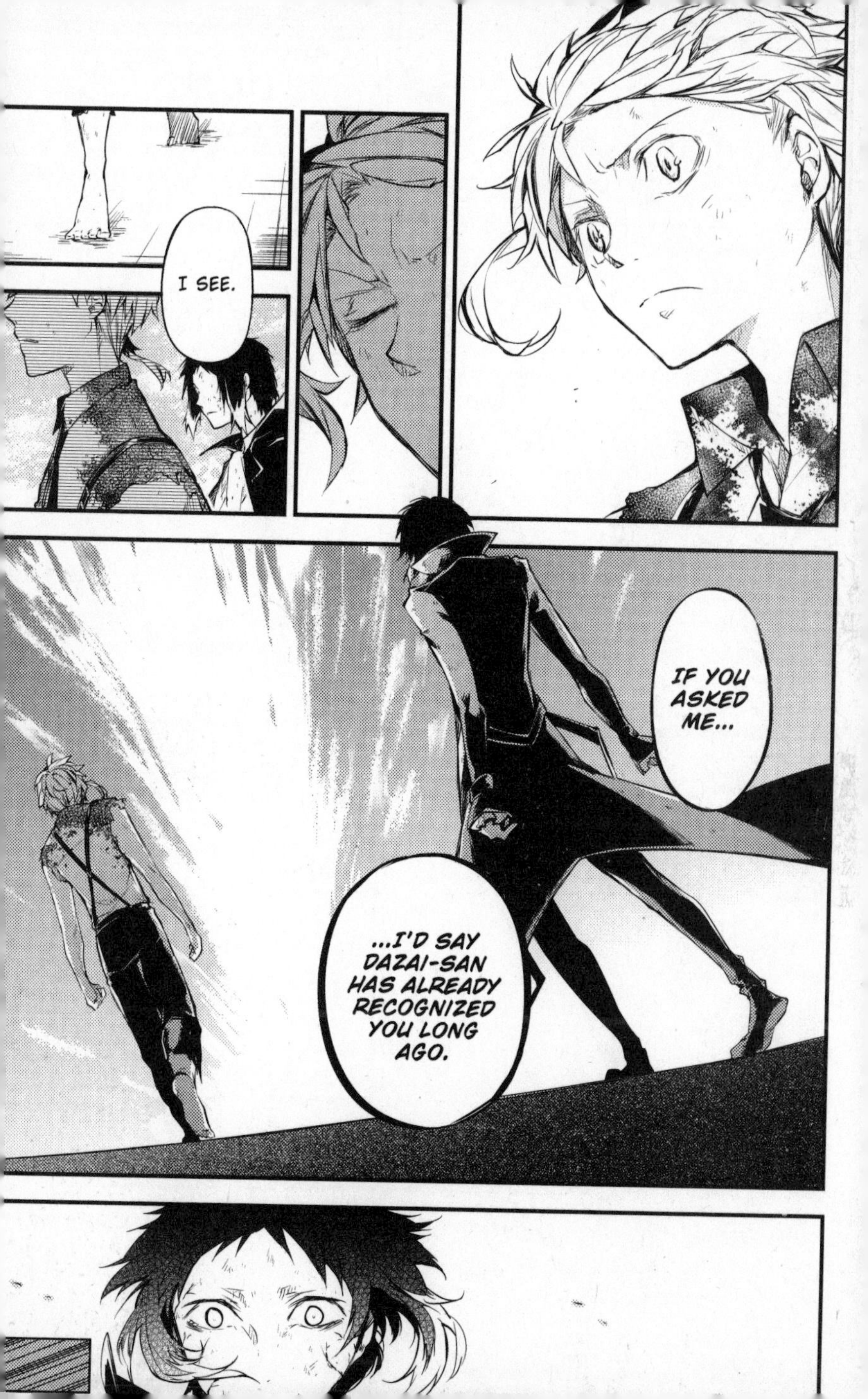
I SEE.
IF YOU ASKED ME...
...I'D SAY DAZAI-SAN HAS ALREADY RECOGNIZED YOU LONG AGO.

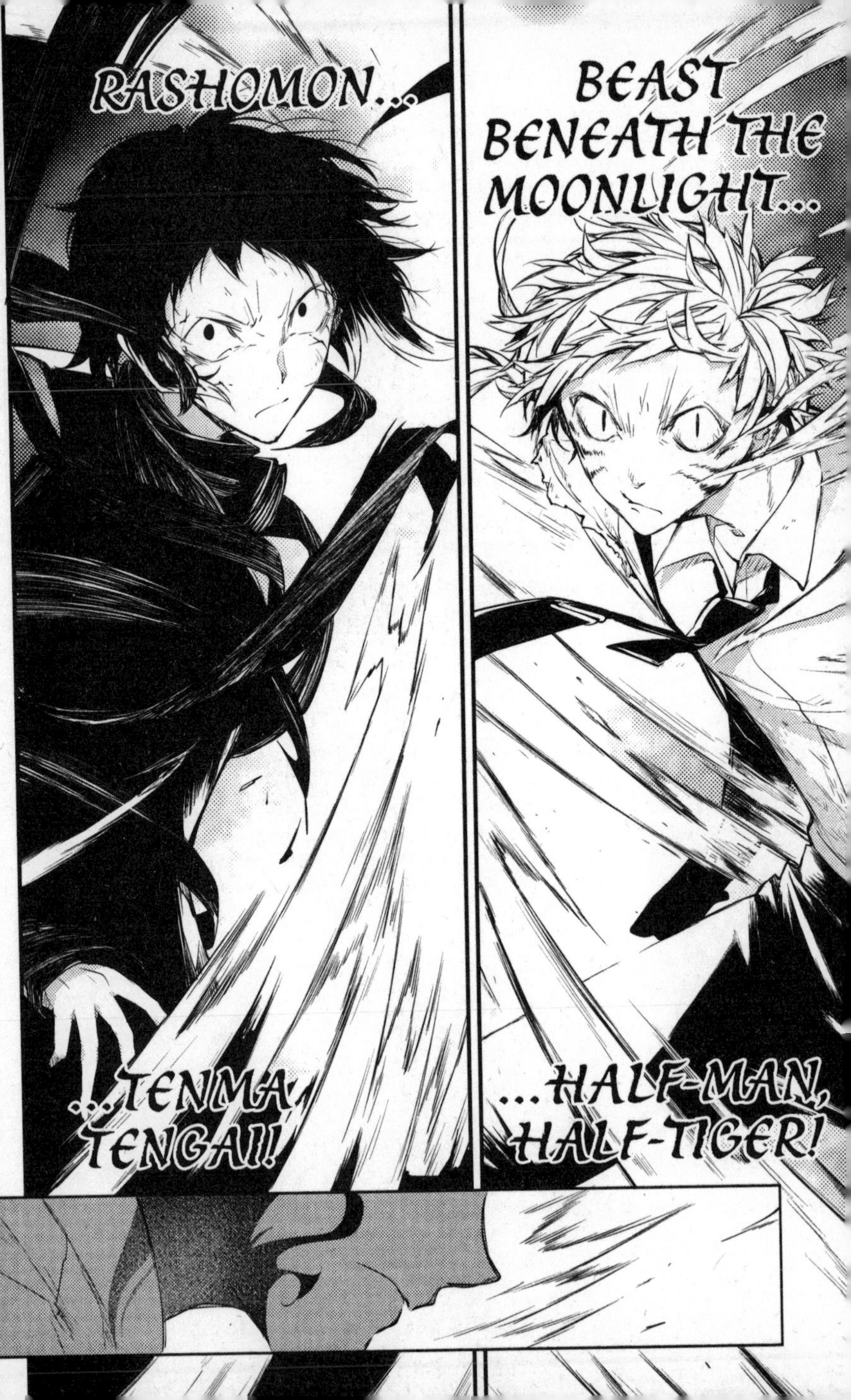
BEAST BENEATH THE MOONLIGHT...
...HALF-MAN, HALF-TIGER!
RASHOMON...
...TENMA TENGAI!

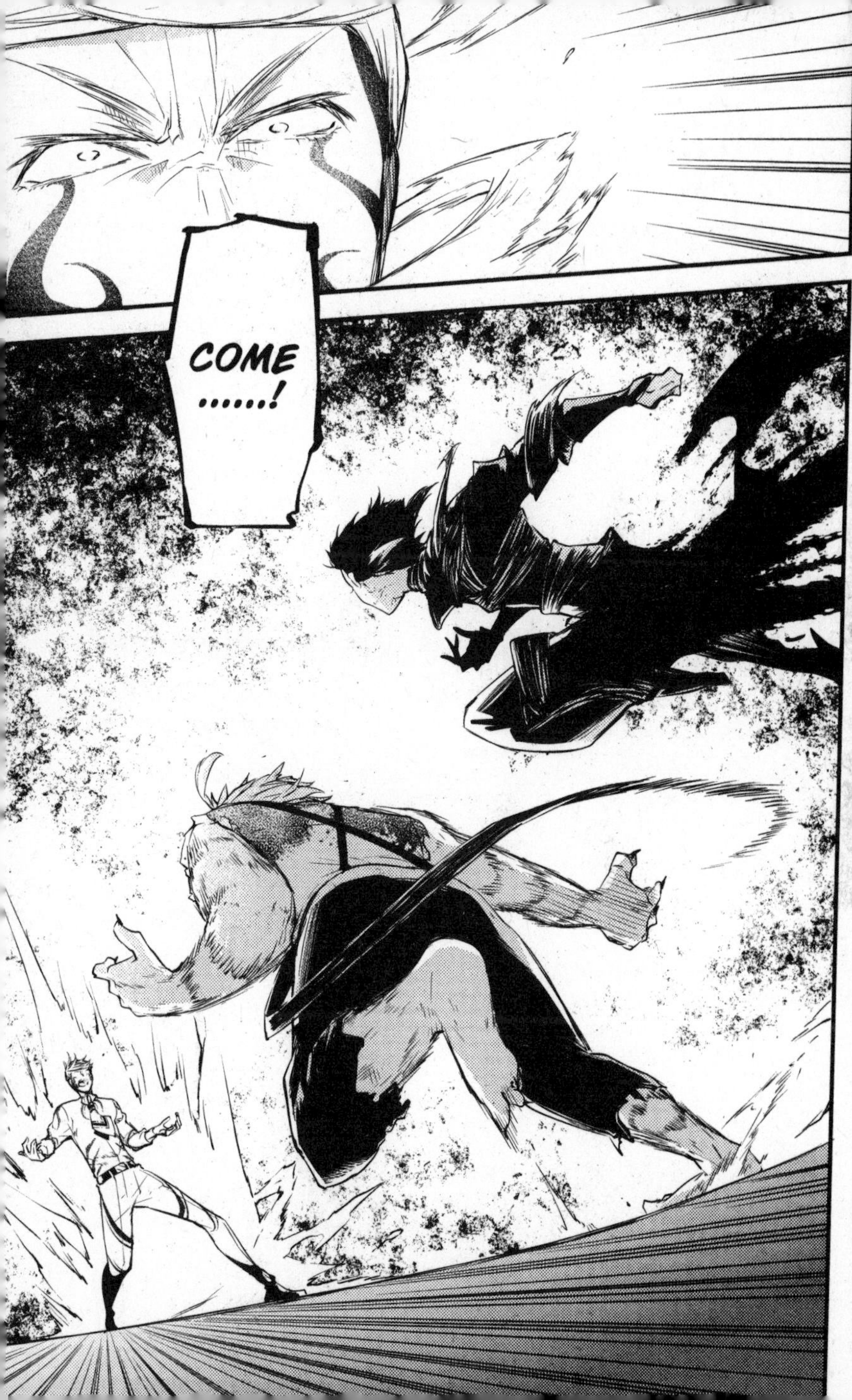
COME ......!

BUNGO
STRAY DOGS

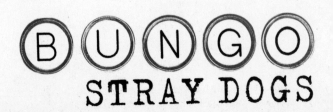

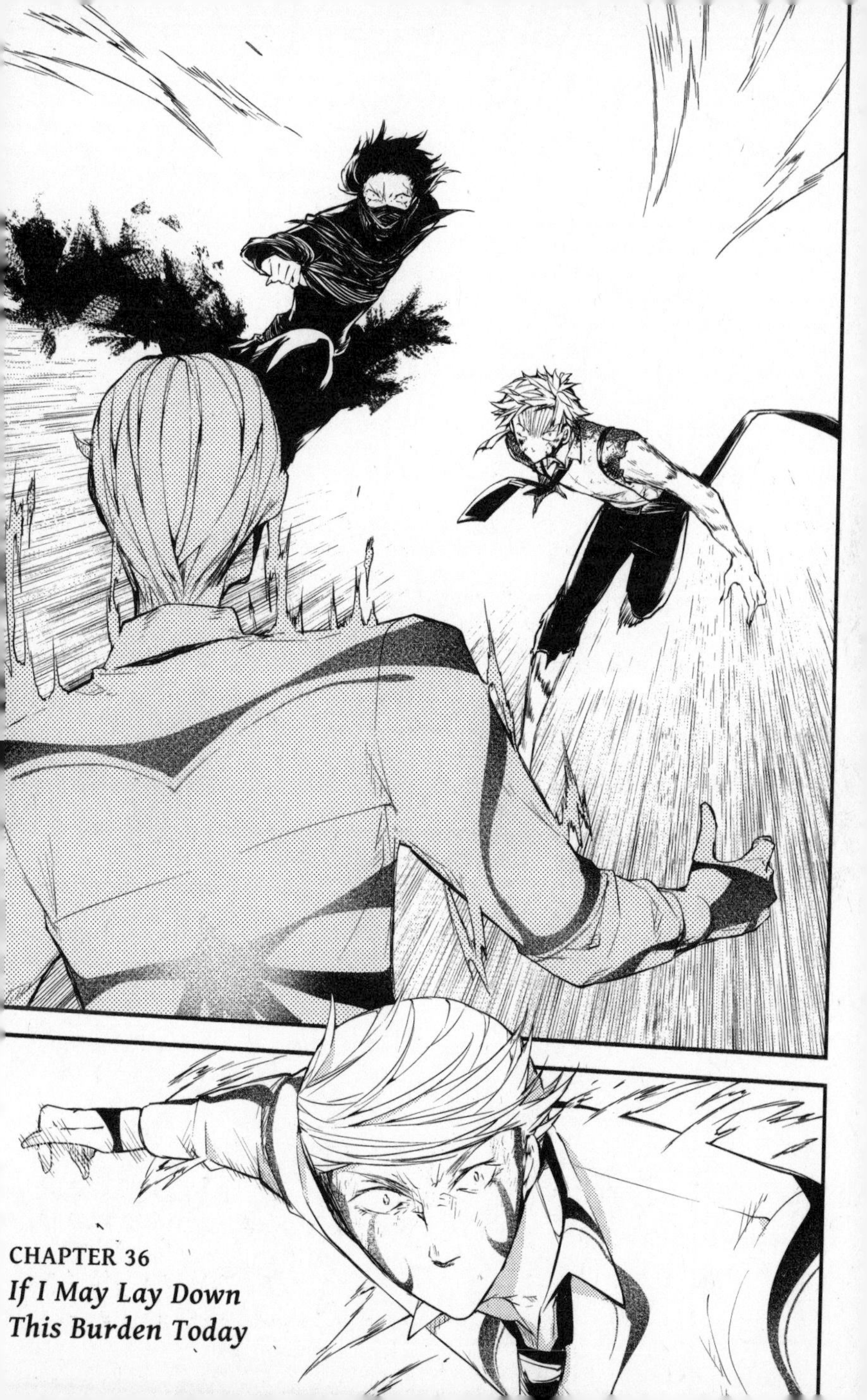

CHAPTER 36

If I May Lay Down This Burden Today

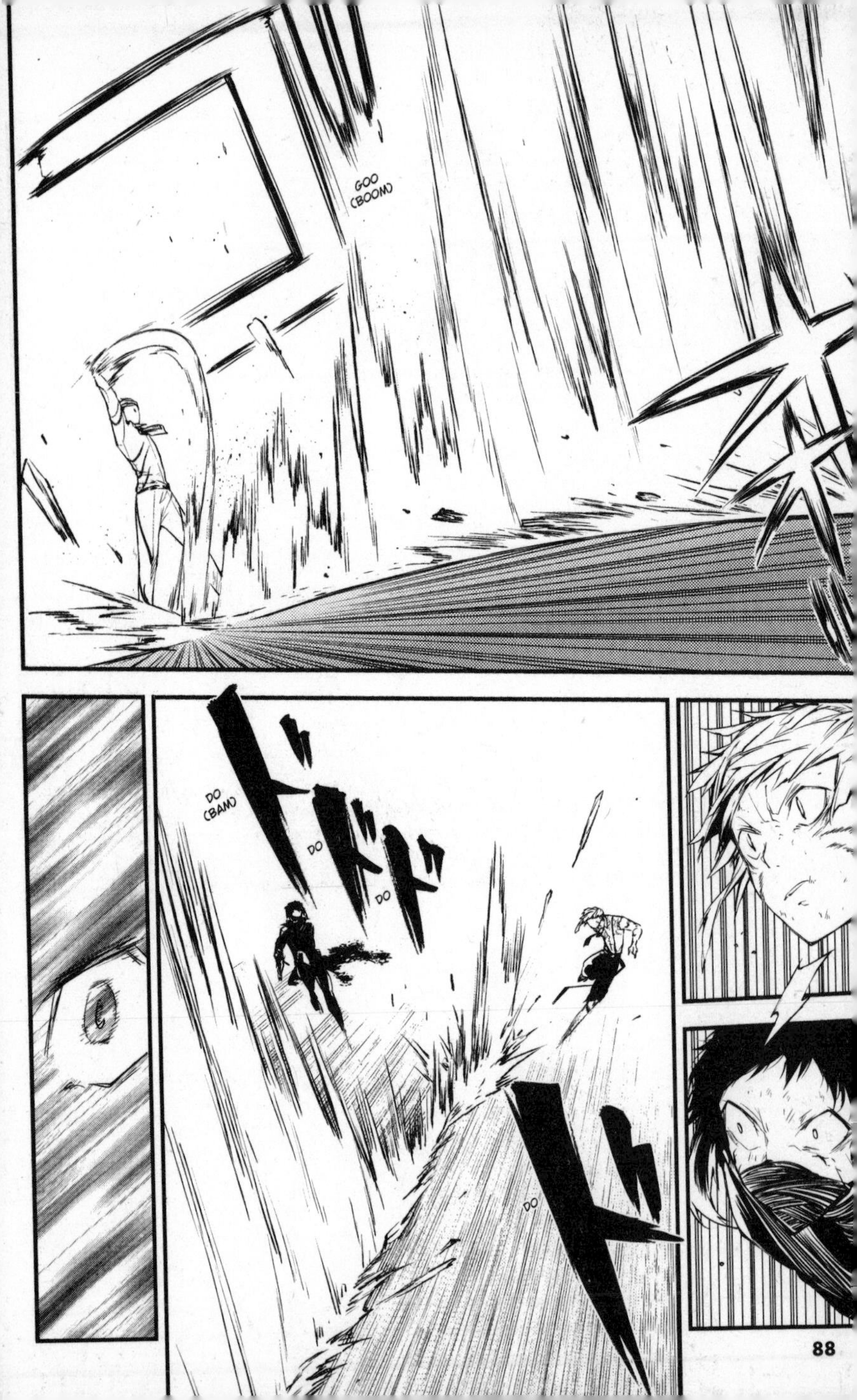
GOO (BOOM)
DO (BAM)
DO
DO
DO

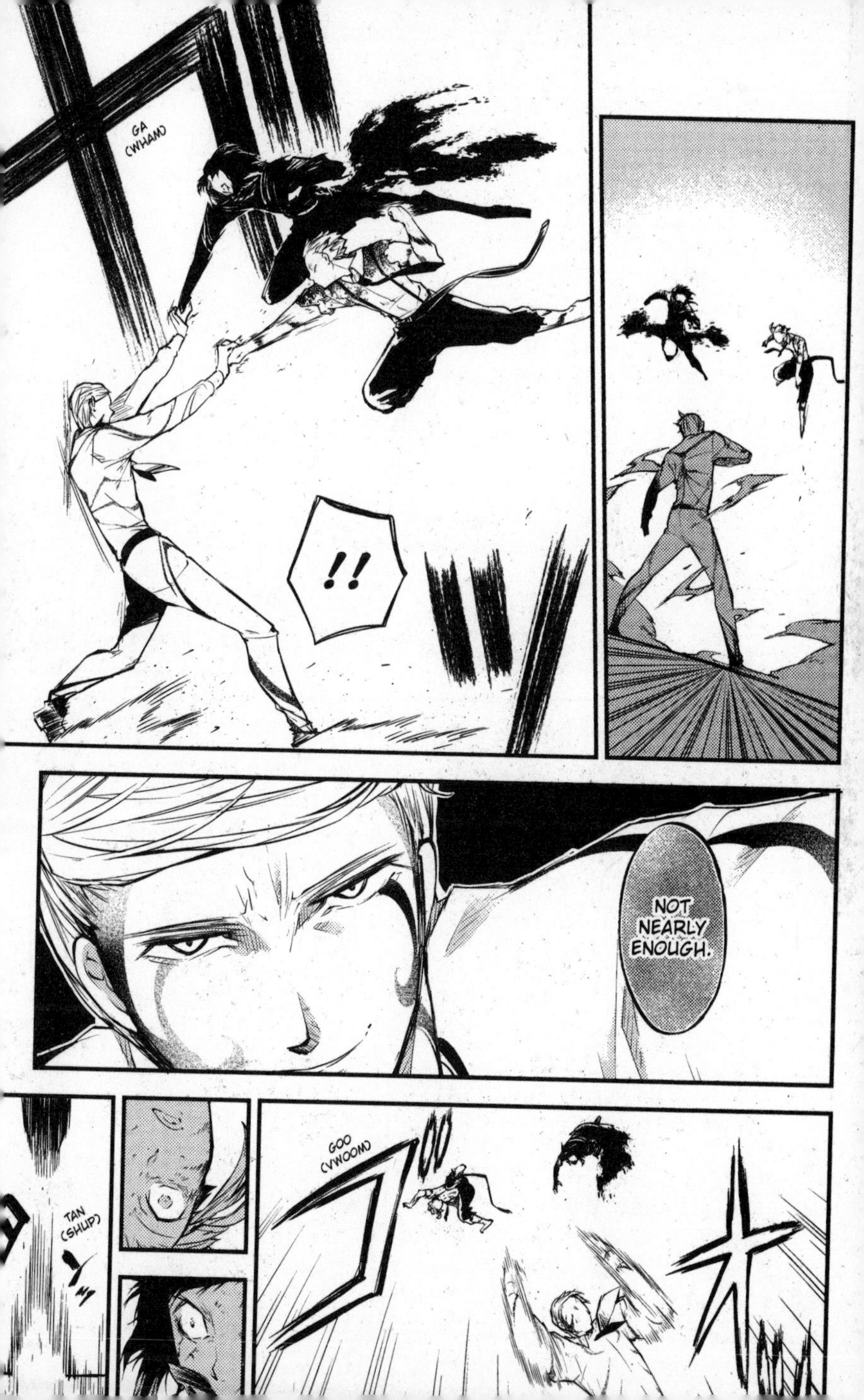
GA (WHAM)
!!
NOT NEARLY ENOUGH.
GOO (VWOOM)
TAN (SHUP)

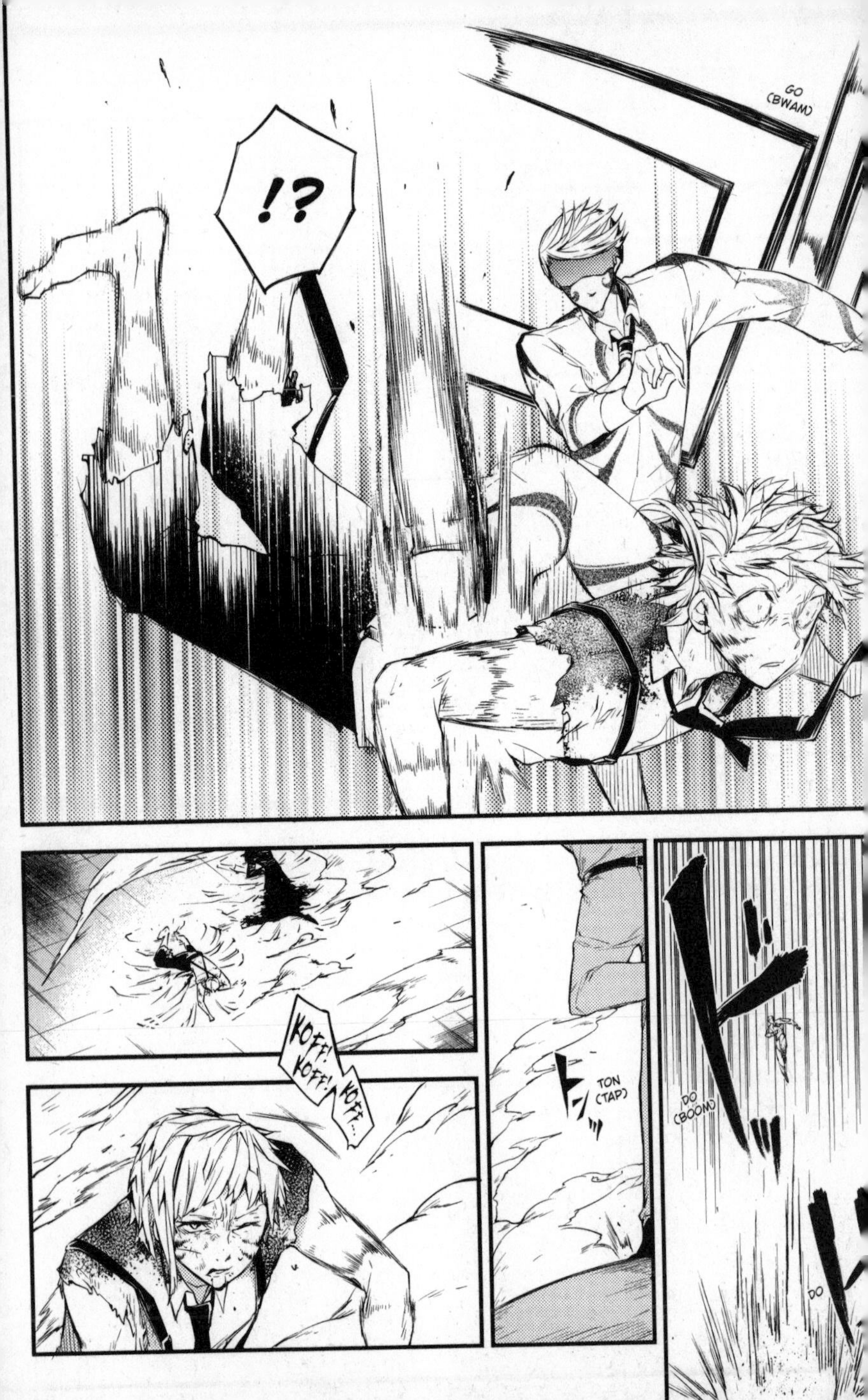
GO
(BWAM)
!?
DO
(BOOM)
DO
TON
(TAP)
KOFF! KOFF! KOFF...

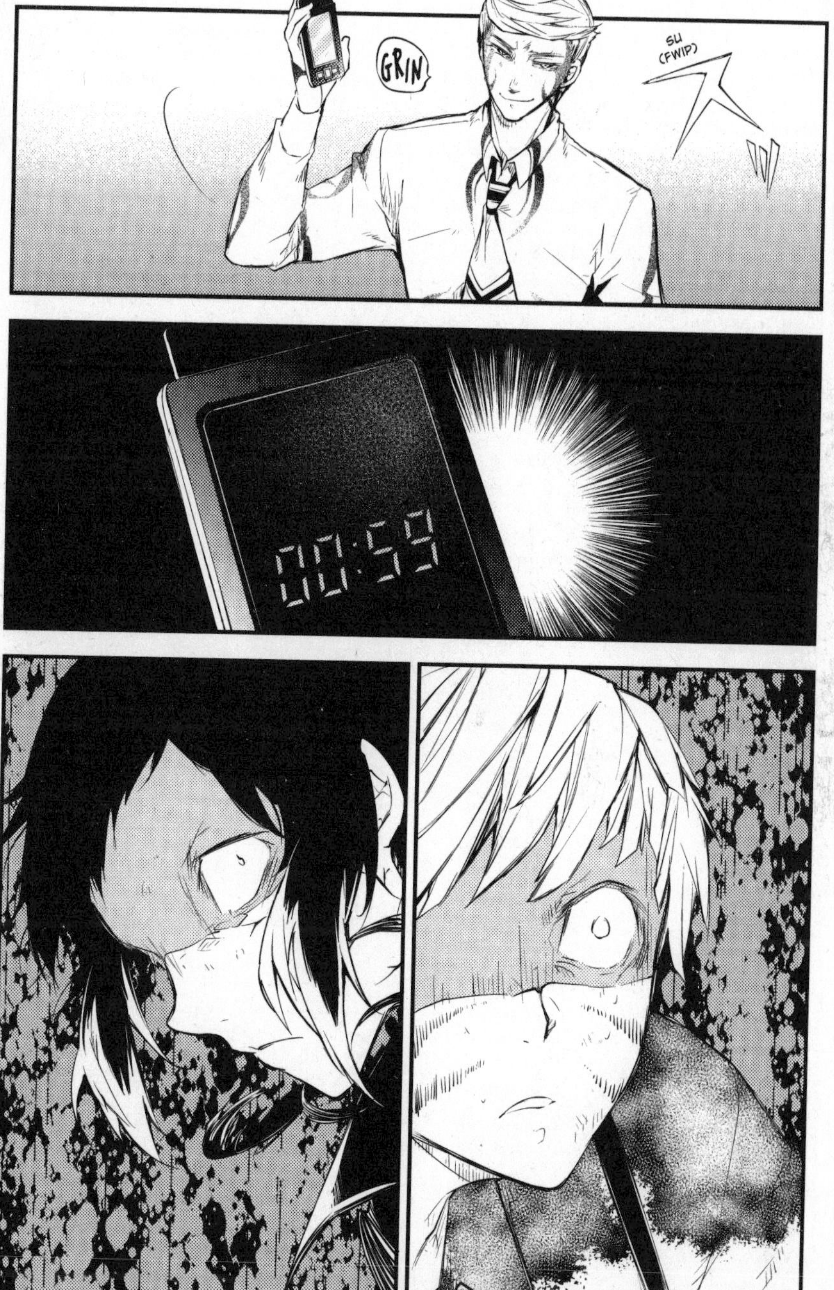
SU
(FWIP)
GRIN
00:59

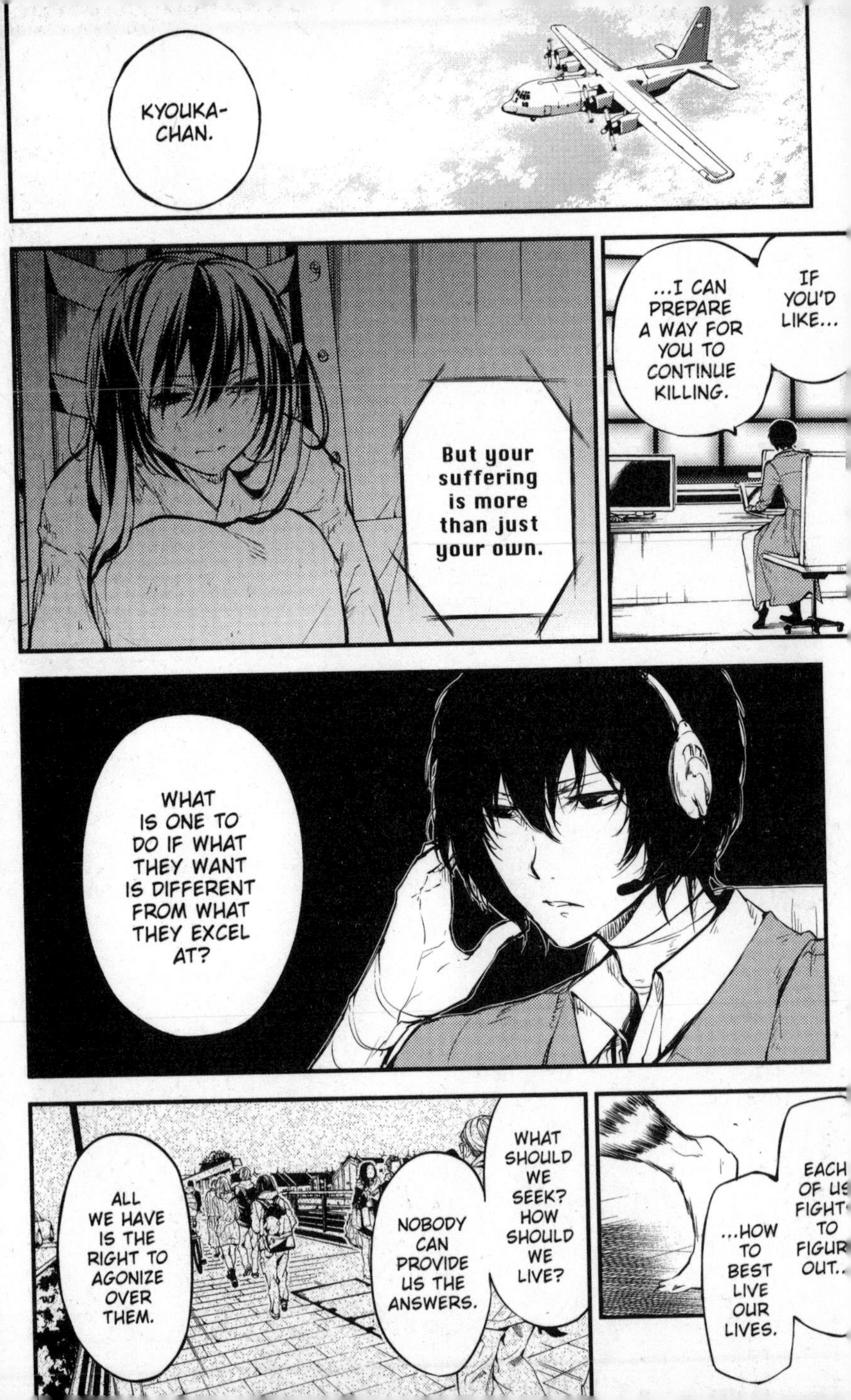
KYOUKA-CHAN.
IF YOU'D LIKE...
...I CAN PREPARE A WAY FOR YOU TO CONTINUE KILLING.
But your suffering is more than just your own.
WHAT IS ONE TO DO IF WHAT THEY WANT IS DIFFERENT FROM WHAT THEY EXCEL AT?
EACH OF US FIGHT TO FIGUR OUT..
...HOW TO BEST LIVE OUR LIVES.
WHAT SHOULD WE SEEK? HOW SHOULD WE LIVE?
NOBODY CAN PROVIDE US THE ANSWERS.
ALL WE HAVE IS THE RIGHT TO AGONIZE OVER THEM.

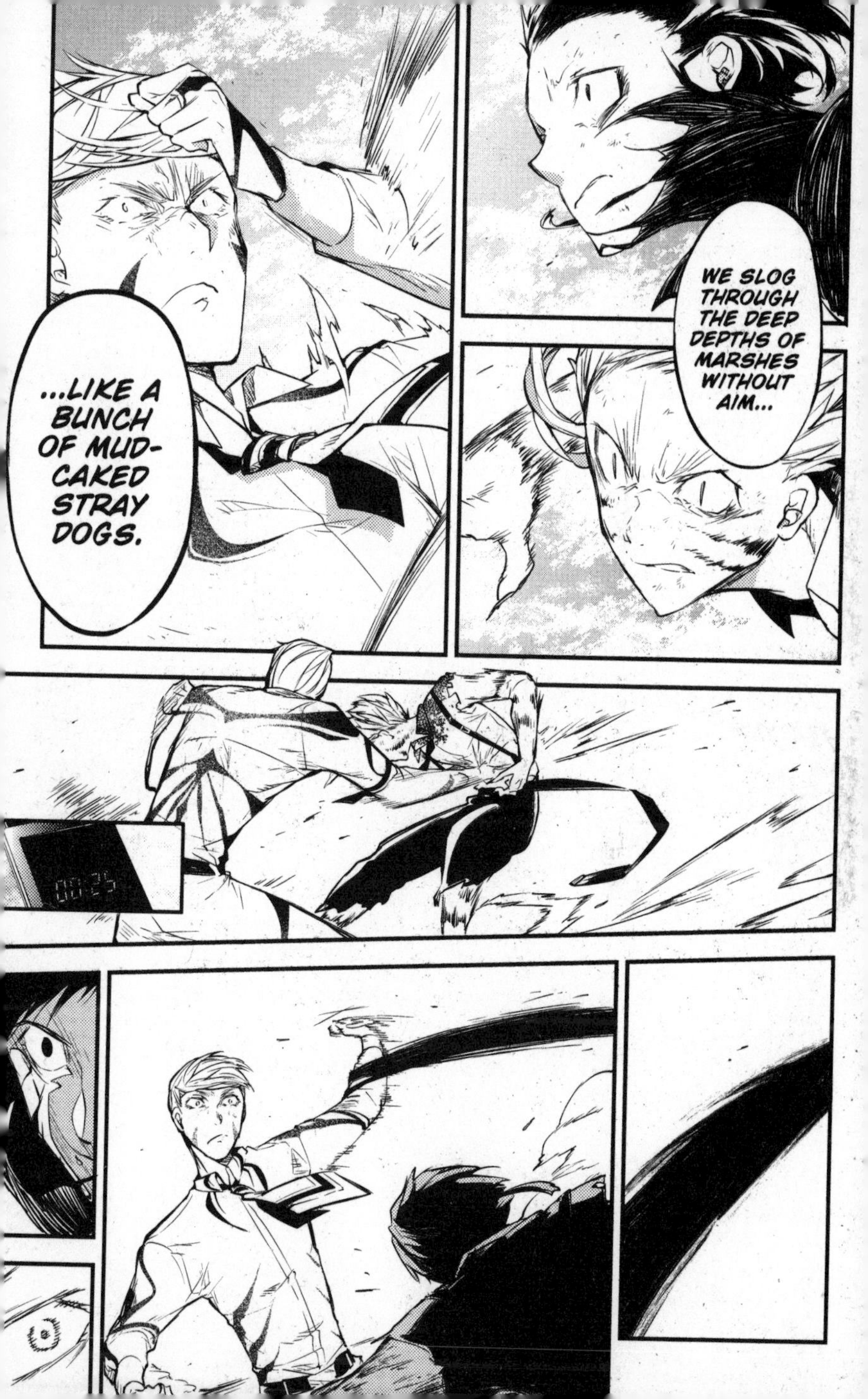
WE SLOG THROUGH THE DEEP DEPTHS OF MARSHES WITHOUT AIM...
...LIKE A BUNCH OF MUD-CAKED STRAY DOGS.

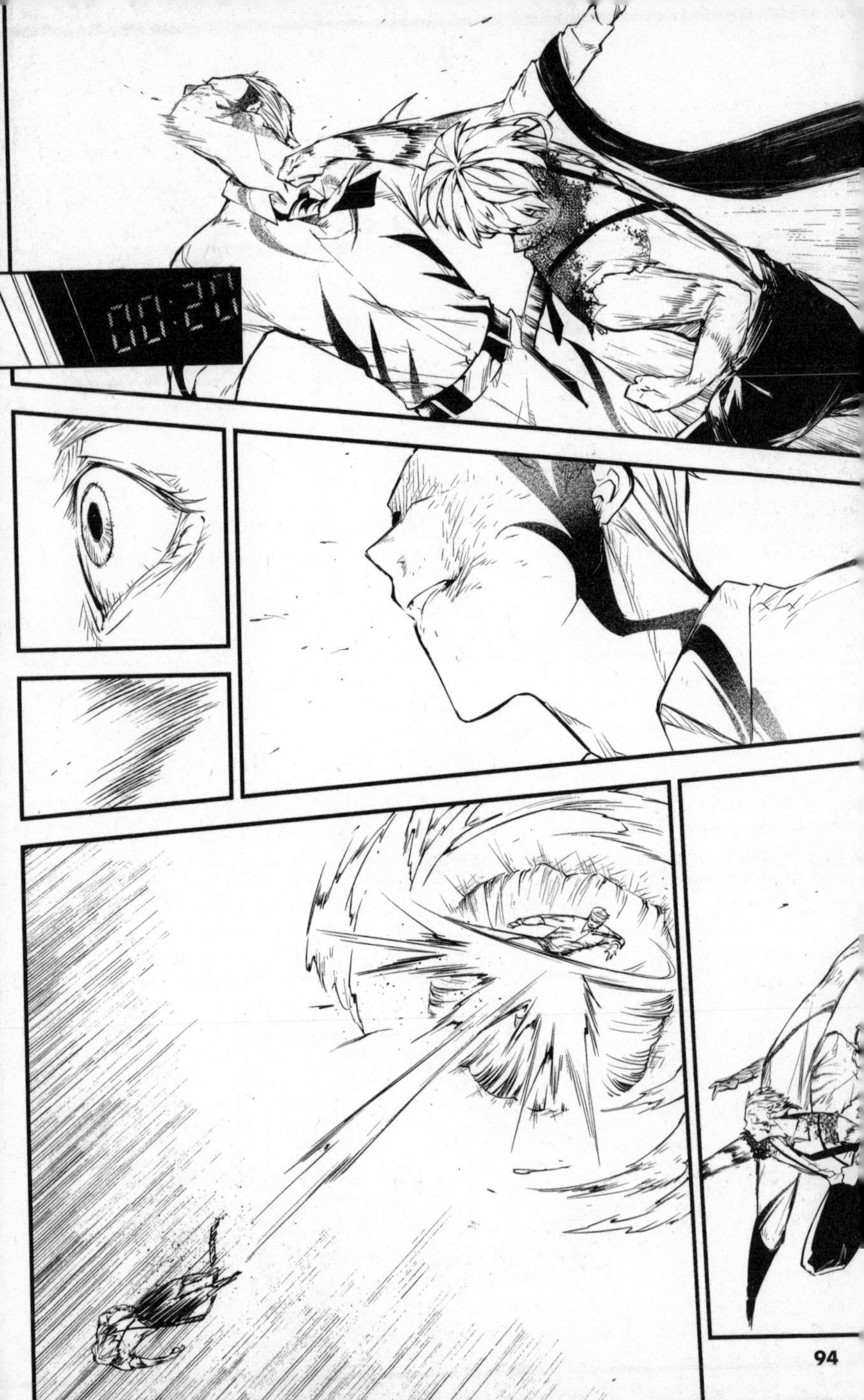
00:20

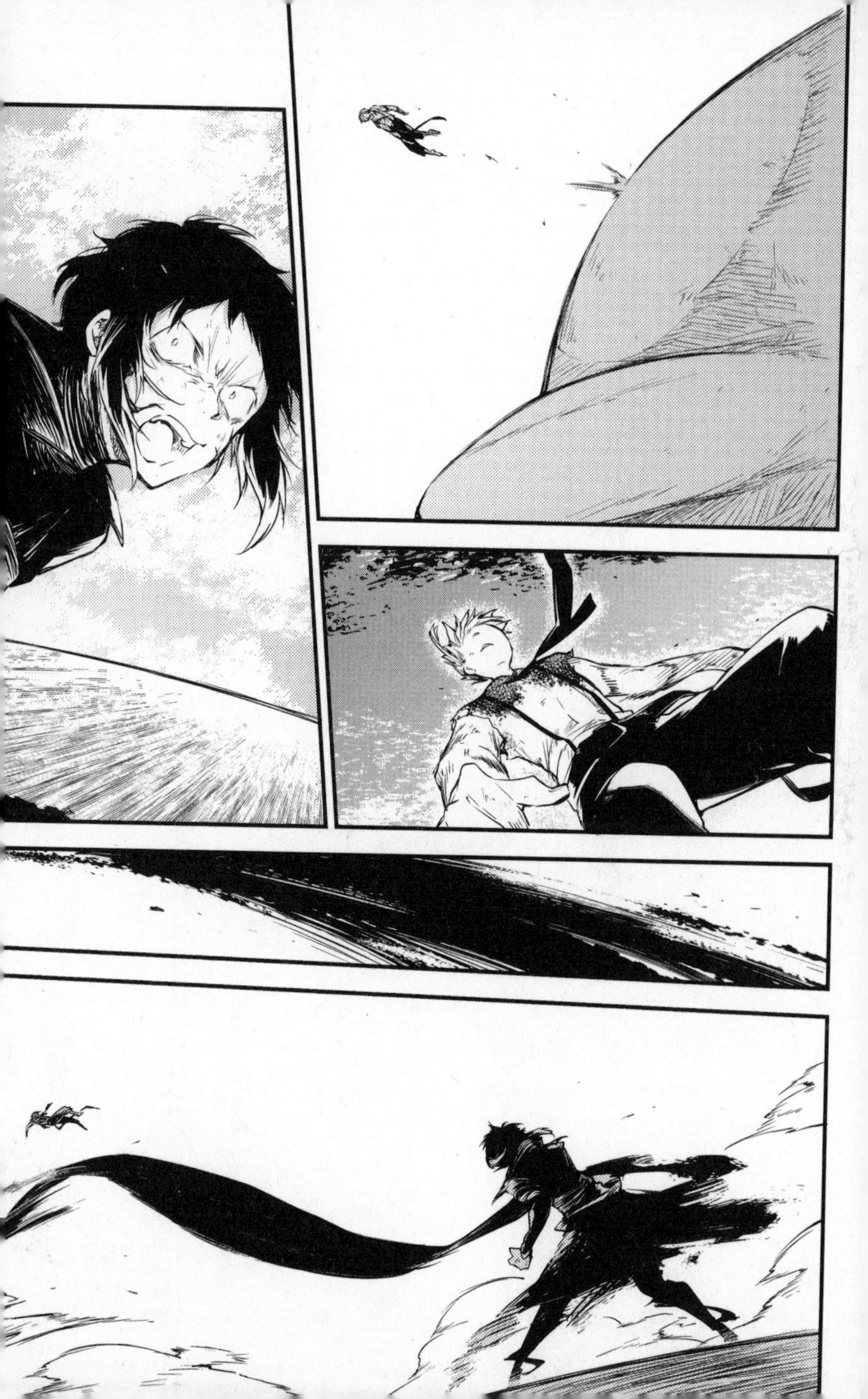

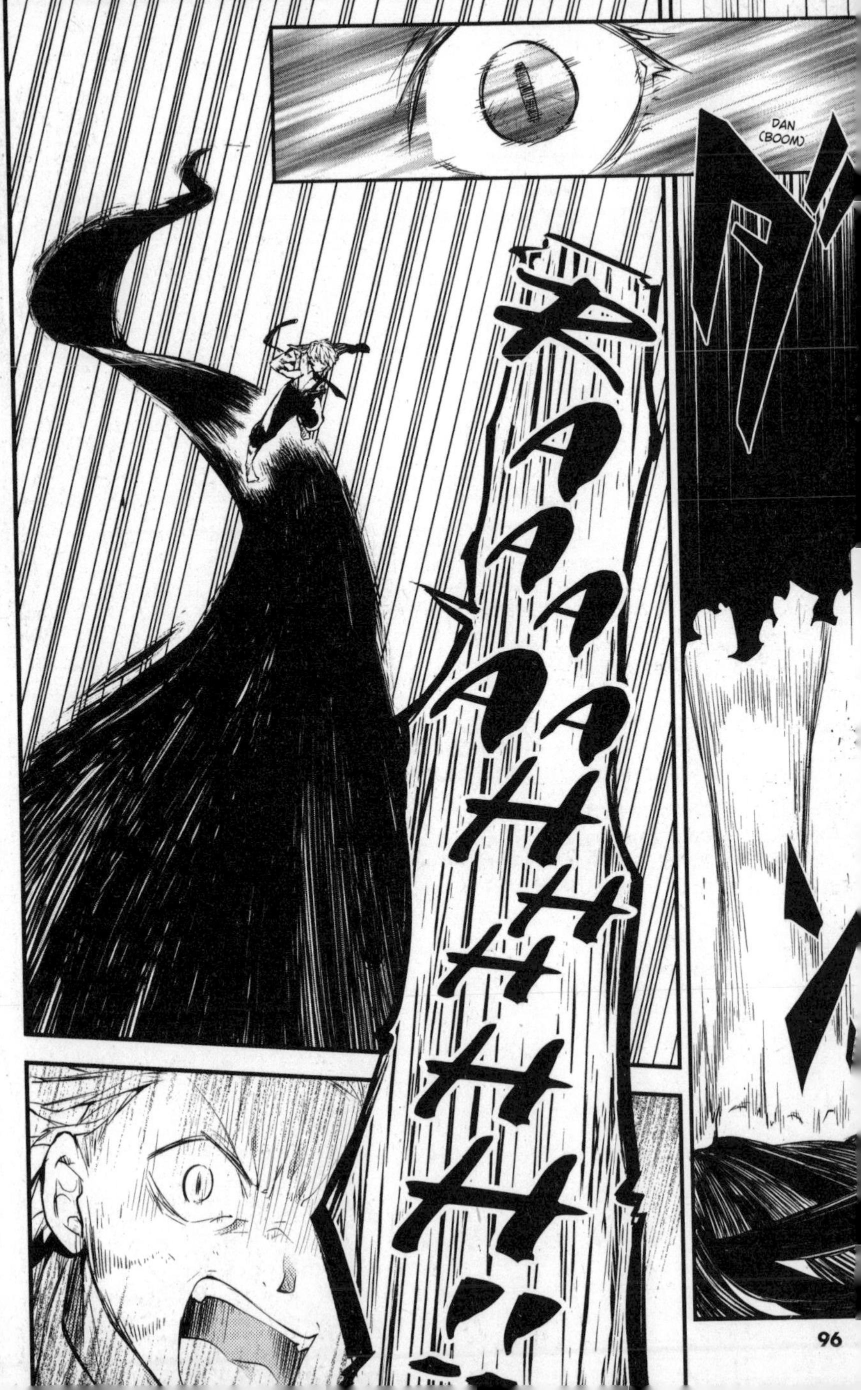
DAN
(BOOM)
AAAAAHHHHH!!

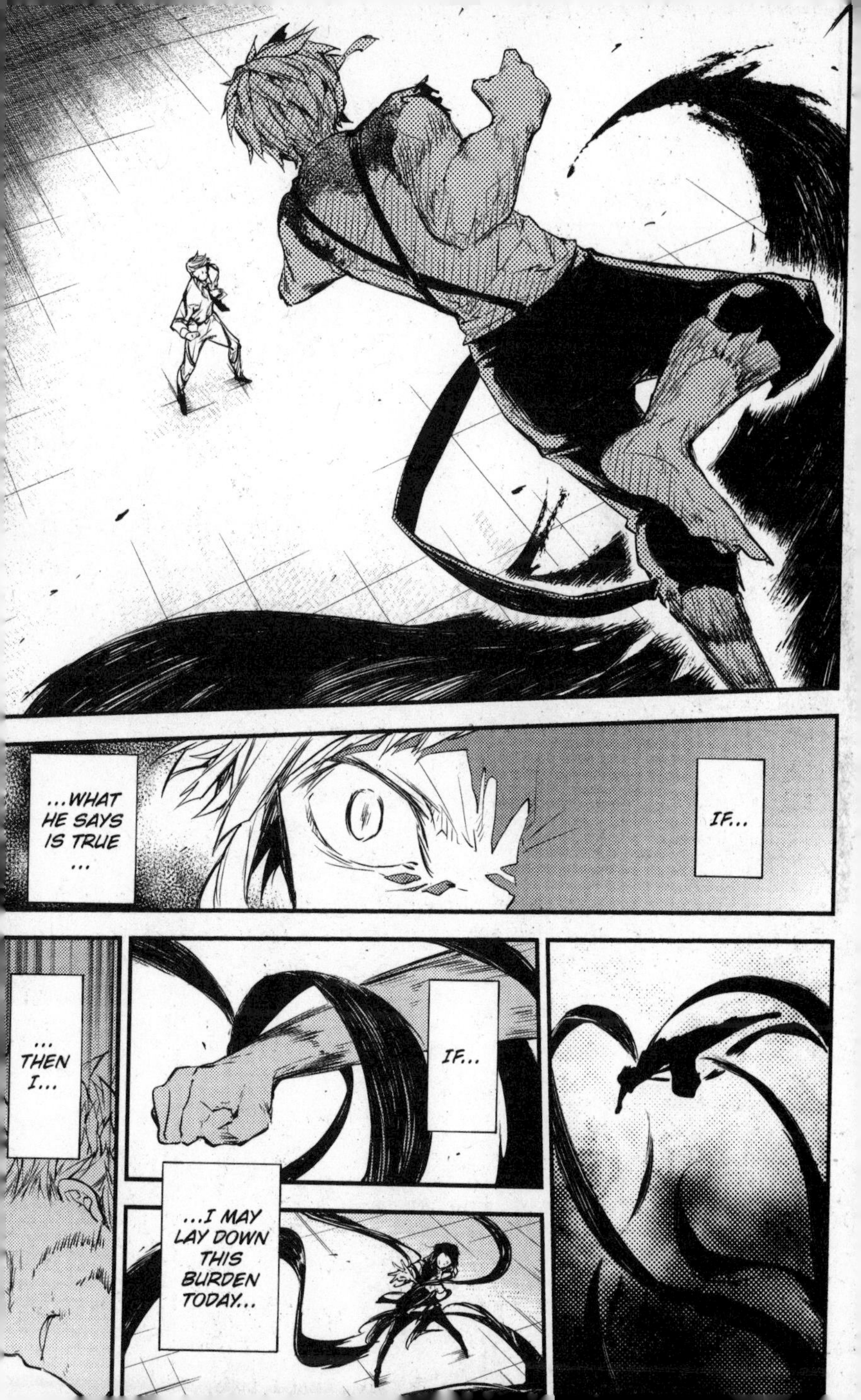
IF...
...WHAT HE SAYS IS TRUE ...
IF...
...I MAY LAY DOWN THIS BURDEN TODAY...
... THEN I...

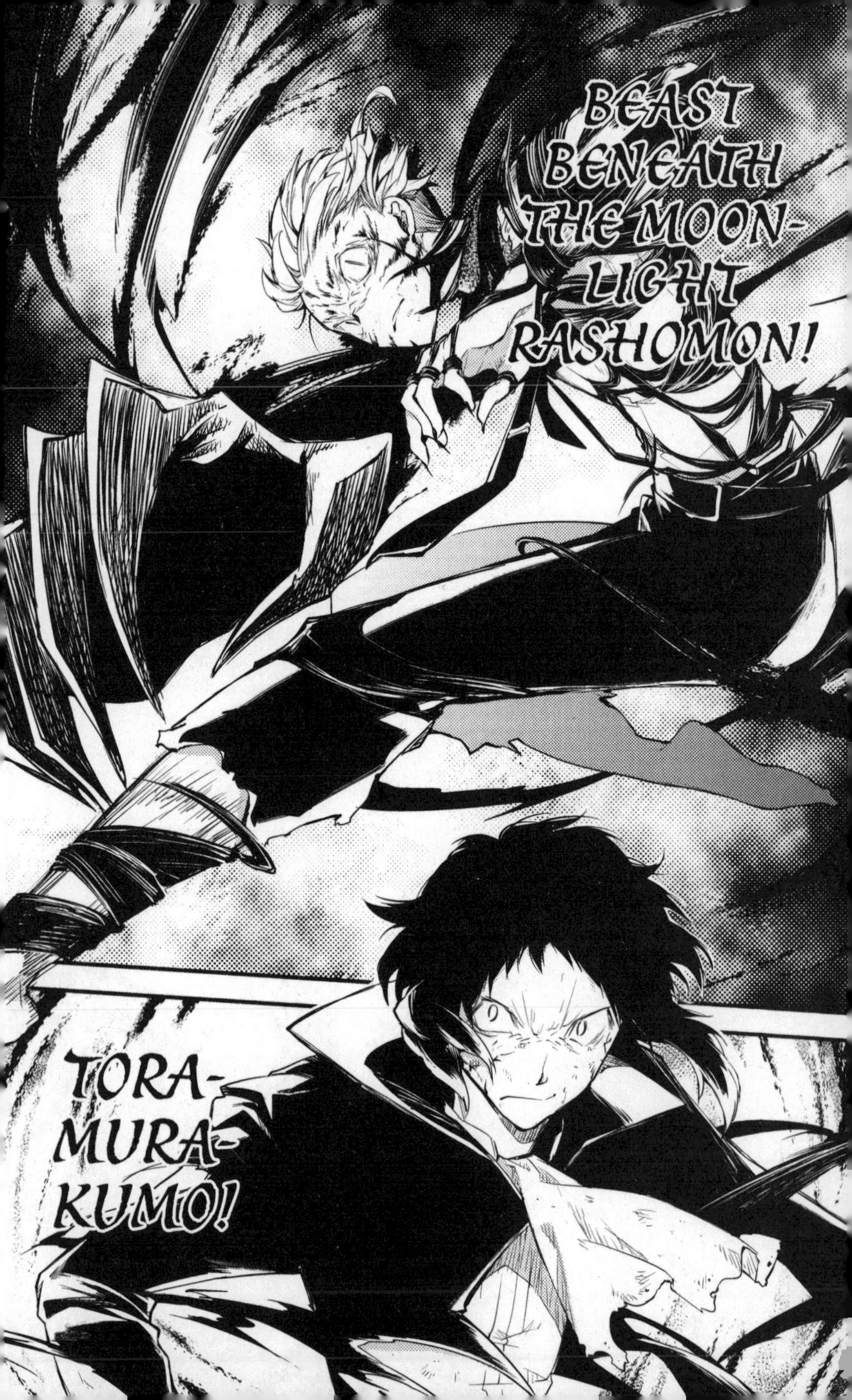
BEAST BENEATH THE MOON-LIGHT RASHOMON!
TORA-MURA-KUMO!

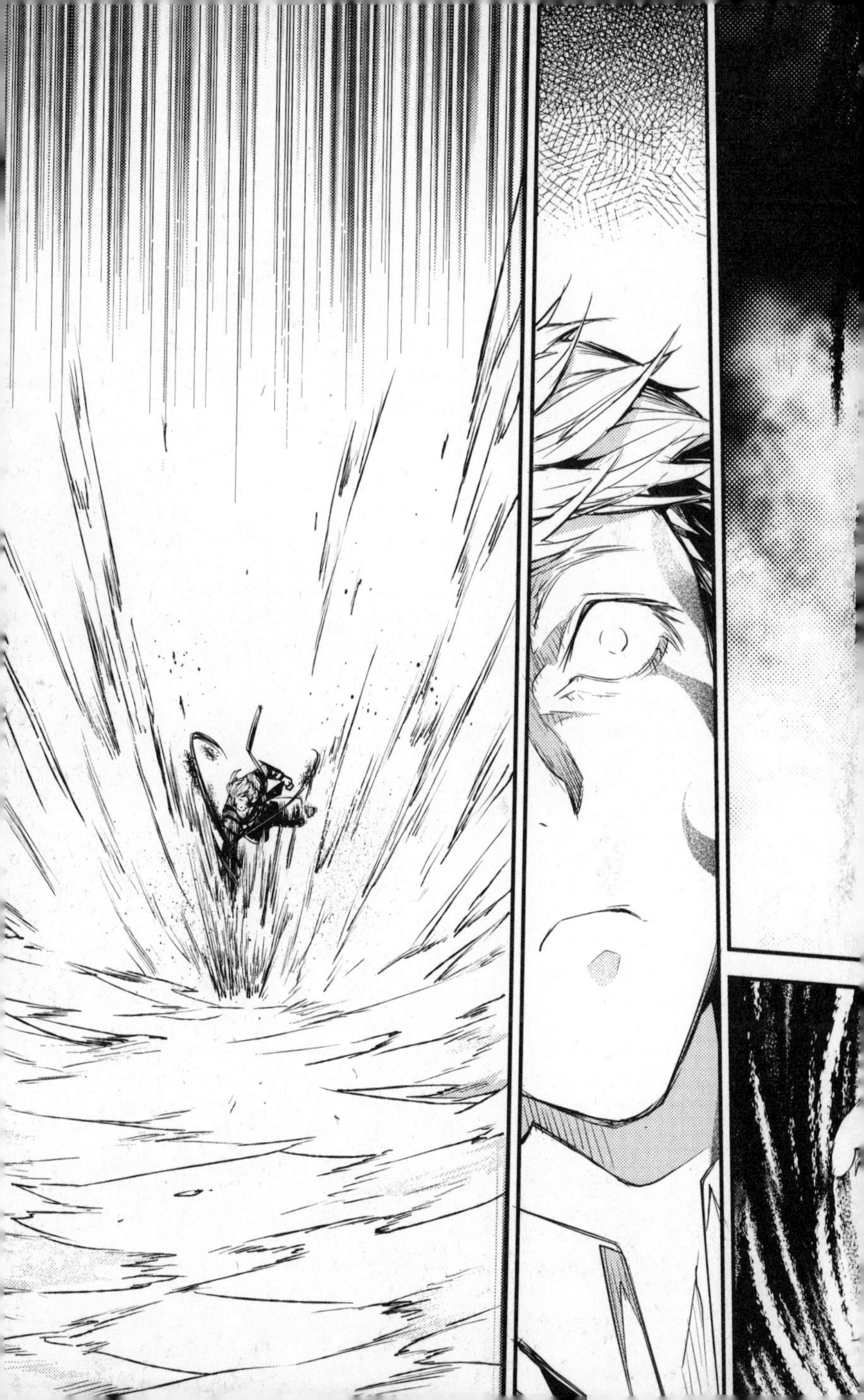

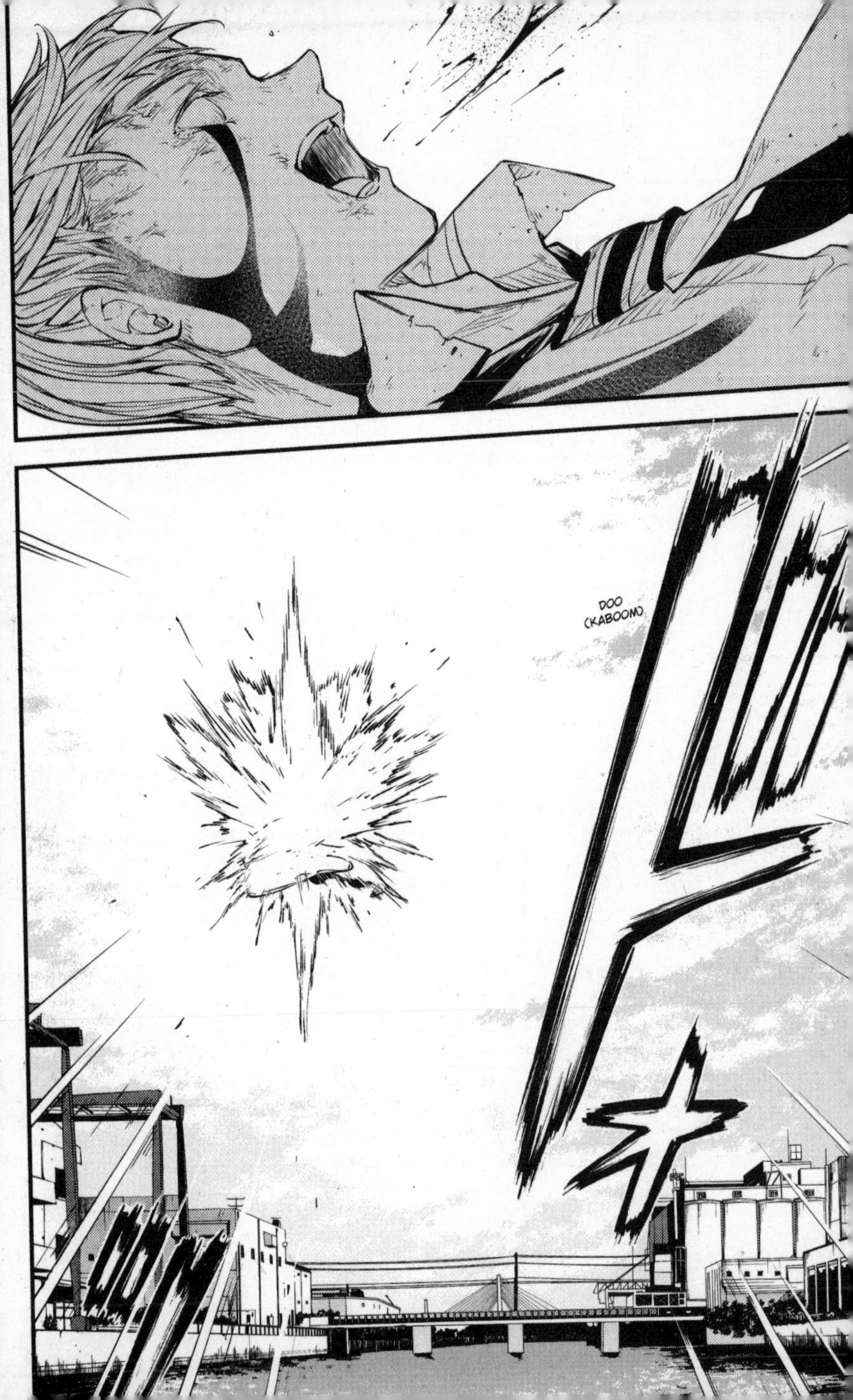
DOO
(KABOOM)

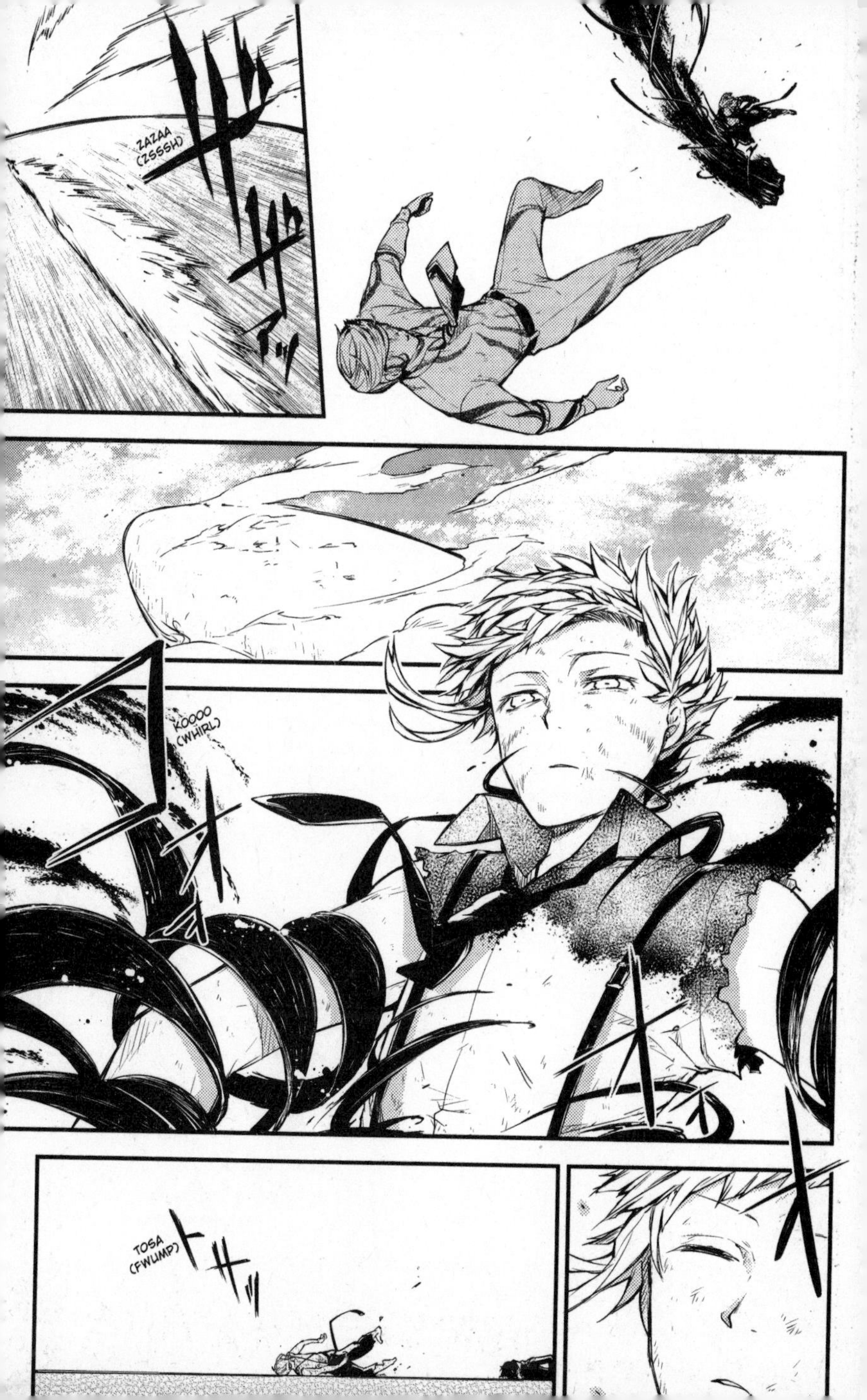
ZAZAA (ZSSSH)
KOOOO (WHIRL)
TOSA (FWUMP)

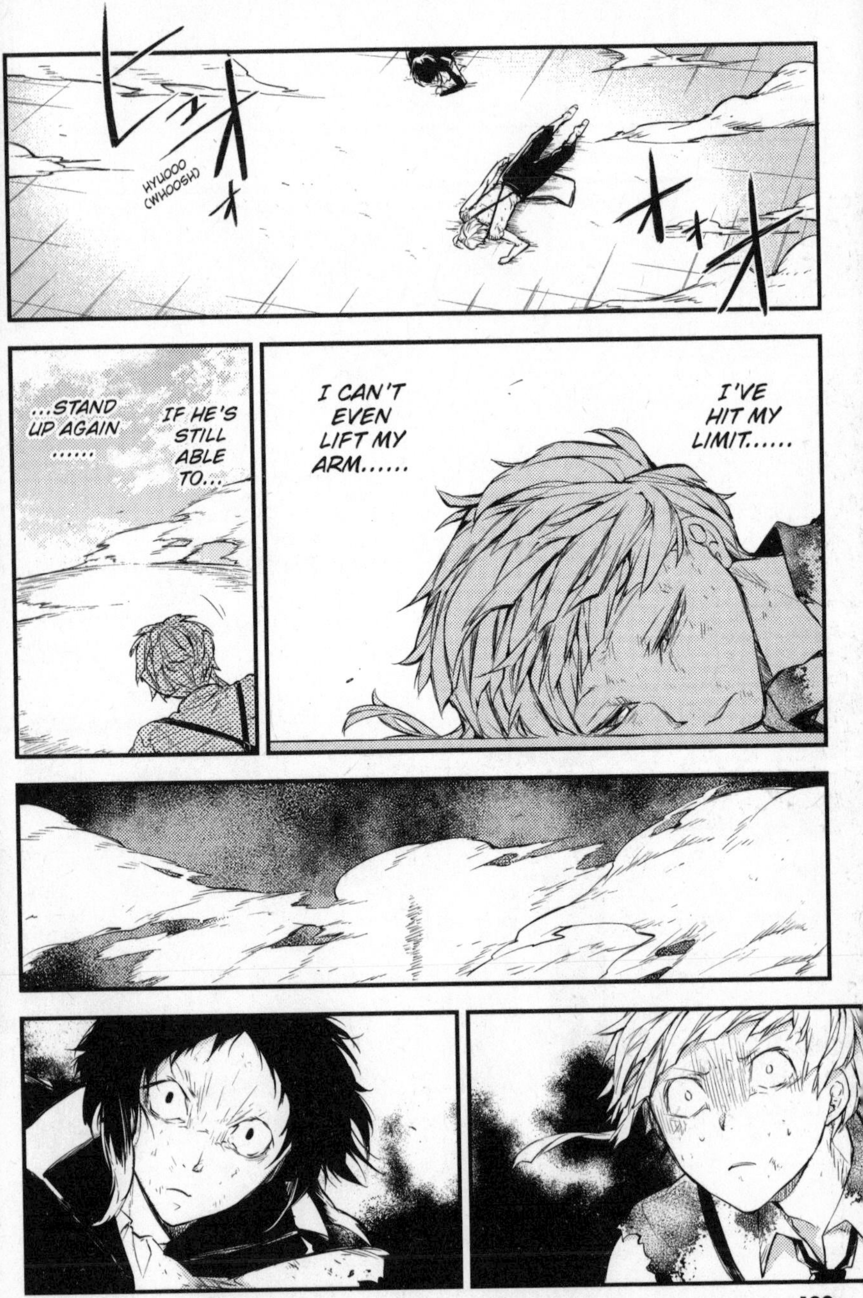
HYUOOO (WHOOSH)
I'VE HIT MY LIMIT......
I CAN'T EVEN LIFT MY ARM......
IF HE'S STILL ABLE TO...
...STAND UP AGAIN ......

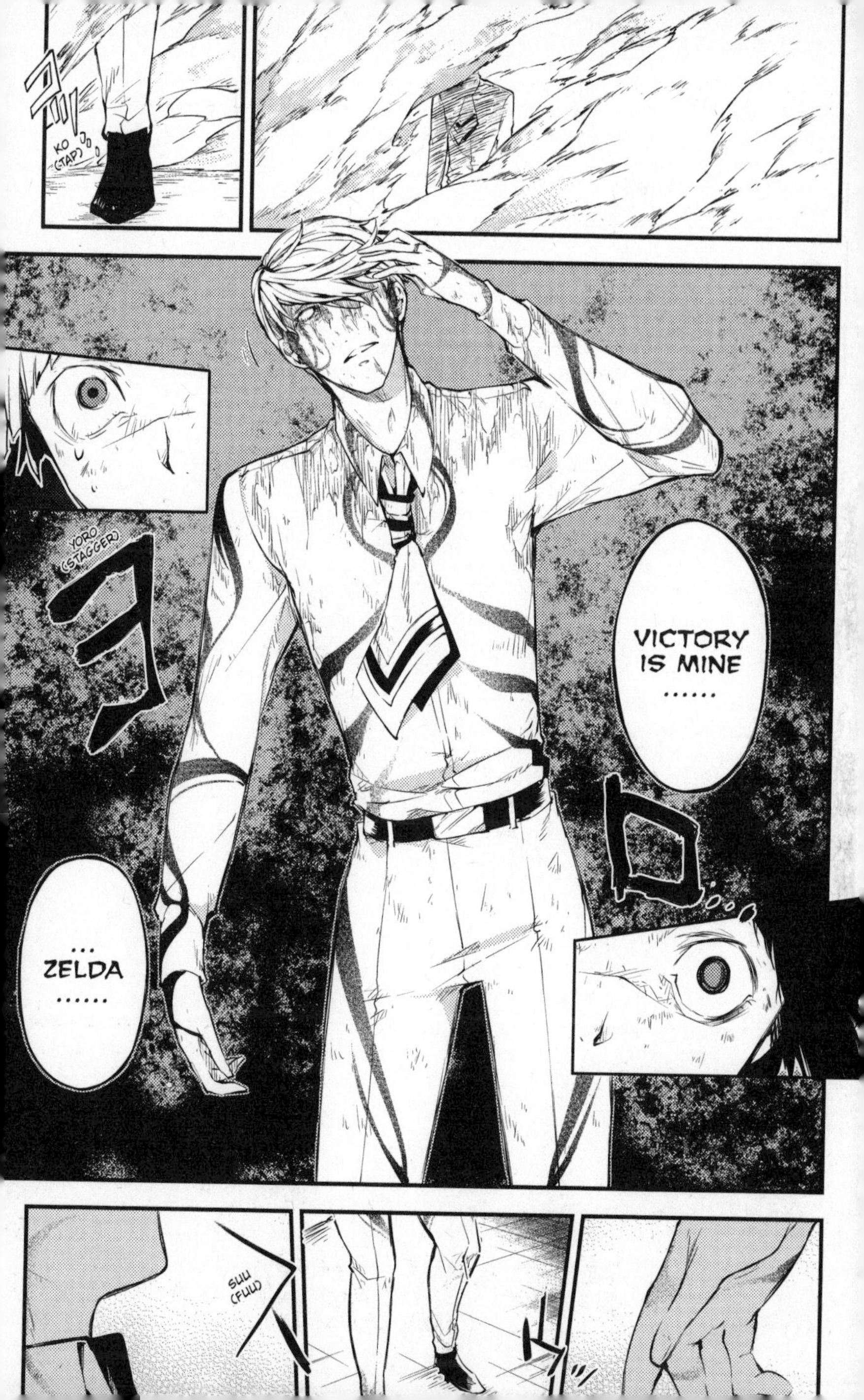
KO (TAP)
YORO (STAGGER)
VICTORY IS MINE ......
... ZELDA ......
SUU (FUU)

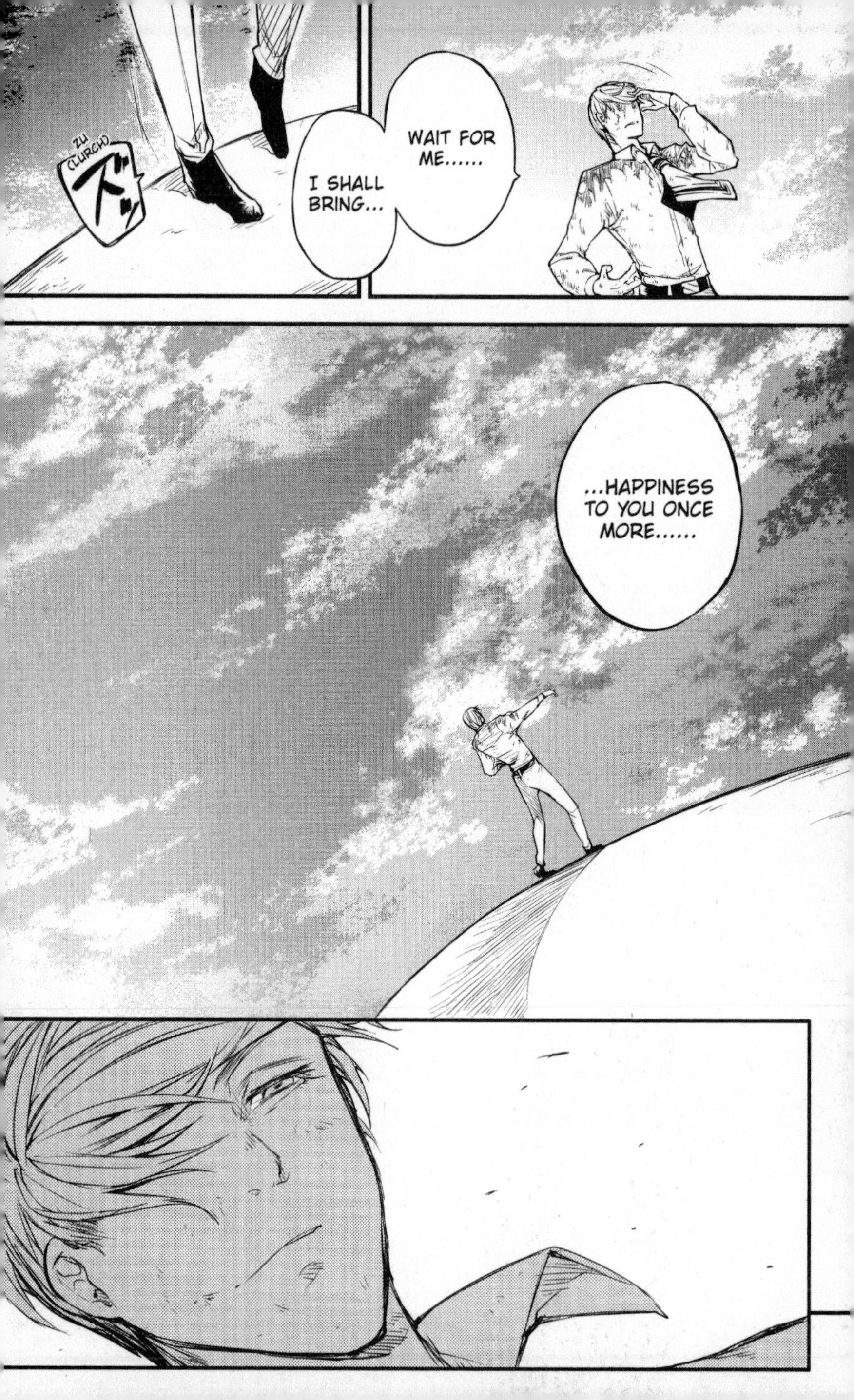
WAIT FOR ME......
I SHALL BRING...
ZU (LURCH) ズッ
...HAPPINESS TO YOU ONCE MORE......

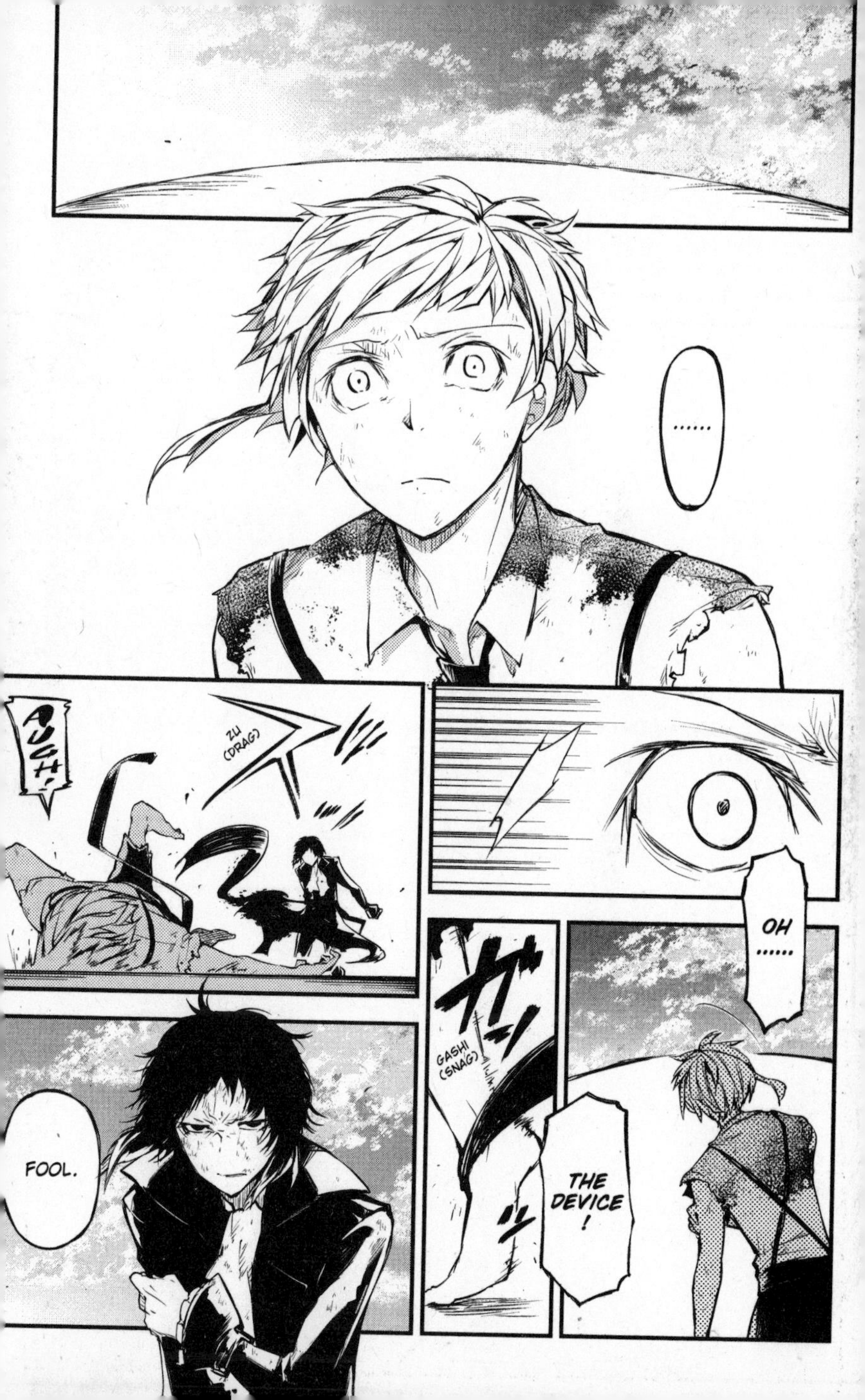

......
AUGH!
ZU (DRAG)
OH ......
GASHI (SNAG)
THE DEVICE!
FOOL.

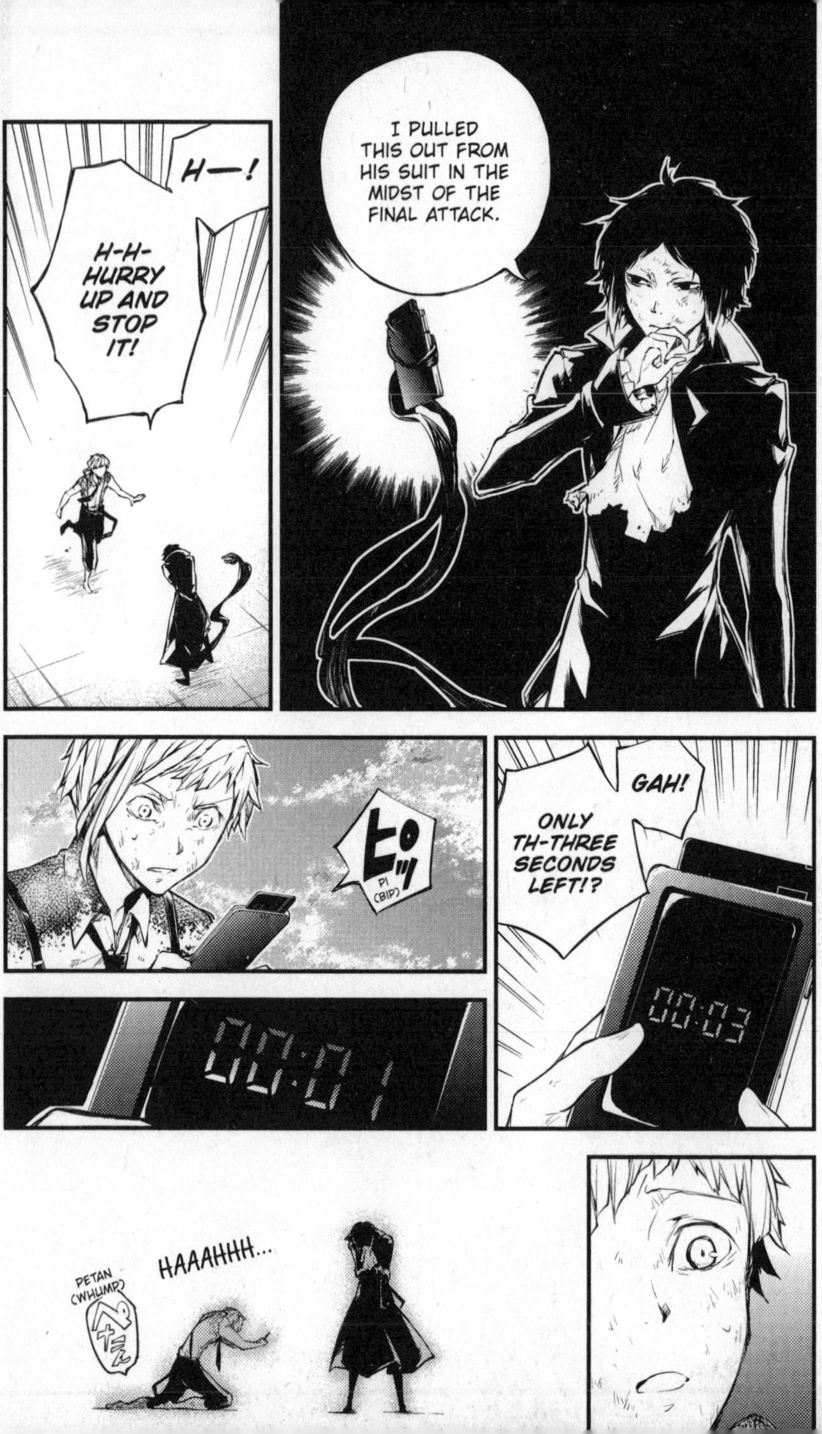
I PULLED THIS OUT FROM HIS SUIT IN THE MIDST OF THE FINAL ATTACK.
H—!
H-H-HURRY UP AND STOP IT!
GAH!
ONLY TH-THREE SECONDS LEFT!?
ピッ
PI (BIP)
HAAAHHH...
PETAN (WHUMP)

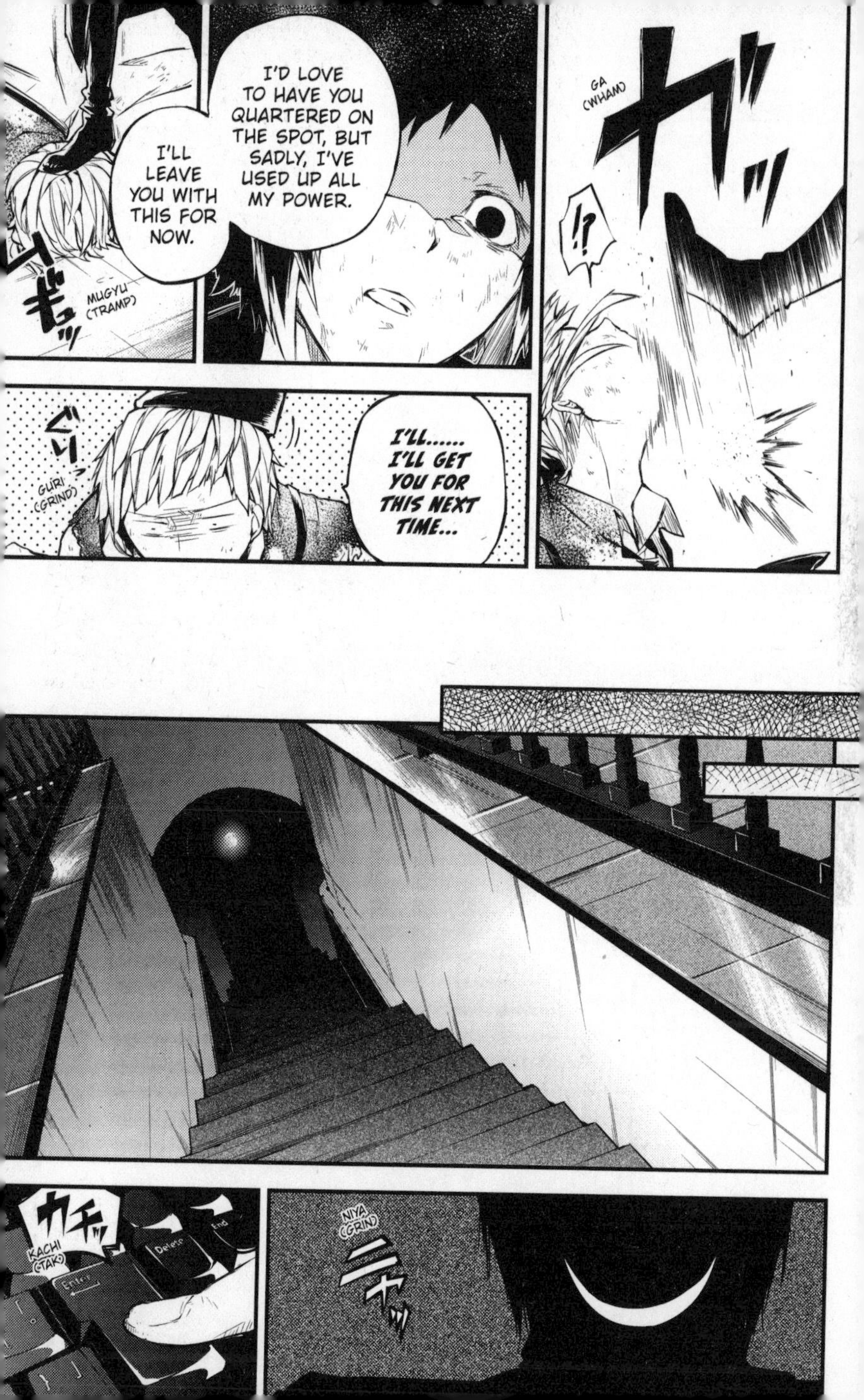
GA (WHAM)
!?
I'D LOVE TO HAVE YOU QUARTERED ON THE SPOT, BUT SADLY, I'VE USED UP ALL MY POWER.
I'LL LEAVE YOU WITH THIS FOR NOW.
MUGYU (TRAMP)
I'LL...... I'LL GET YOU FOR THIS NEXT TIME...
GURI (GRIND)
NIYA (GRIN)
KACHI (TAK)
Delete
End
Enter

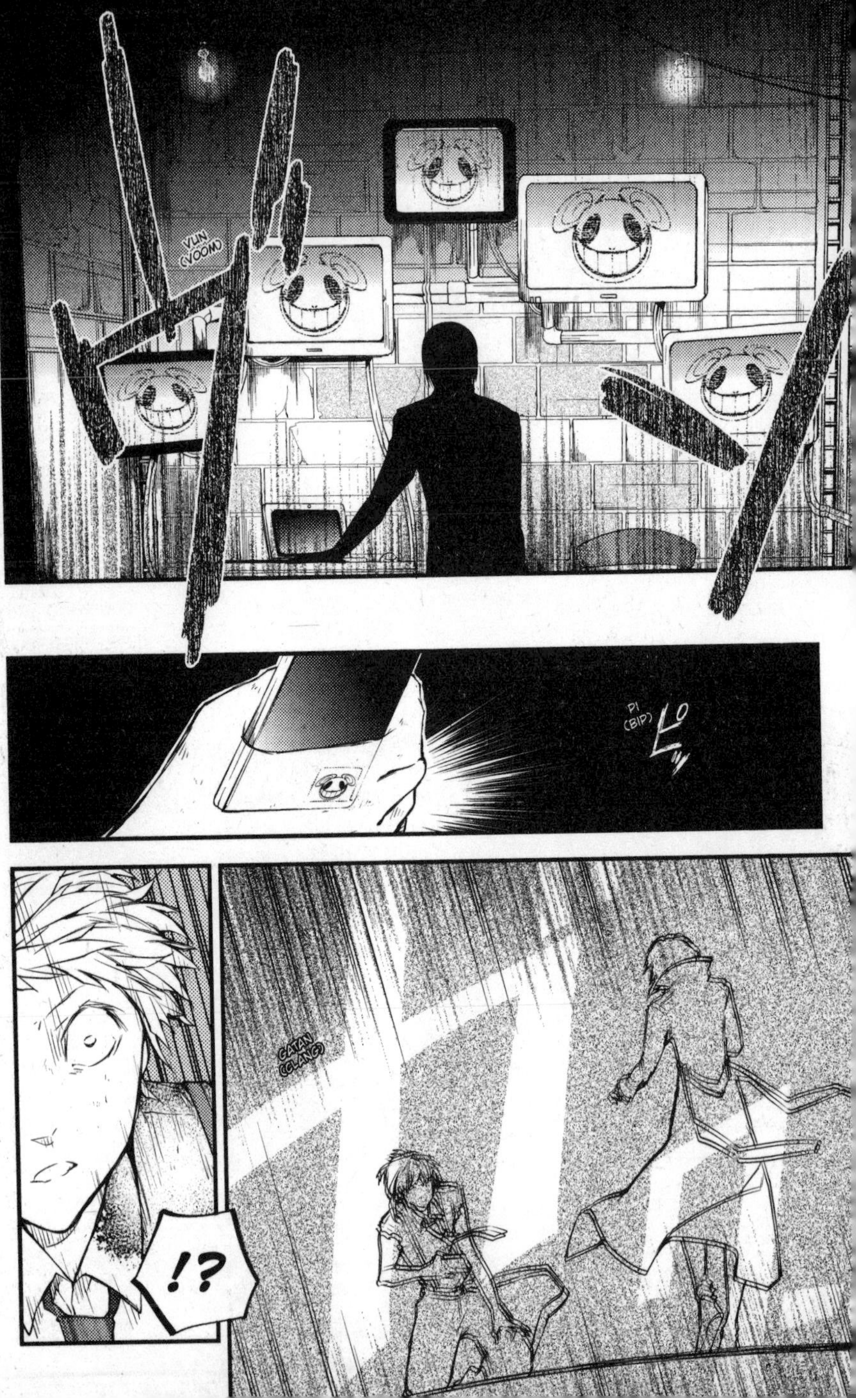
VUN
(VOOM)
PI
(BIP)
GATAN
(CLANG)
!?

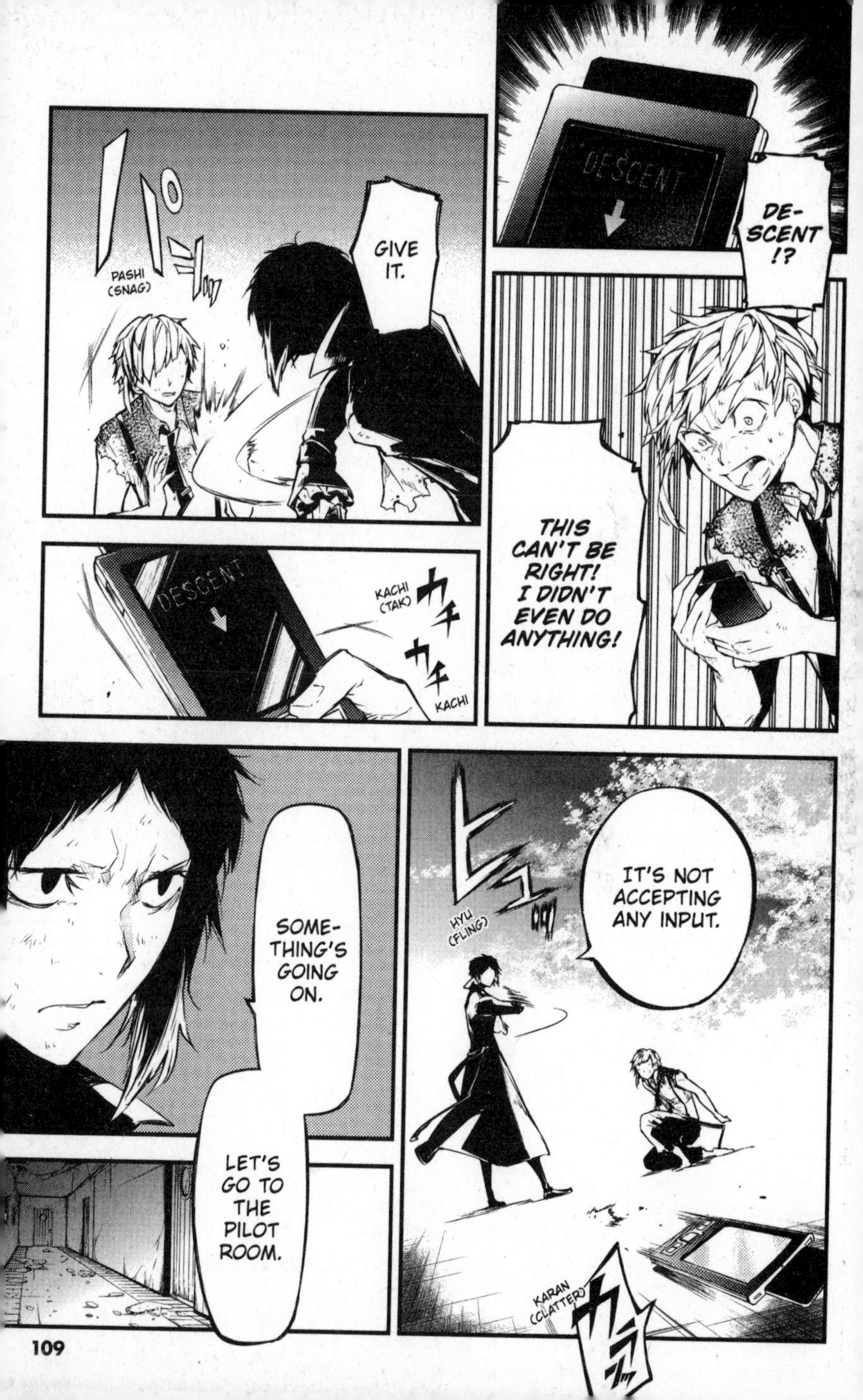
DESCENT
DE-SCENT!?
THIS CAN'T BE RIGHT! I DIDN'T EVEN DO ANYTHING!
GIVE IT.
PASHI (SNAG)
DESCENT
KACHI (TAK)
KACHI
IT'S NOT ACCEPTING ANY INPUT.
HYU (FLING)
KARAN (CLATTER)
SOME-THING'S GOING ON.
LET'S GO TO THE PILOT ROOM.

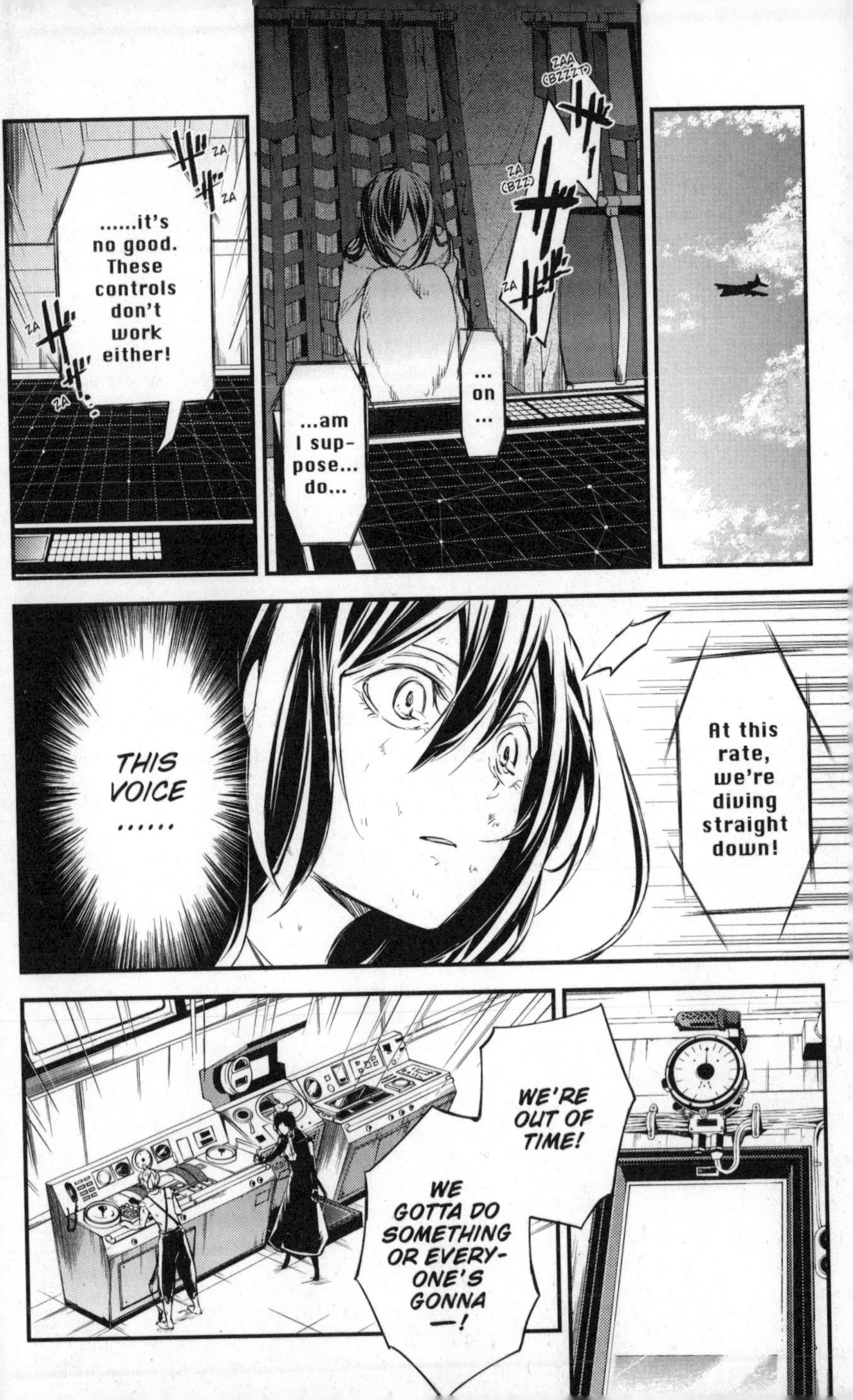

ZAA (BZZZT)
ZA (BZZ)
ZA
... on ...
...am I sup-pose... do...
ZA
ZA
......it's no good. These controls don't work either!
ZA
ZA
At this rate, we're diving straight down!
THIS VOICE ......
WE'RE OUT OF TIME!
WE GOTTA DO SOMETHING OR EVERY-ONE'S GONNA —!

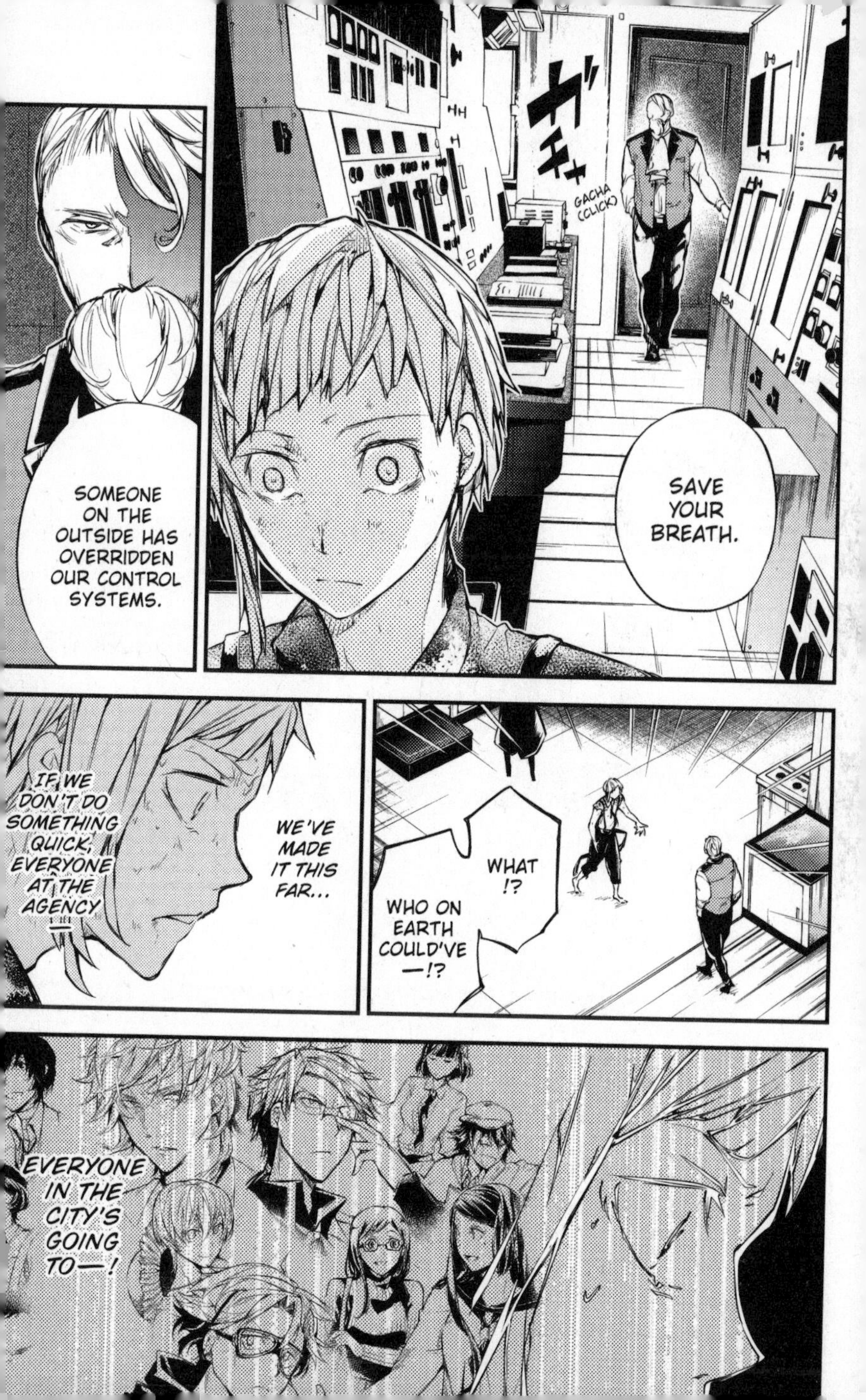

GACHA (CLICK)
SAVE YOUR BREATH.
SOMEONE ON THE OUTSIDE HAS OVERRIDDEN OUR CONTROL SYSTEMS.
WHAT!?
WHO ON EARTH COULD'VE—!?
WE'VE MADE IT THIS FAR...
IF WE DON'T DO SOMETHING QUICK, EVERYONE AT THE AGENCY—
EVERYONE IN THE CITY'S GOING TO—!

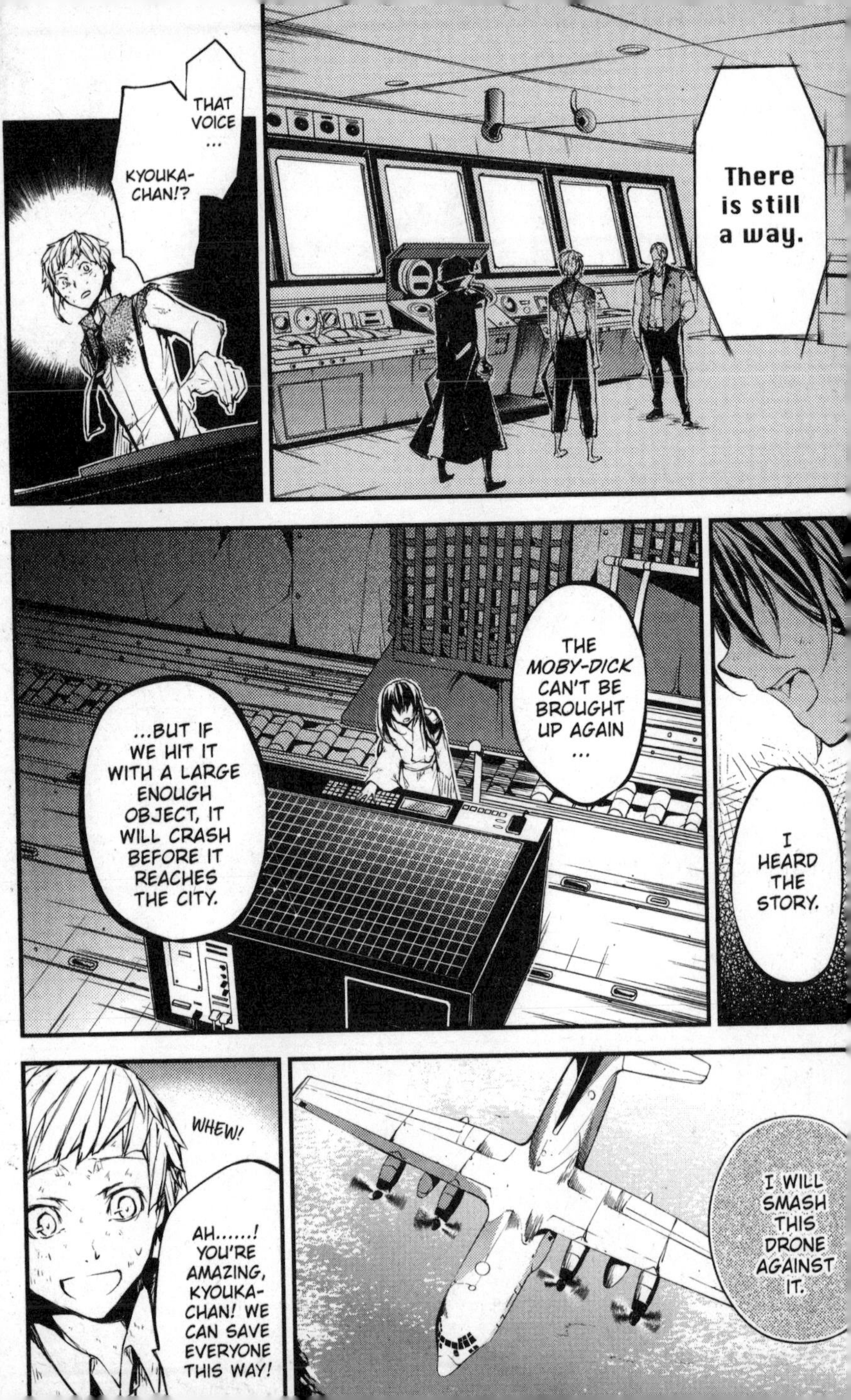
There is still a way.
THAT VOICE ... KYOUKA-CHAN!?
I HEARD THE STORY.
THE *MOBY-DICK* CAN'T BE BROUGHT UP AGAIN ...
...BUT IF WE HIT IT WITH A LARGE ENOUGH OBJECT, IT WILL CRASH BEFORE IT REACHES THE CITY.
I WILL SMASH THIS DRONE AGAINST IT.
WHEW!
AH......! YOU'RE AMAZING, KYOUKA-CHAN! WE CAN SAVE EVERYONE THIS WAY!

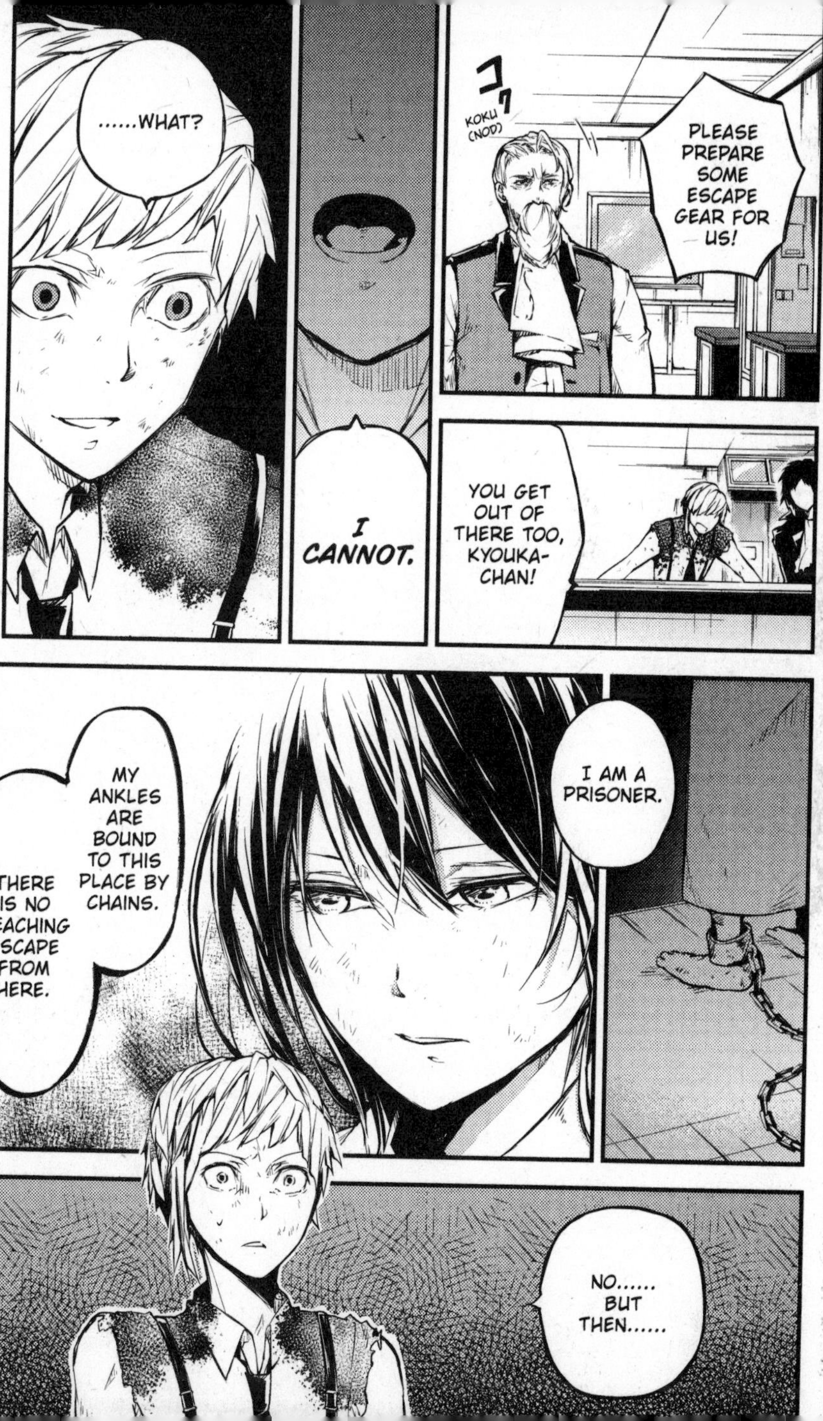
PLEASE PREPARE SOME ESCAPE GEAR FOR US!
KOKU (NOD)
YOU GET OUT OF THERE TOO, KYOUKA-CHAN!
I CANNOT.
......WHAT?
I AM A PRISONER.
MY ANKLES ARE BOUND TO THIS PLACE BY CHAINS.
THERE IS NO REACHING ESCAPE FROM HERE.
NO...... BUT THEN......

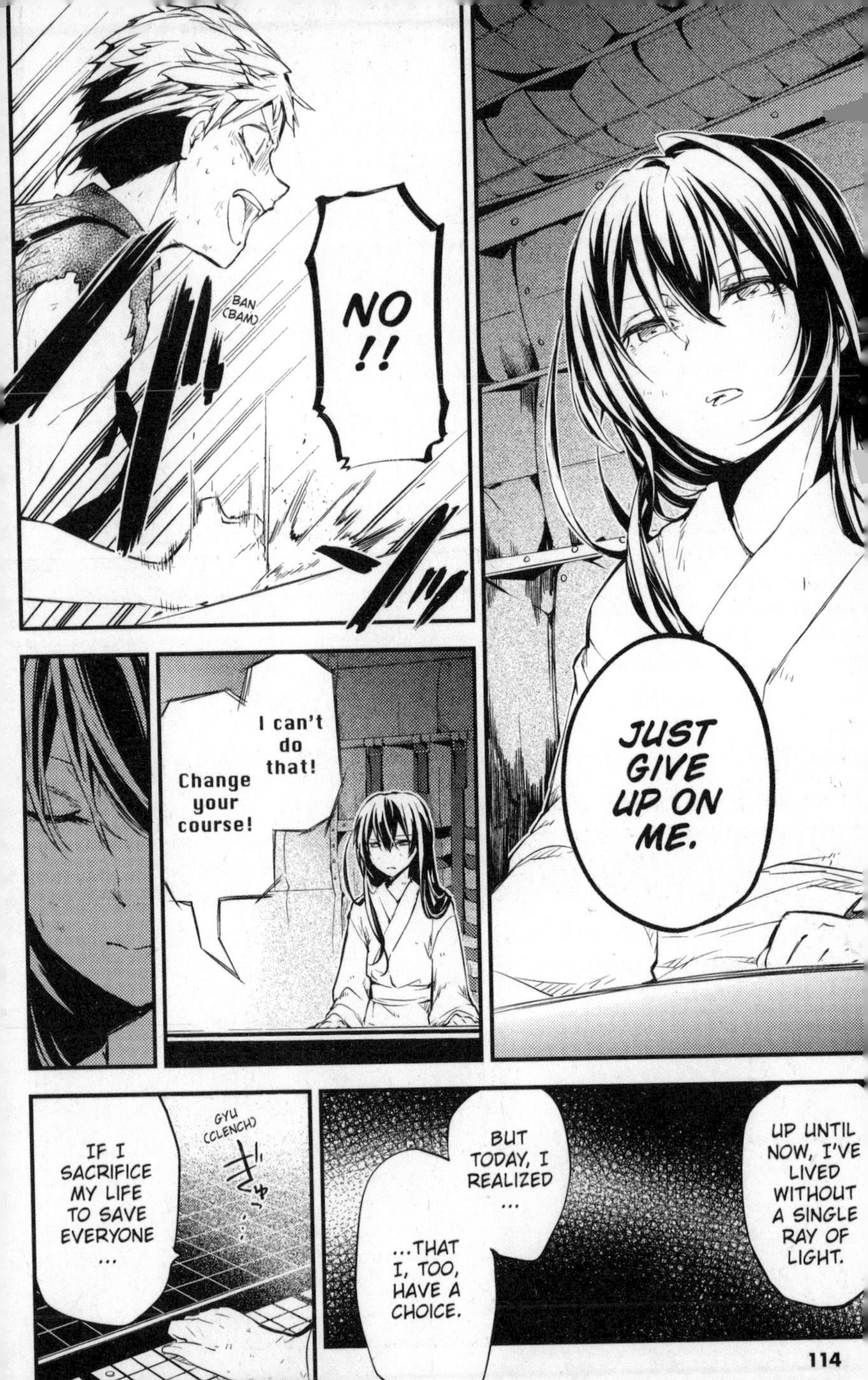

JUST GIVE UP ON ME.
NO!!
BAN (BAM)
I can't do that!
Change your course!
UP UNTIL NOW, I'VE LIVED WITHOUT A SINGLE RAY OF LIGHT.
BUT TODAY, I REALIZED...
...THAT I, TOO, HAVE A CHOICE.
GYU (CLENCH)
IF I SACRIFICE MY LIFE TO SAVE EVERYONE...

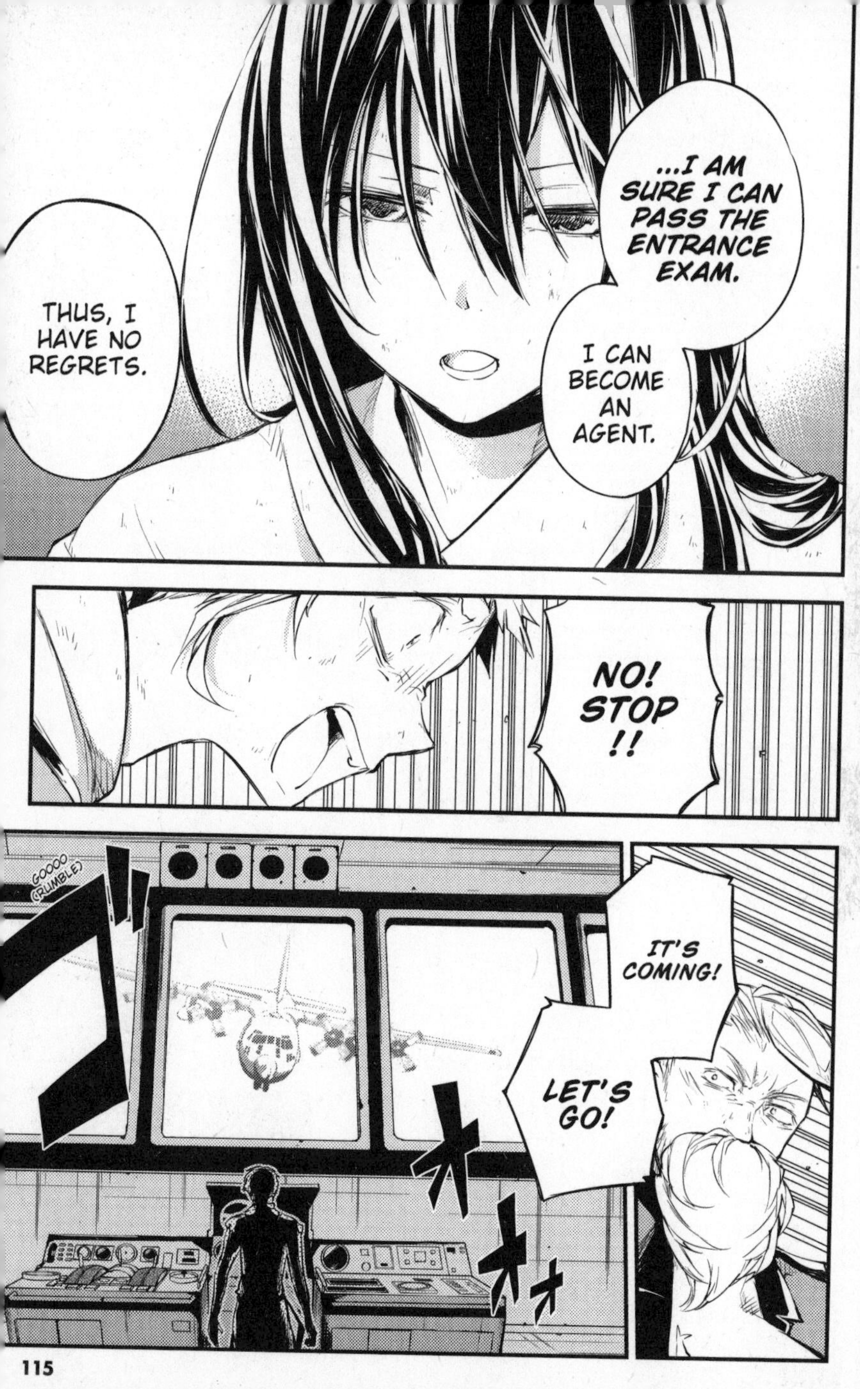
...I AM SURE I CAN PASS THE ENTRANCE EXAM.
I CAN BECOME AN AGENT.
THUS, I HAVE NO REGRETS.
NO! STOP!!
IT'S COMING!
LET'S GO!
GOOOO (RUMBLE)

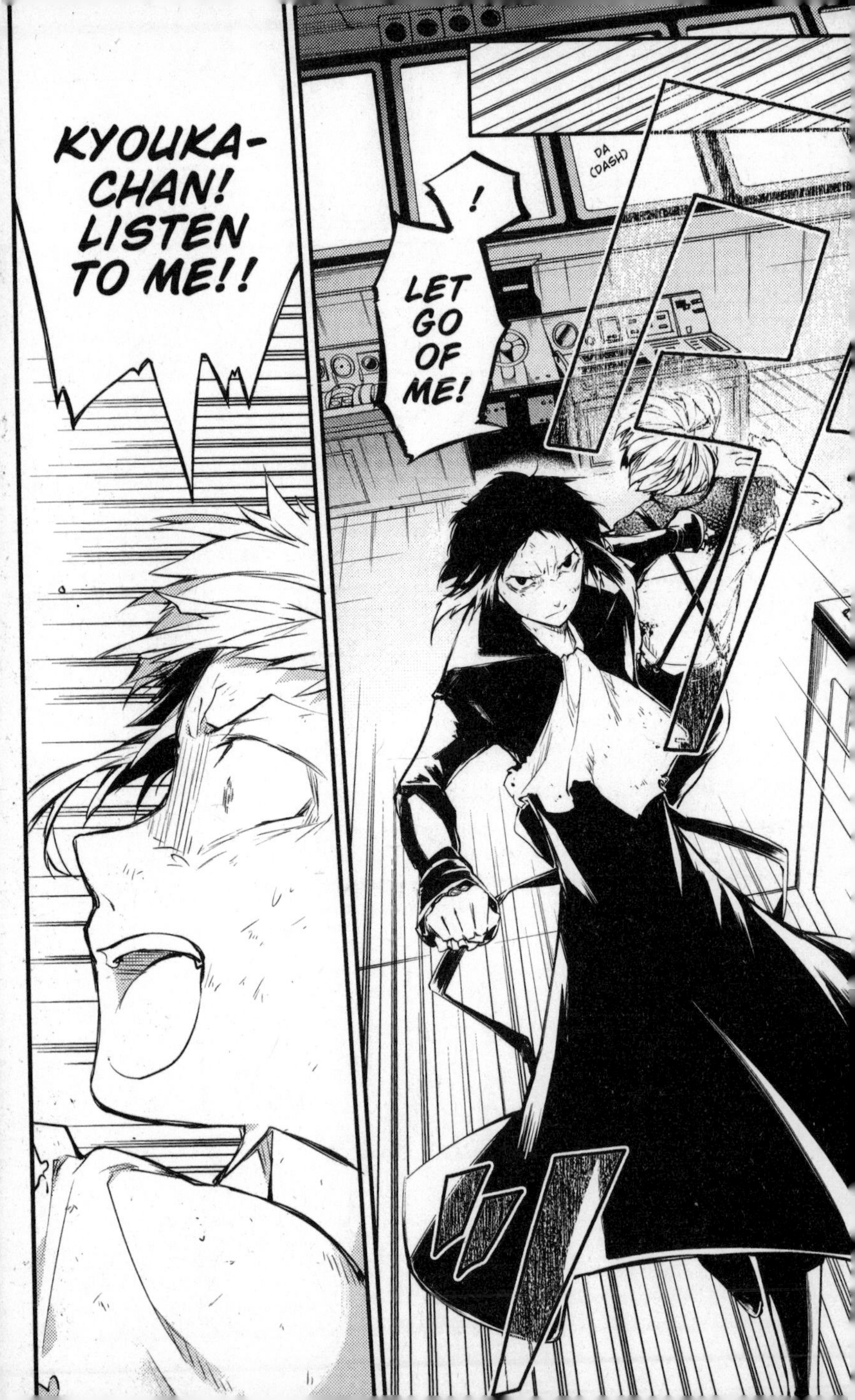
DA (DASH)
!
LET GO OF ME!
KYOUKA-CHAN! LISTEN TO ME!!

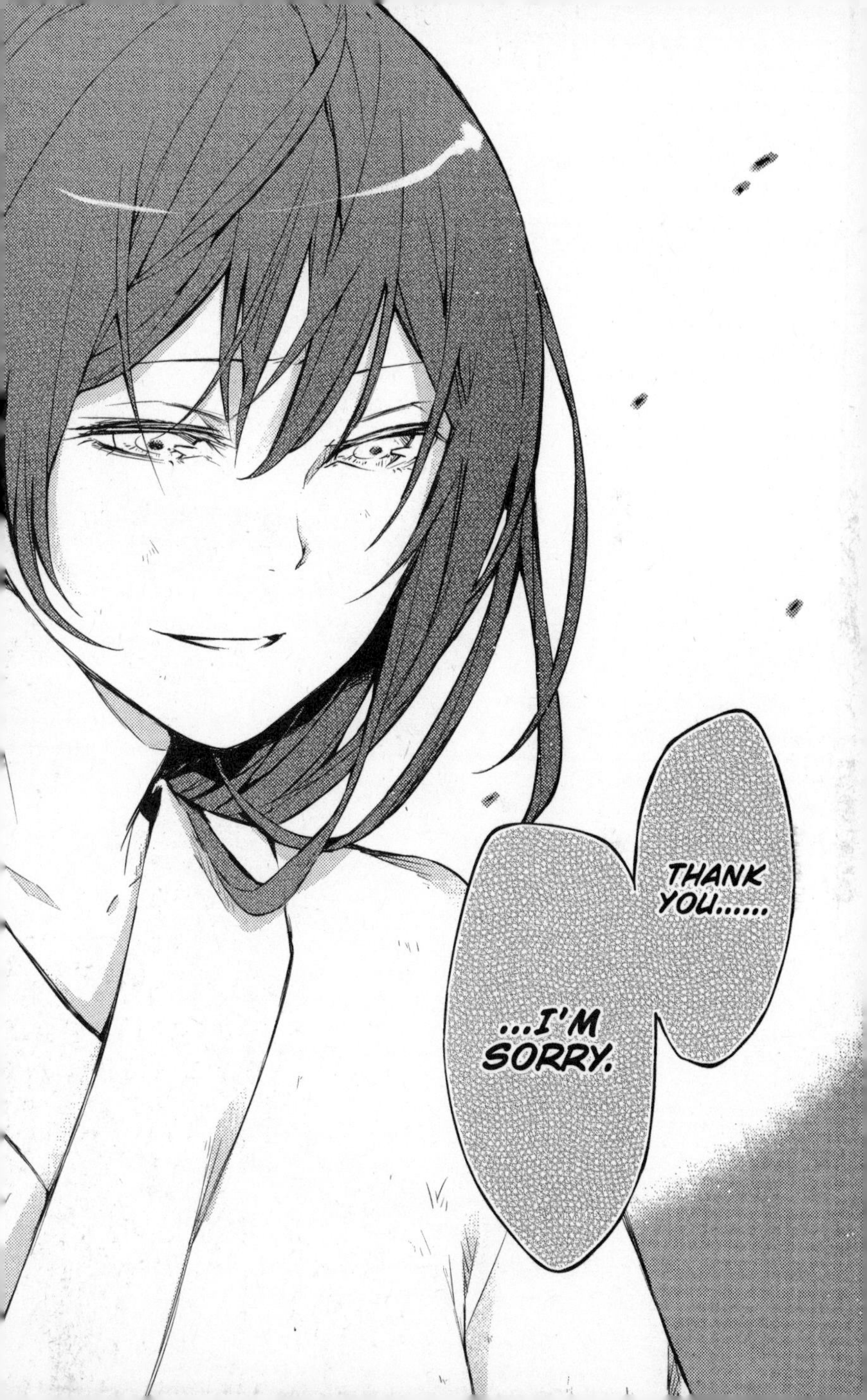
THANK YOU......
...I'M SORRY.

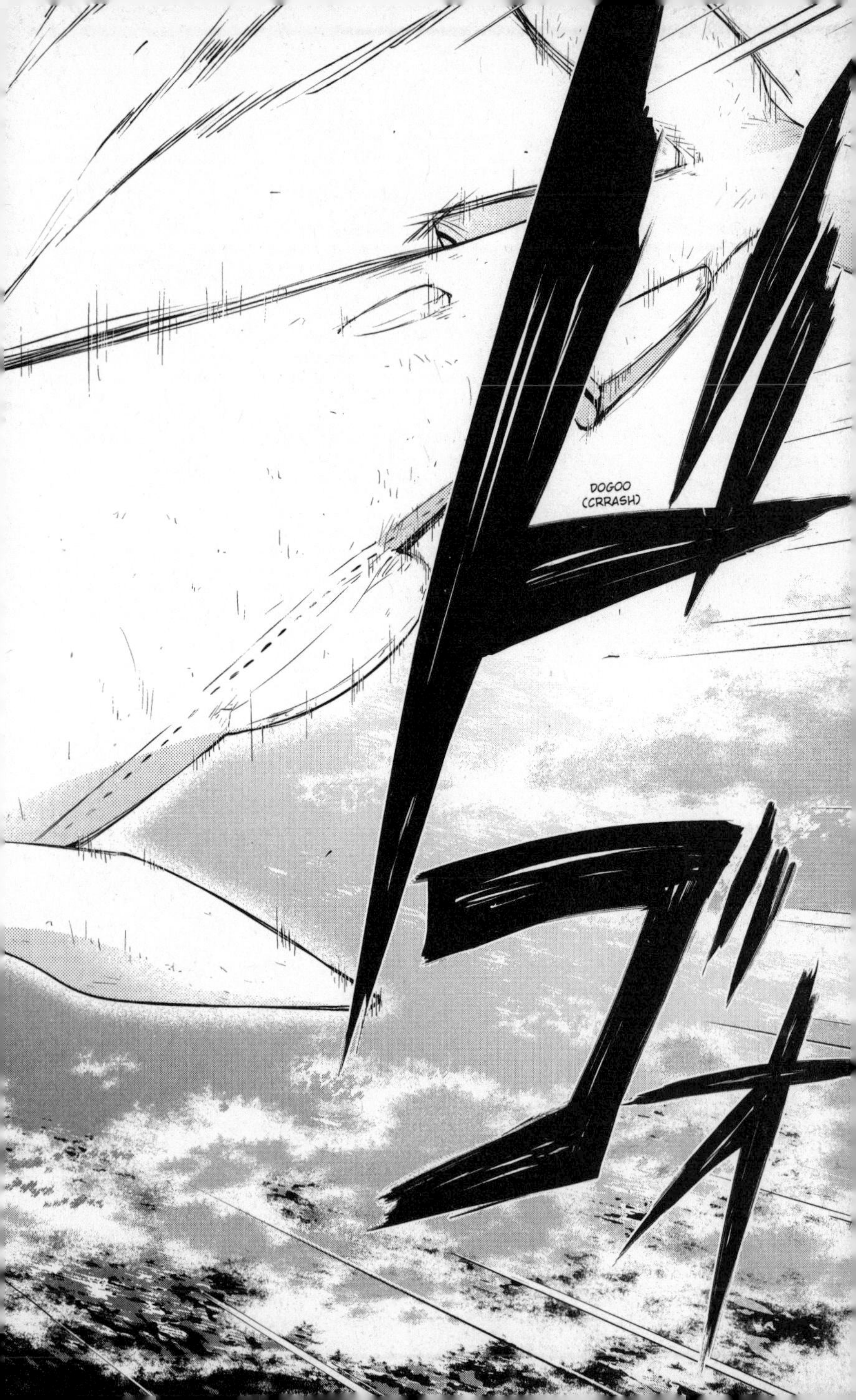
DOGOO
(CRRASH)

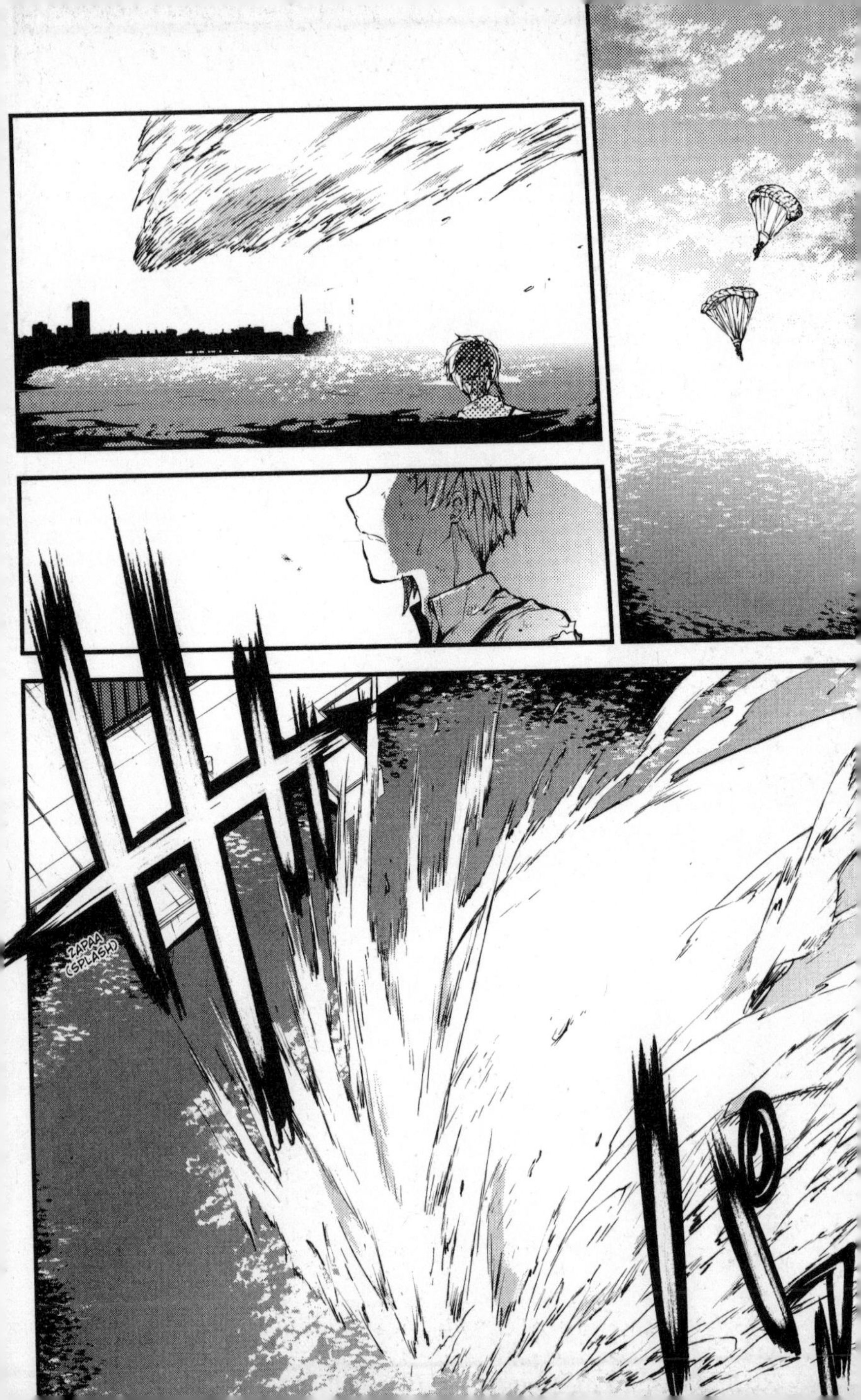
ZAPAA
(SPLASH)

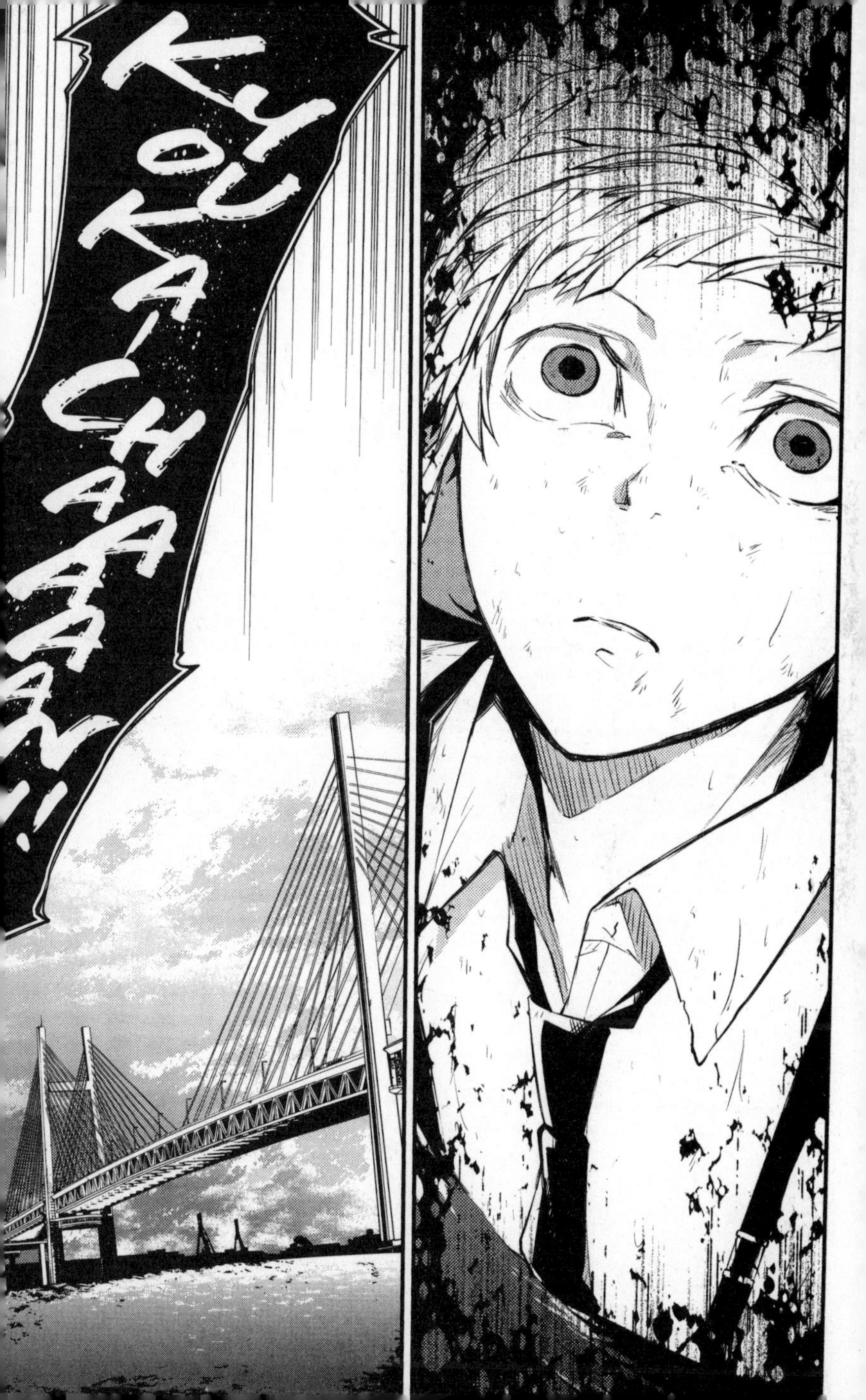
KYOUKA-CHAAAAN!!

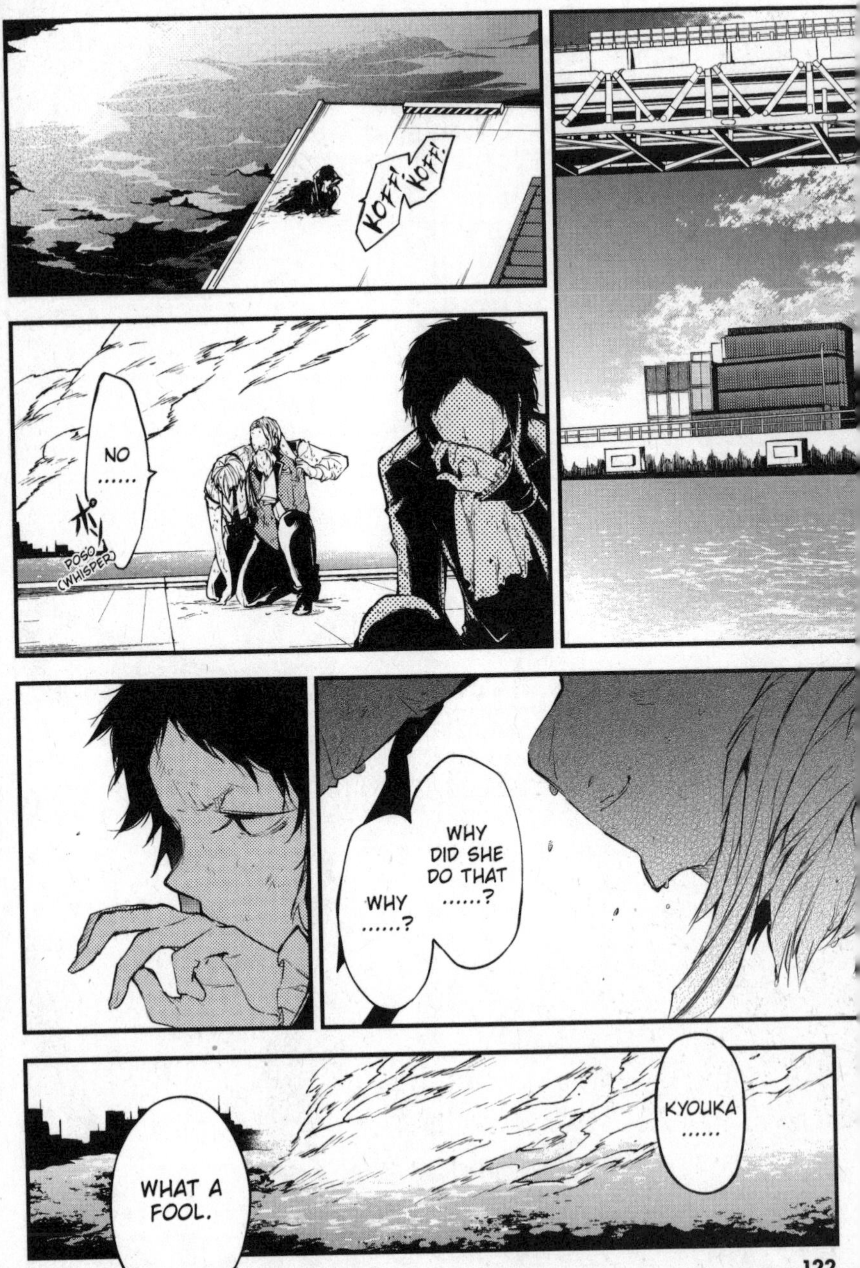
KOFF! KOFF!
NO ......
POSO (WHISPER)
WHY DID SHE DO THAT ......?
WHY ......?
KYOUKA ......
WHAT A FOOL.

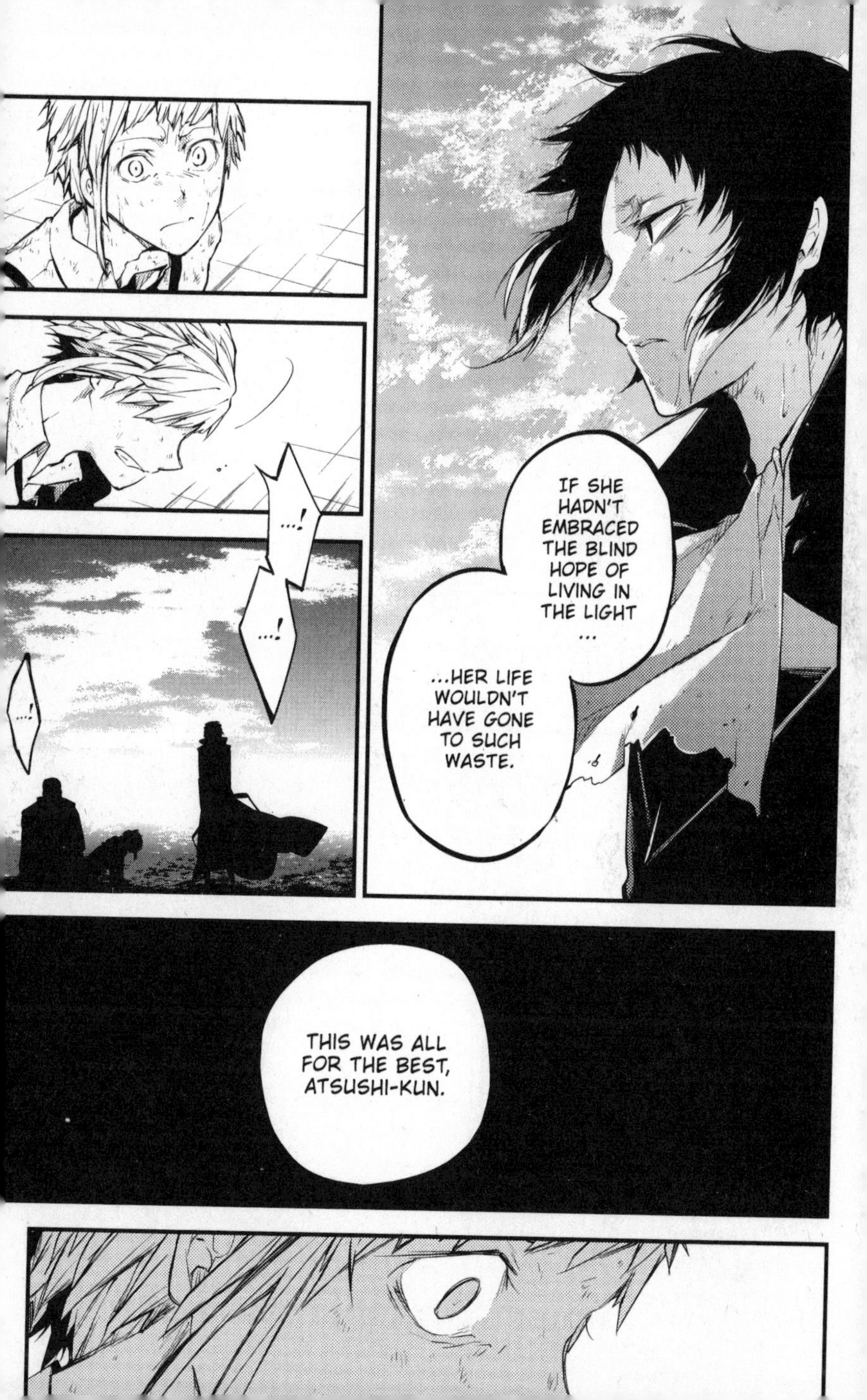
IF SHE HADN'T EMBRACED THE BLIND HOPE OF LIVING IN THE LIGHT ...
...HER LIFE WOULDN'T HAVE GONE TO SUCH WASTE.
...!
...!
...!
THIS WAS ALL FOR THE BEST, ATSUSHI-KUN.

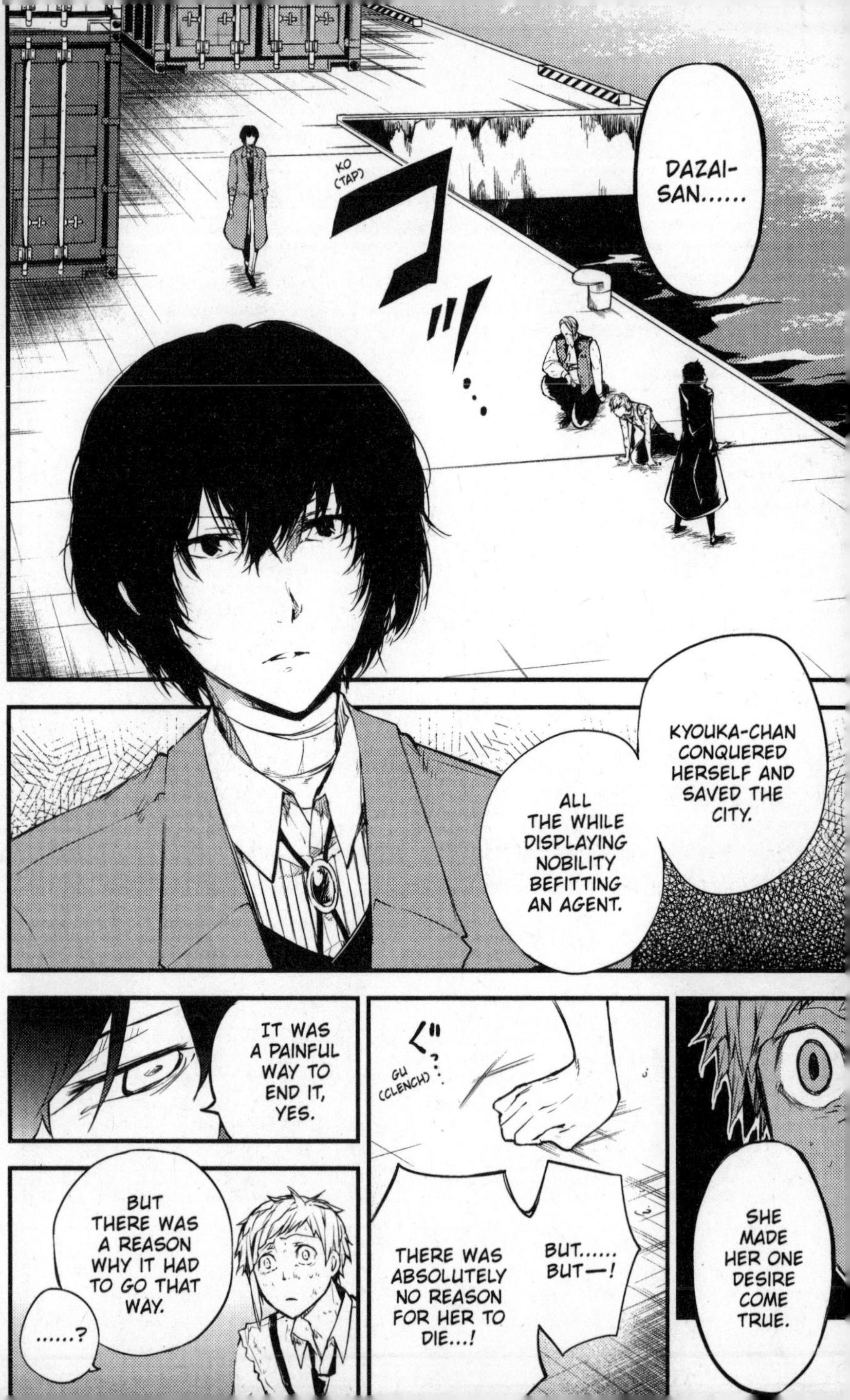
DAZAI-SAN......
KO (TAP)
...
KYOUKA-CHAN CONQUERED HERSELF AND SAVED THE CITY.
ALL THE WHILE DISPLAYING NOBILITY BEFITTING AN AGENT.
SHE MADE HER ONE DESIRE COME TRUE.
GU (CLENCH)
BUT...... BUT—!
THERE WAS ABSOLUTELY NO REASON FOR HER TO DIE...!
IT WAS A PAINFUL WAY TO END IT, YES.
BUT THERE WAS A REASON WHY IT HAD TO GO THAT WAY.
......?

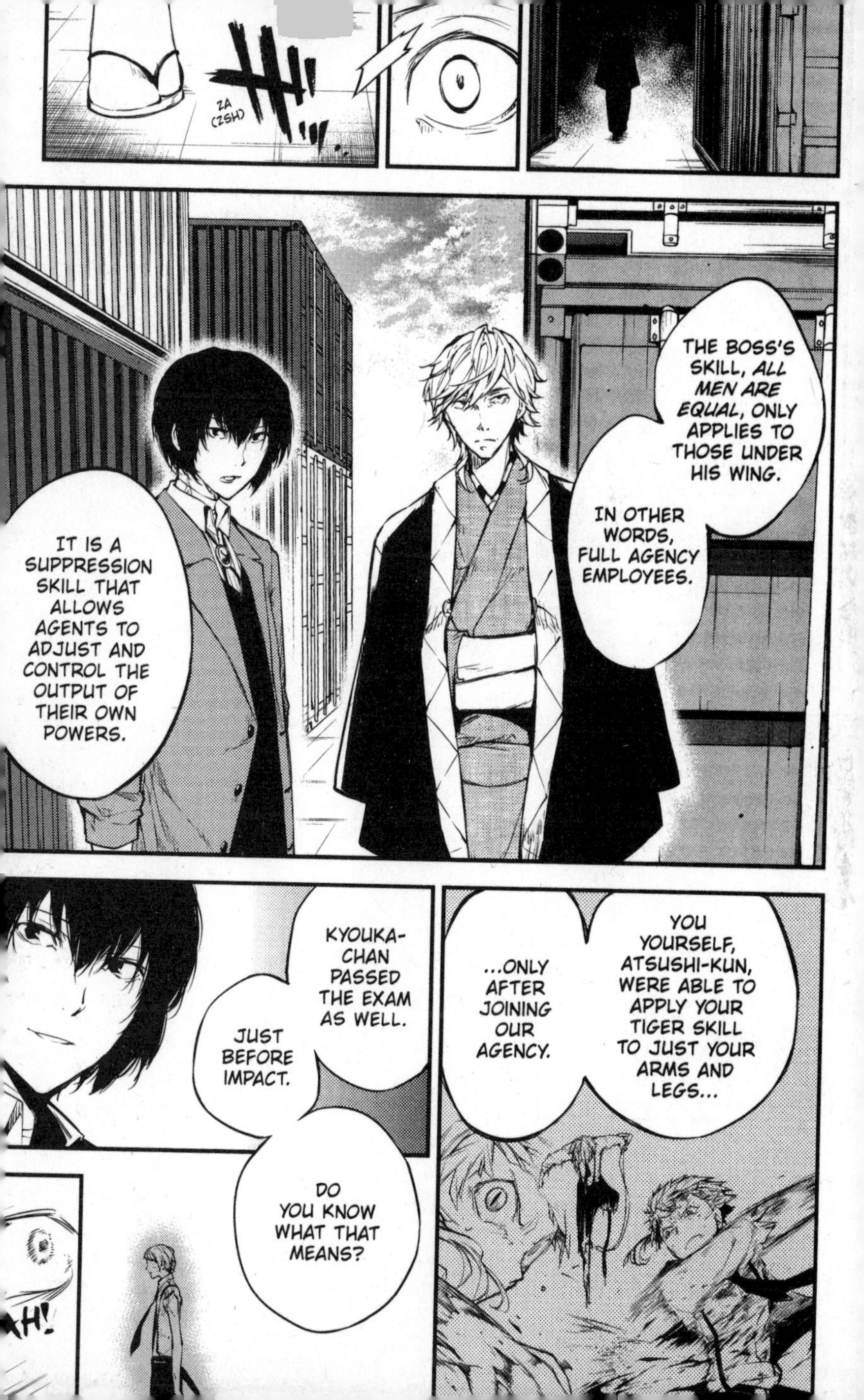
ZA
(ZSH)
THE BOSS'S SKILL, *ALL MEN ARE EQUAL*, ONLY APPLIES TO THOSE UNDER HIS WING.
IN OTHER WORDS, FULL AGENCY EMPLOYEES.
IT IS A SUPPRESSION SKILL THAT ALLOWS AGENTS TO ADJUST AND CONTROL THE OUTPUT OF THEIR OWN POWERS.
YOU YOURSELF, ATSUSHI-KUN, WERE ABLE TO APPLY YOUR TIGER SKILL TO JUST YOUR ARMS AND LEGS...
...ONLY AFTER JOINING OUR AGENCY.
KYOUKA-CHAN PASSED THE EXAM AS WELL.
JUST BEFORE IMPACT.
DO YOU KNOW WHAT THAT MEANS?
AH!

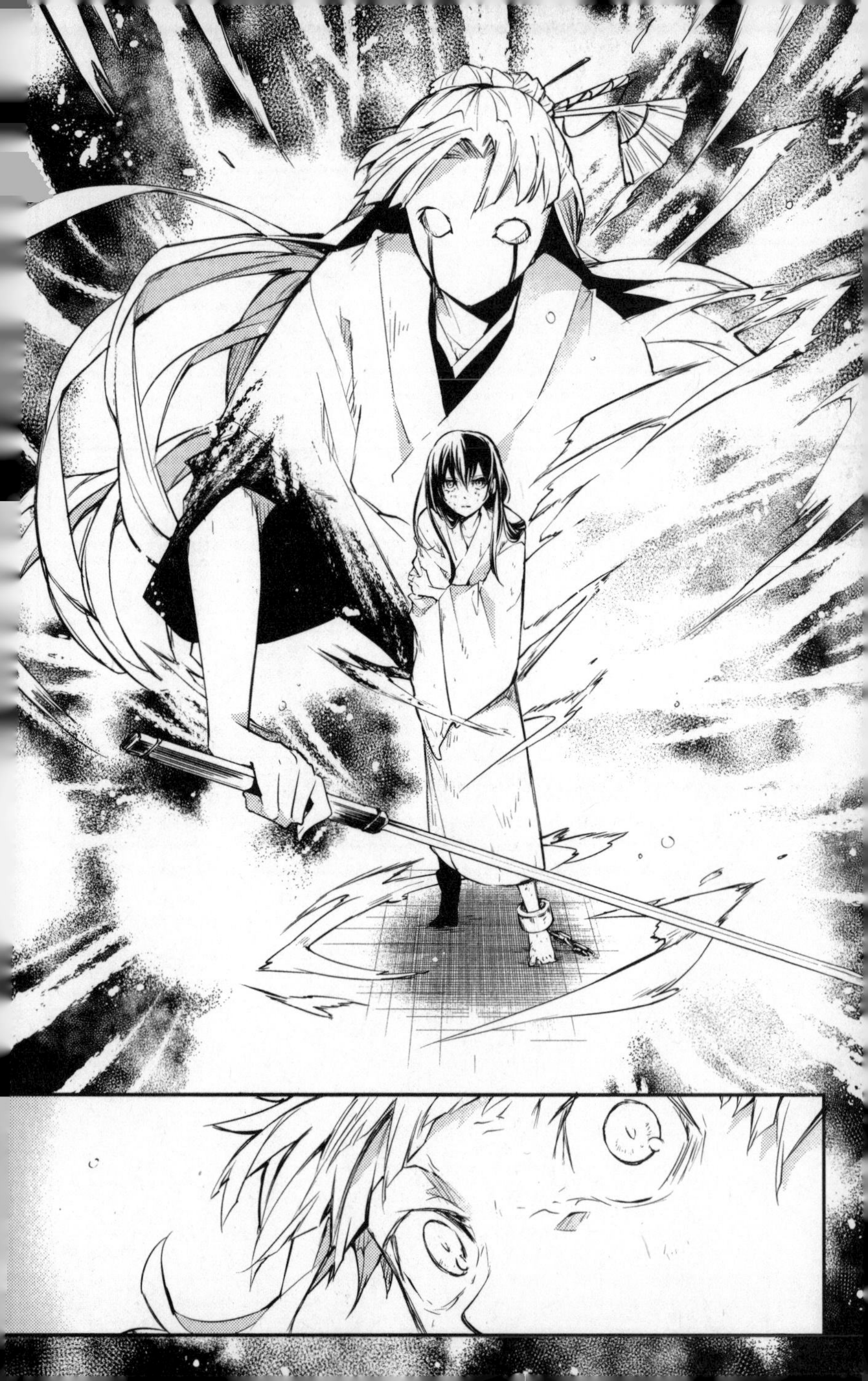

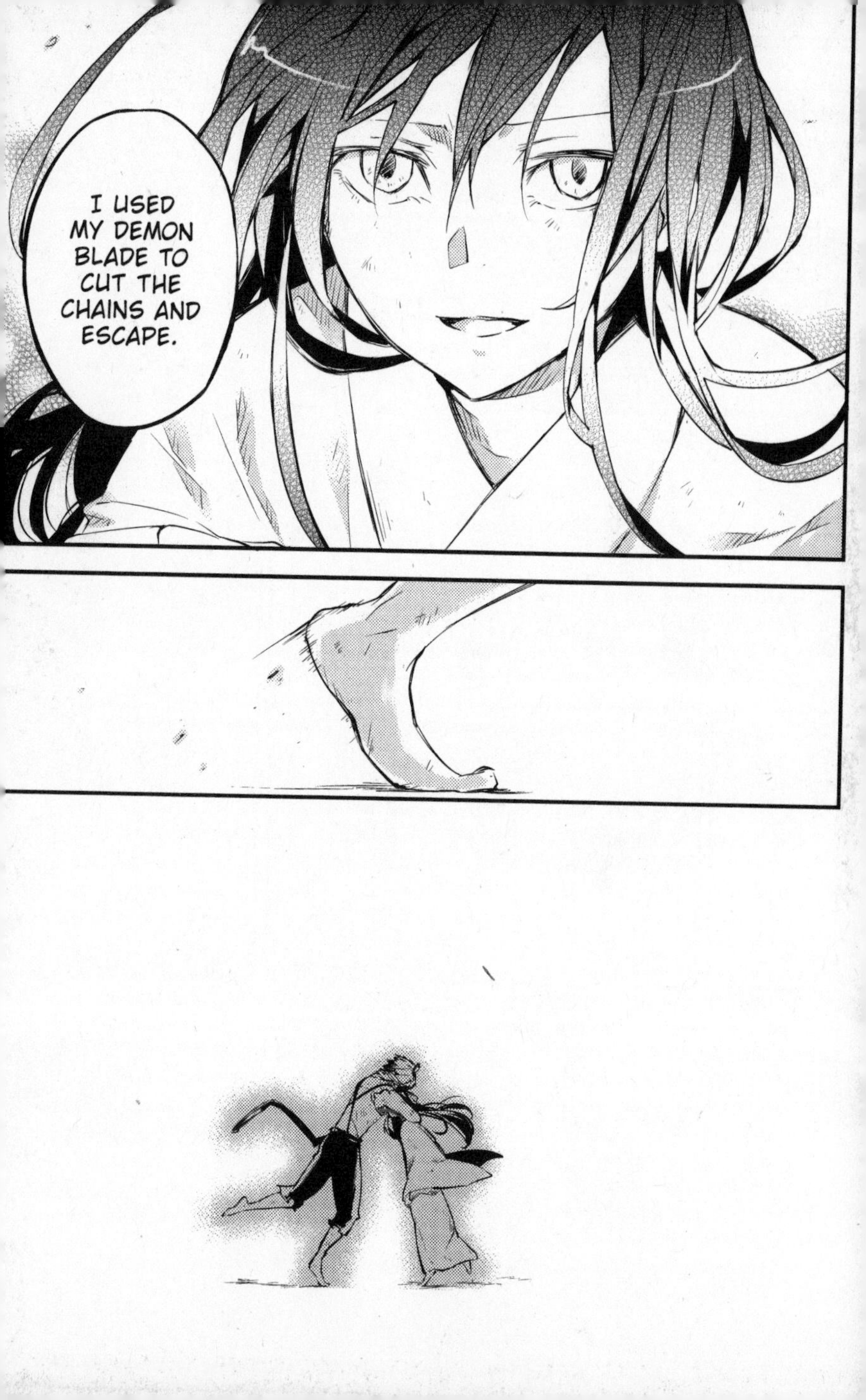
I USED MY DEMON BLADE TO CUT THE CHAINS AND ESCAPE.

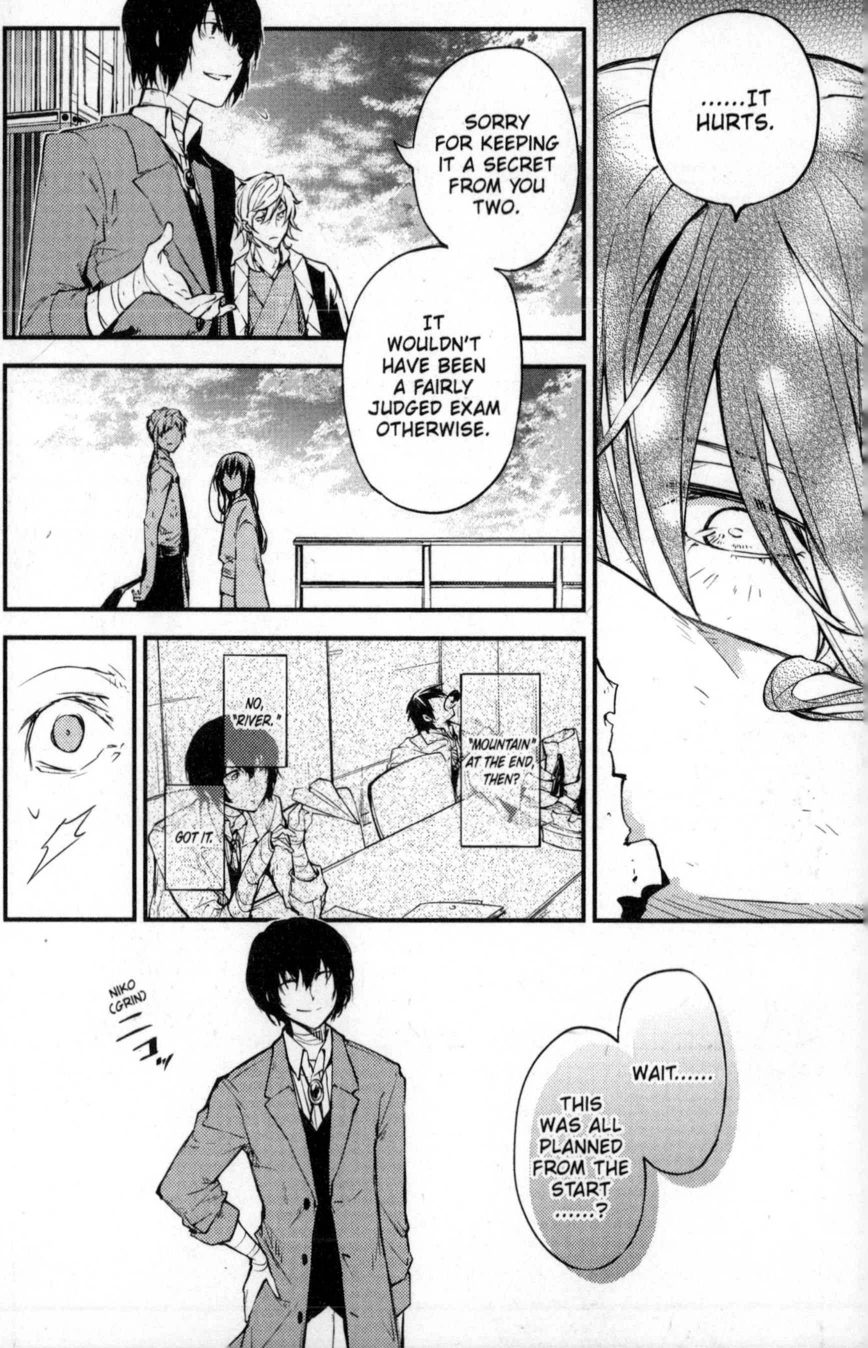
......IT HURTS.
SORRY FOR KEEPING IT A SECRET FROM YOU TWO.
IT WOULDN'T HAVE BEEN A FAIRLY JUDGED EXAM OTHERWISE.
"MOUNTAIN" AT THE END, THEN?
NO, "RIVER."
GOT IT.
WAIT...... THIS WAS ALL PLANNED FROM THE START ......?
NIKO (GRIN)

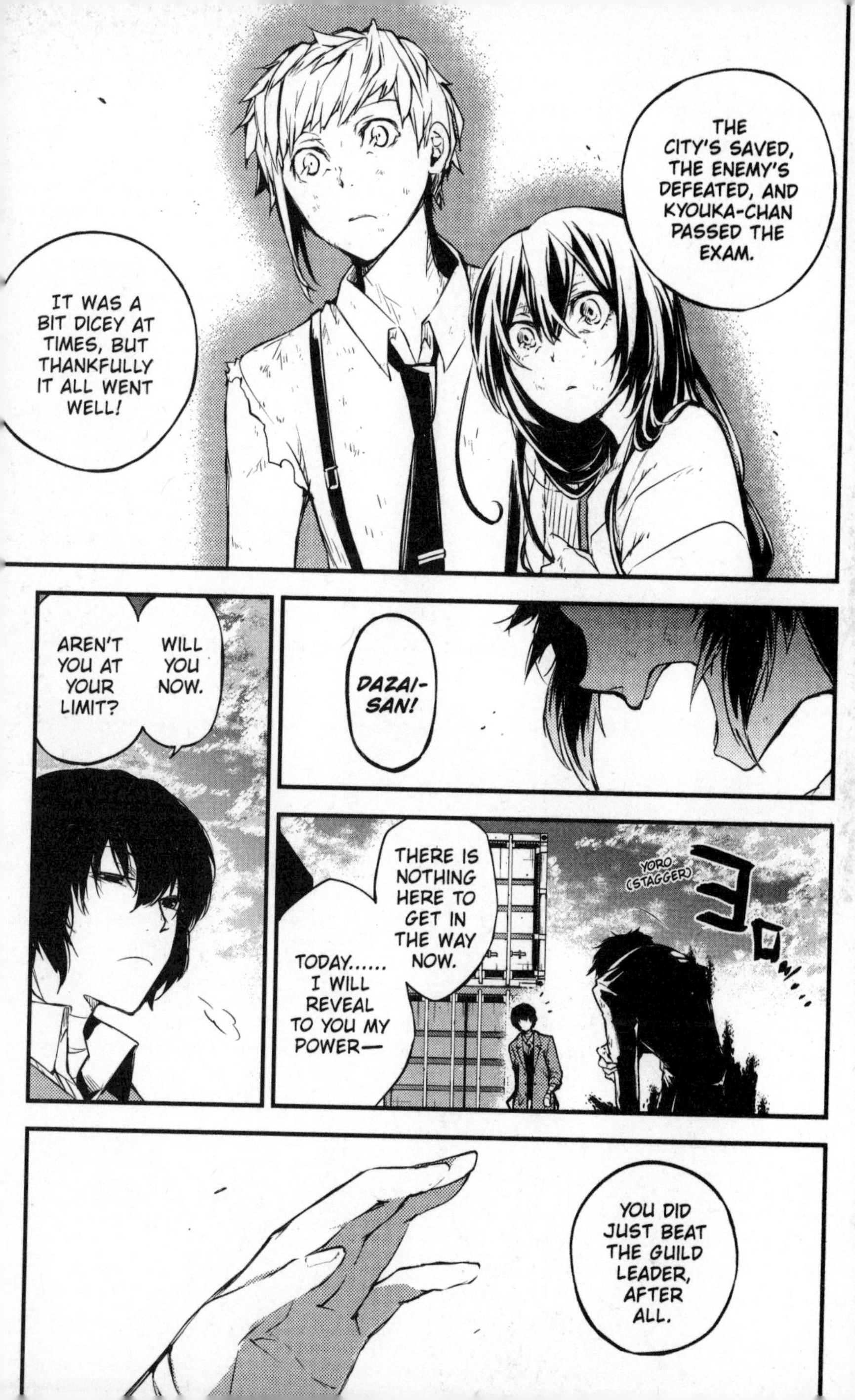
THE CITY'S SAVED, THE ENEMY'S DEFEATED, AND KYOUKA-CHAN PASSED THE EXAM.
IT WAS A BIT DICEY AT TIMES, BUT THANKFULLY IT ALL WENT WELL!
DAZAI-SAN!
YORO (STAGGER)
THERE IS NOTHING HERE TO GET IN THE WAY NOW.
TODAY...... I WILL REVEAL TO YOU MY POWER—
WILL YOU NOW.
AREN'T YOU AT YOUR LIMIT?
YOU DID JUST BEAT THE GUILD LEADER, AFTER ALL.

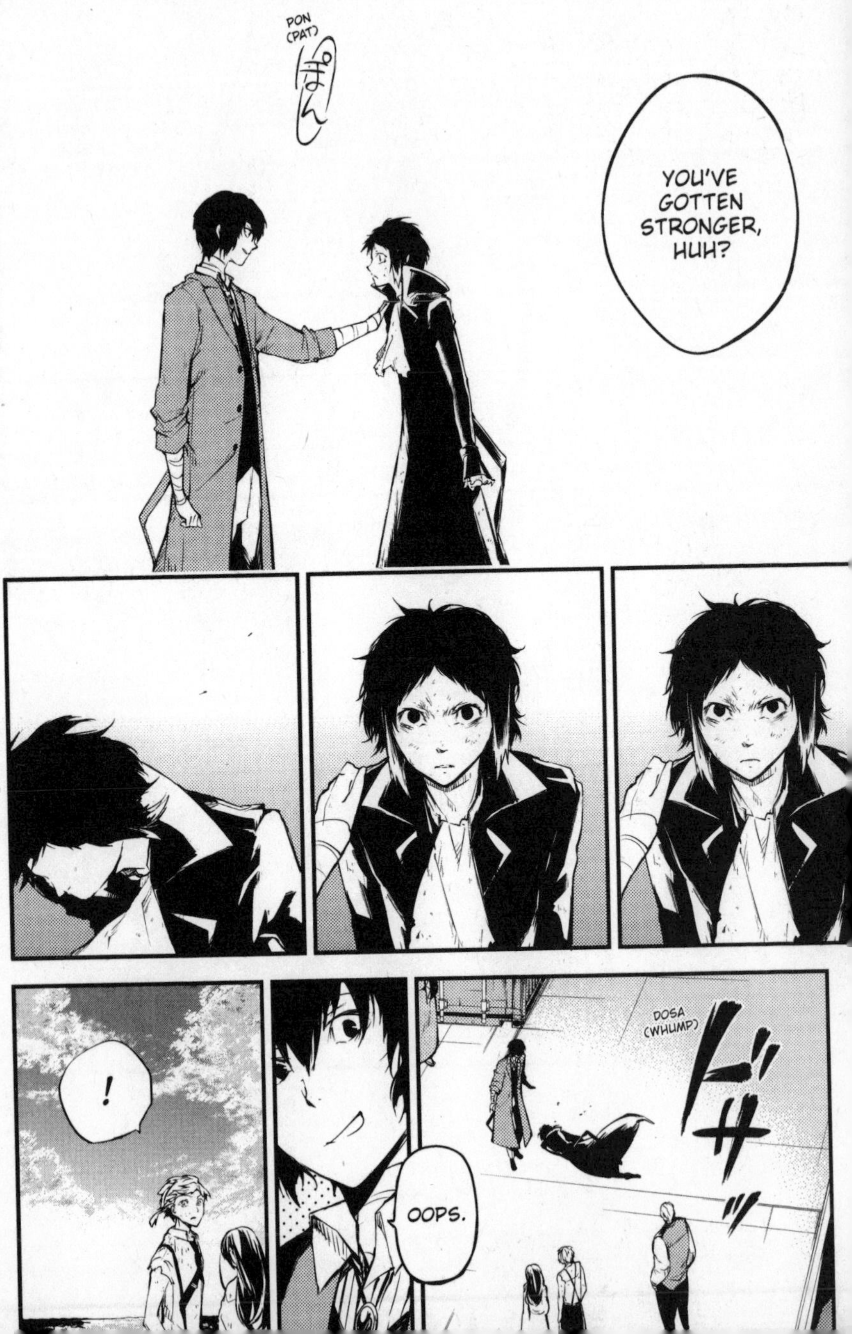
YOU'VE GOTTEN STRONGER, HUH?
PON (PAT)
ぽん
DOSA (WHUMP)
OOPS.
!

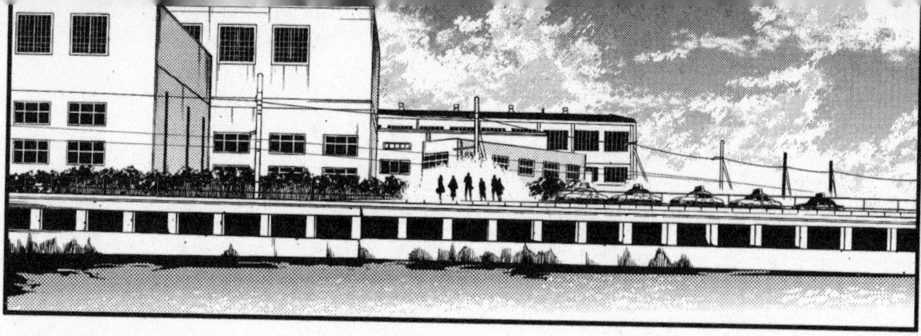

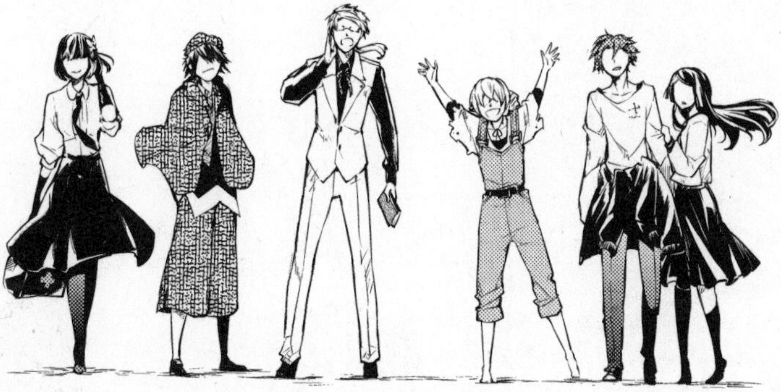

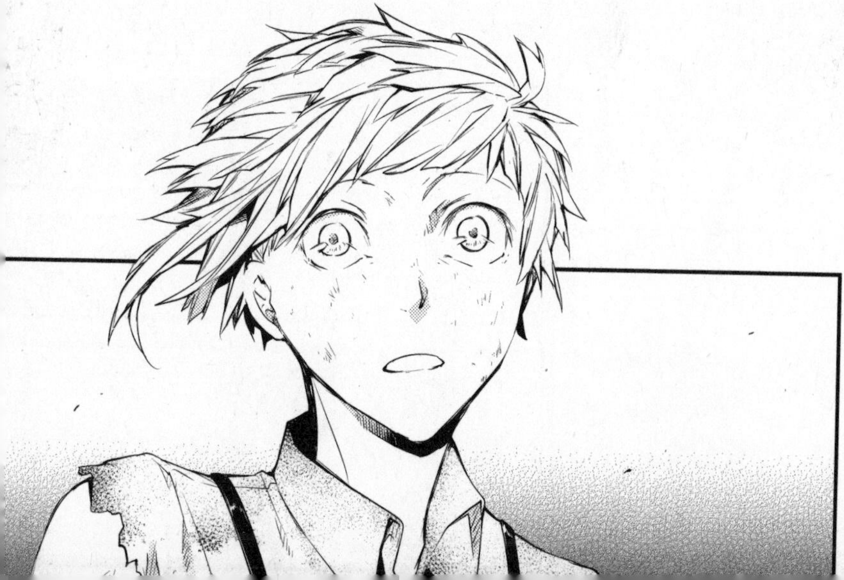

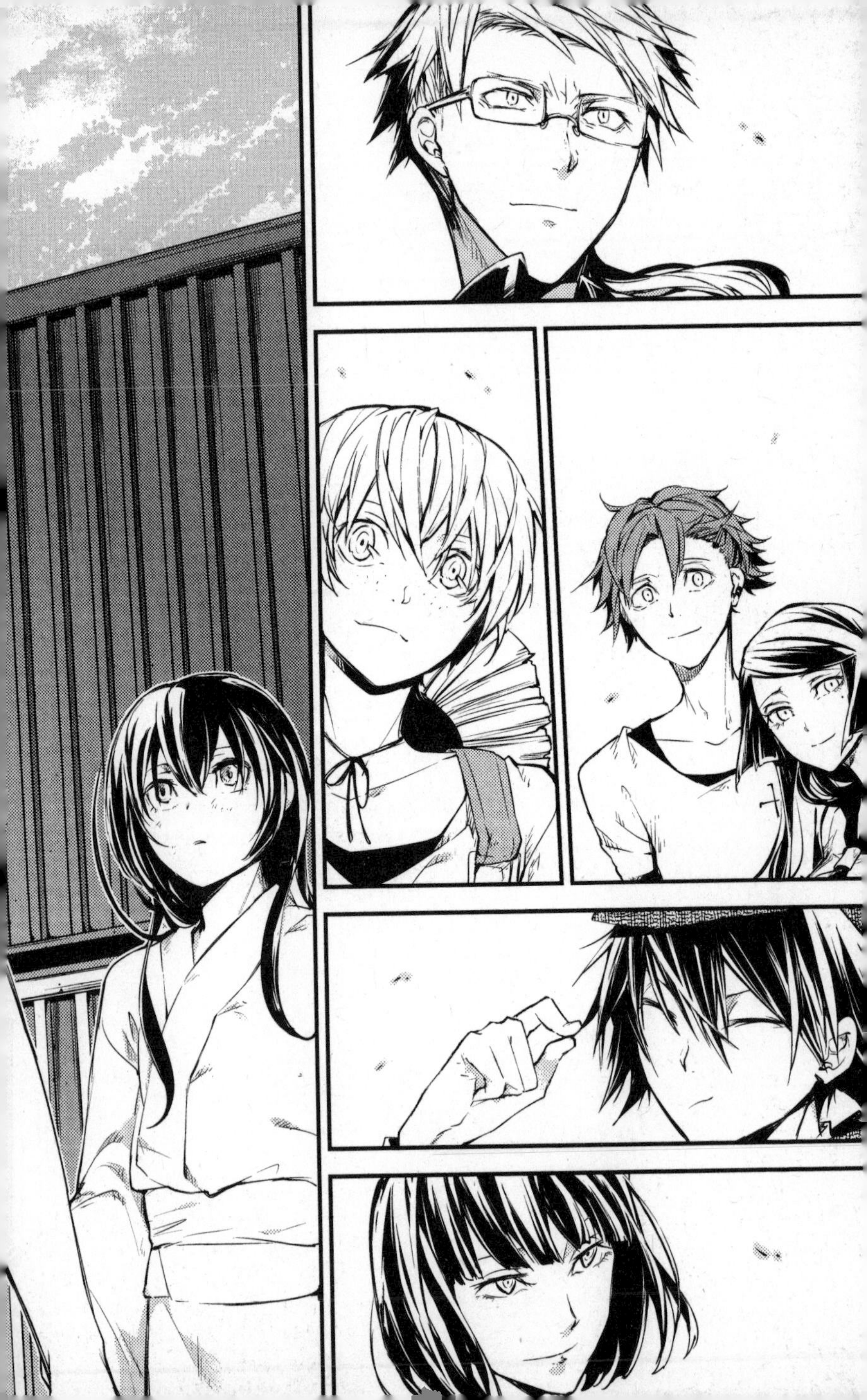

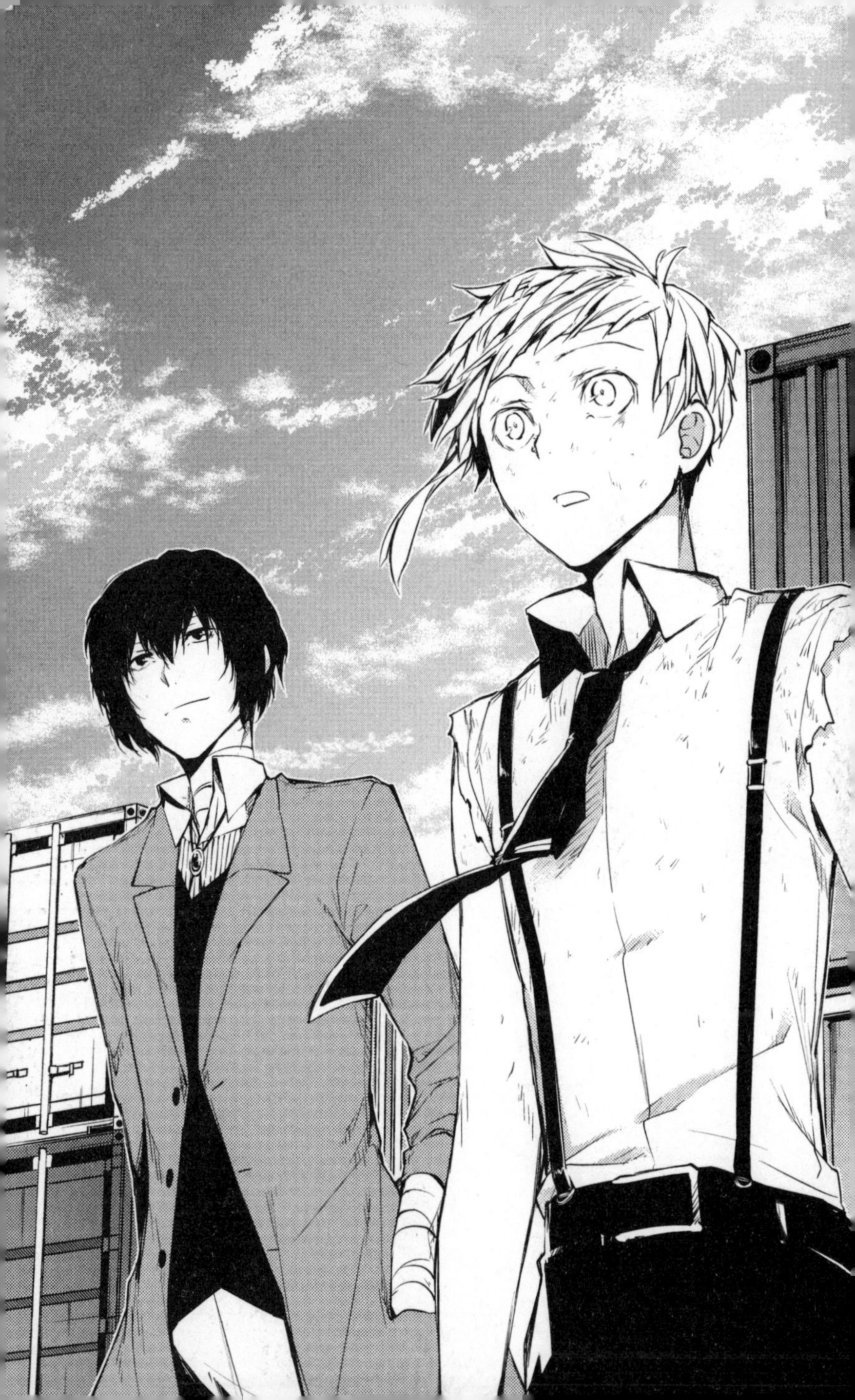

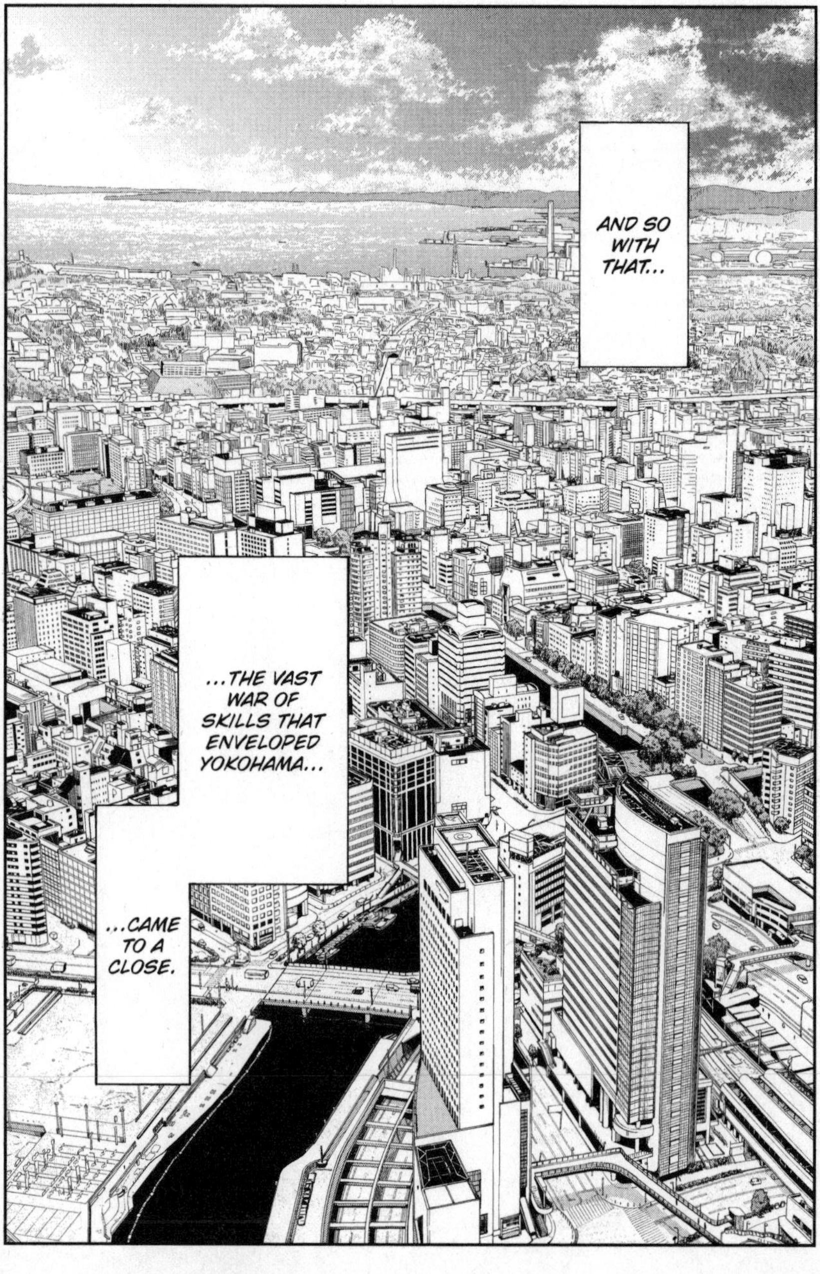
AND SO WITH THAT...
...THE VAST WAR OF SKILLS THAT ENVELOPED YOKOHAMA...
...CAME TO A CLOSE.

FRANCIS SCOTT KEY FITZGERALD

SKILL: **The Great Fitzgerald**
Boosts his physical strength in proportion to the amount of financial assets he consumes.

AGE: *32*

BIRTH DATE: *September 24*

HEIGHT: *191cm*

WEIGHT: *88kg*

BLOOD TYPE: *O*

LIKES: *Money, family, himself*

DISLIKES: *The poor*

BUNGO STRAY DOGS

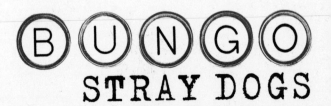

CHAPTER 37

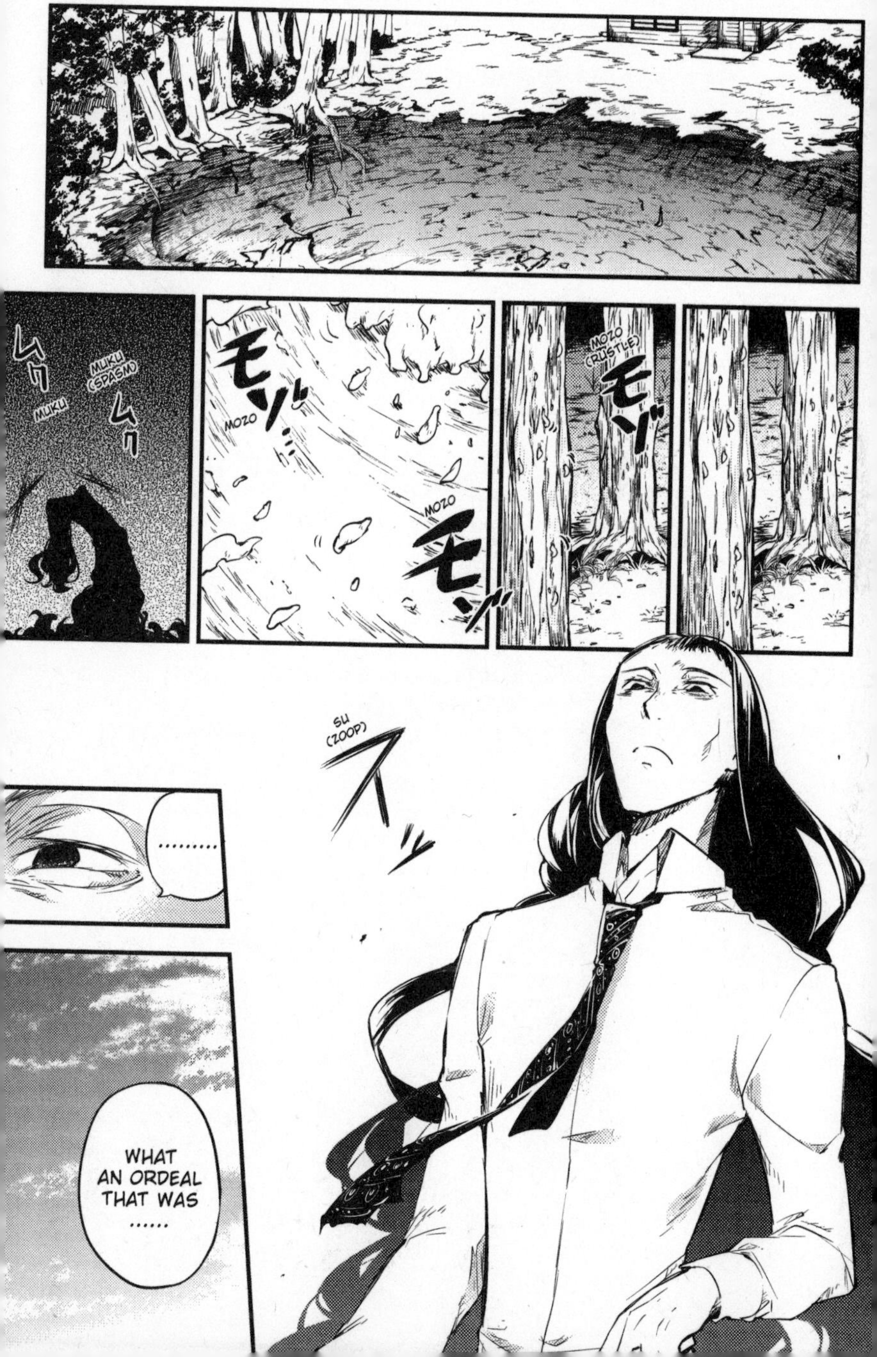
MOZO (RUSTLE)
MOZO
MOZO
MUKU (SPASM)
MUKU
SU (ZOOP)
....
WHAT AN ORDEAL THAT WAS ......

CHAPTER 37
Closing the Party

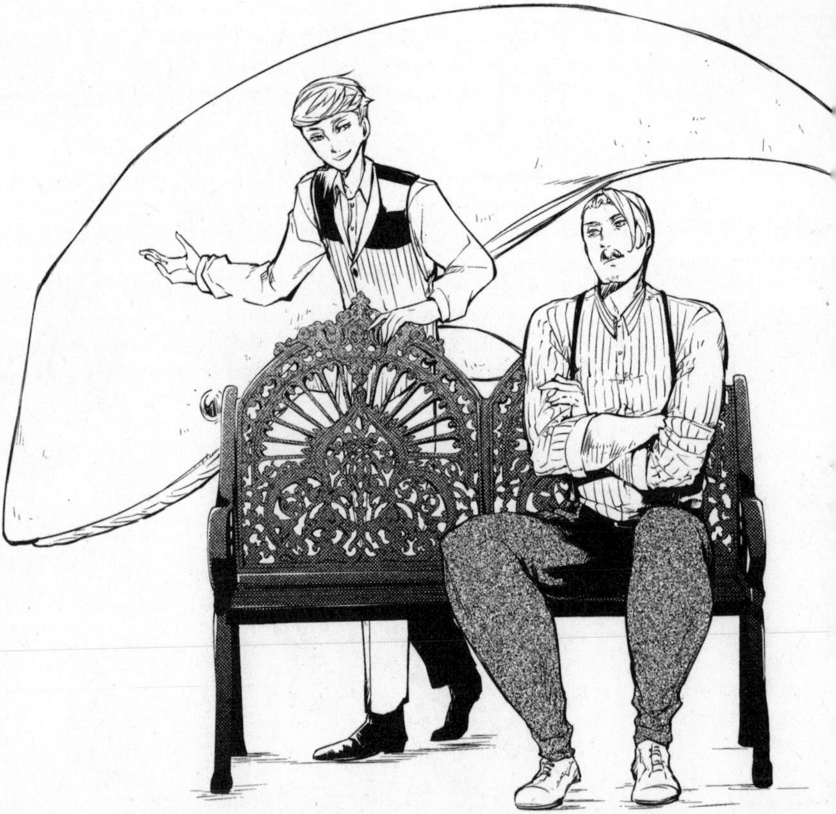

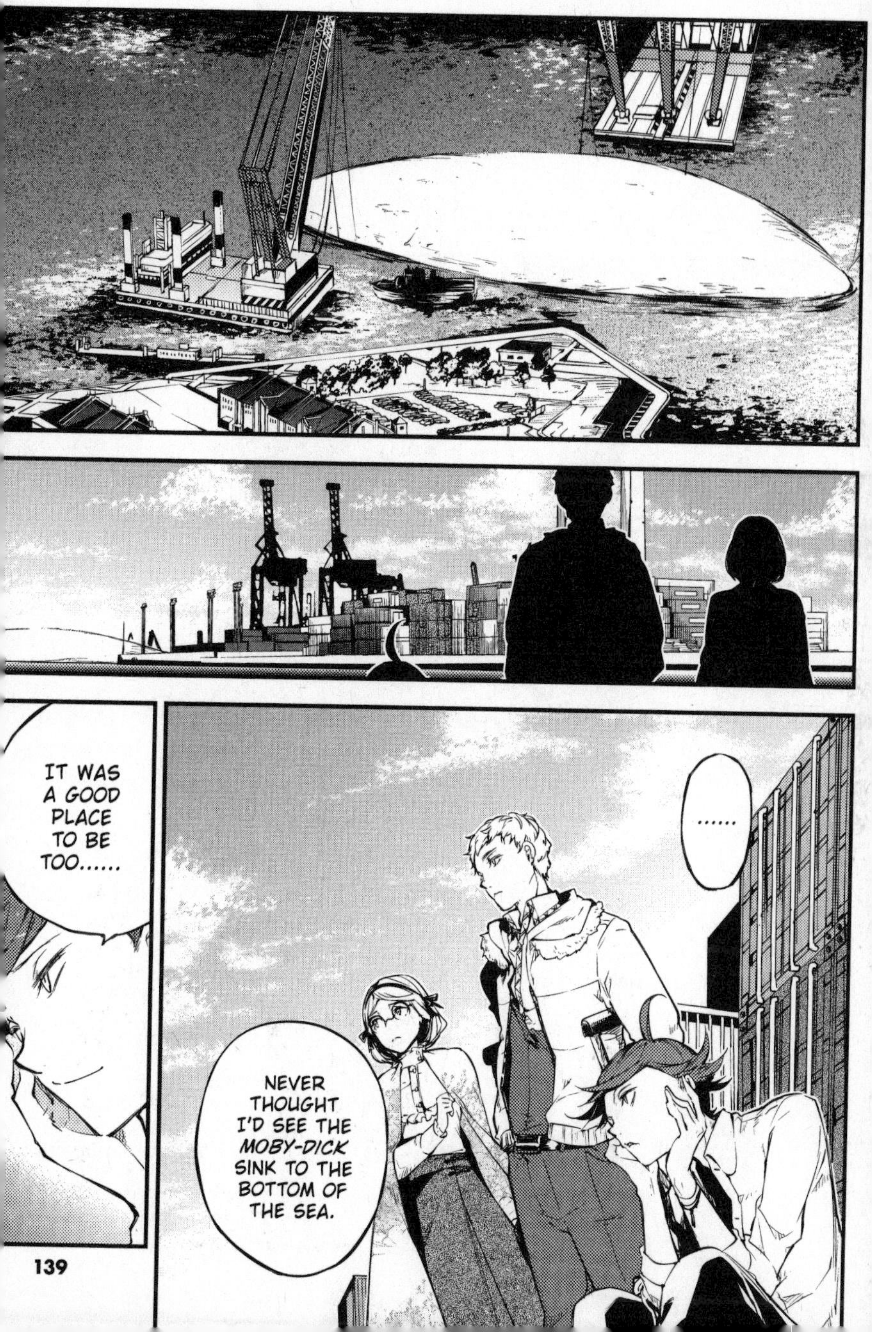

......
NEVER THOUGHT I'D SEE THE *MOBY-DICK* SINK TO THE BOTTOM OF THE SEA.
IT WAS A GOOD PLACE TO BE TOO......

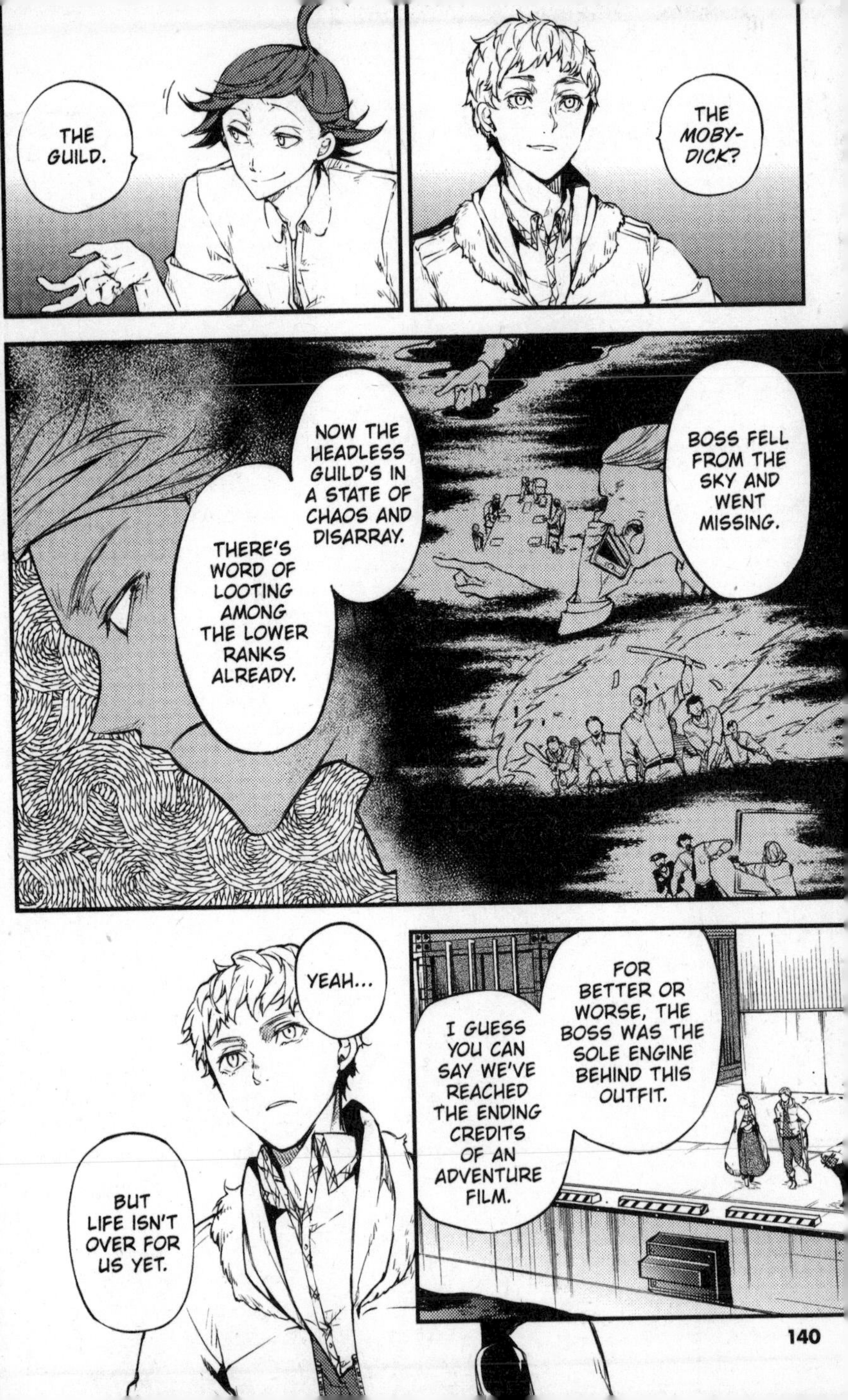
THE *MOBY-DICK*?
THE GUILD.
BOSS FELL FROM THE SKY AND WENT MISSING.
NOW THE HEADLESS GUILD'S IN A STATE OF CHAOS AND DISARRAY.
THERE'S WORD OF LOOTING AMONG THE LOWER RANKS ALREADY.
FOR BETTER OR WORSE, THE BOSS WAS THE SOLE ENGINE BEHIND THIS OUTFIT.
I GUESS YOU CAN SAY WE'VE REACHED THE ENDING CREDITS OF AN ADVENTURE FILM.
YEAH...
BUT LIFE ISN'T OVER FOR US YET.

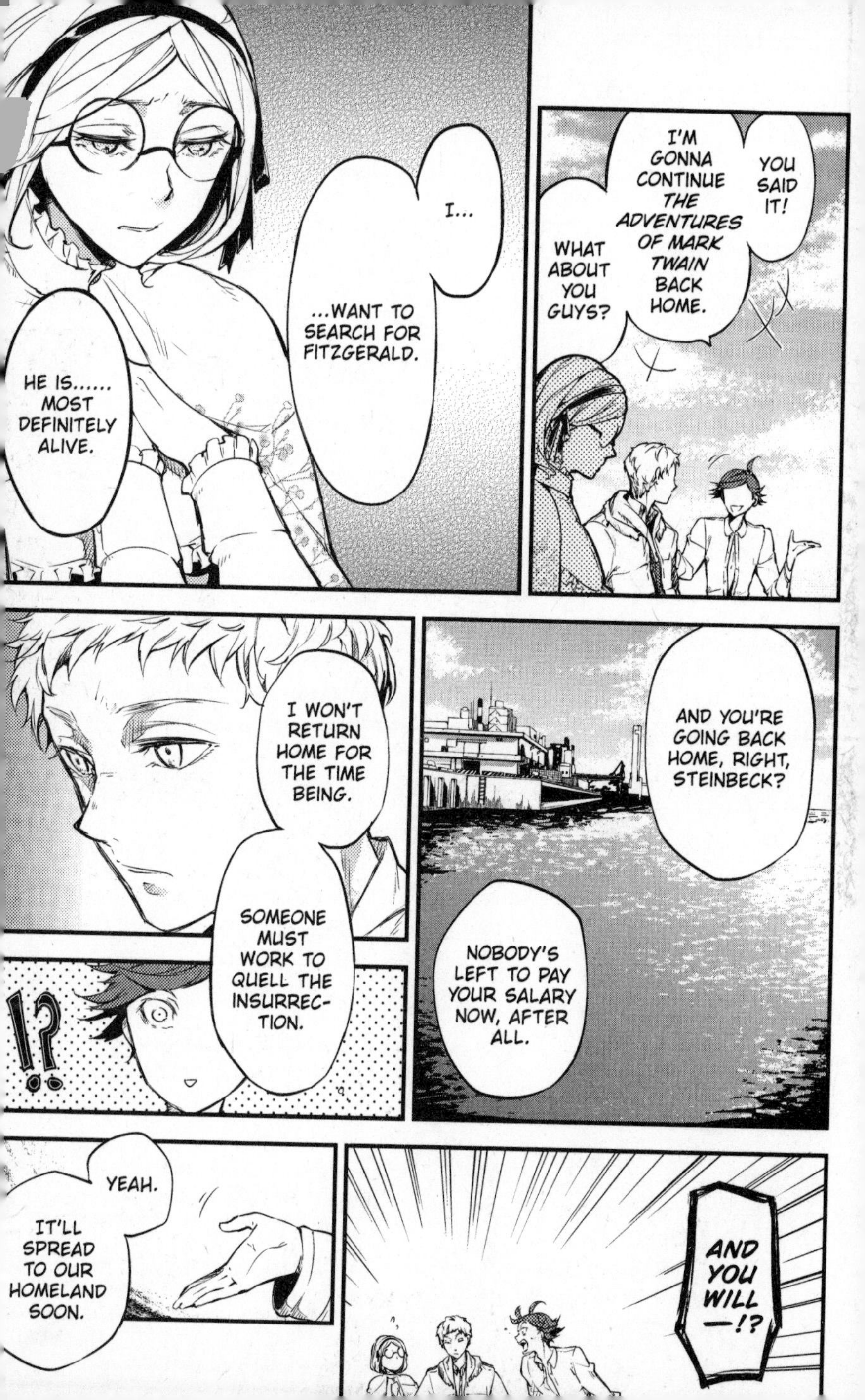
YOU SAID IT!
I'M GONNA CONTINUE THE ADVENTURES OF MARK TWAIN BACK HOME.
WHAT ABOUT YOU GUYS?
I...
...WANT TO SEARCH FOR FITZGERALD.
HE IS...... MOST DEFINITELY ALIVE.
AND YOU'RE GOING BACK HOME, RIGHT, STEINBECK?
NOBODY'S LEFT TO PAY YOUR SALARY NOW, AFTER ALL.
I WON'T RETURN HOME FOR THE TIME BEING.
SOMEONE MUST WORK TO QUELL THE INSURRECTION.
!?
AND YOU WILL—!?
YEAH.
IT'LL SPREAD TO OUR HOMELAND SOON.

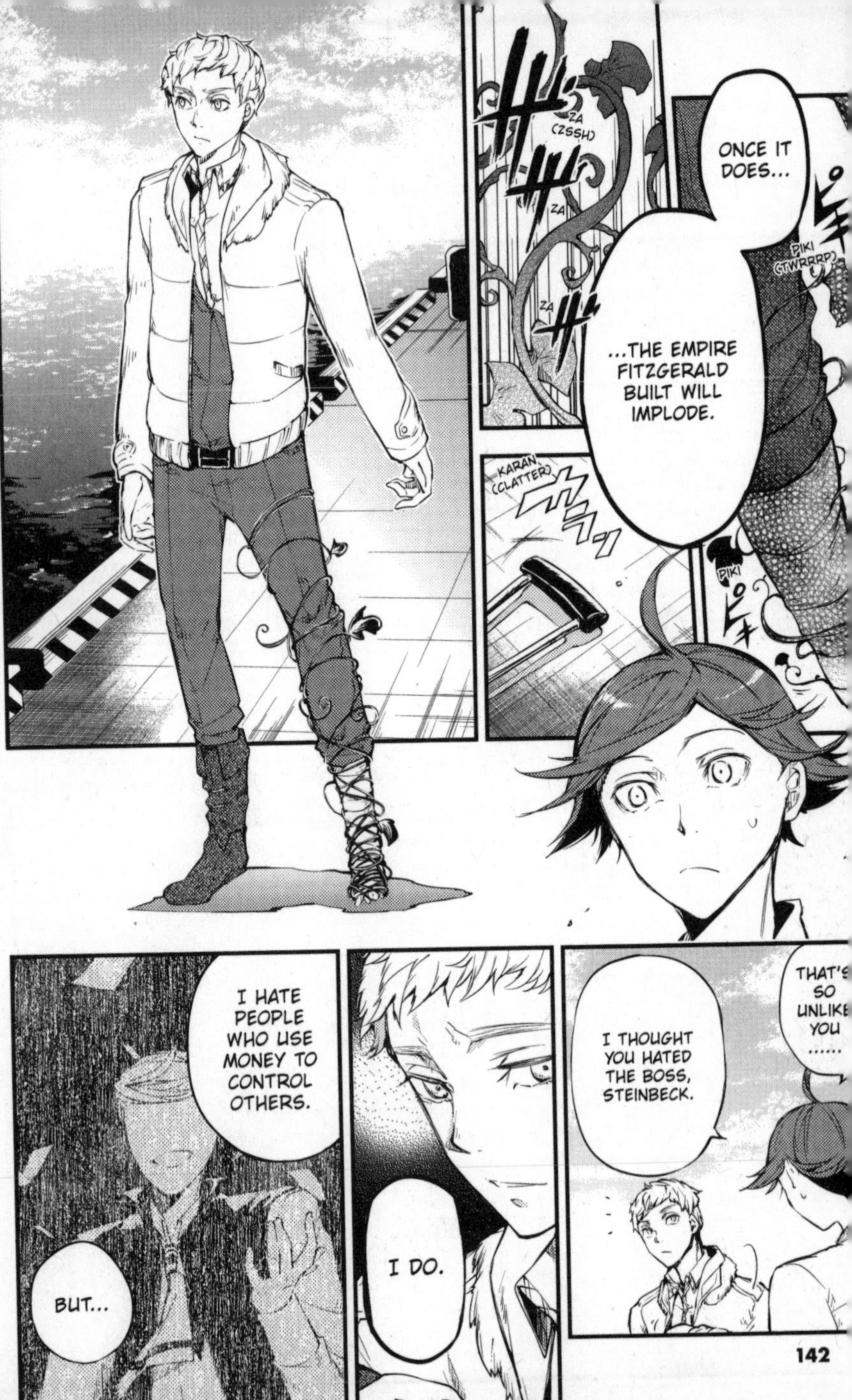
ZA (ZSSH)
ZA
ZA
ONCE IT DOES...
PIKI (TWRRRP)
...THE EMPIRE FITZGERALD BUILT WILL IMPLODE.
KARAN (CLATTER)
PIKI
THAT'S SO UNLIKE YOU ......
I THOUGHT YOU HATED THE BOSS, STEINBECK.
I DO.
I HATE PEOPLE WHO USE MONEY TO CONTROL OTHERS.
BUT...

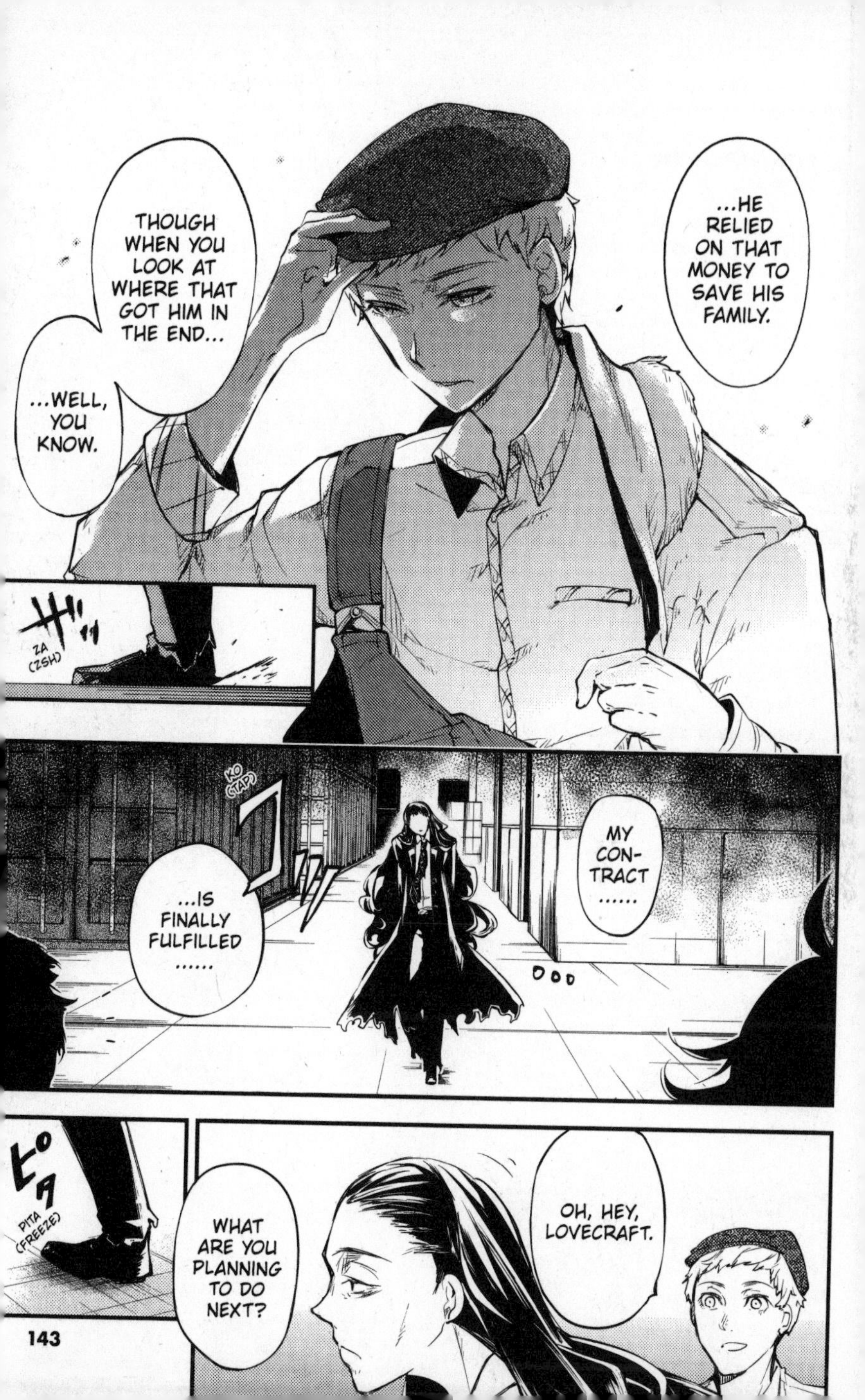
...HE RELIED ON THAT MONEY TO SAVE HIS FAMILY.
THOUGH WHEN YOU LOOK AT WHERE THAT GOT HIM IN THE END...
...WELL, YOU KNOW.
ZA (ZSH)
KO (TAP)
MY CON-TRACT......
...IS FINALLY FULFILLED......
OH, HEY, LOVECRAFT.
WHAT ARE YOU PLANNING TO DO NEXT?
PITA (FREEZE)

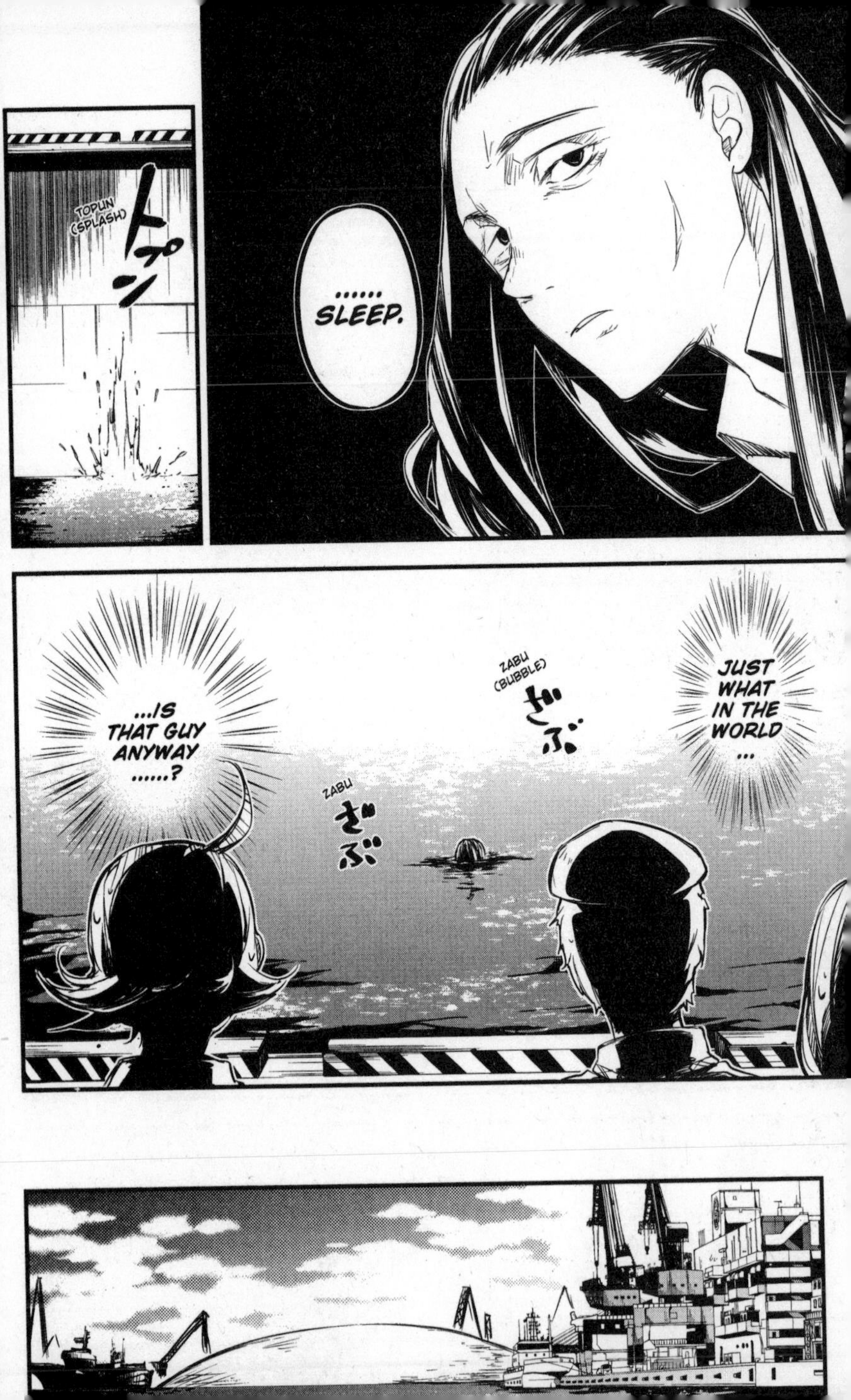
......SLEEP.
TOPUN (SPLASH)
トプン
JUST WHAT IN THE WORLD ...
ZABU (BUBBLE)
ざぶ
ZABU
ざぶ
...IS THAT GUY ANYWAY ......?

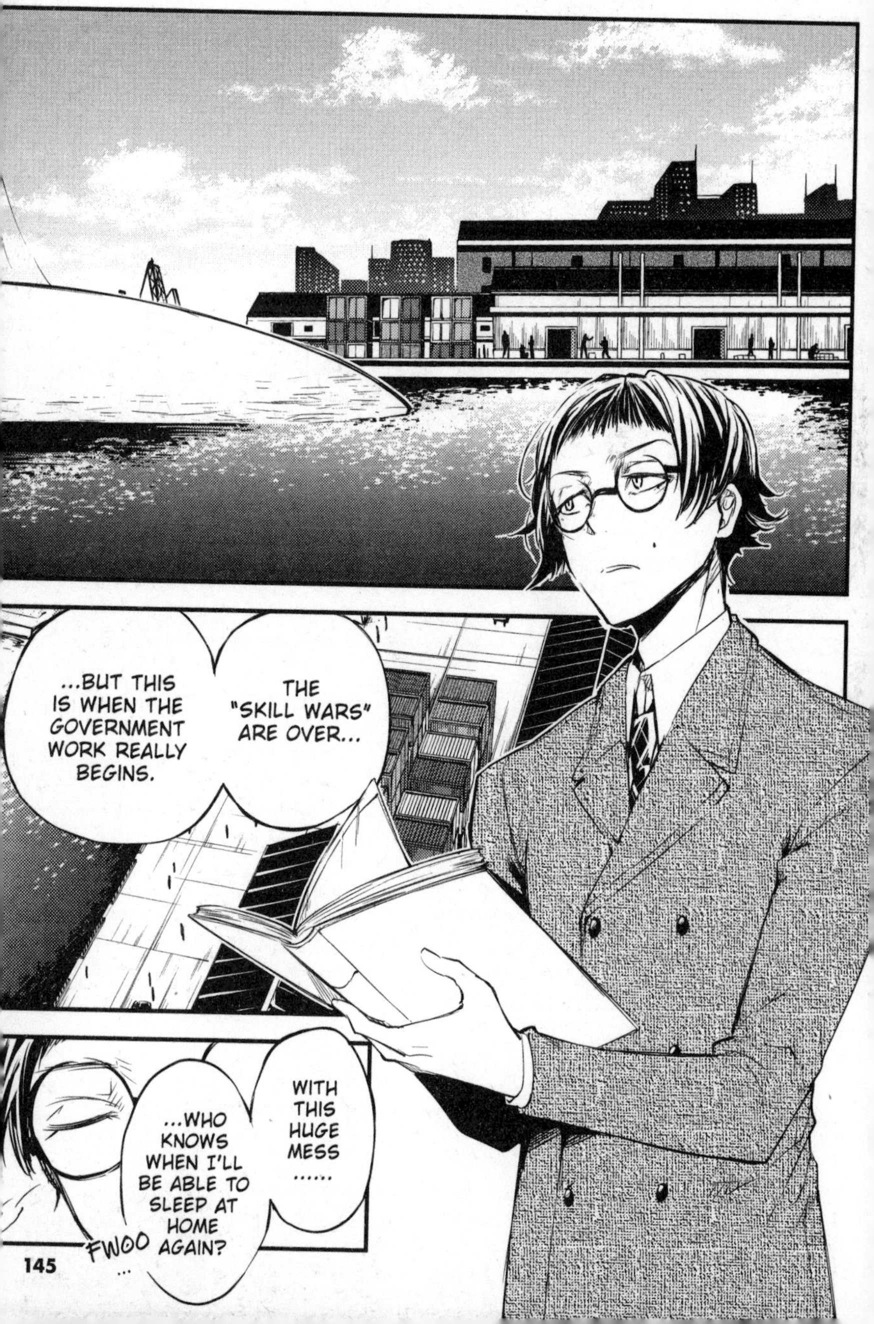
THE "SKILL WARS" ARE OVER...
...BUT THIS IS WHEN THE GOVERNMENT WORK REALLY BEGINS.
WITH THIS HUGE MESS ......
...WHO KNOWS WHEN I'LL BE ABLE TO SLEEP AT HOME AGAIN?
FWOO ...

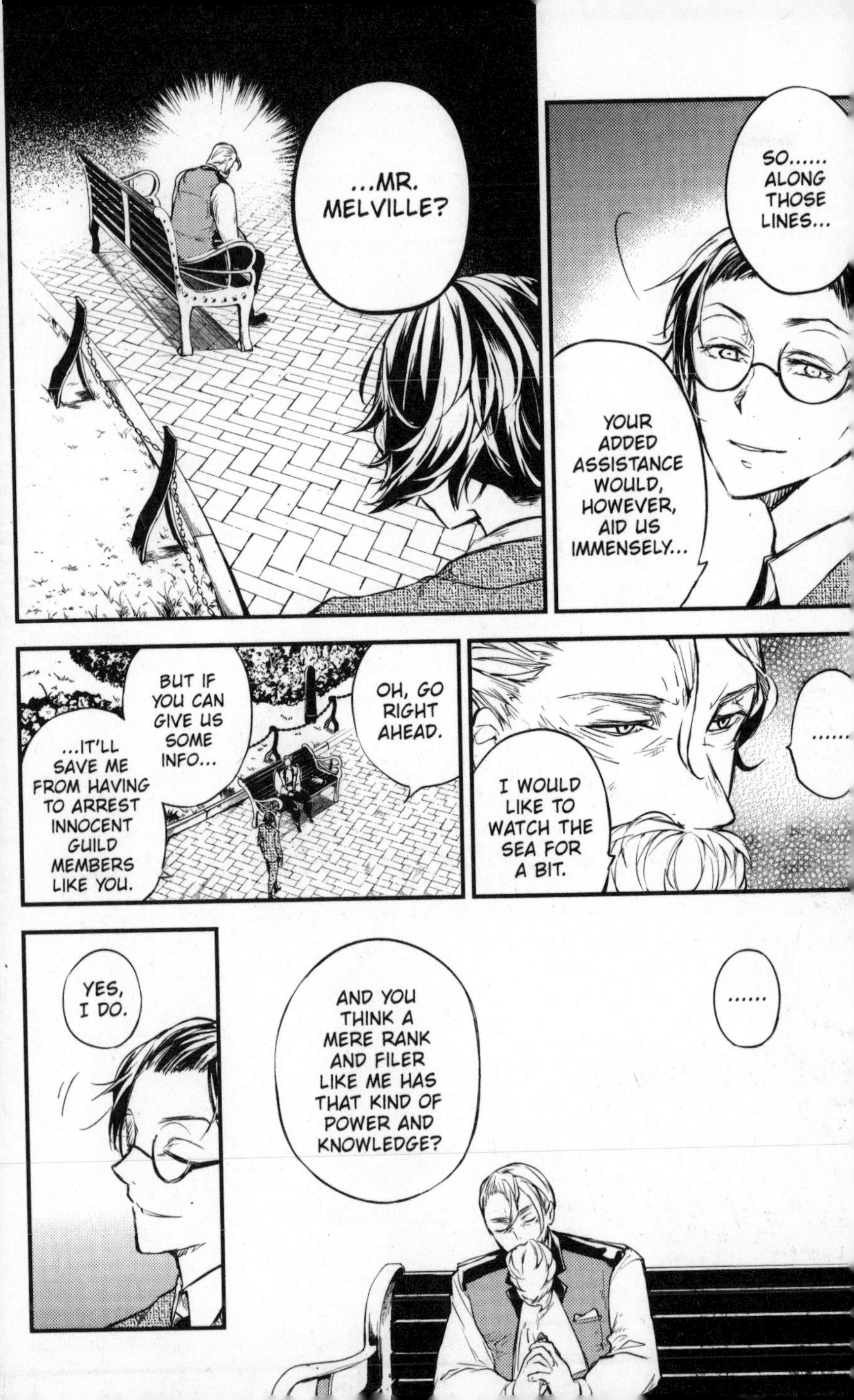
SO...... ALONG THOSE LINES...
YOUR ADDED ASSISTANCE WOULD, HOWEVER, AID US IMMENSELY...
...MR. MELVILLE?
......
I WOULD LIKE TO WATCH THE SEA FOR A BIT.
OH, GO RIGHT AHEAD.
BUT IF YOU CAN GIVE US SOME INFO...
...IT'LL SAVE ME FROM HAVING TO ARREST INNOCENT GUILD MEMBERS LIKE YOU.
......
AND YOU THINK A MERE RANK AND FILER LIKE ME HAS THAT KIND OF POWER AND KNOWLEDGE?
YES, I DO.

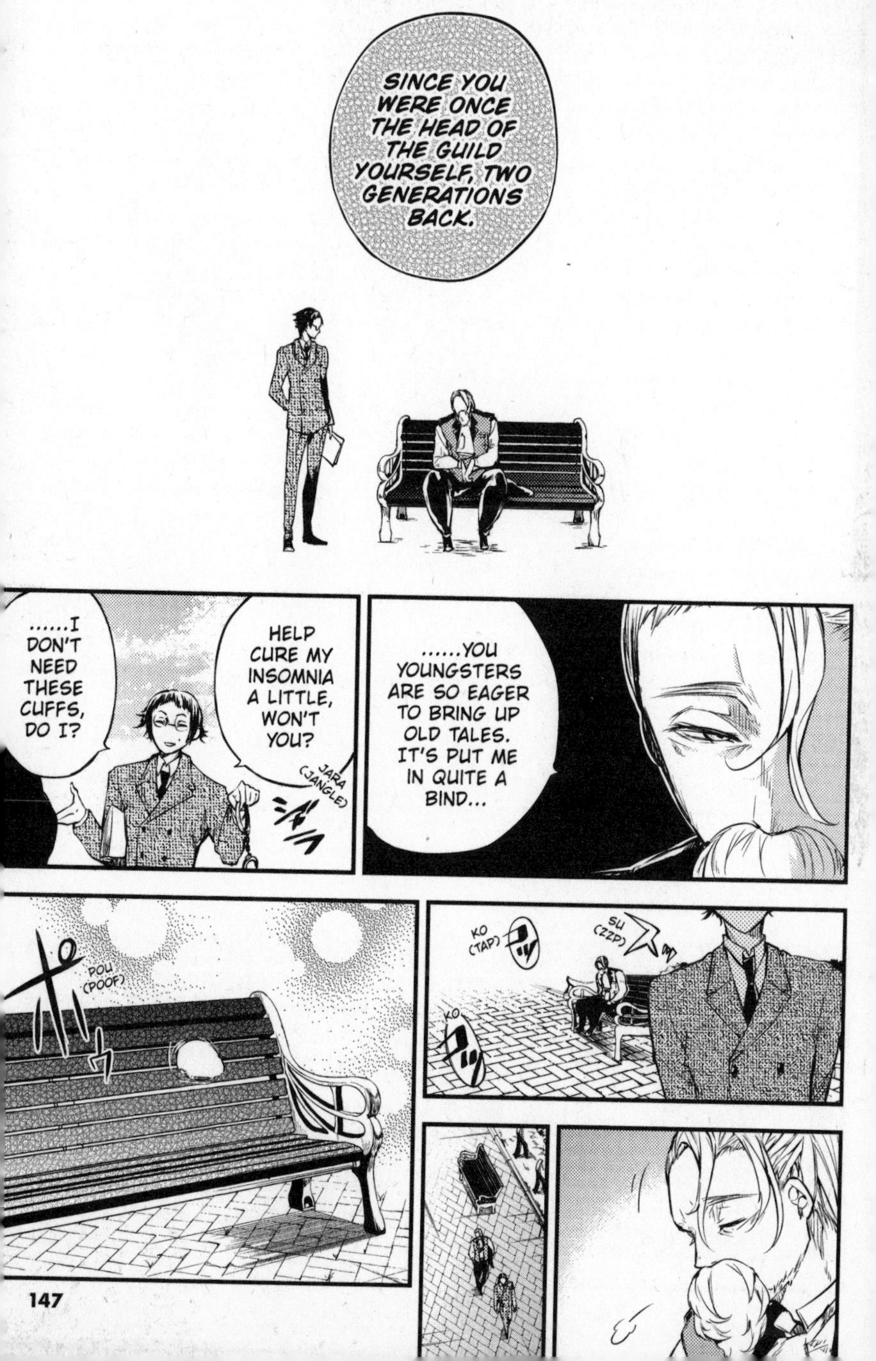
SINCE YOU WERE ONCE THE HEAD OF THE GUILD YOURSELF, TWO GENERATIONS BACK.
......YOU YOUNGSTERS ARE SO EAGER TO BRING UP OLD TALES. IT'S PUT ME IN QUITE A BIND...
HELP CURE MY INSOMNIA A LITTLE, WON'T YOU?
JARA (JANGLE)
......I DON'T NEED THESE CUFFS, DO I?
SU (ZZP)
KO (TAP)
KO
POU (POOF)

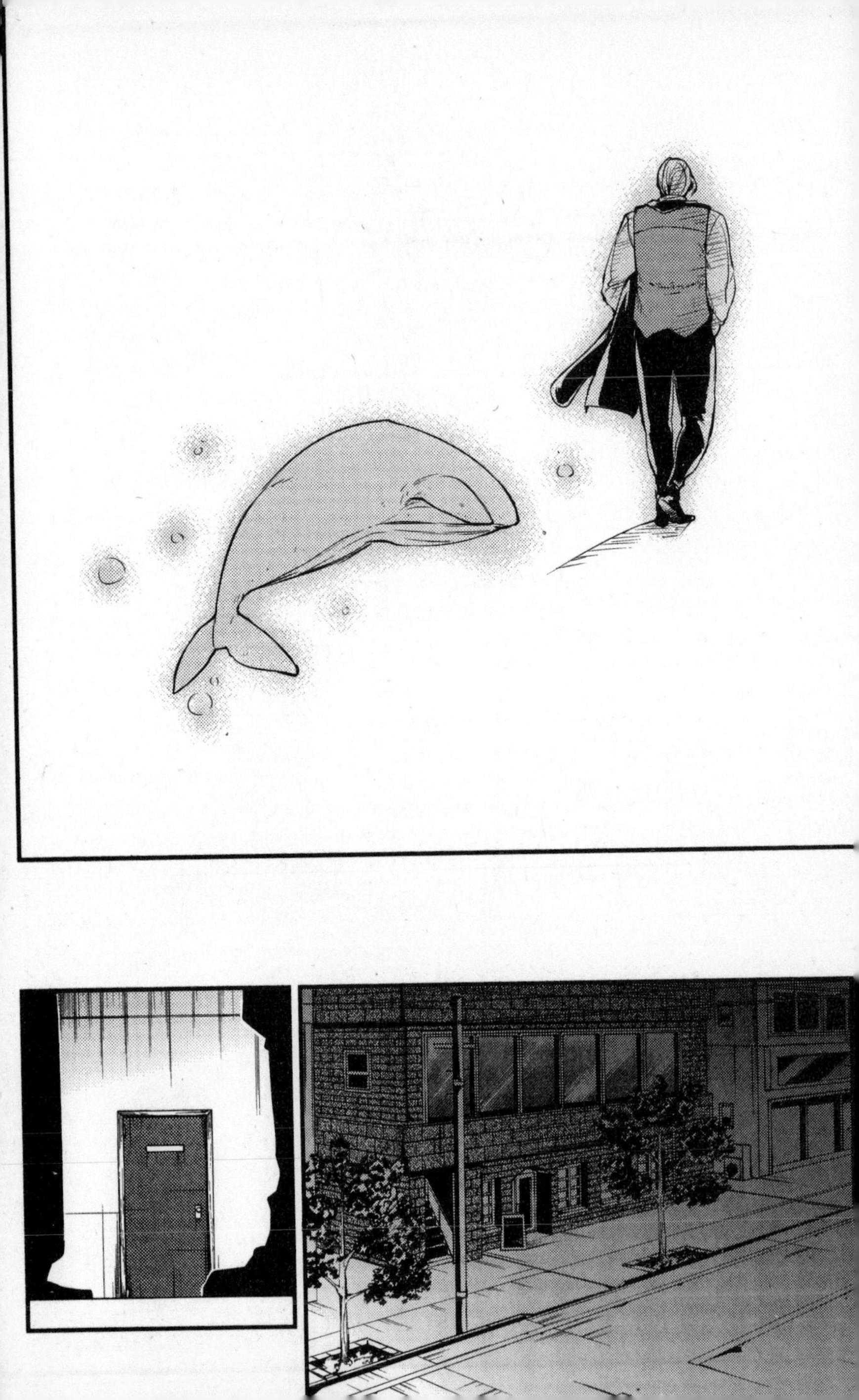

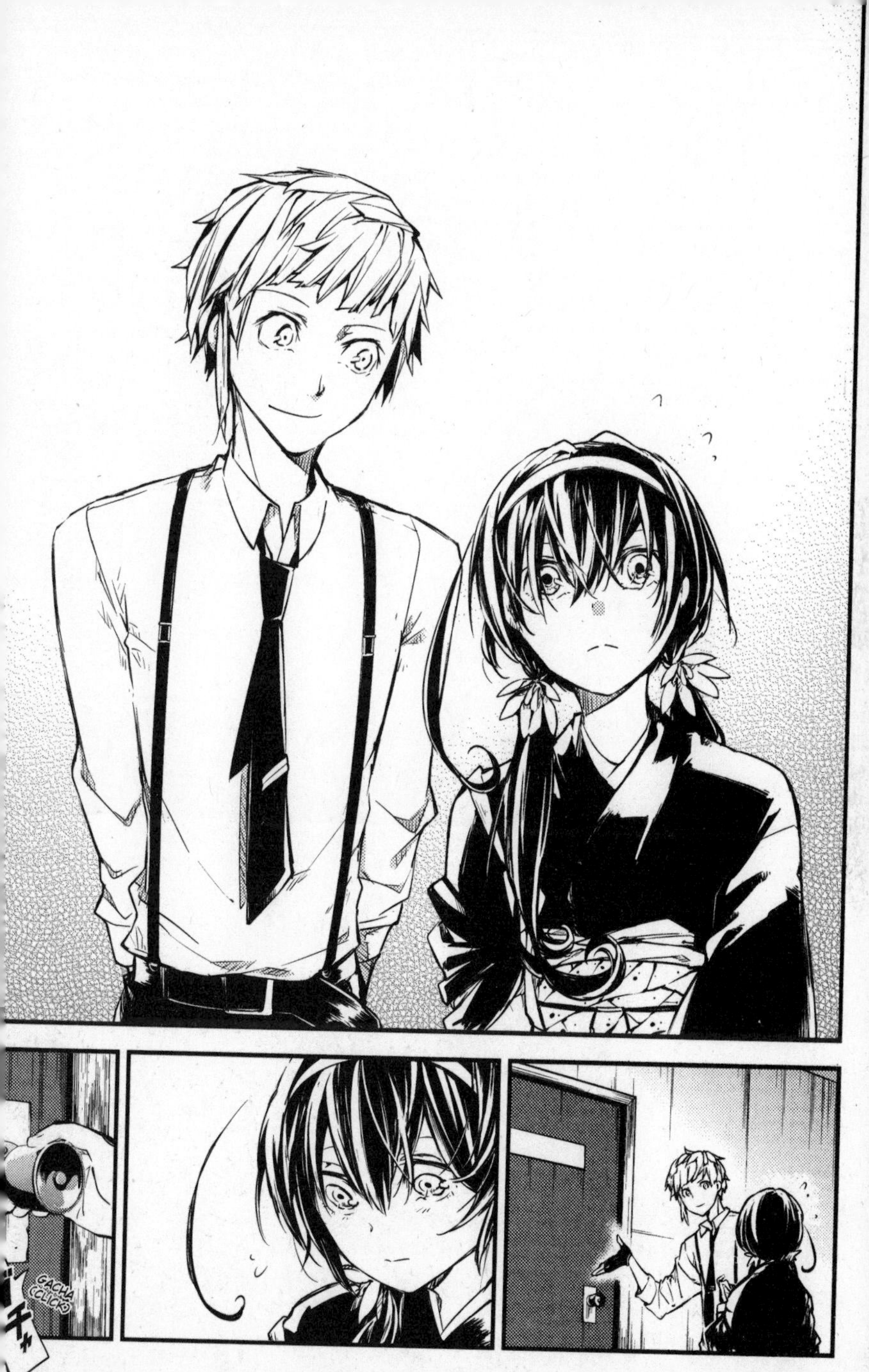
GACHA (CLICK)

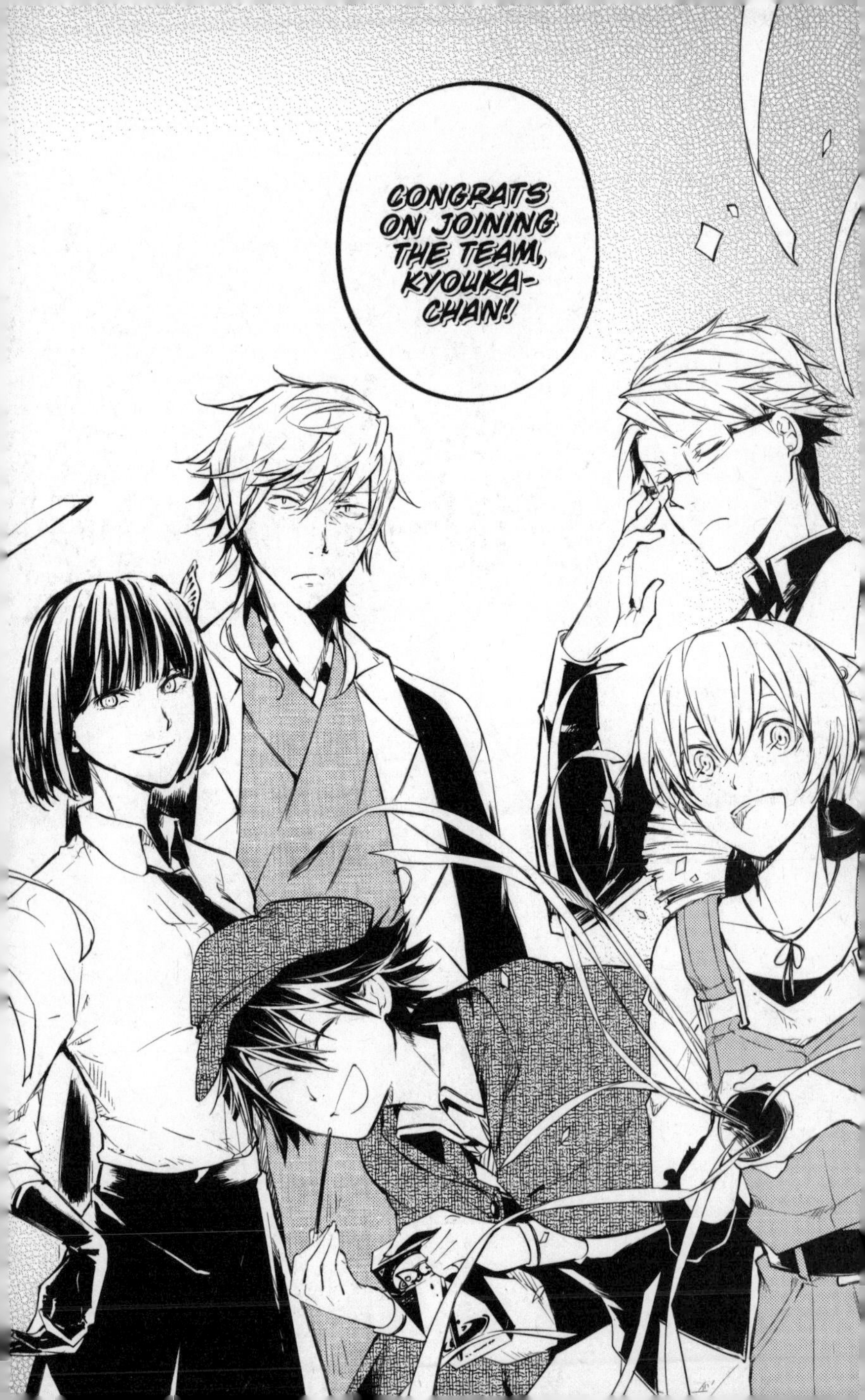
CONGRATS ON JOINING THE TEAM, KYOUKA-CHAN!

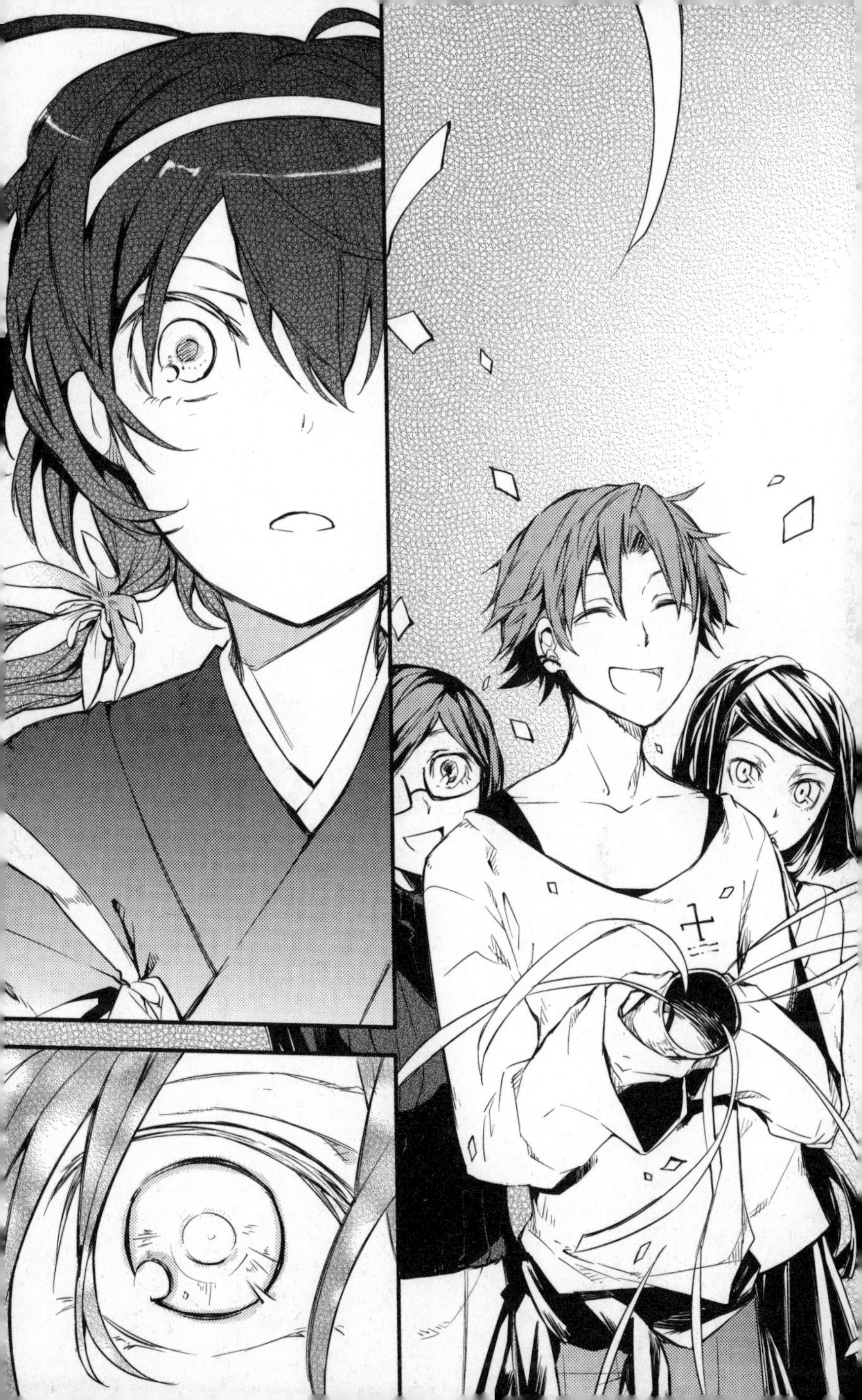

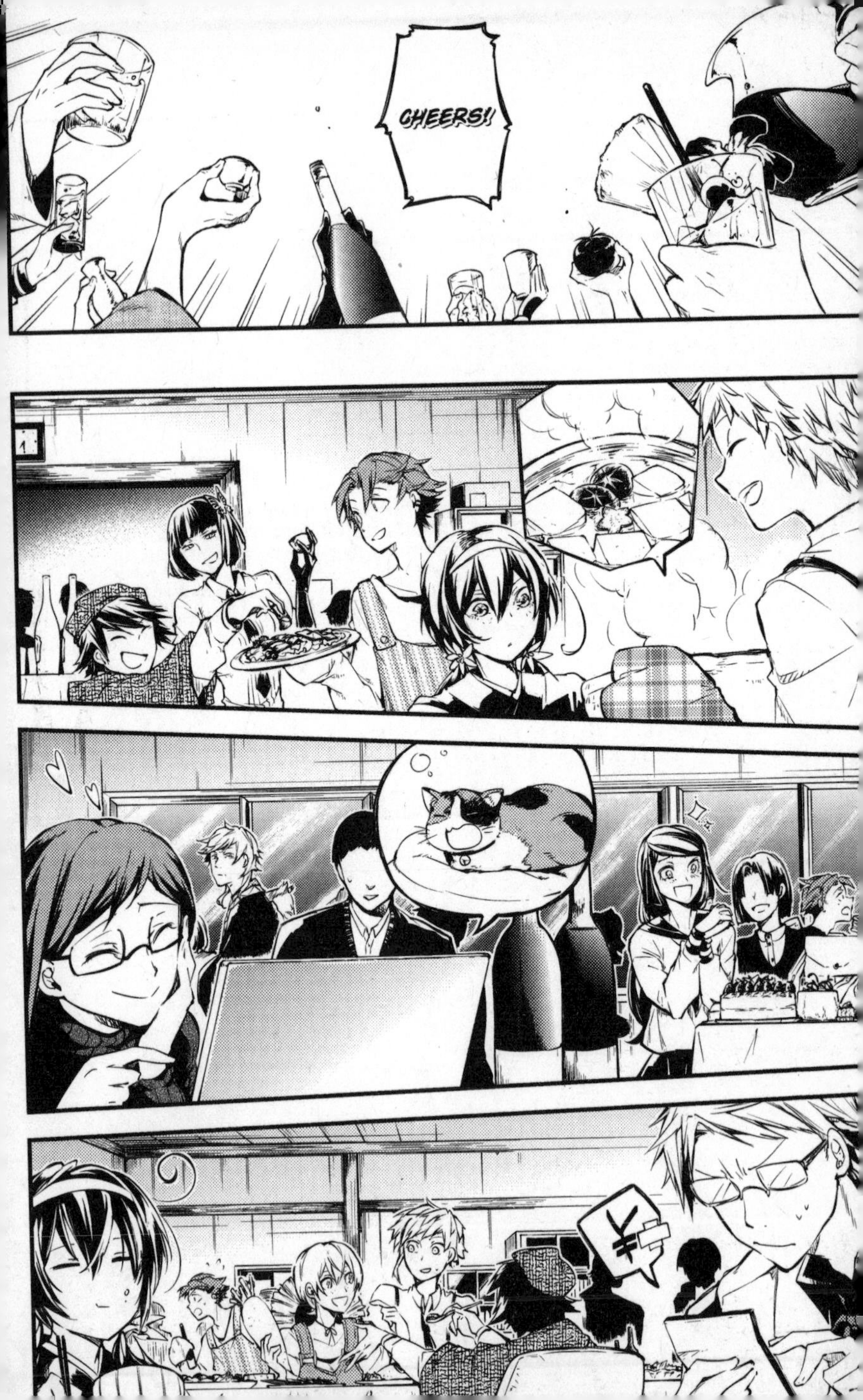
CHEERS!
¥

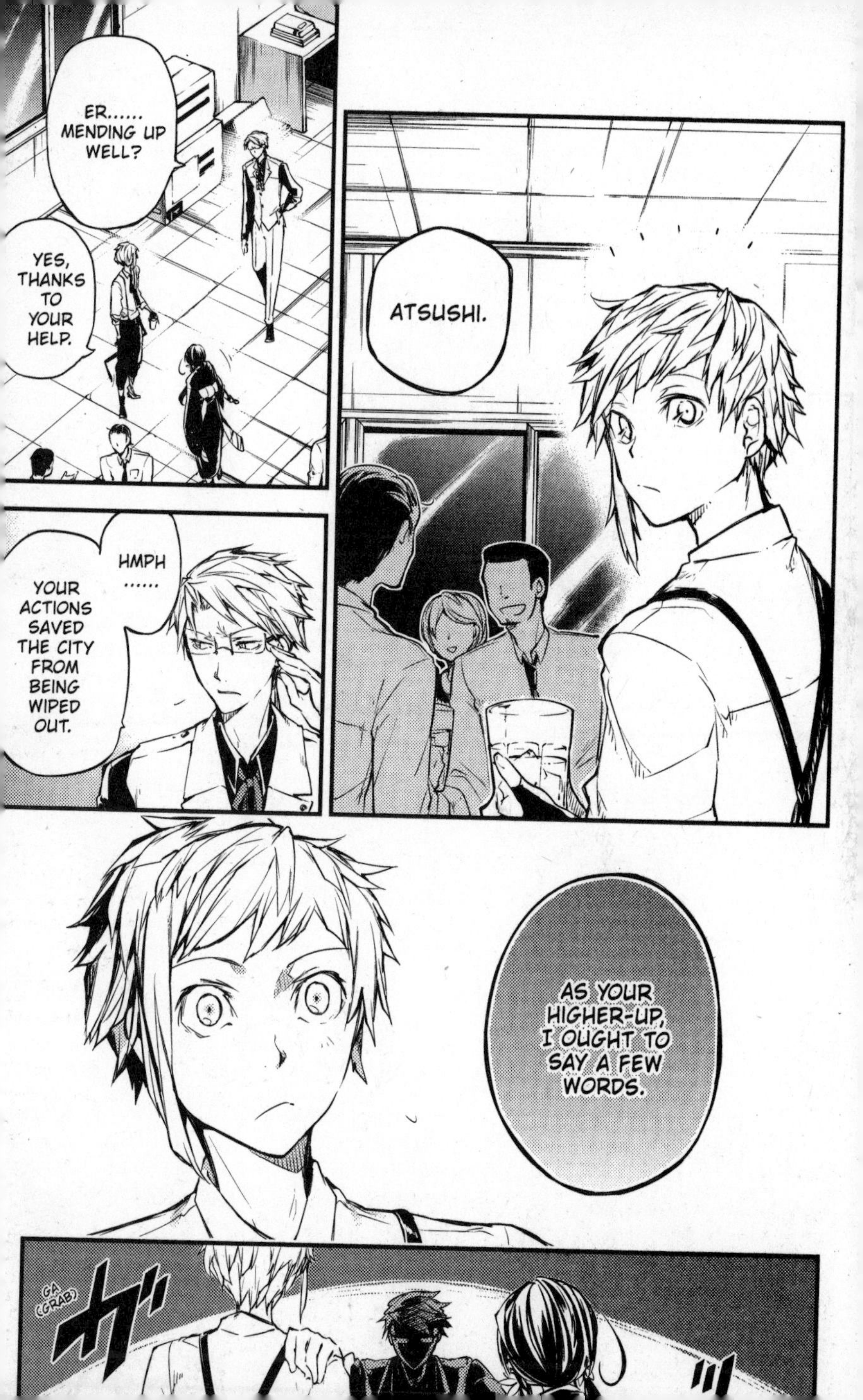
ATSUSHI.
ER...... MENDING UP WELL?
YES, THANKS TO YOUR HELP.
HMPH ......
YOUR ACTIONS SAVED THE CITY FROM BEING WIPED OUT.
AS YOUR HIGHER-UP, I OUGHT TO SAY A FEW WORDS.
GA (GRAB)

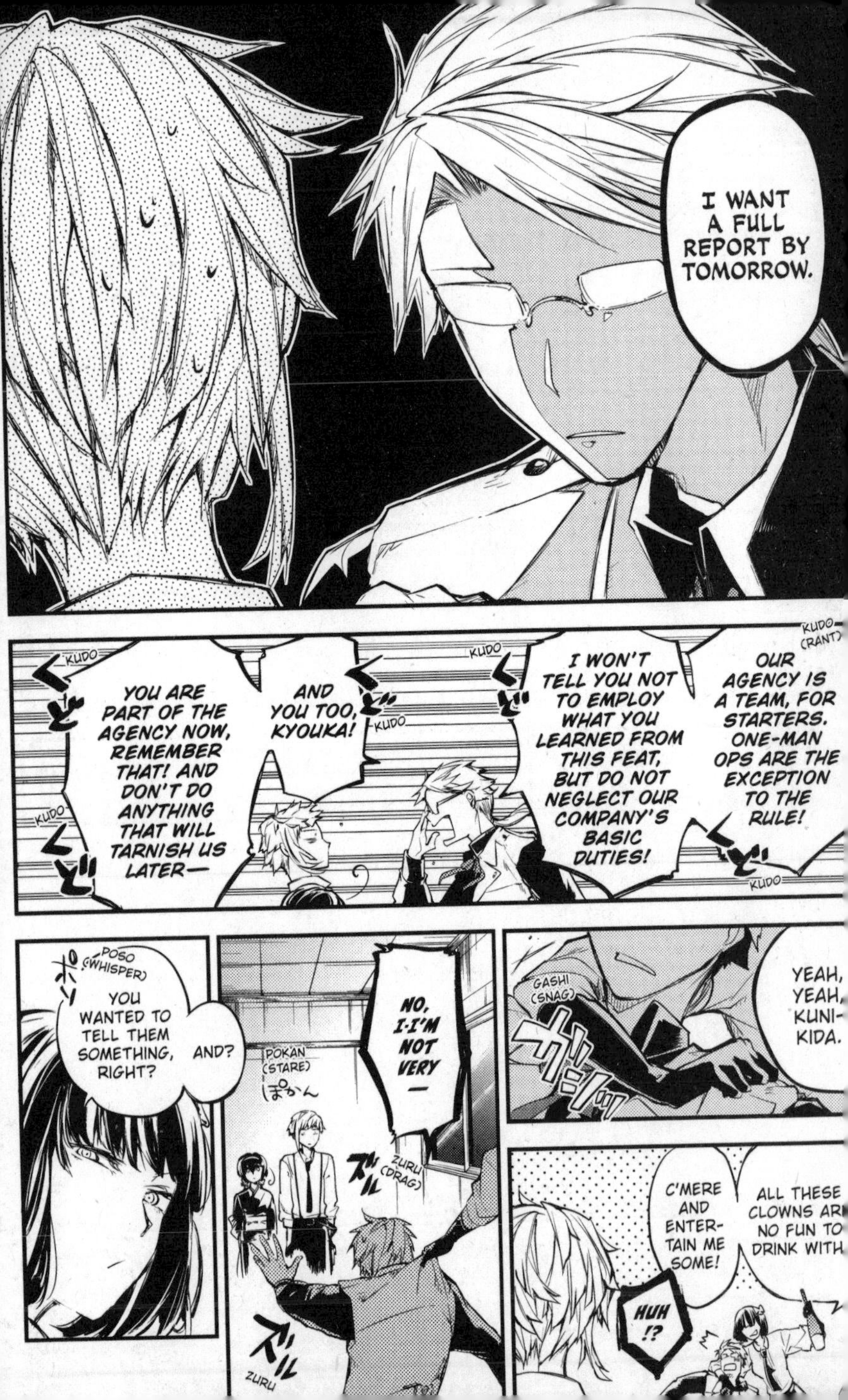
I WANT A FULL REPORT BY TOMORROW.
KUDO (RANT)
OUR AGENCY IS A TEAM, FOR STARTERS. ONE-MAN OPS ARE THE EXCEPTION TO THE RULE!
KUDO
KUDO
I WON'T TELL YOU NOT TO EMPLOY WHAT YOU LEARNED FROM THIS FEAT, BUT DO NOT NEGLECT OUR COMPANY'S BASIC DUTIES!
AND YOU TOO, KYOUKA!
KUDO
KUDO
YOU ARE PART OF THE AGENCY NOW, REMEMBER THAT! AND DON'T DO ANYTHING THAT WILL TARNISH US LATER—
KUDO
YEAH, YEAH, KUNI-KIDA.
GASHI (SNAG)
ALL THESE CLOWNS AR NO FUN TO DRINK WITH
C'MERE AND ENTER-TAIN ME SOME!
HUH!?
NO, I-I'M NOT VERY—
POKAN (STARE)
ZURU (DRAG)
ZURU
POSO (WHISPER)
YOU WANTED TO TELL THEM SOMETHING, RIGHT?
AND?

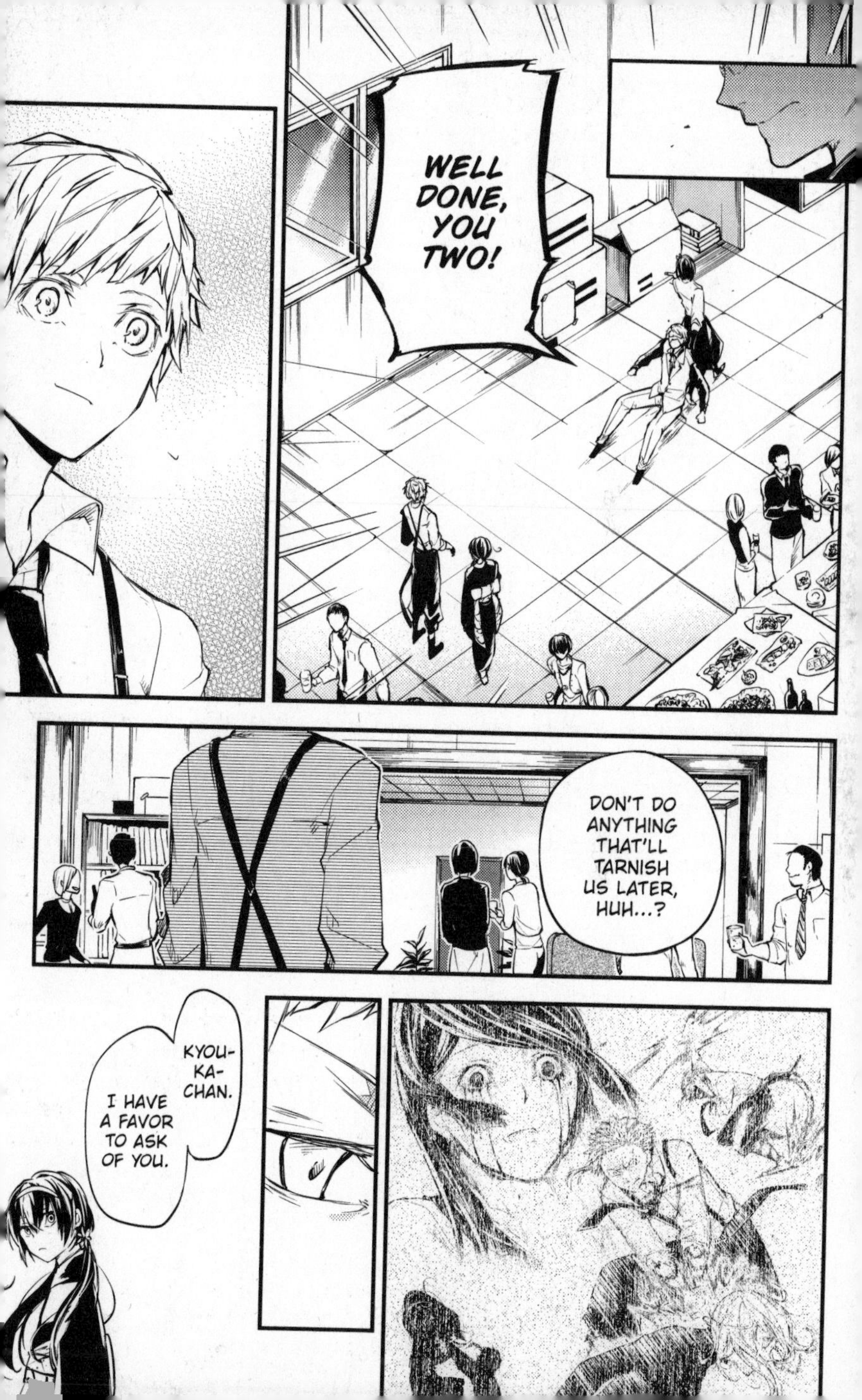
WELL DONE, YOU TWO!
DON'T DO ANYTHING THAT'LL TARNISH US LATER, HUH...?
KYOU-KA-CHAN.
I HAVE A FAVOR TO ASK OF YOU.

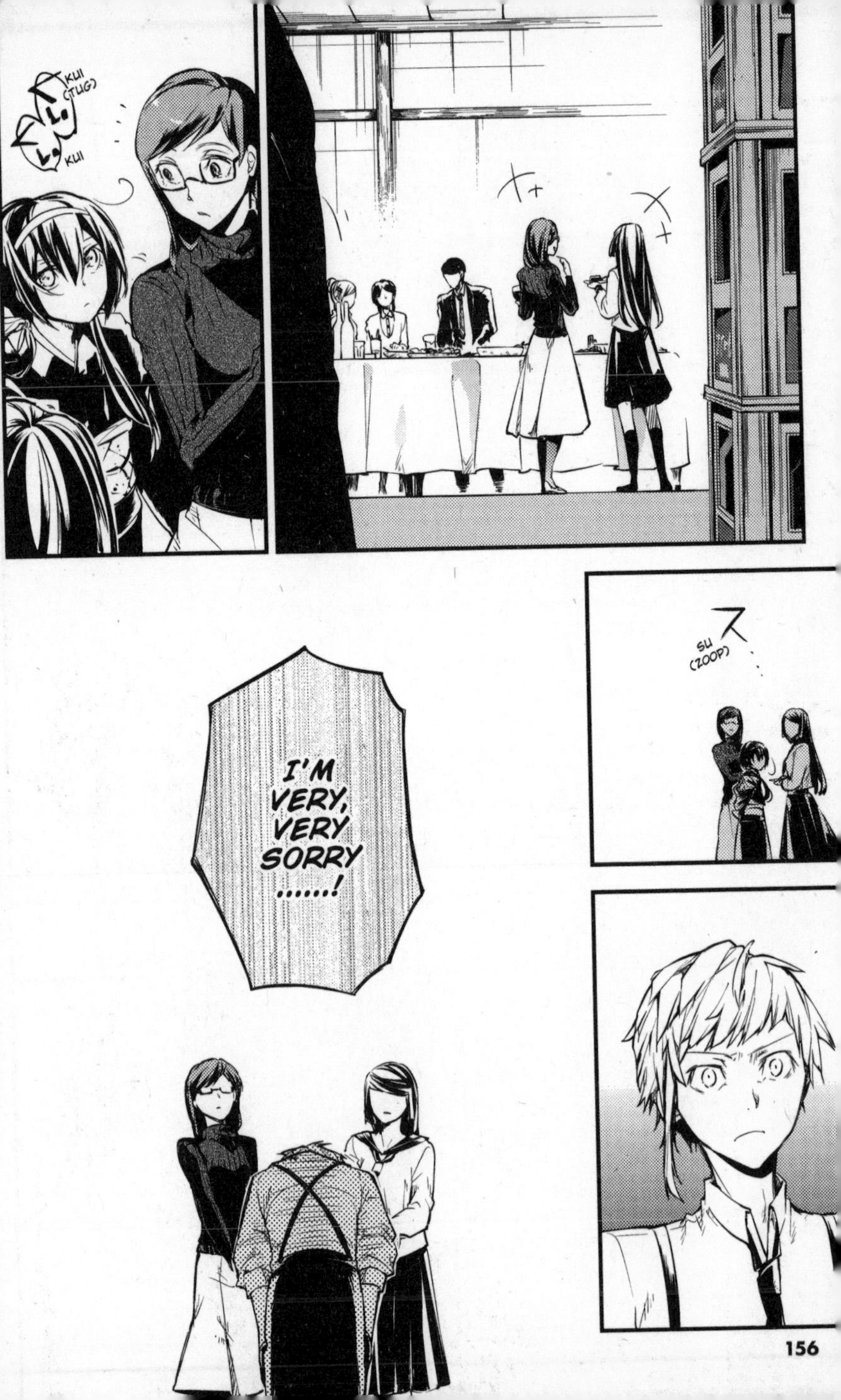
KUI (TUG)
KUI
SU (ZOOP)
I'M VERY, VERY SORRY ......!

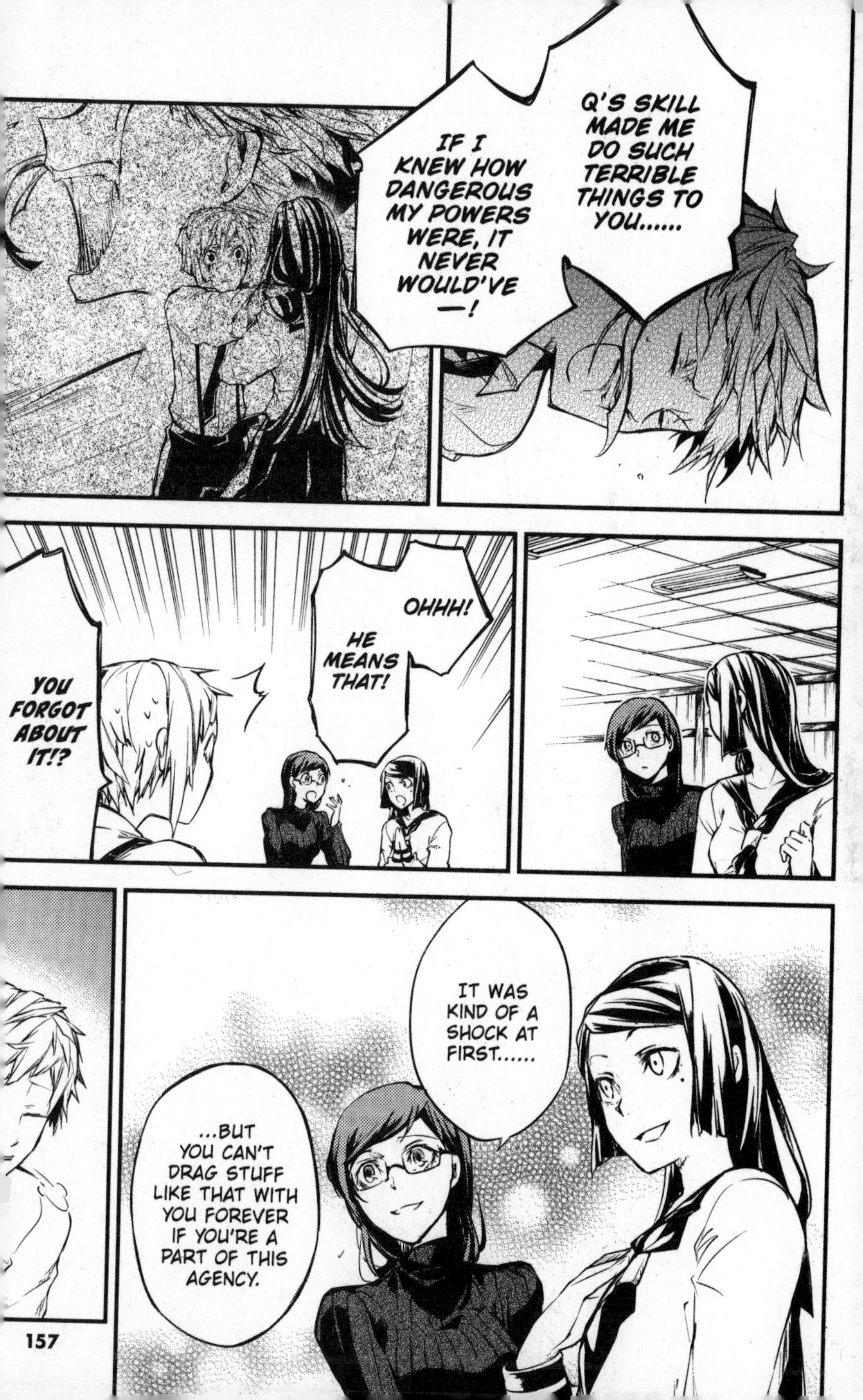

Q'S SKILL MADE ME DO SUCH TERRIBLE THINGS TO YOU......
IF I KNEW HOW DANGEROUS MY POWERS WERE, IT NEVER WOULD'VE —!
OHHH!
HE MEANS THAT!
YOU FORGOT ABOUT IT!?
IT WAS KIND OF A SHOCK AT FIRST......
...BUT YOU CAN'T DRAG STUFF LIKE THAT WITH YOU FOREVER IF YOU'RE A PART OF THIS AGENCY.

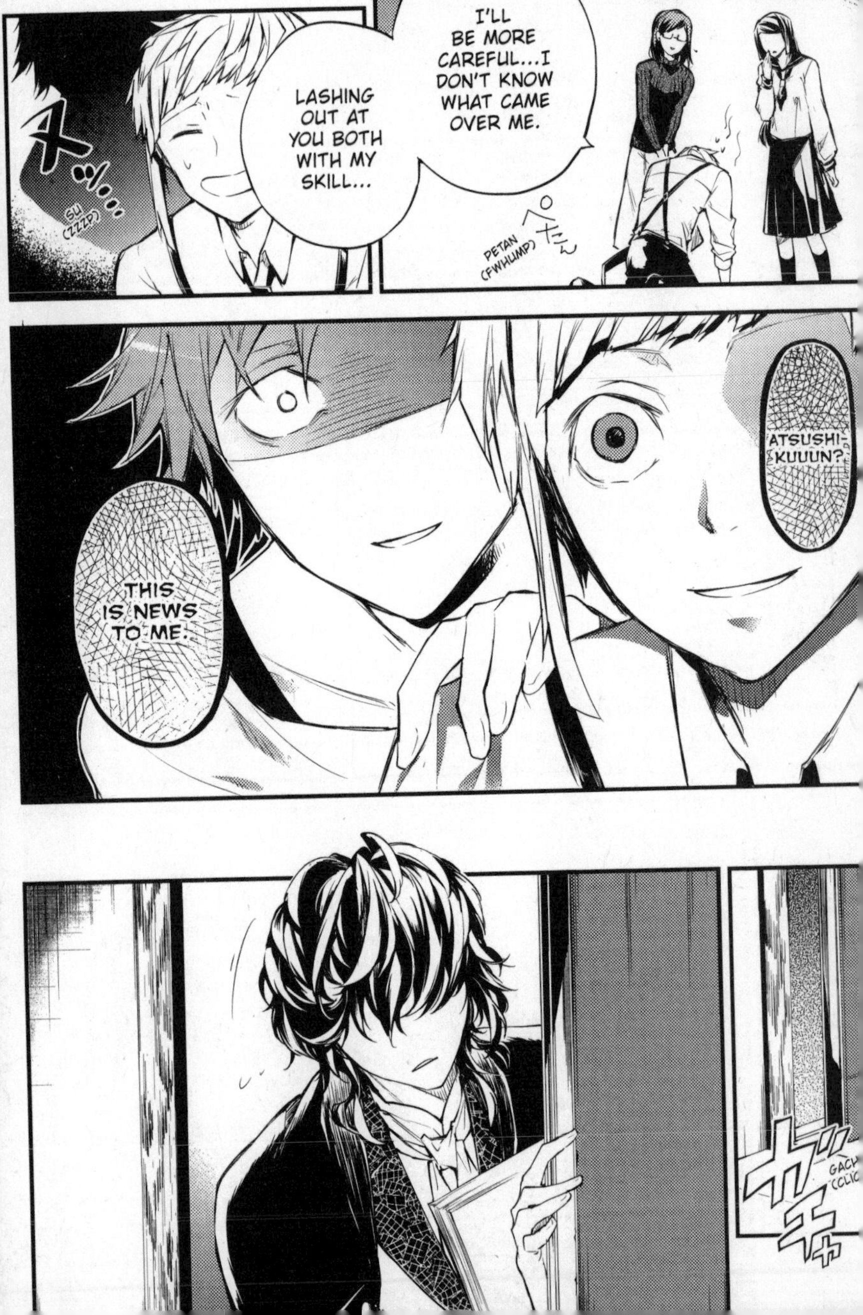
I'LL BE MORE CAREFUL...I DON'T KNOW WHAT CAME OVER ME.
ぺたん
PETAN (FWHUMP)
LASHING OUT AT YOU BOTH WITH MY SKILL...
SU (ZZZP)
ATSUSHI-KUUUN?
THIS IS NEWS TO ME.
ガチャ
GACH (CLIC

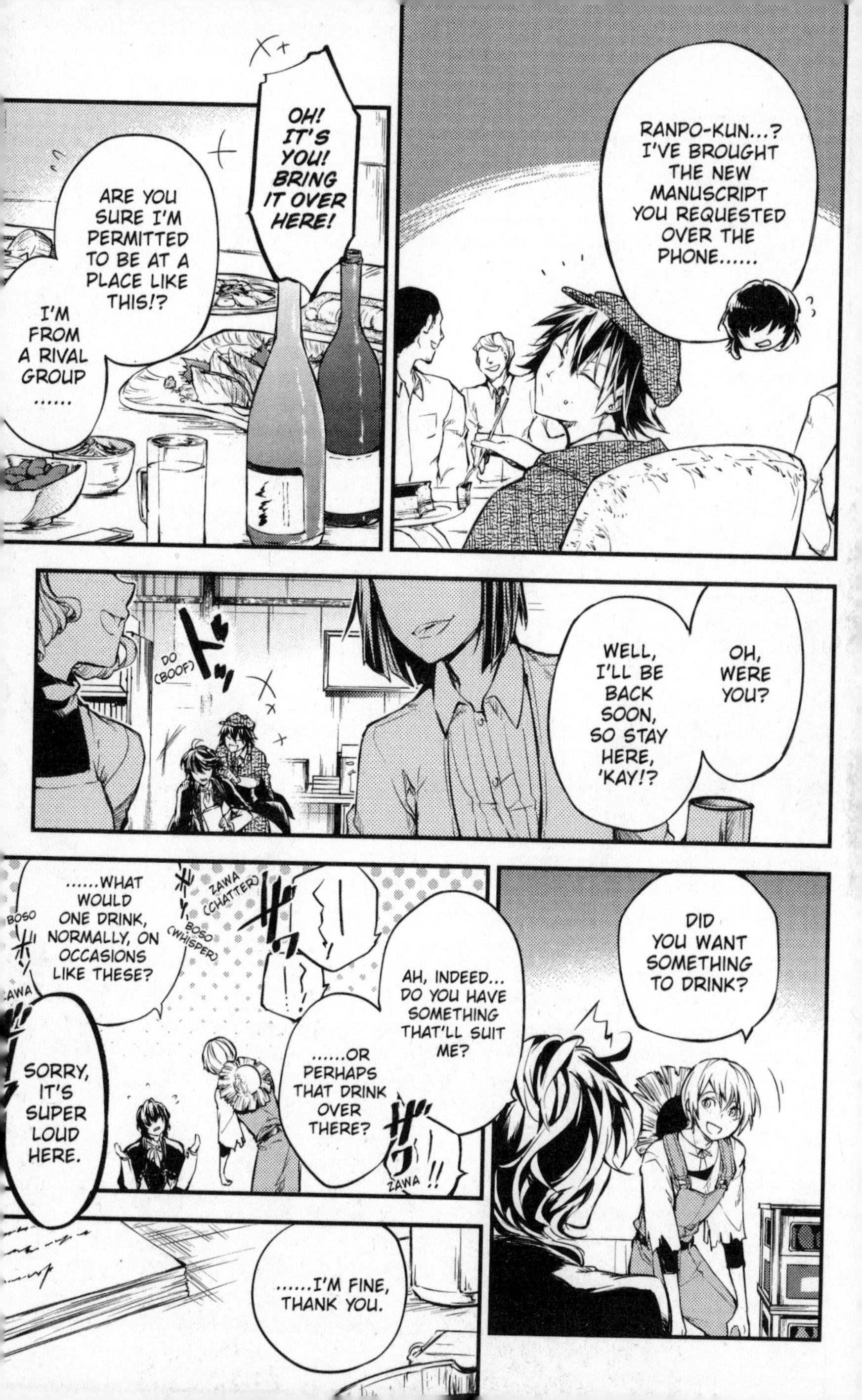
RANPO-KUN...? I'VE BROUGHT THE NEW MANUSCRIPT YOU REQUESTED OVER THE PHONE......
OH! IT'S YOU! BRING IT OVER HERE!
ARE YOU SURE I'M PERMITTED TO BE AT A PLACE LIKE THIS!?
I'M FROM A RIVAL GROUP ......
OH, WERE YOU?
WELL, I'LL BE BACK SOON, SO STAY HERE, 'KAY!?
DO (BOOF)
DID YOU WANT SOMETHING TO DRINK?
AH, INDEED... DO YOU HAVE SOMETHING THAT'LL SUIT ME?
......OR PERHAPS THAT DRINK OVER THERE?
ZAWA!!
ZAWA (CHATTER)
BOSO (WHISPER)
......WHAT WOULD ONE DRINK, NORMALLY, ON OCCASIONS LIKE THESE?
BOSO
SORRY, IT'S SUPER LOUD HERE.
......I'M FINE, THANK YOU.

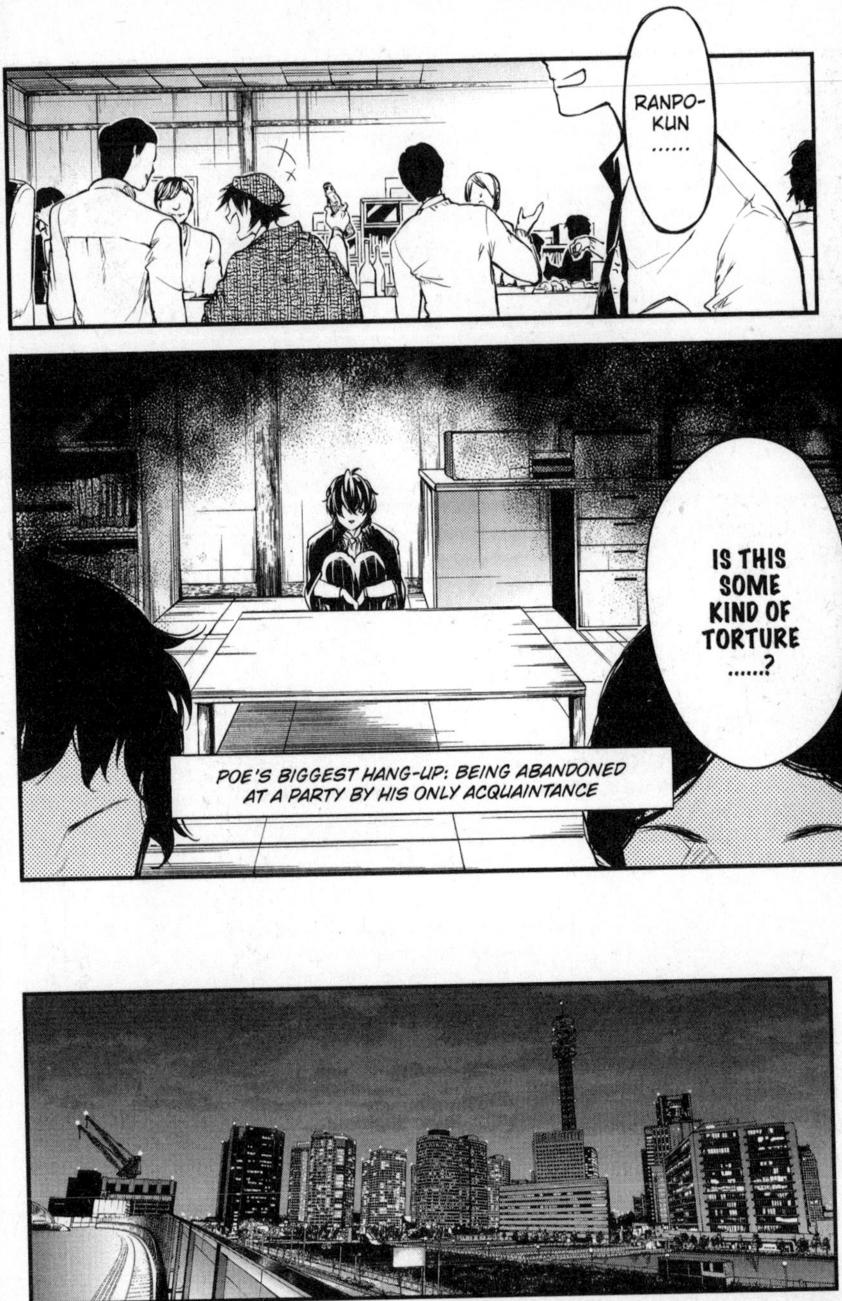
RANPO-KUN ......
IS THIS SOME KIND OF TORTURE ......?
POE'S BIGGEST HANG-UP: BEING ABANDONED AT A PARTY BY HIS ONLY ACQUAINTANCE

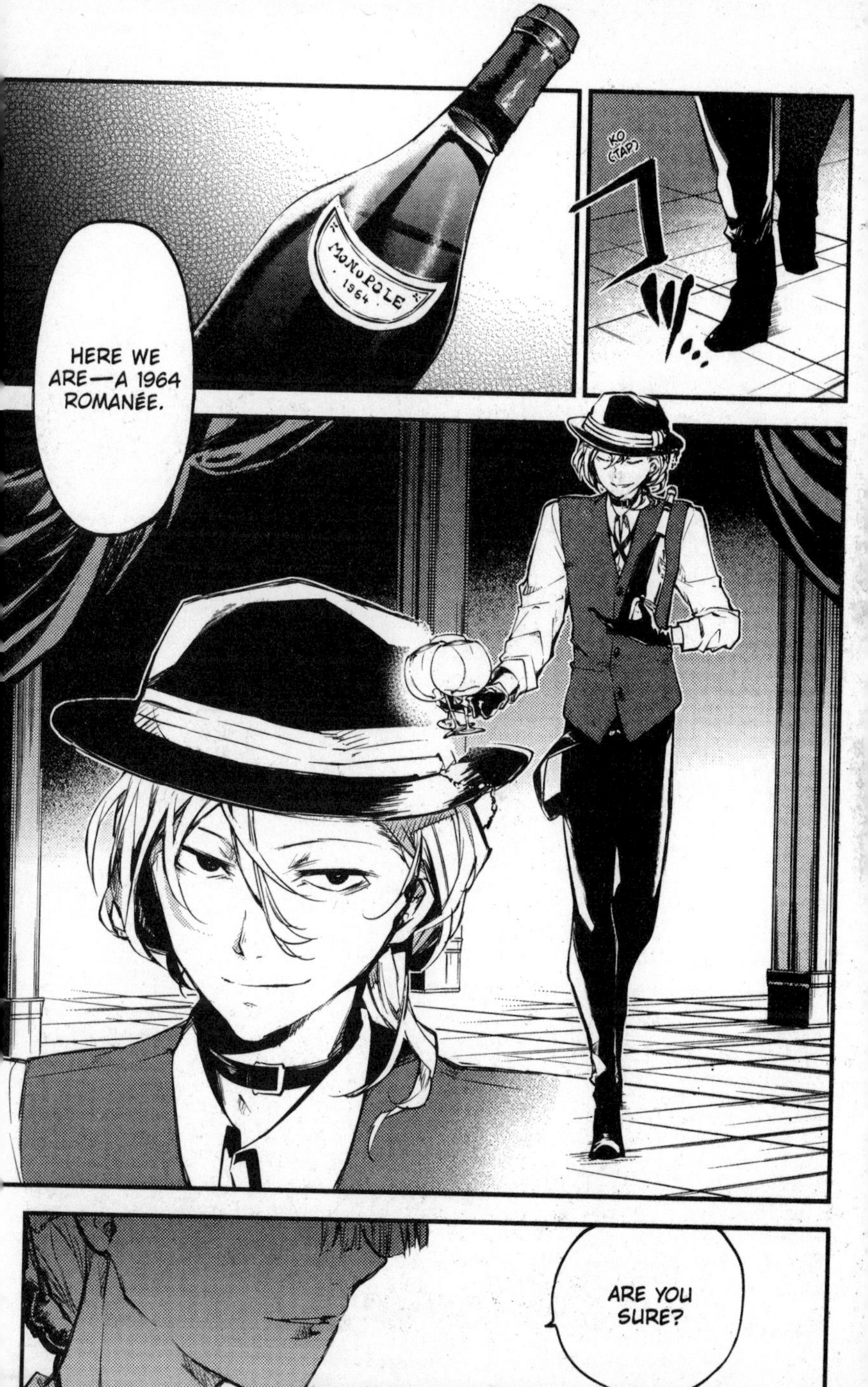
KO (TAP)
MONOPOLE 1964
HERE WE ARE—A 1964 ROMANÉE.
ARE YOU SURE?

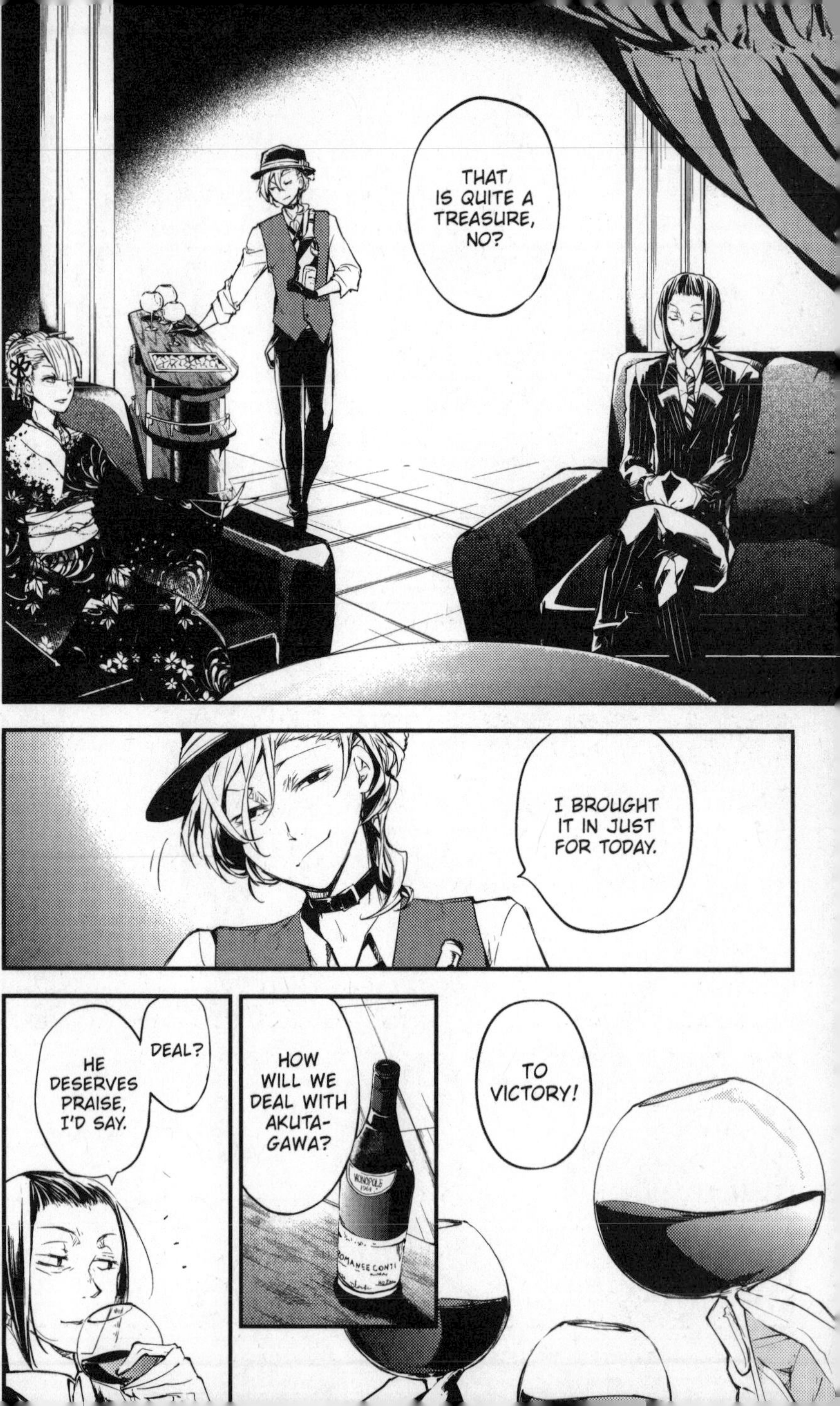
THAT IS QUITE A TREASURE, NO?
I BROUGHT IT IN JUST FOR TODAY.
TO VICTORY!
HOW WILL WE DEAL WITH AKUTA-GAWA?
MONOPOLE
ROMANEE CONTI
DEAL?
HE DESERVES PRAISE, I'D SAY.

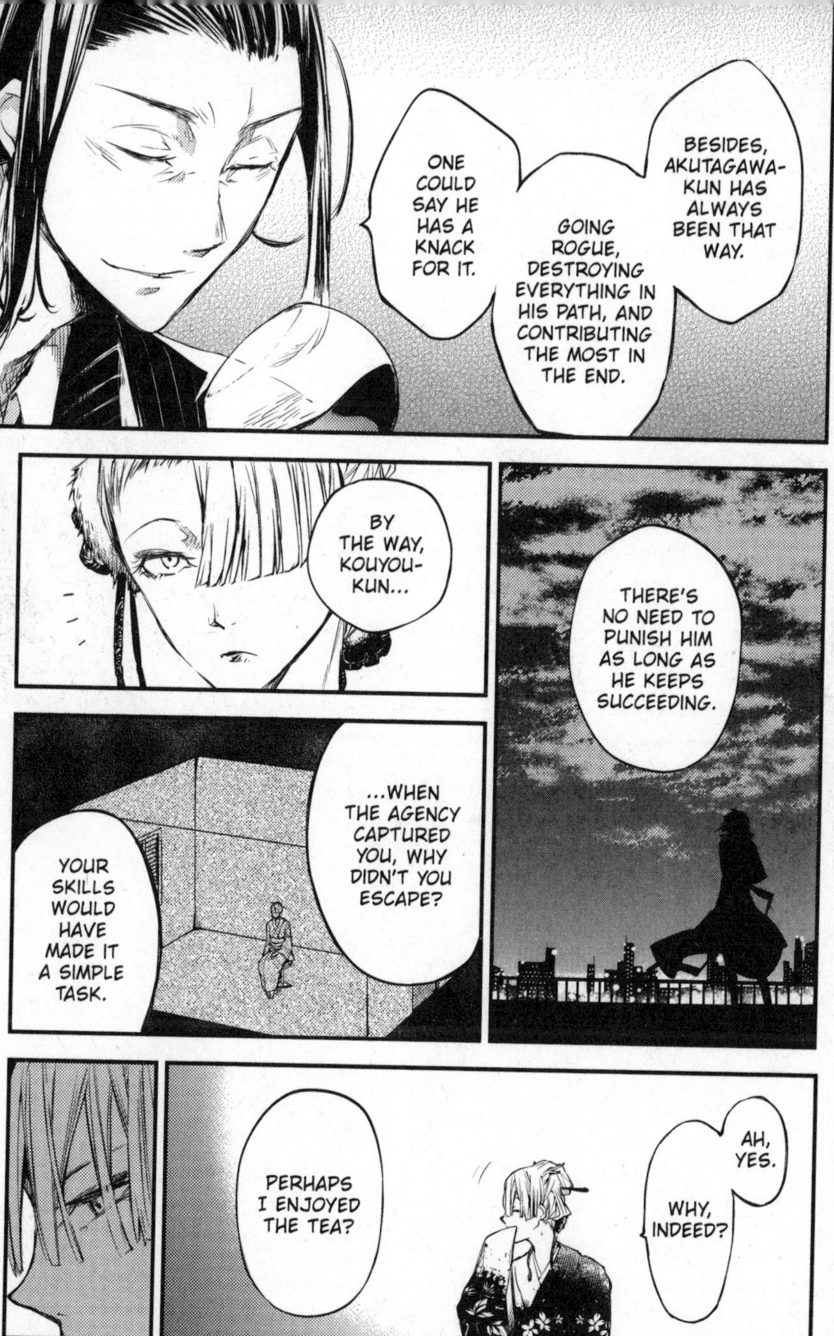
BESIDES, AKUTAGAWA-KUN HAS ALWAYS BEEN THAT WAY.
GOING ROGUE, DESTROYING EVERYTHING IN HIS PATH, AND CONTRIBUTING THE MOST IN THE END.
ONE COULD SAY HE HAS A KNACK FOR IT.
THERE'S NO NEED TO PUNISH HIM AS LONG AS HE KEEPS SUCCEEDING.
BY THE WAY, KOUYOU-KUN...
...WHEN THE AGENCY CAPTURED YOU, WHY DIDN'T YOU ESCAPE?
YOUR SKILLS WOULD HAVE MADE IT A SIMPLE TASK.
AH, YES.
WHY, INDEED?
PERHAPS I ENJOYED THE TEA?

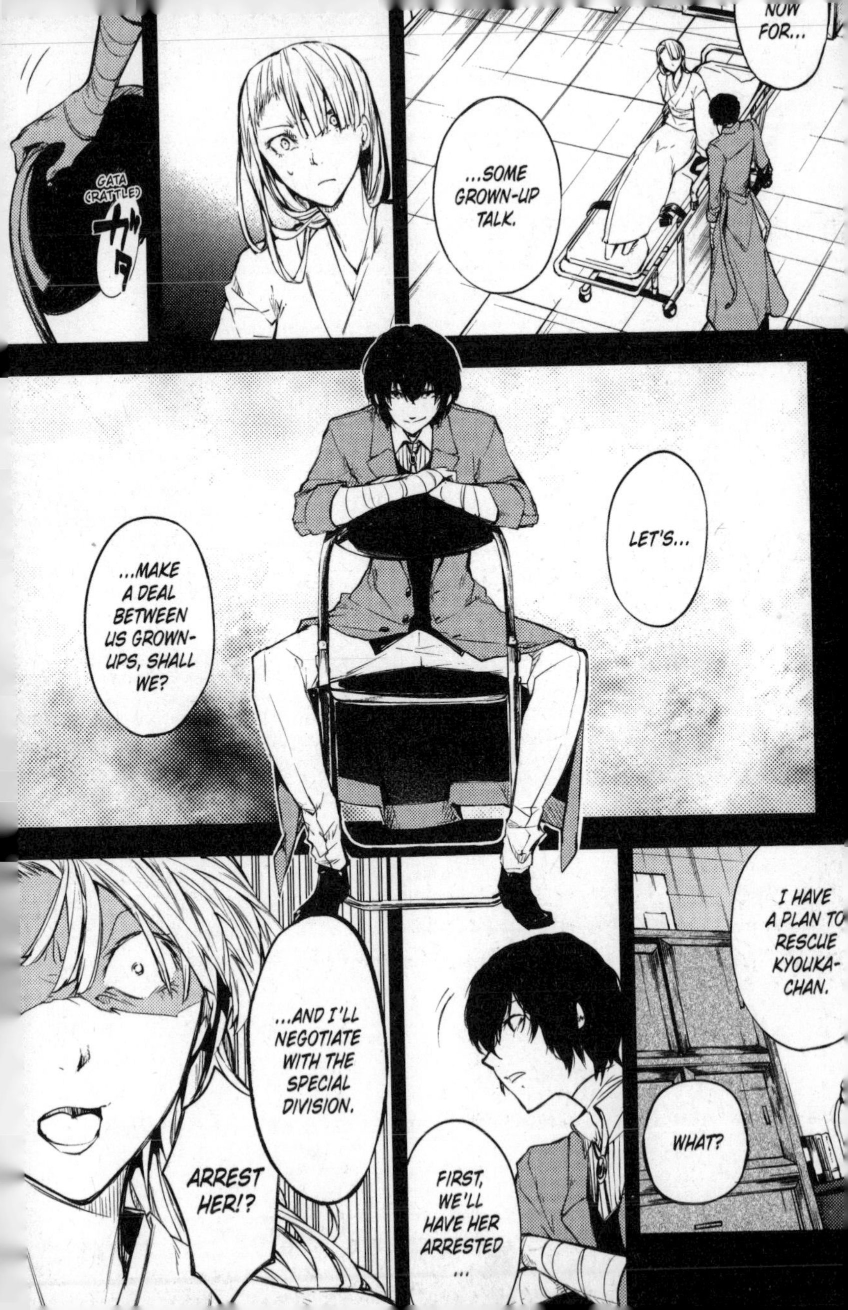
NOW FOR...
...SOME GROWN-UP TALK.
GATA (RATTLE)
LET'S...
...MAKE A DEAL BETWEEN US GROWN-UPS, SHALL WE?
I HAVE A PLAN TO RESCUE KYOUKA-CHAN.
WHAT?
FIRST, WE'LL HAVE HER ARRESTED...
ARREST HER!?
...AND I'LL NEGOTIATE WITH THE SPECIAL DIVISION.

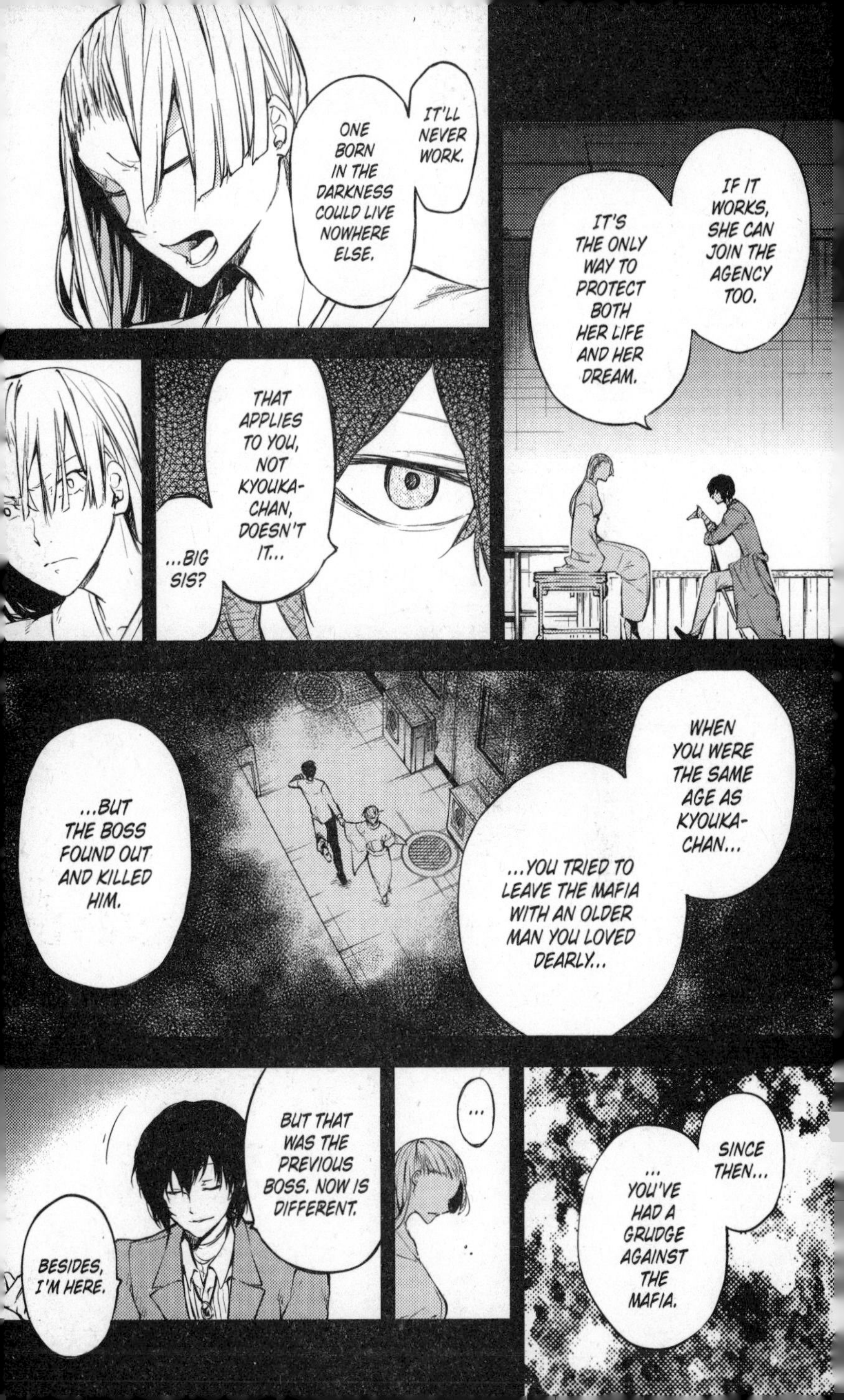
IF IT WORKS, SHE CAN JOIN THE AGENCY TOO.
IT'S THE ONLY WAY TO PROTECT BOTH HER LIFE AND HER DREAM.
IT'LL NEVER WORK.
ONE BORN IN THE DARKNESS COULD LIVE NOWHERE ELSE.
THAT APPLIES TO YOU, NOT KYOUKA-CHAN, DOESN'T IT...
...BIG SIS?
WHEN YOU WERE THE SAME AGE AS KYOUKA-CHAN...
...YOU TRIED TO LEAVE THE MAFIA WITH AN OLDER MAN YOU LOVED DEARLY...
...BUT THE BOSS FOUND OUT AND KILLED HIM.
SINCE THEN...
... YOU'VE HAD A GRUDGE AGAINST THE MAFIA.
...
BUT THAT WAS THE PREVIOUS BOSS. NOW IS DIFFERENT.
BESIDES, I'M HERE.

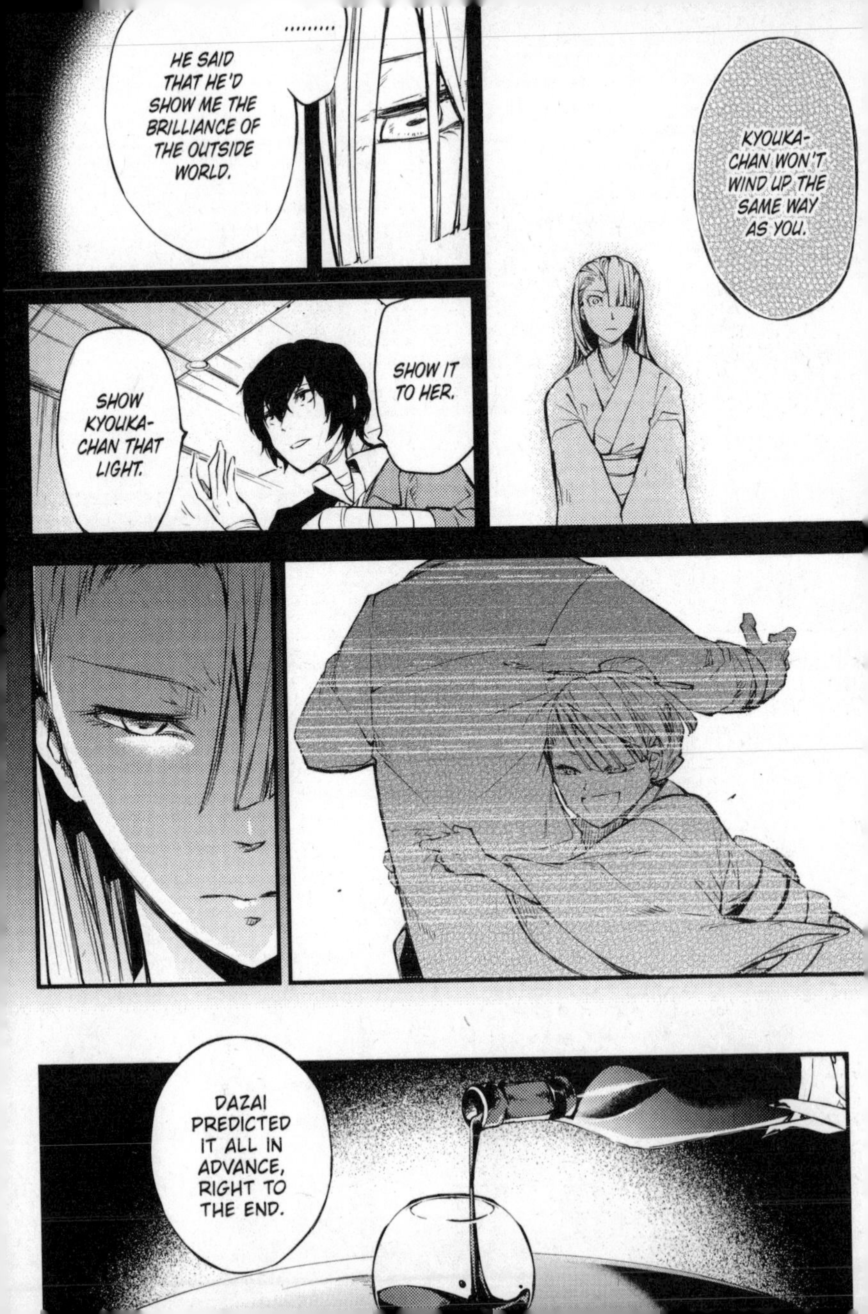
KYOUKA-CHAN WON'T WIND UP THE SAME WAY AS YOU.
....
HE SAID THAT HE'D SHOW ME THE BRILLIANCE OF THE OUTSIDE WORLD.
SHOW IT TO HER.
SHOW KYOUKA-CHAN THAT LIGHT.
DAZAI PREDICTED IT ALL IN ADVANCE, RIGHT TO THE END.

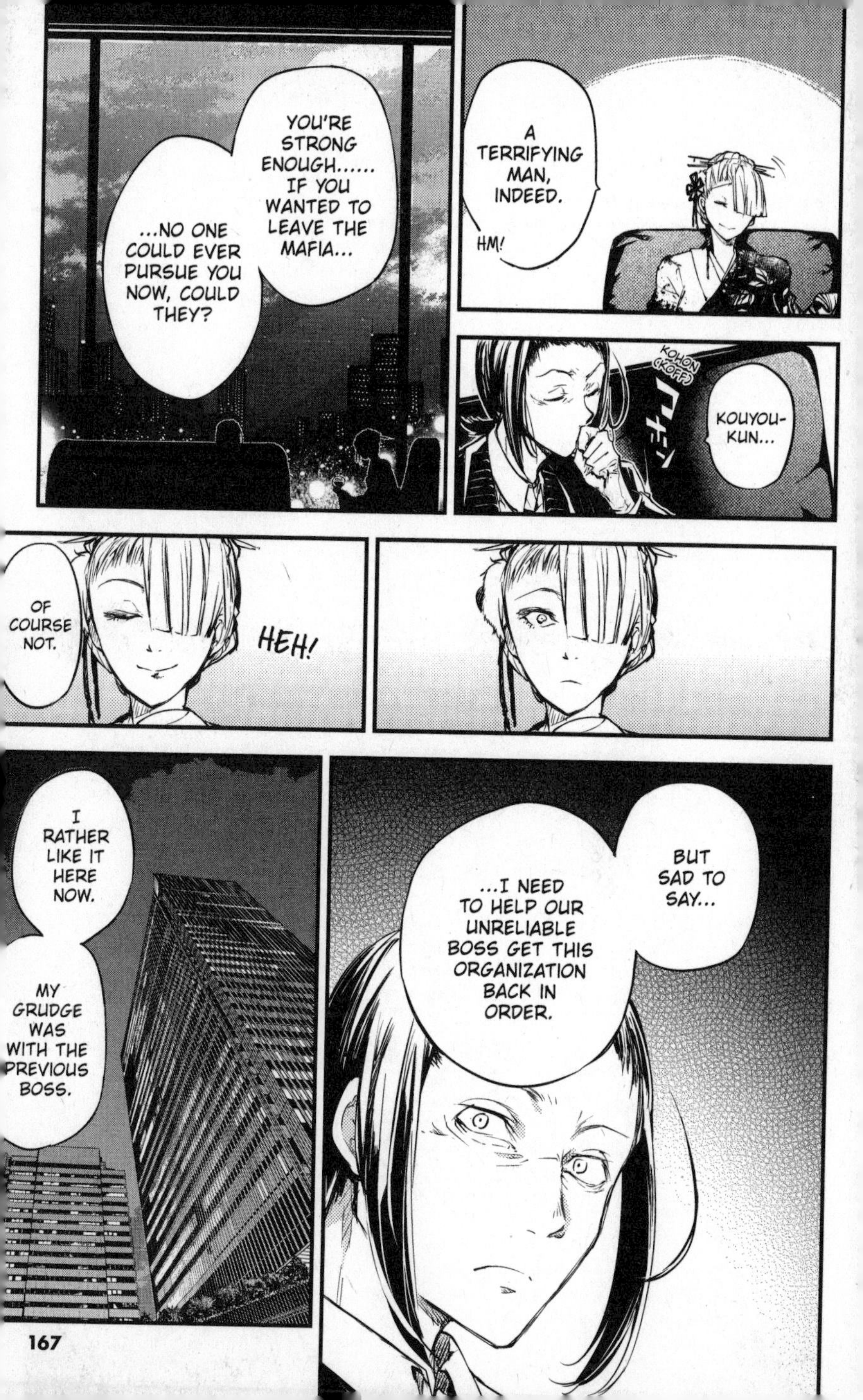
A TERRIFYING MAN, INDEED.
HM!
KOHON (KOFF)
KOUYOU-KUN...
YOU'RE STRONG ENOUGH...... IF YOU WANTED TO LEAVE THE MAFIA...
...NO ONE COULD EVER PURSUE YOU NOW, COULD THEY?
HEH!
OF COURSE NOT.
BUT SAD TO SAY...
...I NEED TO HELP OUR UNRELIABLE BOSS GET THIS ORGANIZATION BACK IN ORDER.
I RATHER LIKE IT HERE NOW.
MY GRUDGE WAS WITH THE PREVIOUS BOSS.

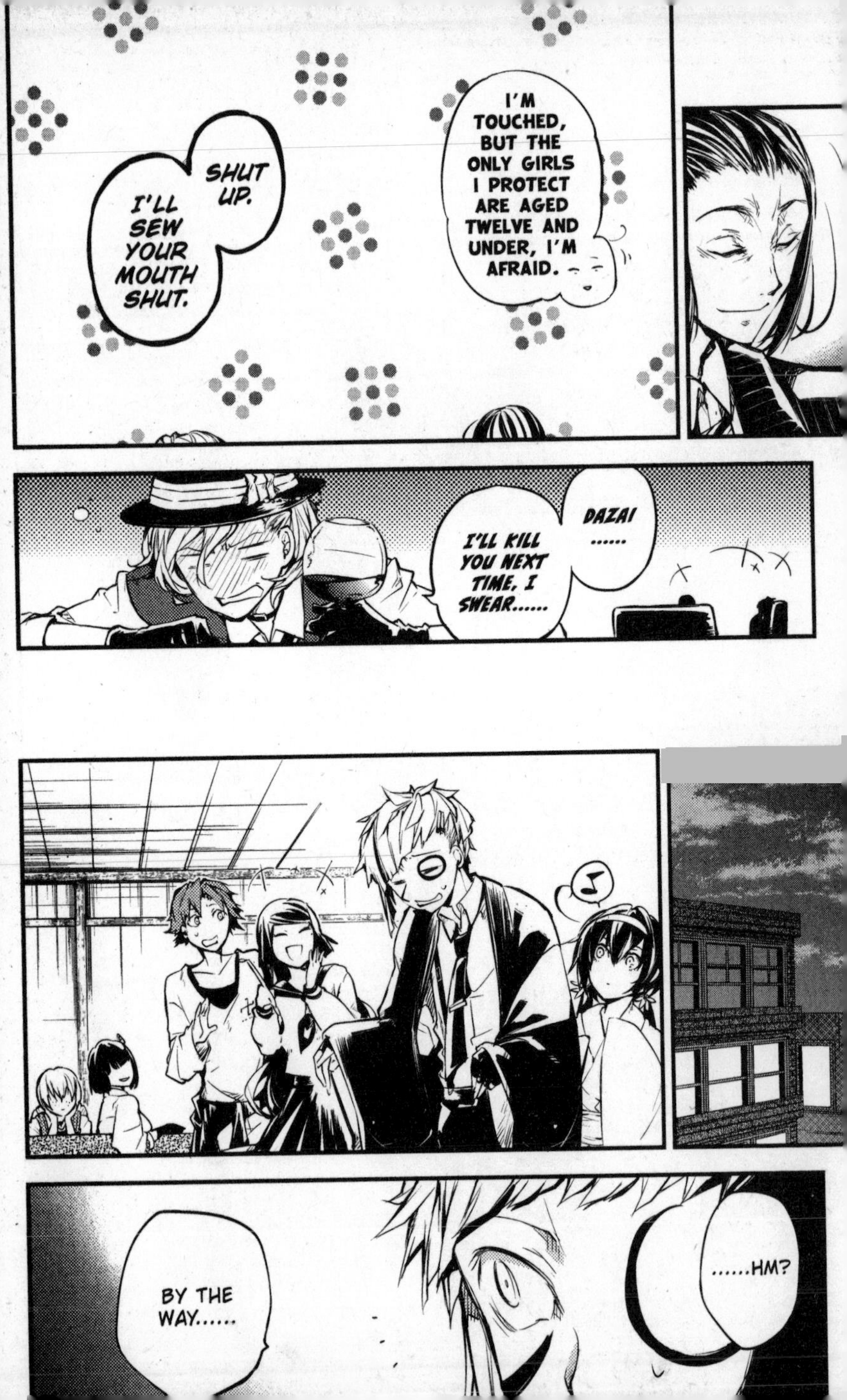
I'M TOUCHED, BUT THE ONLY GIRLS I PROTECT ARE AGED TWELVE AND UNDER, I'M AFRAID.
SHUT UP.
I'LL SEW YOUR MOUTH SHUT.
DAZAI ......
I'LL KILL YOU NEXT TIME, I SWEAR......
......HM?
BY THE WAY......

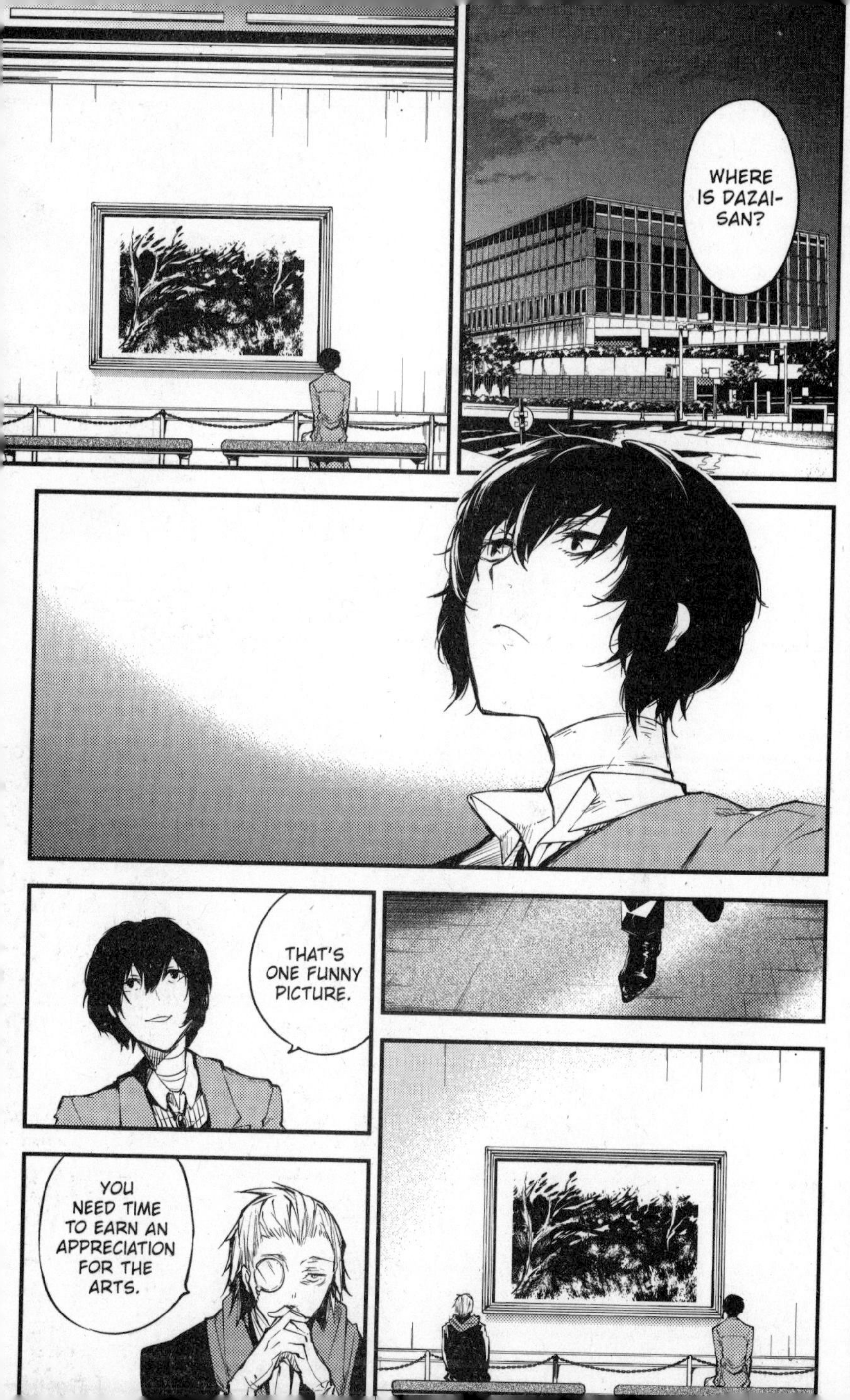
WHERE IS DAZAI-SAN?
THAT'S ONE FUNNY PICTURE.
YOU NEED TIME TO EARN AN APPRECIATION FOR THE ARTS.

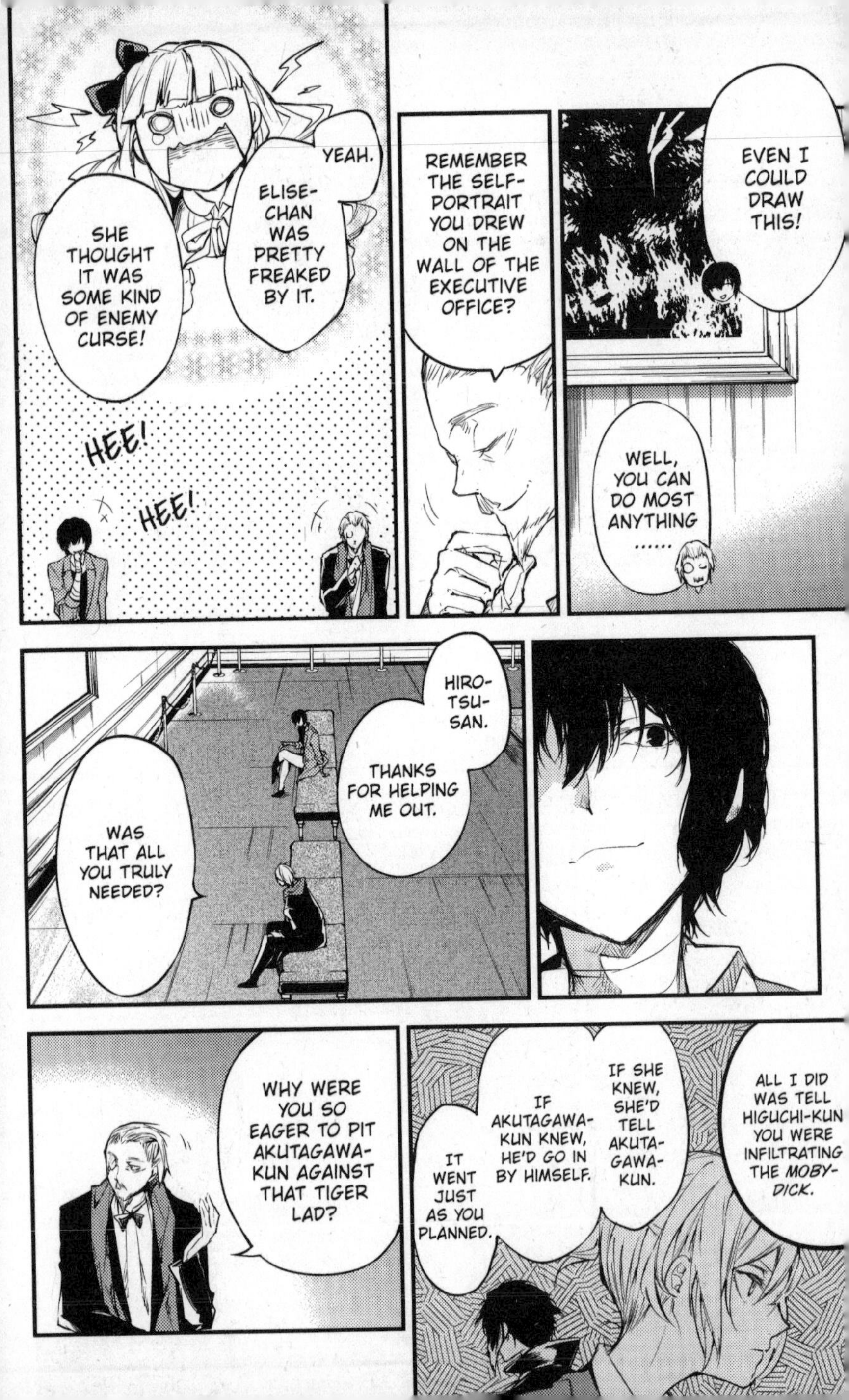
EVEN I COULD DRAW THIS!
WELL, YOU CAN DO MOST ANYTHING ......
REMEMBER THE SELF-PORTRAIT YOU DREW ON THE WALL OF THE EXECUTIVE OFFICE?
YEAH.
ELISE-CHAN WAS PRETTY FREAKED BY IT.
SHE THOUGHT IT WAS SOME KIND OF ENEMY CURSE!
HEE!
HEE!
HIROTSU-SAN.
THANKS FOR HELPING ME OUT.
WAS THAT ALL YOU TRULY NEEDED?
ALL I DID WAS TELL HIGUCHI-KUN YOU WERE INFILTRATING THE *MOBY-DICK*.
IF SHE KNEW, SHE'D TELL AKUTAGAWA-KUN.
IF AKUTAGAWA-KUN KNEW, HE'D GO IN BY HIMSELF.
IT WENT JUST AS YOU PLANNED.
WHY WERE YOU SO EAGER TO PIT AKUTAGAWA-KUN AGAINST THAT TIGER LAD?

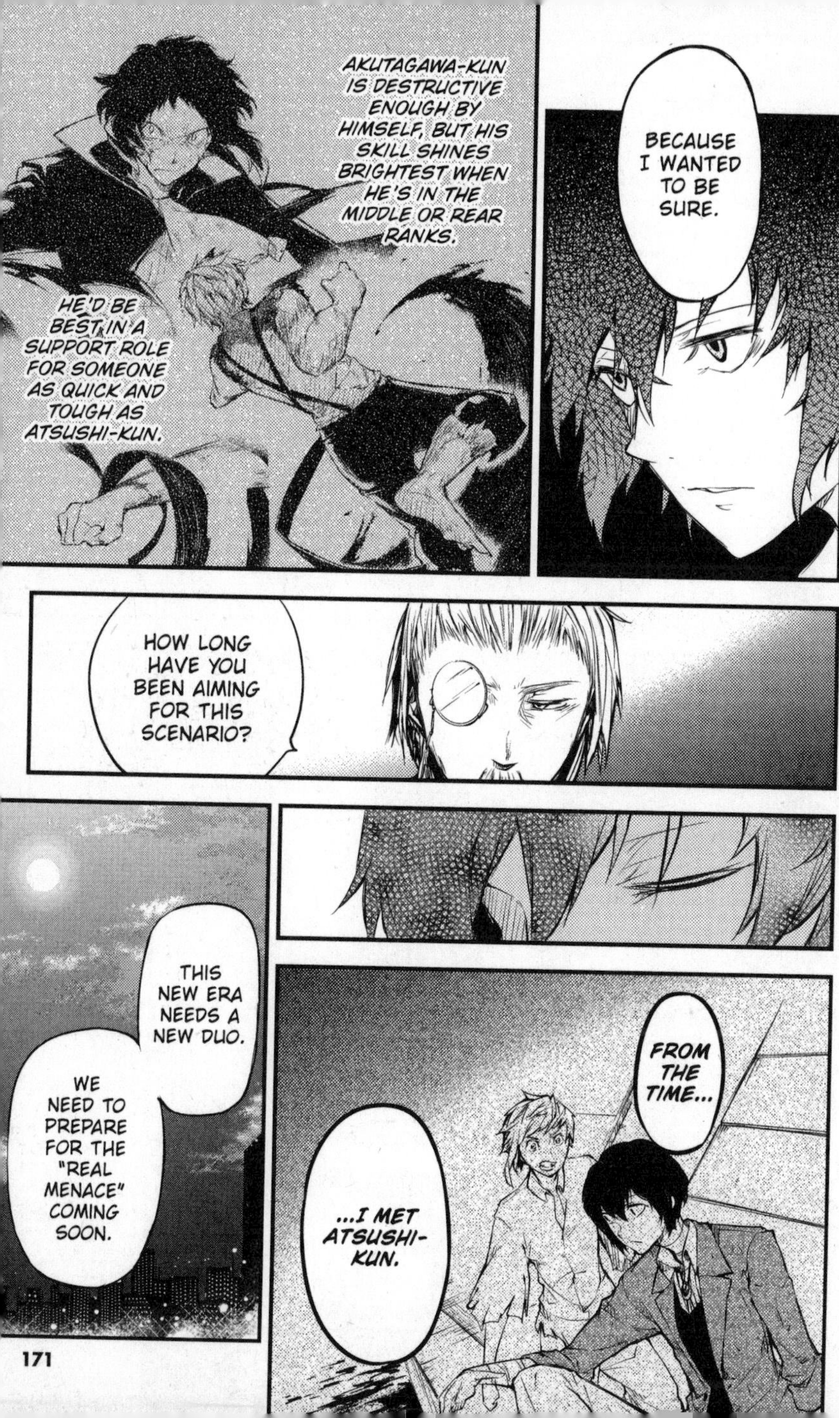
BECAUSE I WANTED TO BE SURE.
AKUTAGAWA-KUN IS DESTRUCTIVE ENOUGH BY HIMSELF, BUT HIS SKILL SHINES BRIGHTEST WHEN HE'S IN THE MIDDLE OR REAR RANKS.
HE'D BE BEST IN A SUPPORT ROLE FOR SOMEONE AS QUICK AND TOUGH AS ATSUSHI-KUN.
HOW LONG HAVE YOU BEEN AIMING FOR THIS SCENARIO?
FROM THE TIME...
...I MET ATSUSHI-KUN.
THIS NEW ERA NEEDS A NEW DUO.
WE NEED TO PREPARE FOR THE "REAL MENACE" COMING SOON.

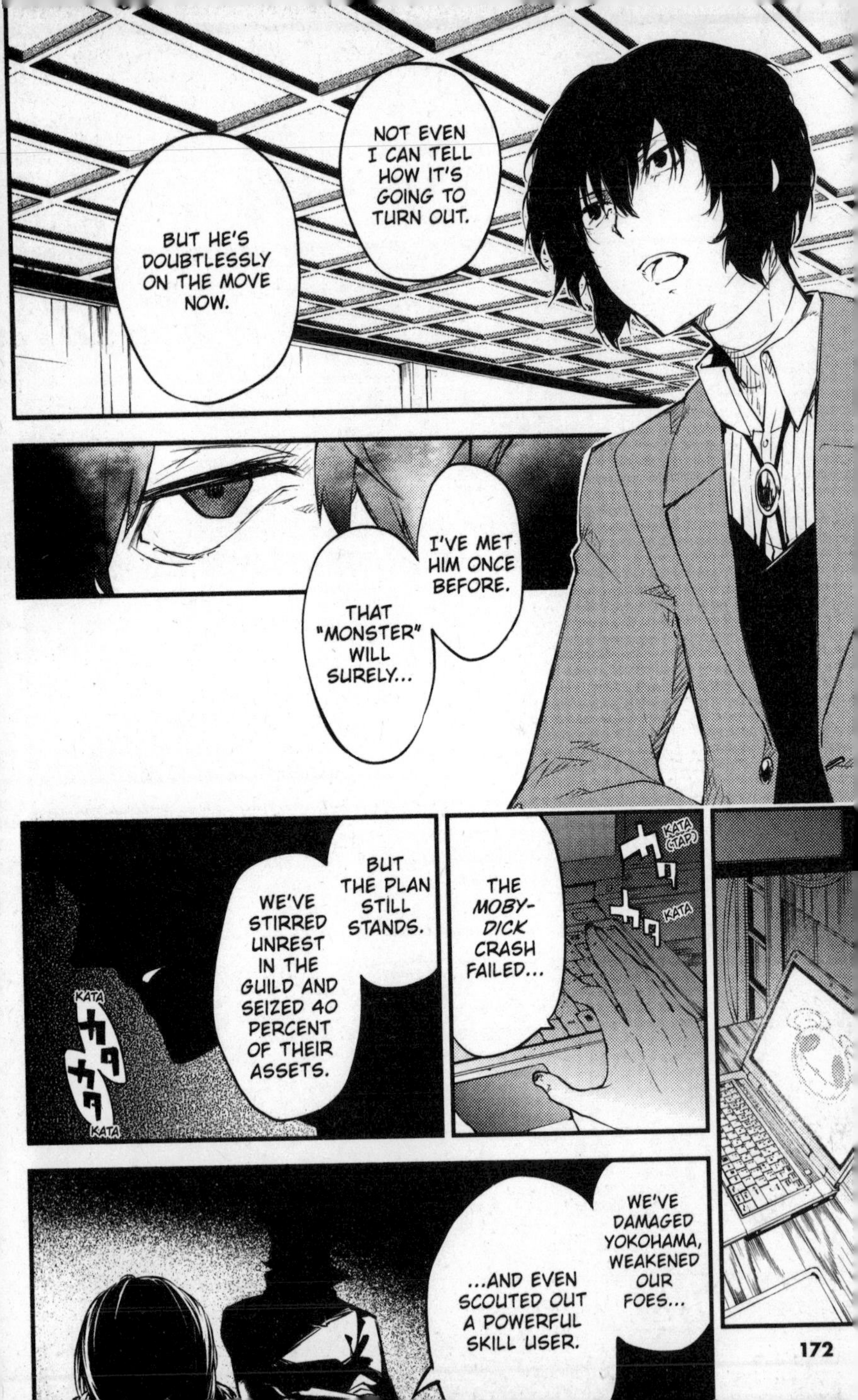
NOT EVEN I CAN TELL HOW IT'S GOING TO TURN OUT.
BUT HE'S DOUBTLESSLY ON THE MOVE NOW.
I'VE MET HIM ONCE BEFORE.
THAT "MONSTER" WILL SURELY...
KATA (TAP)
KATA
THE *MOBY-DICK* CRASH FAILED...
BUT THE PLAN STILL STANDS.
WE'VE STIRRED UNREST IN THE GUILD AND SEIZED 40 PERCENT OF THEIR ASSETS.
KATA
KATA
WE'VE DAMAGED YOKOHAMA, WEAKENED OUR FOES...
...AND EVEN SCOUTED OUT A POWERFUL SKILL USER.

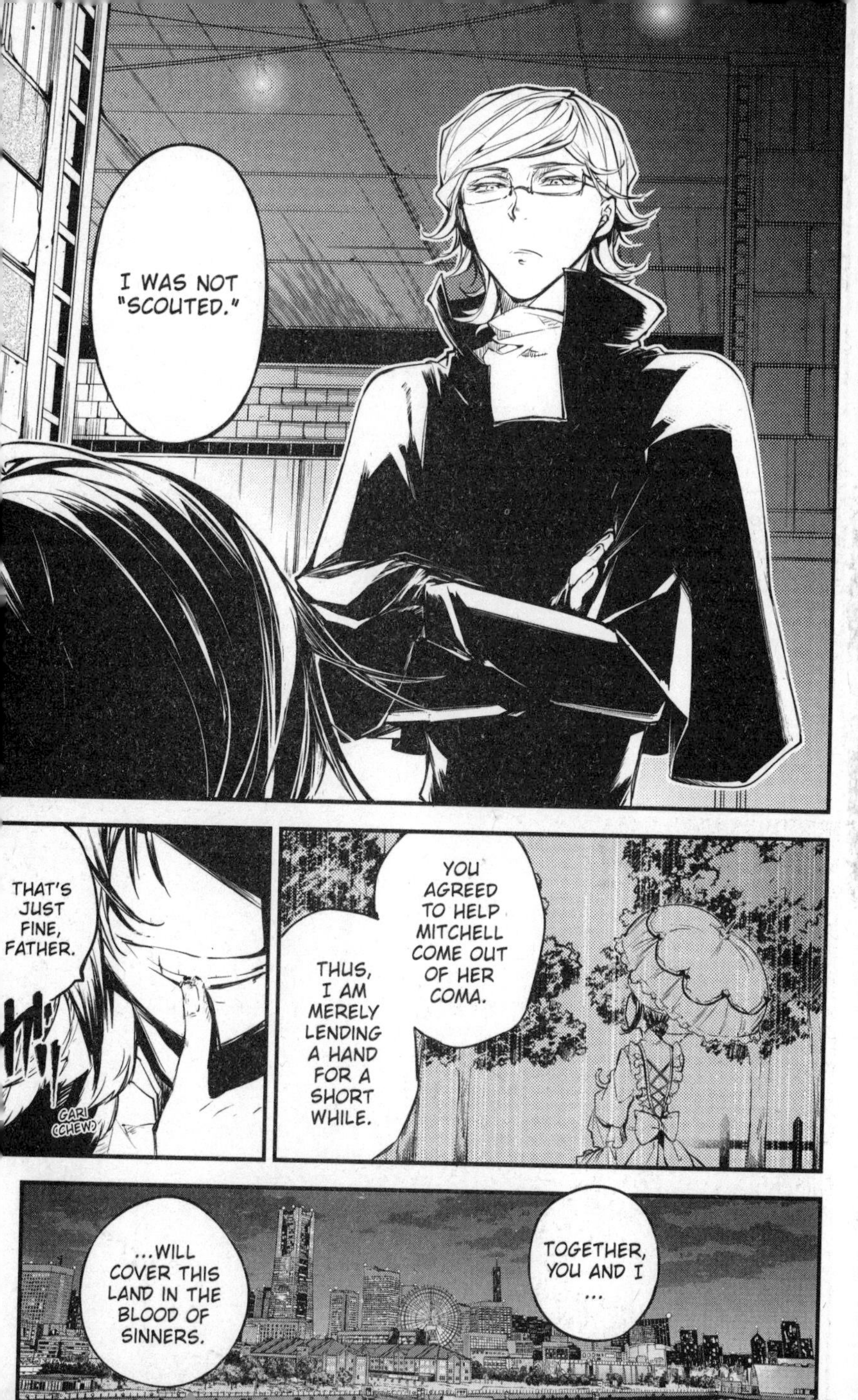
I WAS NOT "SCOUTED."
YOU AGREED TO HELP MITCHELL COME OUT OF HER COMA.
THUS, I AM MERELY LENDING A HAND FOR A SHORT WHILE.
THAT'S JUST FINE, FATHER.
GARI (CHEW)
TOGETHER, YOU AND I ...
...WILL COVER THIS LAND IN THE BLOOD OF SINNERS.

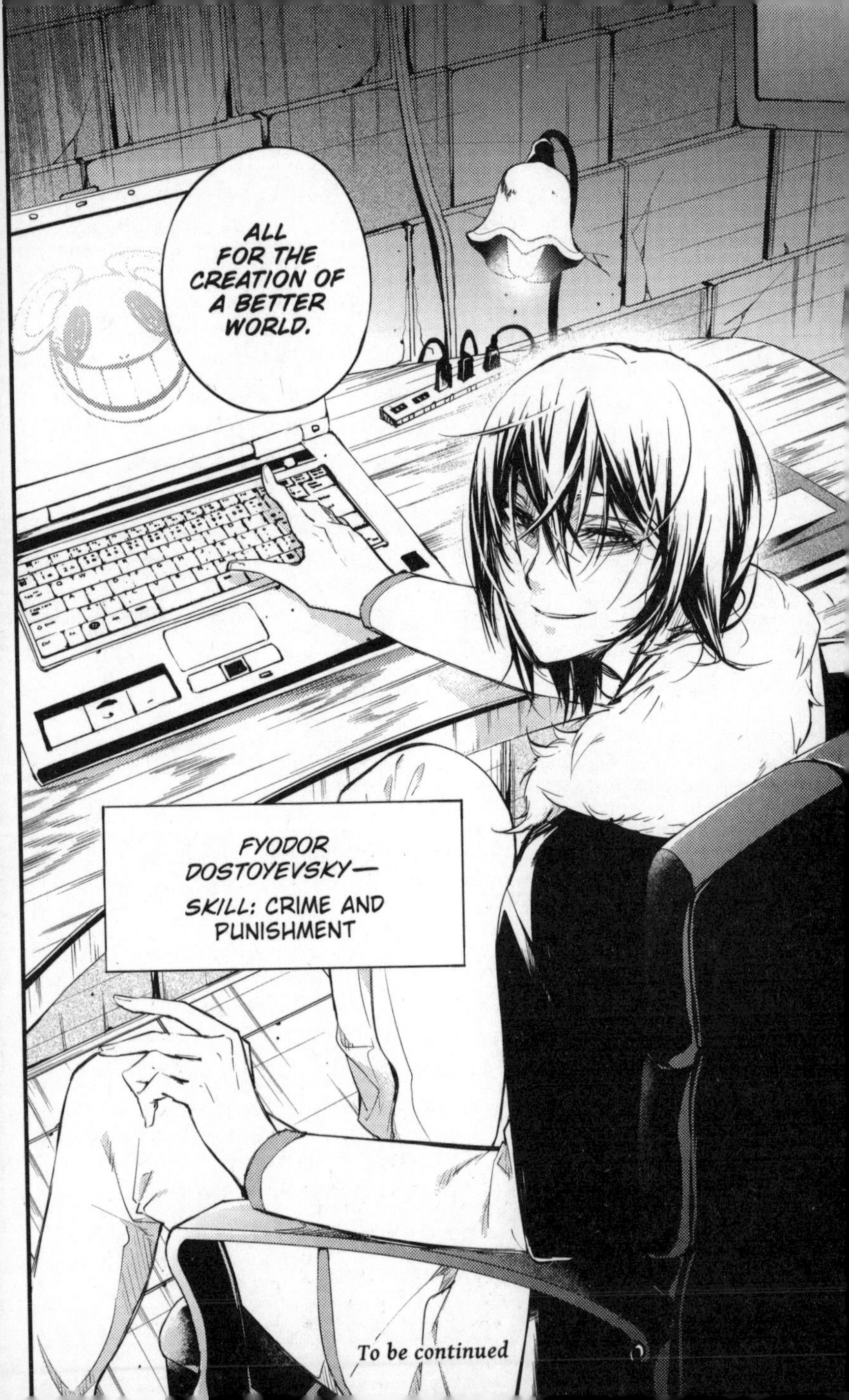
ALL FOR THE CREATION OF A BETTER WORLD.
FYODOR DOSTOYEVSKY—
SKILL: CRIME AND PUNISHMENT
To be continued

BUNGO

STRAY DOGS

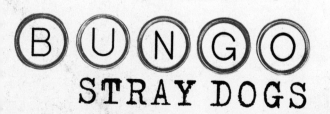

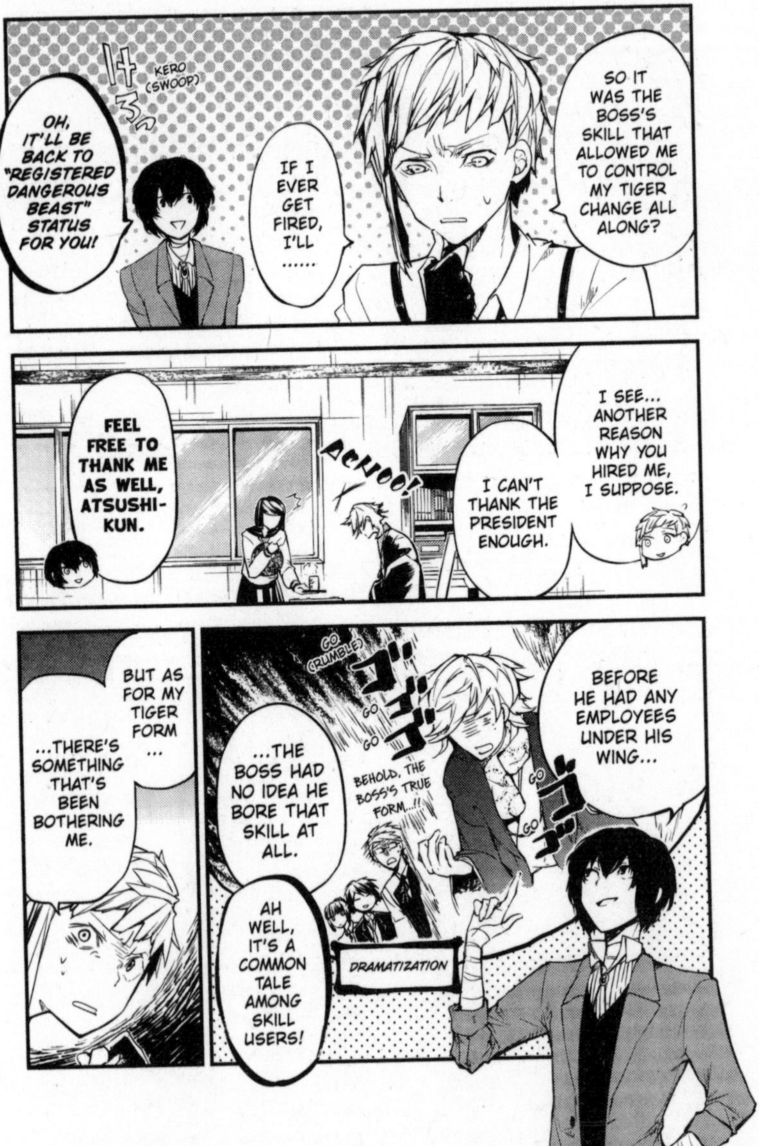
SO IT WAS THE BOSS'S SKILL THAT ALLOWED ME TO CONTROL MY TIGER CHANGE ALL ALONG?
IF I EVER GET FIRED, I'LL ......
KERO (SWOOP)
OH, IT'LL BE BACK TO "REGISTERED DANGEROUS BEAST" STATUS FOR YOU!
I SEE... ANOTHER REASON WHY YOU HIRED ME, I SUPPOSE.
I CAN'T THANK THE PRESIDENT ENOUGH.
ACHOO!
FEEL FREE TO THANK ME AS WELL, ATSUSHI-KUN.
BEFORE HE HAD ANY EMPLOYEES UNDER HIS WING...
GO (RUMBLE)
GO
GO
GO
GO
...THE BOSS HAD NO IDEA HE BORE THAT SKILL AT ALL.
BEHOLD, THE BOSS'S TRUE FORM..!!
DRAMATIZATION
AH WELL, IT'S A COMMON TALE AMONG SKILL USERS!
BUT AS FOR MY TIGER FORM ...
...THERE'S SOMETHING THAT'S BEEN BOTHERING ME.

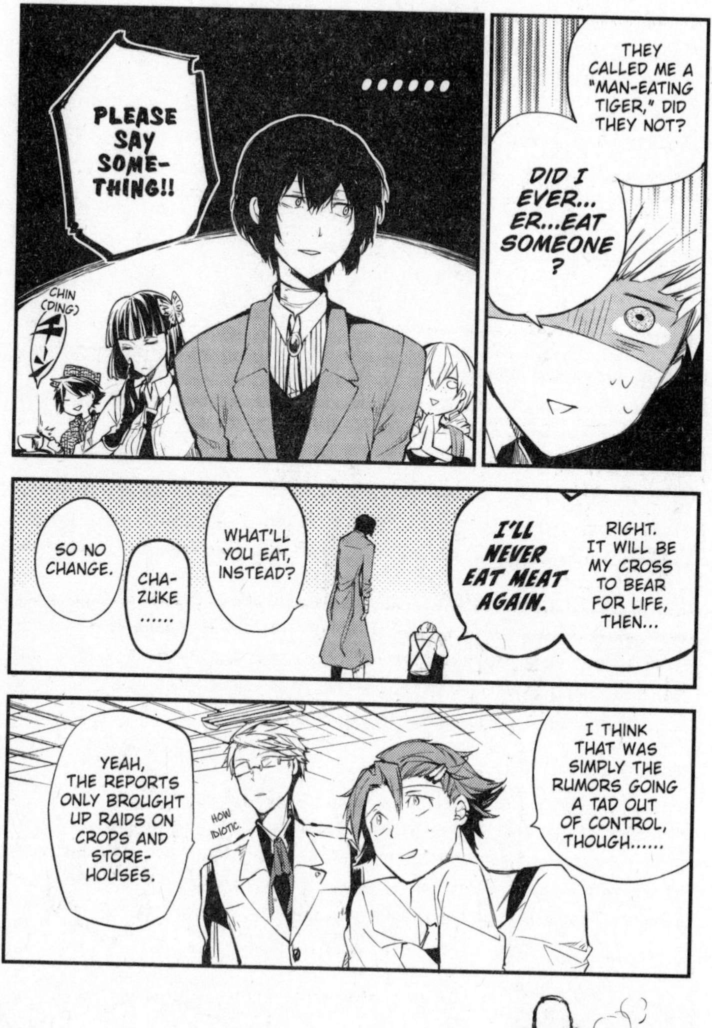
THEY CALLED ME A "MAN-EATING TIGER," DID THEY NOT?
DID I EVER... ER...EAT SOMEONE?
......
PLEASE SAY SOME-THING!!
CHIN (DING)
RIGHT. IT WILL BE MY CROSS TO BEAR FOR LIFE, THEN...
I'LL NEVER EAT MEAT AGAIN.
WHAT'LL YOU EAT, INSTEAD?
CHA-ZUKE......
SO NO CHANGE.
I THINK THAT WAS SIMPLY THE RUMORS GOING A TAD OUT OF CONTROL, THOUGH......
HOW IDIOTIC.
YEAH, THE REPORTS ONLY BROUGHT UP RAIDS ON CROPS AND STORE-HOUSES.

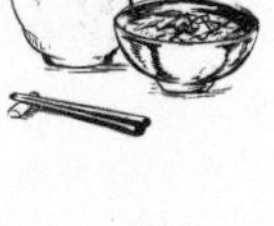

BUNGO STRAY DOGS

AUTHOR GUIDE (PART 4)

The characters of *Bungo Stray Dogs* are based on major literary figures from Japan and around the world! Here's a handy guide to help you learn about some of the writers who inspired the weird and wonderful cast of this series!

HERMAN MELVILLE (1819–1891)

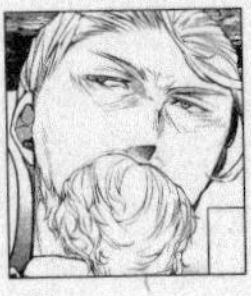

After having published his masterpiece *Moby Dick* in 1851 at the age of thirty-two, Herman lived the rest of his life writing poetry, though much of his work and existence never saw the light of fame until death. He was once friends with writer Nathaniel Hawthorne and spent most of his life taking up various jobs to support his family.

MARK TWAIN (1835–1910)

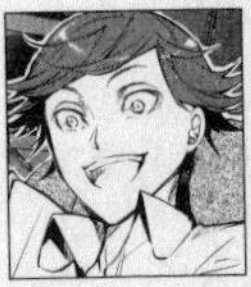

A witty writer and adventurous intellectual, Twain lived his early life in Hannibal, Missouri—a vibrant, bustling river city where trade practices and violence were commonplace. Growing up in the city inspired the setting for many of his works such as *The Adventures of Tom Sawyer* and *Adventures of Huckleberry Finn*.

JOHN STEINBECK (1902–1968)

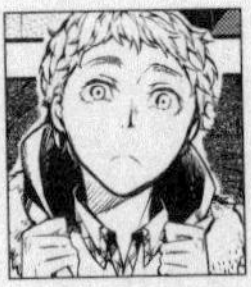

Steinbeck was an outspoken writer who touched upon the social and economic issues of his time through his well-known works *Of Mice and Men* and *The Grapes of Wrath*. He wrote about migrant workers during the Great Depression and was a manual laborer himself before taking up writing.

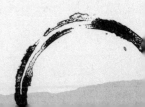

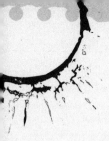

H. P. LOVECRAFT (1890-1937)

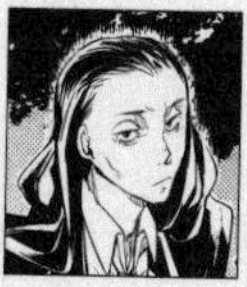

Though plagued by poor health throughout his life, Lovecraft was known as one of the masters of gothic tales and macabre novels. His writing career was spent hidden away behind the scenes as a ghostwriter, his own works only recieving fame after his death. His short stories often involved characters and their encounters with extraterrestrial beings and morbid phenomenons.

NATHANIEL HAWTHORNE (1804-1864)

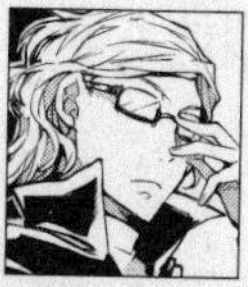

Hawthorne grew up in Salem, Massachusetts—a Puritan environment he would criticize in his work, *The Scarlet Letter*. His book explores the romance and the effects of public shame and guilt on his two main characters: the adulteress Hester and minister Dimmesdale.

MARGARET MITCHELL (1900-1949)

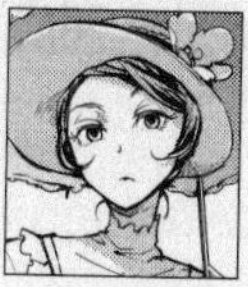

Born in Atlanta, Georgia, to descendants of Civil War veterans, Mitchell's first published work was *Gone with the Wind*. Her book, which talks about the aftermath of the Civil War and Southern love affairs of a young, spoiled daughter who falls into poverty, was published in 1936 and quickly became the most loved novel of her time.

EDGAR ALLAN POE (1809-1849)

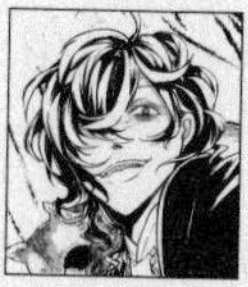

Poe was a transformative writer of his time who wove tales of horror and mystery in profound works such as "The Black Cat" and "The Murders in the Rue Morgue," which was the first modern detective story and gave inspiration for the deductive reasoning employed by Sir Arthur Conan Doyle's Sherlock Holmes. Poe's name is also the inspiration for the pen name "Ranpo Edogawa."

BUNGO STRAY DOGS

Story: Kafka Asagiri   Art: Sango Harukawa

Translation: Kevin Gifford   †   Lettering: Bianca Pistillo

BUNGO STRAY DOGS Volume 9
©Kafka ASAGIRI 2015
©Sango HARUKAWA 2015
First published in Japan in 2015 by KADOKAWA CORPORATION, Tokyo.
English translation rights arranged with KADOKAWA CORPORATION, Tokyo through TUTTLE-MORI AGENCY, INC., Tokyo.

English translation © 2018 by Yen Press, LLC

Yen Press
1290 Avenue of the Americas
New York, NY 10104

Visit us at yenpress.com
facebook.com/yenpress
twitter.com/yenpress
yenpress.tumblr.com
instagram.com/yenpress

First Yen Press Edition: December 2018

Yen Press is an imprint of Yen Press, LLC.
The Yen Press name and logo are trademarks of Yen Press, LLC.

Library of Congress Control Number: 2016956681

ISBNs: 978-0-316-46823-7 (paperback)
       978-0-316-46841-1 (ebook)

10 9 8 7 6 5 4 3 2 1

WOR

Printed in the United States of America